Social Work Practice
with Families and Children

Social Work Practice
with Families and Children

Anthony N. Maluccio
Barbara A. Pine
Elizabeth M. Tracy

COLUMBIA UNIVERSITY PRESS   NEW YORK

COLUMBIA UNIVERSITY PRESS
Publishers Since 1893
New York   Chichester, West Sussex
Copyright © 2002 Columbia University Press
All rights reserved

Library of Congress Cataloging-in-Publication Data

Maluccio, Anthony N.
    Social work practice with families and children / Anthony N. Maluccio,
  Barbara A. Pine, Elizabeth M. Tracy
      p. cm.
    Includes bibliographical references and index.
    ISBN 0-231-10766-8 (cloth : alk. paper)
      1. Family social work — United States. 2. Social work with children — United
  States. I. Pine, Barbara A. II. Tracy, Elizabeth M. III. Title.

  HV699 .M334 2002
  362.82′53′0973 — dc21
                                                                    2002022712

Casebound editions of Columbia University Press books are printed on permanent
and durable acid-free paper.

Printed in the United States of America

c 10 9 8 7 6 5 4 3 2 1

Contents

About the Authors

Anthony N. Maluccio, D.S.W., is professor of social work at Boston College, Graduate School of Social Work, Chestnut Hill, Massachusetts. His teaching and research interests focus on service delivery and outcome evaluation in the area of child and family services, particularly family preservation, family foster care, residential treatment of children and youths, and family reunification of children in out-of-home care. He has coauthored a number of books on the above topics, including, most recently, *Teaching Family Reunification, Reconnecting Families: A Guide to Strengthening Family Reunification Services, The Child Welfare Challenge: Policy, Practice, and Research*, and *Child Welfare Outcome Research in the United States, the United Kingdom, and Australia*.

Barbara A. Pine, Ph.D., is professor of social work at the University of Connecticut, School of Social Work, West Hartford, Connecticut. She teaches in three main areas of social work: social work management, child welfare, and professional ethics, and consults with public and private child welfare agencies. She has coauthored four books on child welfare practice, including three on family reunification and one on preparing adolescents in foster care for adulthood. She also has authored or coauthored a number of articles on topics such as special needs adoption, ethical decision making, family preservation and reunification, and child welfare policy.

Elizabeth M. Tracy, Ph.D., is associate professor of Social Work at Case Western Research University, Mandel School of Applied Social Sciences, Cleveland, Ohio, where she directs the School Social Work Program. She teaches courses in social work practice methods and is especially interested in social work models that support families and make use of natural helping networks. She consults, conducts research, and writes extensively on family preservation services, family-centered child welfare practice, and substance abuse issues in child welfare. She is coeditor of *Reaching High Risk Families* and coauthor of *Person-Environment Practice: The Social Ecology of Interpersonal Helping.*

Preface

Social work with families and children in the United States — as elsewhere — is increasingly complex, controversial, and changing, especially as it seeks to face challenges such as oppression and discrimination against vulnerable populations; social problems such as substance abuse, family violence, child abuse and homelessness; and diminishing funding for critical social supports. This book will address these emerging and cutting-edge issues in addition to more traditional family and child welfare topics such as adoption and family foster care.

Our main purpose is to help social work students and practitioners understand and work with vulnerable families and children. The focus is on intervention at different levels and with different systems — from the child and family to their social networks as well as broader ecological environment. As suggested by Palmer (1995:1): "The term *children* is used generically and is intended to include adolescents when the use of both terms would be cumbersome. When the focus is on children age 13 and over, they are generally termed *adolescents* or *youths*."

Our emphasis is on preparing social workers for direct and indirect practice with clients from vulnerable populations, especially the poor, people of color, and recent immigrant groups, within the context of cross-system and multidisciplinary collaboration. These clients come to the attention of social work practitioners in a variety of settings, including public and voluntary child welfare agencies, family support programs, residential treatment programs, public schools, and other organizations working with or on behalf of children and families.

Recurring themes in the text include a family-centered orientation, an empowerment and strengths perspective, attention to human diversity (cultural, ethnic, and racial), particularly to the value of diversity, the impact of racism and sexism, issues of social justice and oppression, micro and macro practice issues, and achieving a balance between family preservation and child protection in the course of service delivery. Attention is also paid to the role of theory and research in providing guidelines for social work practice. Most important, the text reflects the profession's commitment to social justice and ethical principles. Such concern is especially appropriate at this time, as welfare reform legislation and related movements in contemporary society threaten to "push some children into deeper poverty" and to "further accelerate the permanent separation of children from their parents" (Pelton 1999:1479).

The contents are related to practice through discussion questions focusing on micro and macro aspects at the end of various chapters. There are practice examples and case illustrations involving families experiencing problems to help readers draw connections between selected ideas and concepts and the day-to-day concerns and issues facing practitioners.[1] Throughout the book we build on our extensive experiences in teaching, practice, consultation, and research in the field of family and children's services at the baccalaureate, master, and doctoral levels in schools of social work, all of which has helped us to anchor the book in theory, practice, research, and values.[2]

Organization of Book

The book is designed primarily for MSW students and advanced BSW students as well as practitioners who work with children and families in diverse agency settings. It can be used in a range of courses in schools of social work, including foundation courses on practice, human behavior and the social environment, and social welfare and policy; specialized courses in child and family services; and administration, clinical practice, and research courses. It can serve as a primary text in child and family welfare courses and as a supplementary or recommended text for others. We assume that students already have a basic knowledge of social work and of child development.

The book is divided into three parts. In the first part, four chapters deal primarily with the *knowledge* base underlying social work practice with children and families. Accordingly, these chapters include understanding vulnerable families and children, risks and vulnerabilities confronting families in contemporary society, supporting families and their children, and ethical issues in practice. In the second part we focus on the *practice* base, and these four chapters cover engagement, assessment, case planning and goal setting, family-centered intervention, social network intervention, and school-based intervention. In the third part we conclude with two chapters that address evaluation of practice and service delivery and future challenges and opportunities, including the impact of welfare reform and managed care on vulnerable families and children, the role of other federal policies and programs, and the implications for social work education and training.

The appendixes include information in the following areas:

- tools and instruments to support practice,
- child welfare resource centers and other information sources, and
- electronic resources pertaining to family and children's services.

Notes

1. Brown (2002) offers numerous case studies from the field of child welfare.
2. Also see the following recent texts for additional information:

- *Policies and research*: Downs, Moore, McFadden, and Costin (2000); Hill and Aldgate (1996); Pecora, Whittaker, Maluccio, and Barth (2000); and Rykus and Hughes (1998).
- *Clinical theory and practice*: LeVine and Sallee (1999); Mather and Lager (2000); Mattaini (1999); Pecora, Whittaker, Maluccio and Barth (2000); Petr (1998); Rykus and Hughes (1998); and Webb (1996).

Acknowledgments

We deeply appreciate the contributions of many students, agency administrators, field instructors, practitioners, and social work educators to this book. In addition to encouraging us to proceed with writing it, they have generously shared practice examples and enhanced our understanding of policy and practice. We are particularly grateful to the following:

- Jane Aldgate and Wendy Rose — the Open University, School of Health and Social Welfare, and Jenny Gray of the Department of Health in England, for generously sharing their work on a comprehensive system to assess vulnerable children's needs;
- Diane Drachman — the University of Connecticut, School of Social Work, whose work on immigrants and refugees helped us to strengthen our focus on these families;
- Lynne M. Healy — the University of Connecticut, School of Social Work, for her writings on international social work, which led us to think more globally;
- Susan P. Kemp and James K. Whittaker — the University of Washington, School of Social Work, whose earlier collaboration with us strengthened our understanding of environmental issues facing and shaping families.
- Lenora Kola — Case Western Reserve University, Mandel School of Applied Social Sciences, for her guidance on substance abuse issues and the compilation of resources in appendix 10.

- Robin Warsh — Boston College, Graduate School of Social Work, whose earlier collaboration with us enhanced this current endeavor.

We also express our appreciation to Pamela Harrison for her outstanding secretarial service in preparation of this volume. In working with us over many years she has demonstrated exceptional skill and grace in facilitating our collaboration and responding to our diverse styles, frequent demands, and at times unclear directions. Jennifer Bonner greatly assisted us in the preparation of the bibliography and the appendixes on electronic resources.

We gratefully acknowledge permission to adapt the following materials from our previous writings in other publications.

- Aldine de Gruyter, a division of Walter de Gruyter, Inc., for permission to adapt sections of chapter 7 from S. P. Kemp, J. K. Whittaker, and E. M. Tracy, *Person-Environment Practice: The Social Ecology of Interpersonal Helping* © 1997.
- Child Welfare League of America, Inc., for permission to adapt in chapter 9 sections from A. N. Maluccio, R. Warsh, and B. A. Pine, eds., *Together Again: Family Reunification in Foster Care* © 1993.
- Guilford Press, for permission to adapt in chapter 7 a case summary from S. W. Henggeler, S. K. Schoenwald, C. M. Bourduin, M. D. Rowland, and P. B. Cunningham, *Multisystemic Treatment of Antisocial Behavior in Children and Adolescents* © 1998.
- Haworth Press, for permission to adapt in chapter 6 sections from A. N. Maluccio, "Book Review" of *The Family at Risk — Issues and Trends in Family Preservation*, by M. Berry, in *Residential Treatment for Children and Youth*, vol. 17:100–101.
- Wadsworth, an imprint of the Wadsworth Group, a Division of Thomson Learning, for permission to adapt in chapter 5 sections from A. N. Maluccio, "Action as a Vehicle for Promoting Competence," pp. 354–368, and in chapter 6, sections from G. Burford and S. MacLeod, "Family Group Decision Making," pp. 278–283, *Social Work Processes*, 6th ed., edited by B. R. Compton and B. Galaway © 1999.

Finally, in addition to the acknowledgments noted in subsequent chapters, we thank the following for providing us with examples of innovative programs:

- Anna Maria Olezza, coordinator of the Bilingual/Bicultural Department, Public Schools, Hartford, Connecticut, for sharing with us the example of "The New Arrival Migrant Program" in chapter 8.
- Leola McCrorey, school social worker, and Jackie Tedford, formerly student intern, Weaver High School, Hartford, Connecticut, who contributed the example of "Sister, Sister Let's Talk" in chapter 8.

Part 1

Knowledge Base

1   Understanding Vulnerable Families and Their Children

The following examples, drawn from our teaching and practice backgrounds, illustrate the complex situations facing practitioners in seeking to understand vulnerable families and children.

Barbara J has an elementary grade son, Kyle, who is getting into more and more trouble in school. Kyle has a learning disability and is prescribed medication for hyperactivity. However, the school reports that Kyle often arrives at school without having taken his medication. On those days, his behavior is disruptive to his learning as well as his classmates. Kyle's mother is a single parent whose husband is disabled from an injury sustained in a drive-by shooting. Money is tight, and she does not always get Kyle's prescription filled in time. She is frustrated with Kyle's behavior and annoyed that the school is "on her back" all the time.

Sherry K has been referred to the child protective hotline by a hospital social worker. Her infant girl, now just four days old, has tested positive for cocaine. and this results in an automatic referral to the protective services agency. Sherry arrived at the hospital, just hours prior to the delivery of her baby, having had no prenatal care. The hospital social worker is not sure that Sherry will be able to care for the child at home. The neighborhood where the mother and child would return is chaotic and dangerous; Sherry's house has all but been taken over by drug dealers.

Jerry R, age fourteen, has been referred to the juvenile court after a guard at a local mall found that he had taken a pair of sneakers without paying. His parents, very upset and angry with him, threaten to have him put into a juvenile detention home. However, the staff from the home persuades them to meet with a probation officer to discuss ways to deal with Jerry and help him.

In this chapter we introduce the knowledge base that is useful for social work practice with families and children, with emphasis on those that are particularly vulnerable in contemporary society, such as the families in the above examples. These include, in particular, families and children affected by poverty and its correlates, families and children from populations of color, certain recent immigrant groups, and families with issues of substance abuse, family violence, and HIV/AIDS.

After considering what we mean by *family*, we present the following content areas:

- promoting child and family well-being,
- resilience, coping, and adaptation,
- stress, risk, and protective factors,
- developmental perspective on understanding and working with human beings,
- the experiences of new immigrants,
- intergenerational aspects, and
- feminist perspective on families and children.

We conclude with consideration of a child-focused and family-centered approach to service delivery that will be further delineated and illustrated throughout the book.

Defining the "Family"

As Hartman and Laird (1983:4) have noted, "Human beings can be understood and helped only in the context of the intimate and powerful human systems of which they are a part," of which the family is one of the most important. But how do we — or should we — define family? As Gambrill (1997:571) points out, "This is a controversial question that has implications for the way resources are distributed." Moreover, how the family is defined also has important implications for practice, including eligibility for service, distribution of resources, and helping approaches.

In her discussion of family theory from a multicultural perspective, Smith (1995:7) suggests "that there is no single, correct definition of family. . . . Rather, there are multiple definitions derived from particular theoretical perspectives."[1] She further notes, "No one theory could satisfactorily represent "the truth." But the *many* ways we look at families can help us to better understand them" (Smith 1995:7). Similarly, Hartman and Laird (1983:30) adopt a phenomenological stance:

> A family becomes a family when two or more individuals have decided they are a family, that in the intimate, here-and-now environment in which they gather, there is a sharing of emotional needs for closeness, of living space which is deemed "home," and of those roles and tasks necessary for meeting the biological, social and psychological requirements of the individuals involved.

For our purposes in this text we mean by family "two or more people in a committed relationship from which they derive a sense of identity as a family," thus including "nontraditional family forms that are outside the traditional legal perspective . . . families not related by blood, marriage, or adoption" (Nunnally, Chilman, and Cox 1988:11).[2]

As delineated further in chapter 3, families perform a number of essential functions that contribute to adaptation and survival (Giele 1979):

- *nurturance* — "which focuses on sexual gratification, care, feeding, and emotional support of the individual" (Giele 1979:287);

- *economic*, "which links the family group to the material resources that enable it to survive" (Giele 1979:287);
- *residential*, which "locates the family ecologically in social networks, housing, the community, and region" (Giele 1979:287); and
- *legal and cultural*, which "sets the group boundaries, defines the group identity, and symbolically structures all transactions to give them a particular meaning" (Giele 1979:287).

As also discussed in chapter 3, families help to meet a number of needs, such as nutrition and parenting, through a range of instrumental and expressive functions. *Instrumental functions* refer to meeting basic, life-sustaining needs such as food, clothing, and shelter. *Expressive functions* refer to helping family members meet their emotional, intellectual, and spiritual development needs. Some family needs could be considered as being met through a combination of expressive and instrumental functions, such as child care, and health-related supports.[3]

In line with the above, and in recognition of the diversity of contemporary society, we should emphasize that "respect for diversity requires that *family* be defined openly and broadly so as to include whomever the family itself — with its unique culture, circumstances, and history — designates" (Allen and Petr 1998:8). Human diversity — including culture, race and ethnicity, ability, and sexual orientation — must be respected: "Life-styles and child-rearing methods that might be considered different or unusual should be accepted so long as they promote a child's health and safety" (Warsh, Maluccio, and Pine 1994:4). Hill (1997), for example, has elaborated on the strengths of African American families in such areas as dedicated achievement and work orientations, flexibility in family roles, close kinship bonds, and strong religious orientation.

Practitioners should be prepared to understand and account for the special needs of minorities. As reflected throughout this volume, this means that we need to consider carefully in our practice the dimensions of race and ethnicity, including not only their significance for human functioning but also their impact on service delivery.[4] In this regard, Pinderhughes (1997:20) asserts: "Training practitioners for competence with diverse populations is high on the list of corrective initiatives to address . . . inadequacies" in social work practice. A critical component of such training is learning how to promote the well-being of children and families.

Promoting Child and Family Well-Being

To aid in our understanding of what families and children need to thrive in our society, we have developed a framework of needs and resources for family and child well-being. As seen in figure 1.1, the framework is organized as a triangle depicting the three interrelated aspects of child and family well-being:

- what children need for their optimal development,
- what families need to survive and fulfill their functions successfully, and
- the neighborhood, community, and environmental resources that families and their children require.

At the center of the model is the overall goal for family-centered social work practice: safeguarding and promoting the well-being and welfare of children and their families. We will refer to this framework throughout the book, so as to highlight key points about promoting child and family well-being and safety as well as delineate guidelines and principles for assessment and intervention. The model draws from the contributions of a number of sources in an attempt to show the range of interrelated family and child needs that, when met, promote optimal functioning and development.[5]

Resilience, Coping, and Adaptation

In their work with children and families, practitioners can be guided by knowledge regarding resilience, coping, and adaptation — key constructs in understanding human beings and human behavior. Before elaborating on each of these constructs, we find it useful to consider the competence-centered perspective on social work practice, which can serve as a frame of reference for practitioners.

Competence-Centered Perspective

The competence-centered perspective builds upon ecology as a metaphor guiding the study of the interactions between living organisms and their

FIGURE 1.1 Framework of Needs and Resources for Family and Child Well-Being

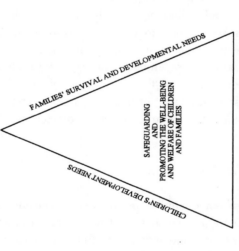

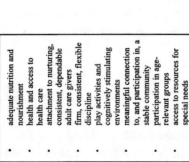

FAMILIES' SURVIVAL AND DEVELOPMENTAL NEEDS

CHILDREN'S DEVELOPMENT NEEDS

SAFEGUARDING
AND
PROMOTING THE WELL-BEING
AND WELFARE OF CHILDREN
AND FAMILIES

NEIGHBORHOOD, COMMUNITY AND ENVIRONMENTAL RESOURCES

- adequate nutrition and nourishment
- health and access to health care
- attachment to nurturing, consistent, dependable adult care givers
- firm, consistent, flexible discipline
- play activities and cognitively stimulating environments
- meaningful connection to, and participation in, a stable community
- participation in age-relevant groups
- access to resources for special needs

- adequate parenting capacity to:
  - provide basic care
  - ensure child's safety and stability
  - give emotional warmth
  - use appropriate discipline and guidance
  - offer cognitive stimulation
- adequate shelter
- adequate financial resources
- marital and relationship accord
- social and kinship networks and support
- ties to a secure and stable community

- income and income supports (e.g. jobs, training, child care, welfare
- communication and transportation (e.g. mass transit, telephone and computer access
- community (e.g. religious and other organizations to meet affiliation needs)
- safety (e.g. fire, police, personal security)

- health (e.g. clean environment, adequate health care)
- education (e.g. schools, child care, adult education, libraries)
- human services (e.g. child guidance clinics, youth programs, parent education, refugee and resettlement programs)
- culture (e.g. recreation facilities, arts, music and dance)

*This framework draws from Andrews and Ben-Arieh (1999), Department of Health, England (2000), Dunst, Trivette, and Deal (1988), Endres (2000), Geismar (1980), and Greenspan (1997).

environments (Bronfenbrenner 1979). In particular, such a metaphor calls attention to the "influence of external environments on the functioning of families as contexts of human development" (Bronfenbrenner 1986:723). As an orientation to practice, ecology helps us to appreciate that human beings are engaged in continuous transaction with their environment; furthermore, the ecological view provides insight into the nature and consequence of such transactions both for human beings and for the physical and social environments in which they function (Germain and Gitterman 1996:5–19).

By offering a broad conceptual lens to view human functioning and needs, ecology underscores that social work intervention should address the interface between human beings and their impinging environments: practitioners focus on improving the transactions between people and environments in order to enhance adaptive capacities as well as enrich environments for all who function within them (Germain and Gitterman 1996). In using such an orientation, practitioners can help mobilize the actual and potential strengths and resources of individuals, families, and groups while simultaneously seeking to render environments more responsive to the adaptive and coping needs of human organisms (Kemp, Whittaker, and Tracy 1997; Maluccio 1981, 1999). In addition, workers are helped to understand the relationships between families and their environments and identify the significant sources of support as well as stress and conflict. They can then assess more objectively the complex personal and environmental factors affecting parents and children and arrive at more appropriate treatment plans and recommendations.

Flowing from the ecological orientation is a competence-centered and strength-oriented approach to practice that contrasts with the more traditional pathology or deficit model (Early and GlenMaye 2000; Hodges and Pecora 2000; Maluccio 1981 and 1999; Norman 2000; Rapp 1998; Reynolds, Walberg, and Weissberg 1999; and Saleebey 1997b, 2002).[6] While the metaphor of ecology provides a way of perceiving and understanding human beings and their functioning within the context of their environment, knowledge about competence development offers specific guidelines for professional practice and service delivery.

The competence perspective draws from ego psychology; psychodynamic psychology; and learning, developmental, and family systems theories. In social work as in other fields, competence is generally defined as the repertoire of skills that enable the person to function effectively. However, a distinction should be made between the notion of discrete competencies or skills and the broader, ecological or transactional concept of competence. The latter may be defined as the outcome of the interplay among:

- a person's capacities, skills, potentialities, limitations, and other characteristics,
- a person's motivation — that is, her or his interests, hopes, beliefs, and aspirations, and
- the qualities of the person's impinging environment — such as social networks, environmental demands, and opportunities (Maluccio 1981).

The competence perspective is akin to the strength perspective delineated by such theorists as Maluccio (1999), Norman (2000), and Saleebey (1997b, 2002). As Gutheil and Congress (2000:40) explain: "The strengths perspective focuses on capabilities, assets and positive attributes rather than problems and pathologies. The assumption is that clients have within them the qualities and resources necessary to grow and develop."

Resilience, coping, and adaptation are key constructs in the competence-centered perspective and will be considered in the next section.

Resilience, Coping, and Adaptation

Resilience refers to the application or operationalization of the strengths perspective in human functioning (Saleebey 1997a, b, 2002) and is defined variously by theorists. Along with such authors as Wolin and Wolin (1994), Walsh (1998:4) views it "as the capacity to rebound from adversity strengthened and more resourceful. It is an active process of endurance, self-righting, and growth in response to crisis and challenge." Masten, Best, and Garmezy (1991:430) describe resilience as "efforts to restore or maintain internal or external equilibrium under significant threat." Werner (1995) indicates that resilience consists of good developmental outcomes despite high-risk status; sustained competence under stress; and/or recovery from trauma. McCubbin and McCubbin (1988:247) define *family resilience* as "characteristics, dimensions and properties of families which help families to be resistant to disruption in the face of change and adaptive in the face of crisis situations."

Others regard resilience more broadly "as a general frame of reference or belief system through which individuals appraise events and situations in the environment. It allows them to define situations from their environment as a challenge and as an opportunity" (Richman and Bowen 1997:101). At any rate, resilient persons are characterized by such attributes as social competence, problem-solving skills, autonomy and self-esteem, a sense of purpose, and an orientation to the future (McCubbin et al. 1998). The concept of resilience is closely related to other perspectives such as the strength perspective, the empowerment perspective, and the social justice perspective. These perspectives emphasize "the bedrock of social work, the importance of the environment and . . . social justice" (Perez-Koenig 2000:143).

We agree with Garmezy (1994) that resilience is a promising concept that is nevertheless "dangerous" because it is based in drama: "The drama is that of the 'American dream,' the Horatio Alger legend — the mistaken view that any and all can succeed were they to work hard" (Garmezy 1994:3). Despite various questions and the need to substantiate its meaning through further research evidence, we consider resilience to be a useful construct for child and family services. Moreover, "using resilience as the knowledge base for practice creates a sense of optimism and hope" (Benard 1994:4).

The concept of resilience is also useful in conjunction with related constructs such as Bandura's "self-efficacy," Rotter's "locus of control," and Antonovsky's "sense of coherence."[7] Particularly noteworthy is the *saluto-genic* orientation to health in human beings proposed by Antonovsky (1994), including the "sense of coherence" construct, that is, the person's or family's degree of confidence that the world is comprehensible, meaningful, and manageable. The child's sense of coherence affects her or his coping and adaptation.

As noted in classical writings by such theorists as Dubos (1968), Erikson (1963), Hartmann (1958), and White (1963), human beings are active participants in their interactions with the environment. The constructs of *coping* and *adaptation* are useful in this regard. Coping refers to the person's cognitive and behavioral efforts to meet new or difficult demands or stresses, such as when a child begins to go to school or a couple enters into marriage.

Adaptation involves a reciprocal relationship between people and their environments. It is the process through which the person's biologically endowed potentialities emerge and develop in response to her or his environmental situation. As Hartmann (1958) indicates, adaptation is a creative endeavor that is influenced by the environment, the person's constitution, and her or his developmental phase. Human beings not only adapt to their environment but also are capable of changing it in accordance with their needs and attributes.

Coping and adaptation connote a complex process requiring a range of personal resources, constructive life experiences, and social and environmental supports. For example, upon entering foster care, children are faced with numerous challenges and demands that call for increased supports from their families, foster parents, and social workers.

Stress, Risk, and Protective Factors

In the course of their development, families and children encounter a variety of stresses and risks that need to be considered in any interventive plans or services. Stress and risk are closely related concepts. As Roskies (1991:412) indicates, "In spite of its widespread use, there is no single, precise definition of the term *stress.*" Selye (1956), who is regarded as the father of modern stress theory, focuses on physiological reactions of the human organism in its struggle to resist noxious stimuli or stressors. Along with other theorists, Locke and Taylor (1991:157) define stress as "the emotional response, typically consisting of fear and/or anxiety and associated physical symptoms resulting from" perceived threats to one's well-being or self-esteem. We think of stress as internal tension or strain produced in the human being in response to any one or more factors.

Risk has been defined as "any influence that increases the probability of onset, digression to a more serious state, or the maintenance of a problem condition" (Fraser 1997a:3). "Risk or vulnerability represents a heightened probability of negative outcome based on the presence of one or more" factors such as "genetic, biological, behavioral, socio-cultural, and demographic conditions, characteristics, or attributes" (Kirby and Fraser 1997:10). Examples of environmental risks are family dysfunction, child abuse, parental illness, and, above all, poverty.

Protective factors are "those internal and external forces that help children resist or ameliorate risk" (Fraser 1997a:13). Rutter (1985:600) further defines protective factors as "influences that modify, ameliorate, or alter a person's response to some environmental hazard that predisposes to a maladaptive outcome." Problem-solving skills, a sense of self-efficacy, and an internal locus of control are examples of internal forces found in resilient children and youths. Examples of external forces are the strong family presence of a caring, supportive adult in the family and a safe and supportive school setting. As Benard (1997) explains, schools can provide a protective environment for many youths and children through the caring and support and high expectations of teachers and other school personnel as well as the opportunities available for meaningful participation in the life of the classroom, school, or community.

Under certain conditions the interplay between risk factors and protective mechanisms leads to successful coping and adaptation: "An individual is able to cope so long as the balance among risks, stressful life events, and protective factors is manageable. But when risk factors and stressful life events outweigh the protective factors, even the most resilient children can develop problems (Werner 1989:80)."

Through her longitudinal, life span study of 618 children, Werner (1994 and 1995) has demonstrated the role of protective factors within the family and community, such as socioeconomic supports, in childhood, adolescence, and adulthood. As considered in subsequent chapters, social workers can play important roles in promoting resilience in children and youths. In particular, in conjunction with the concepts delineated in the preceding section, the constructs of risk, stress, and protective factors suggest several interrelated themes that can help guide social work practice with families and children:

- Human beings are engaged in ongoing, dynamic transactions with their environment and in a continuous process of growth and adaptation.
- Human beings are "open systems" that are spontaneously active and motivated to achieve competence in their coping with life demands and environmental challenges.
- Varied environmental opportunities and social supports are necessary to sustain and promote a human being's efforts to grow, to achieve self-fulfillment, and to contribute to others.
- Appropriate supports should be matched to the human being's changing qualities and needs in order to maximize the development of her or his competence, identity, autonomy, and self-fulfillment.[8]

Developmental Perspective

The developmental perspective[9] represents a certain frame of reference for understanding the growth and functioning of human beings in the context of their families and their families' transactions with their environments. Building on the ecological view of human behavior and social functioning within an environmental context, it incorporates such aspects as the stages and tasks of the family's life cycle, the biopsychosocial principles of individual growth and development, the goals and needs that are common to all human beings and families, and the particular aspirations, needs, and qualities of each person and each family in light of diversity in such areas as culture, ethnicity, race, class, and sexual orientation.

There is an extensive body of knowledge from such disciplines as anthropology, psychology, and sociology related to the developmental perspective. For example, various texts delineate the development stages of human beings through the life cycle, from infancy to adulthood, and the tasks associated with each stage (cf. Germain and Bloom 1999; Newman and Newman 1995; Zastrow and Kirst-Ashman 1997). Other authors focus on the life cycle of the family (cf. Carter and McGoldrick 1999), the linkages among developmental, family, and life cycle theories (cf. Freed 1985), and comparative analysis of traditional and alternative perspectives on human behavior and development (cf. Schriver 1995).

The above texts consider the tasks and challenges associated with different individual and family developmental cycles, the repetition of the family life cycle in blended families, the role of family routines and rituals, the significance of cultural, ethnic, racial, and gender relativity, and the ways in which family functioning (cohesion, adaptability, communication, and role fulfillment) is in part dependent upon the developmental levels of individual family members. For our purposes a number of themes flowing from the developmental perspective should be highlighted:

- Practitioners should take into account the concept of development by explicitly considering this question: Which interventions are effective, with which specific child/family problems, in which environmental settings, and at what particular developmental stages?
- Policies, services, and practice should reflect current knowledge about the development of women, minorities, and other special populations rather than rely primarily on traditional models such as those derived from psychoanalysis. For example, Okun (1996) and Devore and Schlesinger (1996), among others, have focused on human diversity and its significance for ethnic-sensitive social work practice.

- There should be special attention to the developmental needs and challenges faced by families with gay or lesbian parents or children and adolescents (Mackey, O'Brien, and Mackey 1997; Mallon 1997 and 2000). For example, Parks (1998) underscores the heterogeneity and strengths of lesbian-parent families and notes that "though 'non-traditional' in structure, lesbian families confront many 'traditional' dilemmas in early family formation and ongoing function" (386). As Parks (1998:386) indicates, these families "also confront several complications to, or variations on — these traditional family themes," as a result of societal homophobia.
- Individual as well as family development is multiply determined and always occurring, and change is inevitable. At the same time, there may be some underlying individual characteristics that are particularly difficult to change, especially in troubled families (Cadoret et al. 1995).
- Practitioners should be guided by an optimistic view of the capacity of children — and adults — to overcome early deprivation and other adverse early life experiences through nurturing and supportive experiences throughout the life cycle, particularly as they are provided with competent and innovative services. (See, for example, Biegel and Blum 1999; Rhodes and Brown 1991; Weissbourd 1996.) In short, human development is a dynamic process that involves complex and interdependent connections among human beings, their families, and their social and physical environments (Germain and Bloom 1999). Human beings actively shape — and are also shaped by their social contexts (Garbarino 1992).

The Immigrant Experience

In providing services to families and children in the increasing population of immigrants from developing countries, we need to pay explicit attention to their unique needs and circumstances and the consequent impact on their development. As Drachman (1992:68) explains:

The newcomers, who are diverse in age, language, country of origin, and culture, have been arriving mainly from Asia, the West Indies, Central America, Africa, and Eastern Europe. Their immigration status varies and includes refugees, immigrants, undocumented aliens, entrants, and parolees.

As social workers, in keeping with our historical involvement with immigrant populations, we can play an important role in providing services and promoting policies and programs on behalf of these newer groups. In this regard, Drachman (1992:68) proposes a comprehensive framework for understanding new immigrants and helping them with their development and adaptation: "The framework helps workers obtain knowledge of the needs, experiences, and circumstances of new immigrant groups and future newcomers." As outlined below, it consists of three phases, each of which includes a number of critical variables (Drachman 1992:69):

1. *Premigration and departure*

- Social, political, and economic factors
- Separation from families and friends
- Decisions regarding who leaves and who is left behind
- Act of leaving a familiar environment
- Life-threatening circumstances
- Experiences of violence
- Loss of "significant others"

2. *Transit*

- Perilous or safe journey of long duration
- Refugee camp or detention center stay of short or long duration
- Act of awaiting a foreign country's decision regarding final relocation
- Immediate and final relocation or long wait before final relocation
- Loss of significant others

3. *Resettlement*

- Cultural issues
- Reception from host country
- Opportunity structure of host country
- Discrepancy between expectations and reality
- Degree of cumulative stress throughout the migration process.

As Drachman (1992:72) indicates, the above framework can be used to learn about the needs, experiences, and circumstances of new immigrant groups as well as understand the situations of individual immigrants. Such understanding is crucial, for the United States is in the midst of the largest wave of immigration in over seventy years. Various themes are noteworthy in this regard, as explained further by Ferguson, Tracy, and Simonelli (1993).

First, one of the basic tasks that immigrant families face is connecting with and integrating themselves into the new culture. They must do this in the face of several stressors: language barriers, homesickness, lack of ethnic contacts, and adjusting to American lifestyles. Second, most of the immigrant families who come to the attention of social agencies also struggle against poverty, joblessness, and discrimination. Third, some refugees have experienced severe hardships in their country of origin: forced relocation, threats, imprisonment, deaths of family members. They bring these past fears with them. Some go through "exile shock" when they realize how suddenly and permanently their lives have changed. Most people feel good when they first immigrate, but later, maybe in the second year, they feel estranged from their country and family.

Fourth, migration is inevitably disruptive to family life, and the readjustment to a new culture can be a prolonged process. All who migrate must deal with conflicting norms of the country of origin and the United States. Some of the factors influencing adjustment are

- facility with the new language,
- economic and political situations,
- flexibility in making new connections with work, friends, and organizations, and
- connections to the country of origin.

Fifth, in their efforts to cope with these and other challenges, some families wall off the past, forcing their children to learn English and never talk about the country they left behind. Some wall off the new country, working in an enclave and never making an effort to adapt to America. A middle approach is *biculturality*, which involves maintaining old traditions while at the same time learning new ways. However, families that migrate with young children are vulnerable to role reversals in that children often acculturate more quickly than parents. The children become the interpreters for the parents, threatening parental leadership of the family. The pressure on children can be immense. They must adapt to a new culture and do well in school as well as maintain loyalties to their family and culture. The children may feel trapped between conflicting messages from the family and the new culture.[10] In addition, immigrant families of color must cope with the impact of racism throughout the acculturation process.

Intergenerational Aspects

Throughout human history and across societies, parents have relied on the extended family, especially grandparents, for help in care of their children. Such reliance is becoming increasingly problematic, due to such factors as the geographic mobility of families and, above all, growing societal problems in such areas as housing, poverty, substance abuse, and family violence. In addition, there is an increasing proportion of mothers at an early age, including early adolescence; the families of these young mothers are often struggling with their own issues, problems, and challenges.

It has been estimated that, as of the early 1990s, between 2.3 and 4.3 million children lived in the homes of relatives without their parents (Everett 1995). The U.S. Bureau of the Census (1995) reports that approximately 3.9 million children were being raised in grandparent-headed households in 1995. While kinship caring is more common among families of color, it is seen also among white families. As extensively considered by Hegar and Scannapieco (1999), kinship care is a complex phenomenon — whether provided through informal arrangements or through state supervision. According to these authors, among the issues to be considered are the following: How should formal kinship care differ from informal care arranged by the families? Should kinship care be classified as either out-of-home care or family preservation? Should foster families licensure or certification be required of kinship families? How long should the state subsidize placement with kin?

In view of the above, practitioners need to give increased attention to the intergenerational aspects of family and child welfare services.[11] In particular, agency policies and programs should recognize the crucial role of grandparents in caring partially or fully for their grandchildren, including teenage granddaughters who are pregnant or have children of their own. Since they face multiple tasks during a crucial phase of their own development, parenting grandparents need a social service system that responds to their needs. As recommended by the Child Welfare League of America (Child Welfare League of America 1994; National Commission on Family Foster Care 1991), following are some of the strategies that are especially crucial in promoting intergenerational interventions:

- assessing the capacity of grandparents to provide a nurturing home that can meet the child's developmental needs,
- offering services to the parents as well as the grandparents to meet their own needs as caregivers as well as the child's needs,
- providing adequate financial supports, especially in view of the precarious financial conditions of many grandparents,
- monitoring the child's placement in kinship care, so as to ensure the child's well-being as well as address the needs of the kinship family, and
- encouraging practitioners to appreciate and respect each the child's and family's cultural, racial, and ethnic identity.

In addition, there needs to be attention to the ongoing psychosocial issues that many parenting grandparents experience as they are faced with their own basic physical, emotional, and financial adjustments (Poe 1992), the interaction between parents and grandparents, with its potential for frustration and conflicts, the issue of permanency planning for children placed with relatives, and the parents' own need for help in connection with their own problems as well as their functioning as parents. Various authors consider these issues in detail. For example, Poe (1992) offers implications for policy and treatment in the situations of black grandparents. Doucette-Dudman and LaCure (1996) present guidelines for helping grandparents and social service professionals cope with the challenges inherent in grandparent parenting. Generations United (1998) offers recommendations and strategies for dealing with economic supports, health care, education, child care, and legal issues in the situations of grandparents and other relatives raising children. Larkin (1999) and Power and Maluccio (1999) describe intergenerational approaches to helping families at risk, such as foster grandparent programs, mentoring of young mothers by elderly persons, and having older adults work with families experiencing child abuse or neglect.

Feminist Perspective

A feminist perspective for social work emphasizes social, political, and economic justice for women, who have traditionally and historically been oppressed. Such a perspective is characterized by these key themes: *knowing*, such as use of narratives and stories, *connecting*, such as emphasis on community, coalitions, and collaboration, *caring*, such as showing concern and empathy, and *multiplicity*, such as respect for diversity (Van Den Bergh 1995a:xxxiv). In addition, as others indicate: "A feminist vision for a different society includes the demand for gender equality as well as a commitment to altering the processes and manner in which private and public lives are organized and conducted" (Van Den Bergh and Cooper 1986:1).

Feminism is a lens through which to view the experiences of vulnerable women and their children and critically examine their needs and social responses to them. For example, the concept of the feminization of poverty refocuses attention on the fact that currently most poor people in the United States are women and their children. Even among the elderly the poor are mostly women. A feminist approach would focus on the causes of poverty — what pushes women into poverty or inhibits their escape from it — such as workplace discrimination, lack of child support, premature and single parenting, undereducation and insufficient training, and racism. Such an approach would help to fashion policy and program responses seeking to eliminate oppression of women.

The feminist perspective parallels many of the precepts of social work, such as concern for equity and equality, nondiscrimination, self-determination, and human dignity. However, feminist social workers criticize the profession for focusing more on individualistic, personal change strategies than on advocacy strategies that transform the economic, political, and social structures impeding people from achieving equality (Chandler 1986). As reviewed below, other writers expand on this theme.

Abramovitz (1988:10) explains the oppression of women as being rooted in the "family ethic," which defines proper roles for women as marrying, having children, and being supported by a male breadwinner. "Deviants" from the "family ethic," if they are poor, are considered "undeserving" poor. Current and past attempts at "welfare reform" continue to "reproduce the primacy of women's responsibility for family and home" (Abramovitz 1988:10). Moreover, women who depart from their traditional roles are penalized in various ways, as evidenced by sex discrimination in the social security program (Abramovitz 1986:221–223). Levy (1995) examines violence against women, offering implications for social work practice derived from feminist principles and taking "into account the interplay between sexism and racism and the universality as well as the diversity of women's experiences with violence" (321). Chalk and King (1998) and their collaborators offer a comprehensive view of family violence, including a thorough assessment of a range of prevention and treatment programs. *(See chapter 2 for further discussion of family violence as a life condition for many families.)*

Berry (1993), writing about the dilemmas of work and child care responsibility faced by many women today, speaks of the traditional family ideal in the same voice as Abramovitz (1988:27): "This ideal legitimates gender relations that continue to restrict women's economic opportunities, reproductive choice, sexual freedom, and sense of independent identity." According to Berry (1993), underlying the notion of a family model that assigns child care solely as a woman's responsibility are issues of power, resources, and control (i.e., patriarchy). Even newer employment policies that recognize worker's family care responsibilities (e.g., flextime, parental leave, and child care) are seen primarily as benefits for employed women, not men. Acceptance of men's claims to them is limited.

It is also interesting that this view of women as primarily responsible for caregiving does not extend to single mothers receiving welfare assistance. When their term of eligibility for assistance is expiring, these women are virtually forced to seek employment, sometimes without much support for securing appropriate child care. Because the jobs they are able to find are mostly entry-level and low paying, these mothers may continue to depend on some types of welfare assistance, never becoming fully self-sufficient. Moreover, licensed or formal child care programs may be unavailable to them because of their work schedules (Kisker and Ross 1997). Lacking access to, or information about, child care subsidies, they may leave their children in the care of relatives or neighbors without exploring the full range of child care options and without help in identifying what constitutes quality (Pine 1999). As a result, these women may be viewed as doing neither wage-earning or parenting well enough. As emphasized by Pelton (1999), they are thus discriminated against, as another example of the negative impact of recent welfare reforms, particularly the "Personal Responsibility and Work Opportunity Reconciliation Act" of 1996 (PL 104–193):[12]

[These reforms] will push some children further into deeper poverty, increase charges of "abuse and neglect" against their parents, potentially push more families into the arms of a coercive child welfare system and, in conjunction with the Adoption and Safe Families Act of 1997, will further accelerate the permanent separation of children from their parents.

(Pelton 1999:1479)

Swift (1995) views women who are involved in the child welfare system as doubly blamed. First, in our society the nuclear family form, which has evolved along with urbanization and industrialization, is the primary unit and the one seen as having exclusive responsibility for the rearing of children. This exclusivity is congruent with the "individualistic philosophy" that so defines our society. With self-reliance as the dominant virtue, we label anyone who cannot be self-reliant as a failure. Mothers, who must manage both of the traditional, self-sufficient family roles of caretaker and provider, are blamed for failing to fulfill either one successfully. They must be ruled a failure in order to receive help. Swift (1995) notes that "the discourse of neglect has long since established mothers as the 'crucial variable' in neglect" (101). She further indicates: "The study of child neglect is in effect the study of mothers who 'fail'" (101). Reflecting a feminist perspective on women of color, Gould (1985:302) "asserts that racism and sexism are equally oppressive structural features of society and the child welfare system."

As suggested above, "Feminist practice is described as a perspective and not a technique" (Hanmer and Statham 1989:126). Similarly, Land (1995:5) delineates feminist clinical social work as a philosophy of psychotherapeutic intervention: "Clinical social workers who practice from a feminist philosophy may practice from a variety of theoretical orientations, including cognitive-behavioral, psychodynamic . . . psychosocial . . . problem solving, family systems, constructivism . . . or they may use a variety of treatment modalities."[13] Laird (1995:36), on the other hand, "blends together three metaperspectives for a post-modern family-centered practice: feminist, social constructionist, and cultural." In so doing she stresses a number of themes, including emphasis on strength rather than pathology, dismantling of gender hierarchies, and greater sharing of power between client and worker. Similarly, Lee (2000) stresses the role of empowerment in feminist social work practice.

In child welfare a feminist perspective would "recognize the oppressive forces in society that prevent mothers from adequately caring for their children and attempt to develop policies and programs to rectify the situation" (Brandwein 1986:253). Miller (1991) argues for a fundamental reanalysis of basic policy aims and strategies so as to take into account the fact that the major stakeholders in the child welfare system are women and children.

In addressing this problem, Chandler (1986), like Berry (1993), cited earlier, advocates both role equity and role change as solutions. Role equity is the freedom to adopt a broader variety of lifestyles, while role change aims at changing "sex based distinctions that prescribe primary caretaker roles for women" (Chandler 1986:160). In other words, women are not seen as having inherent responsibilities for child care and homemaking. Freeman, Logan, and Gowdy (1992) propose the development of educational and employment programs that emphasize practitioners helping women clients to empower themselves. Hanmer and Statham (1989:124) argue for finding "ways of working with women which address the issues of women's unequal power, status, privilege and options."

Specific strategies for achieving the kinds of changes proposed by the above authors were delineated nearly fifteen years ago by leading social work writers in a special issue of *Child Welfare*, "Toward a Feminist Approach to Child Welfare" (Costin 1985). These strategies remain important and timely today. In particular, Sarri (1985) suggests federal policy changes for dealing with the "feminization" of poverty, especially by expanding eligibility requirements and benefits for the working poor. Meyer (1985) redefines family foster care in line with a feminist perspective; above all, she argues for counteracting a pejorative view of foster children and foster mothers by developing a practice model that is designed to uplift the economic and social status of foster mothers. Kamerman (1985) examines the status of child care services and implications for gender equity and women's solidarity; she highlights, for example, the need for preschool programs such as nursery school or prekindergarten for at least some part of the day for working mothers of children aged three to five.

More recently Swift (1995) has proposed a range of recommendations for "transforming" child welfare — especially child neglect services and policies — in ways that reflect the views of feminist theorists on child welfare. For instance, she redefines child neglect as a societal problem rather than a personal problem, suggests "viewing poor caregiving as one feature of life, connected to other contextual features" (182), thus taking into account the mother's social circumstances rather than simply her personality characteristics, and stresses the importance of assisting mothers in empowering themselves. Similarly, Van Den Bergh (1995b) and her collaborators set forth feminist perspectives on social work theory and practice and discuss the feminization of poverty and its impact on child rearing. They also consider feminist practice with special populations, including women of color, homeless women, lesbian clients, elderly women, and women with substance abuse problems.[14]

Child-Focused and Family-Centered Practice

Social work practice requires that we maintain a principal focus on the child within a family-centered context. As discussed more extensively elsewhere,[15] such a focus suggests that, in most cases, the child can best be helped by regarding the family as the central unit of service or focus of attention, whenever and as much as possible. Human beings can best be understood and helped within their significant environment, and the family is the most intimate environment of all. It is here that the child develops and forms her or his identity and basic competence. The family has the potential to provide resources throughout the life cycle, especially as its members are sustained and supported by various services (Germain and Bloom 1999). The family's own environment can be employed as the arena in which practitioners intervene to help strengthen communication, parenting skills, and parent-child relationships.

As reflected throughout this volume, we consider the following guidelines as especially important in implementing child-focused and family-centered practice:

- There is emphasis on prevention and intervention strategies that reduce stress and risk and promote coping and resilience in children and families.
- Practitioners must understand the relationship between race/ethnicity and issues such as family norms, child-rearing practices, childhood and family poverty, discrimination, and funding of social services.
- Assessment and intervention focus on the family's transactions with its kinship system, school, community institutions, and other social networks that affect its functioning. Intervention strategies are directed not only toward engaging the family in treatment but also

toward changing the social systems that influence it. There is emphasis on case management strategies and community-based approaches that help empower vulnerable clients (Rothman 1994).

- Many parents can be helped to become rehabilitated or to plan responsibly for their children through family treatment approaches as alternatives to placement of children out of their homes or as methods of speeding up the reunification of placed children with their families. For example, birth parents of children at risk can be empowered through the use of group training.

- When children are separated as a result of hospitalization, imprisonment, foster home placement, or residential placement, family ties between them and their families should be preserved as much as possible, through such means as consistent parental visiting. The natural bonds between children in care and their parents may continue to be important for most parents and children long after they are physically separated for either short-term or long-term periods.

- Foster family, group care, or residential placement of a child should be seen as a part of the overall service rather than as *the* service — as a tool, rather than as an end in itself. In line with this, there should be efforts to have parents, foster parents, or other child care personnel regard themselves as partners in a shared undertaking, with common goals and mutually supportive and complementary roles.

- A major source of help often can be the family's extended kinship system. (Danzy and Jackson 1997; Everett, Chipungu, and Leashore 1991), as in situations involving parental substance abuse. As another example, in many cases the extended family, with agency support, can help a parent avert placement or reduce the duration of placement in an unfamiliar setting.

- Mutual aid groups, such as those for vulnerable adolescents, gay and lesbian youths, sexual abuse survivors, or bereaved children, can be therapeutic as well as empowering (Gitterman and Shulman 1994).

- Children and youths themselves can also be actively involved in the helping process, including reaching decisions regarding the best permanent plan for them. As practitioners become more comfortable in asking about their views, they find that children and youths have a lot to say that should be taken into account in planning services on their behalf (cf. Martin and Palmer 1997; Mech and Rycraft 1995).

- Above all, the child's and family's safety is always a paramount concern, and there should be vigorous efforts to provide a safe environment for the child wherever he or she may be living. As described in the next chapter, risks and vulnerabilities in children's environments go beyond family conflict or parental inadequacy and include many other factors such as poverty, inadequate housing, and community violence.

We have introduced the knowledge base useful in understanding and working with vulnerable families and children through a child-focused, family-centered orientation that can be applied to service provision in diverse agency and community settings. In the next chapter we focus on the risks and vulnerabilities that children and families face. Historically, social workers have been extensively involved with these families, in line with the profession's unique focus on the transactions between people and their environments, emphasis on self-determination of clients, and commitment to promoting the competence and strengths of children and their families.

Work with these families in greatest need is consistent with the primary mission of the profession as stated in the NASW *Code of Ethics*: to enhance human well-being and help meet the basic needs of all people, with particular attention to the needs and empowerment of people who are vulnerable, oppressed, and living in poverty (National Association of Social Workers 1999:1). The framework of needs and resources presented in this chapter is also consistent with social work's mission. It directs the practitioner to both the child and family and "the environmental forces that create, contribute to, and address problems in living" (NASW 1999:1).

Notes

1. See Smith (1995) for an overview of major family theories, including structural-functional theory, family systems theory, human ecology theory, and family development theory.
2. As Gambrill (1997: 571) further observes: "Families may be defined by biological relatedness and/or living arrangements. There are many kinds of families including step-families, nuclear families, extended

families, gay/lesbian families, single-parent families, families without children, families with grown children, and bicultural families."

3. See Billingsley (1968); Caldwell, Greene, and Billingsley (1994); and Carter and McGoldrick (1999) for further discussion of family functions.

4. For discussion of the dimensions of race and ethnicity in social work practice with families and children, see Anderson, Ryan, and Leashore (1997); Cohen (1992); Courtney et al. (1996); Everett (1997); Ewalt, Freeman, and Fortune (1999); Fong and Fuzuto (2001); Gutiérrez and Lewis (1999); Iglehart and Becerra (1995); and Pinderhughes (1997).

5. In developing the "Framework of Needs and Resources for Family and Child Well-Being," we have drawn on the contributions of our colleagues in Britain who have worked extensively to develop a child-centered assessment framework aimed at improving outcomes for children in need (Department of Health, England — Department for Education and Employment, Home Office 2000). Because of this emphasis, the British framework places children at the center of the three-sided model. Currently the assessment framework is being used throughout Britain by local social service providers to assess needs and plan interventions with children and families.

In attempting to create a model showing the most complete set of needs and attributes for well-being, we have also drawn on the work of Dunst, Trivette, and Deal (1988), who developed a set of twelve categories of need ranging from economic to cultural/social. Geismar's (1980) framework for developing his "Profile of Family Functioning" with its delineation and discussion of nine areas of functioning was also helpful, as was Endres's (2000) "Family Development Matrix Outcomes Model." Endres's model serves both as an assessment tool and as a means of helping families recognize their strengths and is organized on a five-point scale from "thriving" to "in-crisis." Our thinking about what children need in order to thrive was especially enhanced by Greenspan's (1997:264–267) seven "irreducible needs of childhood," which range from consistent, nurturing relationships to stable neighborhoods and communities. Andrews and Ben-Arieh's (1999) work to delineate sixteen variables associated with positive child development worldwide was also extremely useful as we developed the child dimension of the three-sided model.

6. See "Special Issue on the Strengths Perspective," *Families in Society:*

The Journal of Contemporary Human Services, Vol. 82, No. 3 (May–June 2001): 217–324.

7. For further consideration of these and other constructs related to "resilience," see Antonovsky (1994).

8. For more extensive consideration of the concepts of stress, risk, and protective factors, see Fraser (1997b), Haggerty et al. (1994), and Monat and Lazarus (1991). Also see Smokowski (1998) for description of prevention and early intervention programs that help promote coping and resilience in disadvantaged children and Walsh (1998) for a comprehensive approach to family resilience, with guidelines for recognizing and fostering core elements of resilience.

9. For further details regarding the developmental perspective, see Pecora et al. (2000), from which this section has been adapted.

10. For a sampling of information on the values, adaptation, and functioning of members of newer immigrant groups, see Balgopal (2000); Cheung (1996); Drachman (1992 and 1995); Drachman, Kwon-Ahn, and Paulino (1996); Fong and Furuto (2001); Fuligni (1998); Guarnaccia and Lopez (1998); Lashley (2000); and Sewell-Coker, Hamilton-Collins, and Fein (1985).

11. For further details on intergenerational approaches to helping families at risk, see Henkin and Kingson (1998–1999).

12. See the Personal Responsibility and Work Opportunity Reconciliation Act of 1996, P.L. 104–193, 110 Stat. 2105.

13. Noting that feminist clinical social work may reflect a hybrid of theoretical orientations, Land (1995) summarizes a range of theories and core principles that inform feminist practice.

14. See Van Den Bergh and Cooper (1986) and Van Den Bergh (1995b) for suggestions on incorporating feminist issues and strategies into current models of community-based social work practice.

15. See, for example, Maluccio, Warsh, and Pine (1998); Pecora et al. (2000); and Warsh, Maluccio, and Pine (1994).

Questions for Discussion

1. How would you define "family" in contemporary society, and why? How does your definition take into account human diversity?

2. Apply the framework of needs and resources for family and child well-being presented in this chapter to a family on your caseload. How does the

framework help you in understanding this family? How would you revise the framework to make it more useful for families coming to the attention of your agency?

3. Consider a family from your caseload in conjunction with the conceptual model of needs and resources described in this chapter. What assets does this family have for promoting the well-being of its members? What community resources are available to promote optimal functioning and well-being?

4. Choose a family that has been referred to your agency with a presenting problem in the areas of family functioning or child rearing. What do you regard as this family's most resilient features, and why?

5. What do you see as the main needs and challenges confronting recent immigrant families to the United States from a particular developing country, and why?

6. You have been asked to offer for colleagues in your agency a fifteen-minute, selective review of the major implications of the feminist perspective for social work with families and children. Outline the points that you would plan to cover.

Suggestions for Further Information

Anderson, G. R., A. S. Ryan, and B. R. Leashore, eds. 1997. *The Challenge Of Permanency Planning in a Multicultural Society*. New York: Haworth.

Carter, B. and M. McGoldrick, eds. 1999. *The Expanded Family Life Cycle: Individual, Family, And Social Perspectives*. 3d ed. Boston: Allyn and Bacon.

Ewalt, P. L., E. M. Freeman, and A. E. Fortune, eds. 1999. *Multicultural Issues in Social Work: Practice and Research*. Washington, D.C.: NASW.

Germain, C. G. and M. Bloom. 1999. *Human Behavior in the Social Environment: An Ecological View*. 2d ed. New York: Columbia University Press.

Haggerty, R. J., L. R. Sherrod, N. Garmezy, and M. Rutter, eds. 1994. *Stress, Risk, and Resilience in Children: Processes, Mechanisms, and Interventions*. Cambridge: Cambridge University Press.

McCubbin, H. I., E. A. Thompson, A. I. Thompson, and J. Fromer, eds. 1998. *Stress, Coping, and Health in Families: Sense of Coherence and Resiliency*. Thousand Oaks, Cal.: Sage.

Reynolds, A. J., H. J. Walberg, and R. P. Weissberg, eds. 1999. *Promoting Positive Outcomes: Issues in Children's and Families' Lives*. Washington, D.C.: CWLA.

Saleebey, D., ed. 2002. *The Strengths Perspective in Social Work Practice*. 3d ed. Boston: Allen and Bacon.

Van Den Bergh, N., ed. 1995. *Feminist Practice in the Twenty-first Century*. Washington, D.C.: NASW.

2   Risks and Vulnerabilities

In this chapter we focus on some of the risks to which the most vulnerable families and children in today's society are exposed. We build on the family-centered, ecological orientation to social work practice with families and children described in chapter 1, examining risks in the larger social and economic environment, in the families' own neighborhood and community, and in their homes and interpersonal environments. If interventions to mediate these risks and support families in their important roles are to be successful, the importance of viewing these risks to families and their children as deriving from a series of embedded and interrelated contexts and systems cannot be understated. Moreover, for social workers who, alone among human services professionals, are trained to work with systems of all sizes, understanding how these systems impact on and influence the family is critical to successful assessment and intervention. As social workers we must know what are the best ways "to enable families to perform the magic feat of which they alone are capable: making and keeping human beings human" (Bronfenbrenner 1986:738). And, we must recognize and build on people's strengths and potentialities, as emphasized in chapter 1.

This chapter also reflects back to the conceptual framework for promoting well-being described in chapter 1, in which we delineate what families and their children need for optimal functioning and development and show, sadly, how many and which needs go unmet for vulnerable families. The interrelatedness of the framework's three domains — children's needs, family needs, and community resources — becomes clear as the risks are discussed, as does the co-occurrence of multiple risks. After defining poverty as a life condition for many groups in our society, we consider poverty and its association with impoverished neighborhoods, adolescent pregnancy and parenting, school problems, and homelessness. We then examine the impact of violence on families and children. Next, we discuss the risks deriving from family separation because of a child's placement in out-of-home care or parental incarceration. We conclude with a review of health risks and vulnerabilities.

Poverty as a Life Condition

Without question, the greatest of all threats to families is poverty. In fact, all of the risks that will be delineated and described in this chapter are more likely to be associated with, or derive from, a family's economic status. As considered in this section, these include unemployment, inadequate housing or homelessness, divorce and family disintegration, family and community violence, school failure, inadequate health care, teen-aged pregnancy, and a wide range of other health risks and vulnerabilities from HIV/AIDS to lead poisoning and poor nutrition. In short, as Greenspan has indicated, poor families are the most vulnerable to a large "cluster of sorrows" (Greenspan 1997:252).

Defining Poverty

In the United States the official definition of poverty is an absolute measure. The federal poverty line is adjusted each year for both the cost of living and family size. In 1997 the poverty line was $16,400 for a family of four (Children's Defense Fund 1999). This measure of poverty, established in 1964, is based on the the the cost of a minimally nutritious diet as established by the U.S. Department of Agriculture (USDA), multiplied by three, with food assumed to represent one-third of a family's living expenses. Mollie Orshansky, an economist with the Social Security Administration at the time, is credited with this definition of poverty (Handler 1995). Using this measure, families considered extremely poor subsist on incomes of half the poverty line or less, those that are quite poor have incomes between 50 and 100 percent of the poverty line, and those considered near poor have between 100 and 185 percent of poverty line income (National Center for Children in Poverty 1998).

Critics of the poverty line as an accurate measure of economic status note that only cash income and assistance are counted. Neither the Earned Income Tax Credit nor noncash benefits are calculated. At the same time, family income matched to the poverty threshold for purposes of determining eligibility for income and other supports is pre-tax; none of the costs of earning the income (e.g., child care) are deducted from income totals. Also problematic is that no cost of living differences among different parts of the country are factored into the poverty line (Betson and Michael 1997). Other critics point to the formula underlying the poverty line, noting that food no longer represents one-third of a family's budget, especially given the lack of affordable housing and the fact that many poor families may pay as much as half (and sometimes more) of their income on rent and utilities while food has dropped to one-seventh of average family expenditure (U. S. General Accounting Office 1997). Others point to the fact that the USDA's minimally adequate, lowest-cost diet is meant for short-term consumption only; nutritional adequacy of this diet over the long term is highly questionable. Thus the accuracy of the poverty line as a threshold for determining family need has been contested.

A new approach to measuring poverty, recommended by the National Research Council of the National Academy of Sciences in 1995, would take some of the above limitations into account, resulting, some say, in a more accurate national measure of the resources and needs of families (Betson and Michael 1997). For now, however, the federal poverty line that has been used for over thirty years remains the most useful, albeit flawed, absolute measure of the economic status of children and families.

While the poverty line represents a level of deprivation, poverty can also be viewed as representing inequality. The poorest one-fifth of Americans receive less than 5 percent of the national personal income, while the wealthiest one-fifth receive 42.7 percent (DiNitto and Dye 1987). If there were income equality, each group would receive 20 percent of personal income; the current difference represents the extent of inequality. And, as discussed below, this inequality is more likely to be borne by those families with children to support.

Which Families Are Poor?

Families with children are three times as likely to be poor as families without children (Gustavsson and Segal 1994). Over 20 percent of all children, 14.3 million, in the United States are poor (Children's Defense Fund 2001). And, in every state in the nation, children are more likely than adults to be poor. In this "juvenalization of poverty" preschoolers are the poorest Americans (Gustavsson and Segal 1994:59). According to the 2000 census, one in five (19.7 percent) of children under five are poor (Children's Defense Fund 2001).When the number of children living in near poverty (185 percent of the poverty line) is added to those at or below it, the percent of poor preschool children in the U.S. rises to 43 (National Center for Children in Poverty 1998).

Although the largest number of poor children are white, black and Hispanic children are much more likely be poor. In 2000 nearly one in three black children (30.9 percent) and over one in four Hispanic children (28 percent) were poor (Children's Defense Fund 2001). Poverty rates among very young Hispanic children have increased 53 percent in the past twenty years (National Center for Children in Poverty 1998). Black children are more likely than other poor children to experience the deleterious effects of long-term poverty (Corcoran and Chaundry 1997).

Families with only one parent are the most likely to be poor. Among families of young children with two parents, the poverty rate is 11.5 percent, as compared with single-parent families with young children, where the rate is 54.8 percent (National Center for Children in Poverty 1998). The data on families of color are even more bleak. According to 1991 poverty figures, the poverty rate for both black and Hispanic female-headed families was 60.1 percent (Gustavsson and Segal 1994). Moreover, the number of families among the very poor — those living below half of the poverty line — increased in 1997 to 2.7 million. Most of the increase of 426,000 were families headed by single mothers (Children's Defense Fund 1999).

Wilson (1987) has pointed out that sex and marital status of the head of the household are the two key determinants of a family's impoverishment. When families are headed by women, especially younger ones, they are much more vulnerable to poverty than are other types of families. Divorce, separation, and out-of wedlock births all contribute to the growth of female-headed families. However, the proportion of out-of wedlock births is growing. Of the 4.1 million babies born in 1992, 1.2 million, or 30 percent, of them were born to unmarried women. This represents a 2.5 times increase since 1977 (Harris 1996). These figures represent changes in two areas: the decline in percentage of women who are married and the declining rate of births to married women, the result of which is that the proportion of out-

of-wedlock births of the total of all births has grown (Wilson 1987). Wilson
further notes that almost 40 percent of these are to women under twenty
years of age. Although the ratio of out-of wedlock births is much higher for
black women than for white, level of education is highly correlated with the
incidence of such births in both groups. Among college graduates, births to
unmarried black women is 21 percent compared to 2 percent for unmarried
white women; for high school dropouts, it is 83 percent for black women
and 38 percent for white women (Jencks 1991).

Young mothers in female-headed families are more likely to have had
their schooling interrupted, a factor highly associated with underemployment or joblessness. Moreover, they rarely receive child support. Wilson
(1987) suggests that there is a strong relationship between the increasing rate
of joblessness among black men and the rate of black female-headed families
and single mothers.

Schein's (1995) in-depth study of thirty rural women who were impoverished — they were mainly single parents whose average annual income was
less than $8,000 — showed a profile of courage and tenacity as the women
struggled to balance their often competing roles of provider and parent.
Schein illustrates this by quoting the words of one mother: "I was working
at the dog-bone factory. My daughter had so many problems with her ears.
She had gotten sick when I was working and I missed work and I kept missing
work because of taking her to the doctors and getting her operations done,
and I got fired" (Schein 1995:29).

Schein posits an "ABC's of poverty" to explain the macro and micro
factors contributing to the situations of the women in her study. A is the
absence of education and training; B is the betrayal by a mate; and C is the
negative experiences in the women's own childhoods.

Poverty and Impoverished Neighborhoods

Although many poor people live in suburban or rural areas, poverty is
becoming much more of an urban problem. The proportion of poor people
living in cities rose from 27 to 41 percent between 1959 and 1985 (Gephart
1997). Thus, in addition to clustering with the other indicators of disadvantage listed earlier in this chapter, poverty itself is often clustering in urban
neighborhoods with more poor people living in areas where there are other
poor people. In the decade between 1980 and 1990, census data show an

increase in the number of metropolitan census tracts with 40 percent or more people living in poverty. Residents of these communities were more likely to be black and Hispanic: Of the 11.2 million people who lived in poor communities, 50 percent were black, 33 percent Hispanic (Gephart 1997). It stands to reason that poor families without needed goods and services are at greater risk if they live in areas where their neighbors are also in dire need and thus unable to help.

William Julius Wilson (1996) has proposed that the problems in these poor, urban neighborhoods, such as crime, family dissolution, and poverty, can be tied directly to the disappearance of work in these communities. He maintains that high levels of joblessness have resulted in low levels of social organization. "When jobs are scarce, many people eventually lose their feeling of connectedness to work in the formal economy; they no longer expect work to be a regular, and regulating, force in their lives (Wilson 1996:30). The departure of work from urban communities is a major, but not the only, barrier to full employment for their residents. Other factors include the lack of transportation to jobs located outside the community, lack of affordable, available child care, low levels of education and poor job skills, and a wide variety of health problems that impede employment.

Those who lack education and training and access to employment, as well as experience a host of other social problems, are part of the growing group now known as the urban underclass — people who are "socially and economically isolated from the majority of society" (Gustavsson and Segal 1994:65; Ricketts and Sawhill 1988). Jencks (1991) has defined the underclass as "composed of people who lack the social and cultural skills required to deal with mainstream American institutions" (29).

Adolescent Pregnancy and Parenting

As noted above, nearly 40 percent of out-of-wedlock births are to adolescents. Unquestionably, teenaged pregnancy is a high-risk experience for both mother and child. Pregnant adolescents are much less likely to seek or obtain prenatal care than their older counterparts. Complications in childbirth, low birth weight of their children, and increased risk of premature birth are among the health risks to the adolescent and her child. Lack of family and spousal support, poverty, inadequate health care, lack of information about child development and parenting, a scarcity of other needed supports and resources, and the challenge of assuming parenting roles while still maturing herself all serve to constrain an adolescent mother's ability to adequately meet her child's (and her own) needs. Anderson (1991), whose work illuminates various aspects of life in the inner-city neighborhood, points out that for the young woman there is an allure of the street culture around having a baby, such as recognition from peers that a man found her desirable and the change in status to a "grown woman." By the time the baby is three years old, however, the balance between pride in motherhood and the burdens of parenting shifts. By then the child's multiple developmental needs are many, and the adolescent mother may feel trapped with even fewer options for the future than ever. This young mother may then look to her own parents for help. Grandparents raising their grandchildren often have limited resources and may even have their own young children to raise, which adds further risks to children born to adolescent mothers (Henkin and Kingson 1998–1999; Roe and Minkler 1998–1999). Among grandparents raising grandchildren, one in five lives in poverty (Children's Defense Fund 2001).

Children of single adolescent mothers are twice as likely to experience low school achievement and grade repetition, serious discipline problems and unruly conduct in school, and running away, all of which are the precursors for school dropout, joblessness, delinquency, and adolescent parenthood. Hence a cycle of impoverishment is established (Harris 1996). And, while it is difficult to separate the effects of poverty and single parenthood, their result clearly is double jeopardy for both children and their parents (Handler 1995). By the time children enter school, the "buffering power" of parents begins to decline sharply, as the children are exposed to impoverished and destructive settings outside their homes (Handler 1995).

School Dropout and School Failure

School dropout — leaving school without successfully completing a high school program — is another risk factor likely to both a cause and an effect of poverty. Poor children are at much greater risk of leaving school prematurely. In 1996 11.1 percent of students from families in the lowest quintile of income dropped out of high school as compared to 2.1 percent of students from families in the highest-income quintile (National Center for Education Statistics 1996). As with other factors placing children at risk, race and ethnicity are closing linked: Hispanic and black students are at greater risk of dropping out of high school than their white counterparts. In 1996 there were 3.6 million young adults who were between sixteen and twenty-four years of age and out of school without completing high school. Among Hispanics in this age group, 1.3 million or 29.4 percent had dropped out of school. For young adults who were black, 13 percent had dropped out. While whites in this age group accounted for the largest proportion of the school dropouts — 1.6 million — their dropout rate was lowest at 7.3 percent (National Center for Education Statistics 1996).

In addition to income, race, and ethnicity, factors associated with dropping out of school include grade retention (being held back), having a physical, emotional, or learning disability, and being born outside the United States. Young people who have been retained are more likely to drop out of school than those who are promoted each year. This is especially true for students retained in the later grades. Students retained for two or more years were nearly 4 times more likely to drop out of school. Students with disabilities were nearly 1.5 times more likely to drop out than those who were not disabled (National Center for Education Statistics 1995). Not surprisingly, foreign-born young people may experience language as a barrier both to enrolling in, and successfully completing, high school in the United States (National Center for Education Statistics 1996). These risks are compounded when students attend schools that are ill-equipped, are understaffed, and have insufficient resources to meet their needs for remediation, special education, and language and cultural consistency. Moreover, in urban as well as suburban areas violence has made some schools unsafe.

Homelessness and Substandard Housing

The importance of adequate housing to family well-being cannot be overemphasized. Housing is more than merely shelter from the elements. Housing is home, a place where people can find you, the setting for family life, in the neighborhood where you play, shop, and see your friends and neighbors (Mulroy 1995a). Unfortunately, too many families do not have housing adequate for their needs, principally because they lack funds required to purchase or rent it. Cost affects everything about housing: quality, space, location, and neighborhood. For some families housing is in unsafe physical condition in impoverished neighborhoods that lack basic services. Others are forced to share housing with other families, which leads to serious over-crowding. Still others are forced to spend far too much of their limited income on housing, resulting in scarce funds available to meet other basic needs. Finally, some are without housing at all and join the growing numbers of homeless families.

The Department of Housing and Urban Development (HUD) has de-veloped standards for housing in this country that consist of three criteria. First is a home's physical adequacy, which includes heating, plumbing, con-struction. Second is the number of people living in the home; more than one person to a room is considered overcrowding. Third is the cost of the housing. Rent should represent no more than 30 percent of income; in the case of ownership, the mortgage and home maintenance should represent not more than 40 percent of a family's income. Using these standards, nearly one-third of all dwellings in the United States would be problematic; 40 percent of these housing units are occupied by families in which women are the head of the household (Mulroy 1995a).

There currently is a housing crisis in the U.S.; increased demand for afford-able housing has far outstripped its diminishing supply. This is a result of a number of factors. Chief among them are growing numbers of families in poverty, increased competition for inner-city housing stock between poor fam-ilies and wealthier ones seeking to "gentrify" neighborhoods that are conve-nient to city centers, discrimination against families, especially families of color, that limits their ability to relocate to better neighborhoods, a sharp decline in federal funds to build affordable housing in the 1980s, and increases in the cost of housing that are not matched by income increases (Mulroy 1995a).

In the past decade home ownership has declined among all families. In 1980 almost half of all young families owned homes. That proportion de-clined to one-third of families in 1991 (Children's Defense Fund 1992). Few families in single parent households live in their own homes as compared to those with two parents. Only about a third of single parents are homeowners, whereas two-thirds of two-parent families are. Moreover, 5 million poor fam-ilies who rent paid over half their income for housing (Mulroy 1995a).

As found in a study of poor families in Boston, homelessness, the most visible result of the housing crisis, is "the bottom rung of the rental housing crisis for the economically marginal who have the fewest economic and social supports (Mulroy 1995b:57). Nationally, the estimated number of those who are homeless is between 2 and 3 million (Rossi 1990; Children's Defense Fund 1989). We are experiencing the highest rates of homelessness since the Great Depression in the early nineteen thirties. Moreover, families and children are the fastest growing group, representing 34 percent of the homeless; children represent one out of every four homeless persons (Gustavsson and Segal 1994). One study of twenty-nine cities showed the rate to be 38 percent (Harms, Ray, and Rolandelli 1998).

The effects on a family and its children of being homeless and living "on the street" are obvious. There are exposure to the elements and inability to meet the most basic of feeding and personal care needs, not to mention fear and anxiety about real dangers. Even when a family finds a place in a shelter for the homeless, its members are vulnerable. Shelters can be frightening and sometimes dangerous places. Usually, a family ending up homeless and in a shelter has exhausted all other forms of support and/or is escaping family violence. Families seeking shelter services may be separated because of age limits. For example, children over a certain age may not be eligible to stay in a particular facility (Gustavsson and Segal 1994). Shelters may provide overnight accommodations but require clients to leave during the daytime, forcing families to find alternative arrangements.

A number of studies have documented deleterious effects on children of both homelessness and living in a shelter. In either case, children's school performance is likely to be affected. Maza and Hall (1998) found that 30 percent of the children they studied were achieving below their grade level. Moving to a shelter is likely to mean that children are unable to attend their own school. Children living in shelters may lack appropriate clothing to wear to school; they may be subject to teasing about their appearance by other children (Harms, Ray, and Rolandelli 1998). The lack of quiet and privacy in a shelter makes doing homework very difficult. Even worse, when their families become homeless, many children do not attend school at all, as reported in a study by Maza and Hall (1998).

Health and safety are also jeopardized by the need to live in a shelter. Children in shelters have higher rates of upper respiratory illnesses, ear infections, skin ailments, and dental problems (Wright 1991). Lack of preventive health care leads to even higher rates of illness. Health status differences between homeless children and children in general can be dramatic. For example, the National Health Care for the Homeless program found that homeless children were thirty-five times more likely to have head lice than were children from the general population (Kryder-Coe, Salamon, and Molnar 1991). While not life threatening, this is a condition that prohibits school attendance and may easily be spread to others living in the shelter.

And crowded shelter conditions lead to the spread of other illnesses, while the lack of sanitary facilities compromises safe food preparation and, ultimately, good nutrition. Children who are living in shelters to escape family violence may also experience other problems. First and foremost is the fact that these children may have been the victims of abuse. Or they have experienced the trauma of witnessing violence. Their mothers may have been injured and thus less able to care for them. Moreover, these families are at the additional risk of being isolated; social support networks available to other families may not be accessible to these children and their mothers because of the abuser's threats of violence against family and friends or the need to keep their location a secret (Harms, Ray, and Rolandelli 1998).

Homeless adolescents are another group of young people at great risk. Comprising mostly runaways from troubled families, these youth face the multiple hazards of life on the street, including physical assault, sexual assault, HIV/AIDS, and substance abuse (Gustavsson and Segal 1994; Whitbeck and Hoyt 1999). In their study of over six hundred homeless adolescents, Whitbeck and Hoyt (1999) found that these young people had experienced multiple life changes in caretaker and living arrangements, with decreased parental involvement in their lives. The earlier they first left their disorganized families (or were forced out), the greater the risk of experiencing what these researchers call "precocious independence" — premature freedom from adult guidance and support combined with experimentation with adult behaviors the adolescent is not yet equipped to handle. In fact, this premature freedom completely undermines these young persons' ability to move successfully into adulthood, forever casting them into marginal societal roles (Whitbeck and Hoyt 1999).

Homelessness disproportionately affects young people leaving foster care. For instance, Roman and Wolfe (1997) found that persons with a history of foster care placement are overrepresented in the homeless population. In another study, homeless young adults who had been in foster care were the least likely to have an expectation of ever achieving permanent housing (Piliavin et al. 1996).

Violence as a Life Condition

Another risk facing many families is exposure to violence in the community, at school, and at home.[1] This is one of the most significant public health issues in America today. In particular, homicide is the second leading cause of death among fifteen to twenty-four year olds (Marans, Berkman, and Cohen 1996). The homicide rate among males in this age group is ten times that of youths in Canada, fifteen times greater than that for youths in Australia, and twenty-eight times greater than for those in either France or Germany (Osofsky 1999). Moreover, African American young men are eleven times more likely to be killed by guns than their white counterparts (Marans, Berkman, and Cohen 1996). It has been suggested that these high rates of violence are exceeded only in some developing countries, such as Colombia and Brazil, and in countries at war (Osofsky 1999).

As mentioned earlier, schools are not safe either, as evidenced by several recent, well-publicized tragedies. In addition to actual violence, there is a danger posed by threats. An estimated 160,000 children stay home each day for fear of intimidation from their classmates. Teachers are not exempt either. Fried (2000), citing statistics from the National Education Association, points out that over 6,000 teachers are threatened and over 200 are physically assaulted by students each day. Violence in the home in the forms of child abuse and domestic violence, often co-occurring, is also a growing problem of much concern. Some would say that family violence is a major taproot of other forms of societal violence: "Families are the primary incubators of violence today, as they always have been" (Rhodes 2000:11). Others cite the role of the media: "The content of the American media is the most violent in the world" (Osofsky 1999:34, citing the American Academy of Pediatrics 1995 policy statement on the media).

Furthermore, many children and families experience violence in multiple settings at home, in school, and in their communities, which compounds its effects on their well-being. Some children, especially those who are poor and live in low-income communities, are so chronically exposed to violence in their lives that in some neighborhoods it is hard to find a child who has been neither a victim nor a witness to violence (Osofsky 1999). As Garbarino and others have pointed out, for these children "danger replaces safety as the organizing principle" (Garbarino et al. 1992:83).

Community Violence

As noted above, the recent school shootings have received much media attention and have contributed greatly to the perception that no place in

America is safe anymore, no matter what the community's socioeconomic status. In fact, poor children are much more likely than wealthier children to experience violence in their communities, including in their schools. For some of these children, community violence is a chronic feature of their lives. As Guterman and Cameron (1997) have stressed, impoverished physical environments with abandoned buildings and vacant lots may provide a ready setting for violence. Poorer communities, when they are settings for drug distribution and sales, are also the sites for drug violence, from which no one is safe. A study in New Haven, Connecticut with a sample of school children in the sixth, eighth, and tenth grades found that 41 percent had seen someone shot or stabbed in the previous year (New Haven Public Schools 1992). Pynoos and Eth (1986) estimate that children witness between 10 and 20 percent of all homicides in Los Angeles.

Violence at school, as with other settings where children are exposed to violence, has a significant impact on academic achievement, mental health, and well-being. According to Singer et al. (1995), 70 to 80 percent of the children in their study of mainly urban schools had witnessed violence during the previous year. Moreover, it is important to view school violence on a continuum and consider what would constitute violence for a first grader as compared to a high school senior. Violence for younger children would typically include kicking, hitting, or spitting, whereas for older children this may escalate to physical fighting, extortion, bullying, and even homicide (Institute for Urban and Minority Education 1999). Whether at school or in their neighborhoods, children's exposure to violence is a major threat to their well-being. As Fontana (2000:29) has said, "The present environment is poisoning our youngsters." The next section will discuss family violence, followed by a detailed discussion of risk effects, since the risk effects of community violence mirror many of those to children experiencing violence in their own homes.

Family Violence

There are essentially two types of family violence — domestic violence, which has been defined as violence between adults who are intimate partners and includes acts or threats of physical harm (Fantuzzo and Mohr 1999), and child maltreatment, which may be physical, sexual, or emotional abuse or neglect. Domestic violence, now widely recognized as a serious social problem, is both a public health and safety issue and a crime; all states in the U.S. now have laws penalizing abusers (Fantuzzo and Mohr 1999). However, only about half of women who were victims of domestic violence reported their abuse to the police (Culross 1999). And although there is some increasing attention to women who are violent toward their male partners, it is women who are mainly injured as a result of violence (Davis 1995). Estimates about women seeking medical treatment in emergency rooms are that from 4 to 30 percent are there because of injuries caused by their partners (Culross 1999). Davis (1995) stated that each year during the early 1980s over 1.5 million women were severely assaulted by their partners. This number increases substantially each year (Chalk and King 1998). Their injuries seriously compromise these women's lives, health, and functioning, including their ability to parent their children. Even mothers who survive their abuse may, as a result of continued threats and actual harm, become completely preoccupied with their safety or emotionally numb and depressed (Carter, Weithorn, and Behrman 1999).

When women who are battered are immigrants without legal residency status, both they and their children may be vulnerable to even greater risk. First, husbands who are citizens or legal residents may refuse — or threaten to refuse — to file for their spouse's legal permanent resident status if she reports the abuse. Additionally, these women may also be deterred from reporting abuse or leaving an abusive situation by the threat of deportation. If deported, mothers of children who are U.S. citizens could be faced with the solomonic choice of either leaving their children behind or moving them to what is, for them, a new country. Finally, immigrant mothers may be particularly vulnerable to state child protection statutes that define exposure to domestic violence as child neglect or abuse, since such determination is likely to affect their eligibility for legal residency status (Mathews 1999).

While early concerns about domestic violence focused mainly on its impact on women, since the late 1980s there has been increasing attention to its effects on children (Chalk and King 1998; Fantuzzo and Mohr 1999; Seymor and Hairston 1998). Children, especially the very young, are the indirect victims of domestic violence by their exposure to it. In Fantuzzo and Mohr's study children under five were overrepresented in the group of children witnessing violence in their families; also, their families had other risk factors, including poverty, substance abuse, parent's low educational attainment, and the single status of the female head of household (Fantuzzo and Mohr 1999). Children's exposure to violence in their families ranges from hearing it, seeing it, intervening by trying to protect their parent or calling the police, and witnessing its aftermath, including injuries, the arrival of police officers, and even the arrest of one or both adults (Fantuzzo and Mohr 1999). Although study results are varied, an estimated 3 to 10 million children are exposed to domestic violence each year (Carter, Weithorn, and Behrman 1999).

Child Maltreatment

Added to the risk of exposure to domestic violence, and the loss of parental attention because of it, is child maltreatment involving the high co-occurrence of child abuse and domestic violence. Estimates are that between one-third and two-thirds of families experiencing either domestic violence or child maltreatment have both problems (Carter, Weithorn, and Behrman 1999). As mentioned earlier, child maltreatment can take the form of neglect or abuse. Abuse may be physical, sexual, or emotional. According to the American Humane Association (AHA), there was a 132 percent increase in reports of child maltreatment in the decade between 1984 and 1994 (AHA June 1994a). In 1992 almost 3 million children were reported to be maltreated, with nearly a million of these cases substantiated (AHA June 1994a). Of these, just over half (52 percent) were substantiated as neglect. Neglect is failure to provide needed, age-appropriate care (AHA June 1994a). Examples include inadequate nutrition, health care, suitable clothing and hygiene, and failure to supervise safe play and school attendance. As mentioned earlier, the child protection statutes in some states may hold mothers responsible for emotional neglect if their children are exposed to domestic violence and they do not take action to prevent risks of such exposure (Culross 1999). Neglect is highly correlated with poverty, which may greatly impede a parent's ability to provide what her child needs. Thus, those responding to cases of substantiated neglect are called upon to help parents obtain needed resources (AHA June 1994a). Child neglect is a serious risk to children's lives, however. In 1993, of the estimated 1,299 children who died in the U.S. from maltreatment, 43 percent of the deaths were attributed to neglect (AHA June 1994b).

As discussed further by Pecora et al. (2000), Wallace (1996), and Wiehe (1992), there are three forms of child abuse — physical abuse, psychological abuse, and sexual abuse. Physical abuse constitutes acts of aggression against a child by his or her caregiver that result in injury or risk of injury. The aggressive acts may include hitting, slapping, biting, and kicking, and injuries may also result from use of an object such as a belt or stick. The parent may not actually have intended to injure the child, as when using corporal punishment for disciplining purposes. Identification of physical abuse as intentional harm, as distinguished from accidental, unintentional injury, remains a challenge for social workers, medical professionals, and law enforcement officials, however, despite increased awareness about child abuse and the availability of training and reporting guidelines. Moreover, cultural differences may result in a report (and substantiated case) of child abuse for parents whose traditions include extensive use of corporal punishment. Among the factors associated with physical abuse of children are parents who were themselves abused, parents who have inadequate parenting skills, including a lack of empathy regarding their child, social isolation, and stress caused by poverty, lack of resources, and the demands of child care, especially when children have special needs and parents have few resources for meeting them (Wiehe 1992).

Psychological or emotional abuse is harm directed at a child's self-esteem and sense of competence. It includes chronic parental or caregiver belittlement of a child, degrading him or her, and rejection and isolation. It may also include exposing a child to criminal behavior such as drug abuse and prostitution (Wiehe 1992; AHA October 1992). Emotional abuse is more likely to occur in families where there is scapegoating, where communication patterns are poor, and where parents are experiencing emotional problems and/or stress (Wiehe 1992). The causes and correlates of child abuse — either physical or emotional — are multiple, complex, and interactional.

Child sexual abuse — use of a child for an adult's sexual gratification — constitutes about 17 percent of all cases of child abuse and neglect that are reported (AHA May 1993a). It is an area of considerable and growing public concern. The adult's exploitation of the child may range from behaviors that are nontouching, such as filming pornography or exhibitionism (including having a child watch a sexual act), to touching behaviors that may go from fondling to actual sexual intercourse (AHA May 1993b). Most victims of sexual abuse know their abuser, who uses trust as an entrée to the abusive relationship and coercion to maintain it. Increasingly, however, the Internet is being used by strangers to entice children into sexual relationships, causing parents much concern about their children's open access to the computer and prompting police departments around the country to use new detection strategies to trap perpetrators of this emerging form of sexual misconduct.

Effects of Community and Family Violence on Families and Children

The negative effects of violence on the well-being of children and their families can be overwhelming and irreversible, depending upon factors such as the source of the violence, the extent to which violence is a chronic feature in a family or a child's life, and chronic exposure to more than one source of violence (Chalk and King 1998). Thus there is a cumulative risk of exposure to violence when neither the community nor the family environment is a safe one. Some estimates are that as many as one in five American children live with a significant accumulation of risk (Garbarino and Kostelny 1996). Parents may be rendered unable to fulfill their roles as caregivers, and children's cognitive, emotional, and physical development can be severely impeded.

In addition to the dangers of community violence mentioned earlier, parents who live in violence-ridden neighborhoods report feelings of frustration and helplessness when they are unable to protect their children. This helplessness may in turn be communicated to their children, undermining children's sense of security in parents and caregivers. Garbarino and Kostelny (1996) point to the importance of adults as critical resources for children who need predictability and stability in their caregiving relationships. Children who do not experience these qualities may experience a declining trust in the adults around them and in adults in general (Garbarino and Kostelny 1996). In short, "The loss of a childhood and of the opportunity to be nourished in a secure environment are overarching deprivations" (Apfel and Simon 1996:1).

Parents may also respond to dangers in the community by becoming overprotective of their children, thus interfering with their developmental needs to explore and seek increasing independence (Osofsky 1995). Moreover, churches, schools, and social agencies, especially in inner cities, can become overwhelmed by community violence and be rendered less effective as social supports for families. Osofsky (1995:783) notes that "parallels have been drawn between children growing up in inner cities in the U.S. and those living in war zones."

When children are witnesses to or victims of violence at school, in the community, or at home, they have increasing worries about injury and death, and they may suffer grief and the loss of a loved one or friend. They also may be less able to concentrate, especially on their school work (Guterman and Cameron 1997). Singer et al. (1995), in their study of school violence, found that youths exposed to violence were more likely to experience depression, anxiety, anger, dissociation, and symptoms of trauma, including those associated with post-traumatic stress disorder (PSTD). Another source noted that students with repeated exposure, including to violence at home, are difficult to engage in the classroom because they are, among other things, constantly scanning the environment for potential threats (Institute for Urban and Minority Education 1999). Other factors associated with children's exposure to violence include low self-esteem, self-destructive behavior, and anger and aggression (Institute for Urban and Minority Education 1999). Children may adapt to pernicious violence and the constant experience of fear and powerlessness through their own violent acts (Marans, Berkman, and Cohen 1996).

Violence, especially domestic violence, may impede a parent's ability to meet her child's needs, either because she has become obsessed with trying to remain (and keep her children) safe or she has become emotionally numb or depressed by her constant victimization. Thus, parents may become psychologically unavailable to their children. When their parents are injured, children actually lose some or all of their parental care, albeit temporarily. Fantuzzo and Mohr (1999) point out that although there are major gaps in knowledge about the effects of domestic violence on children's behaviors, they may be classified as either internalized or externalized. Internalized behaviors include fears and phobias, insomnia, bed-wetting and depression; externalized behaviors include aggressive acts and conduct problems.

The most serious outcome of child maltreatment is a child's death. Conservative estimates are that each year over one thousand children die from maltreatment (AHA June 1994b). Nationally, tracking the causes of child deaths is problematic since only a handful of states currently have procedures for investigating and reporting child fatalities. Young children are especially at risk of death from abuse or neglect. The American Humane Association reported in 1994 that 86 percent of the children who died were under five years of age; 46 percent were under age one (AHA June 1994b). For children who are repeatedly traumatized, including by abuse, Terr (1991:15) points out that they undertake "massive attempts to protect the psyche and to preserve the self." These coping mechanisms include mental escapes through self-hypnosis and emotional removal, depersonalization and dissociation, as well as rage and aggression turned against the self in suicide or self-mutilation (Terr 1991). In addition to permanent emotional damage, children suffer long-term and sometimes permanent physical damage from abuse and neglect. Physical abuse can result in deformities and disabilities. Neglect, especially medical neglect, can lead to malnutrition, deafness, and debilitating asthma, among other lasting somatic effects. Invariably, these are tied to a child's emotional development in the struggle for self-esteem and a healthy identity.

The following example shows the terrible effects long-term and multiple types of abuse can have on a child.

In March of 1988 eleven-year-old Andrew M., a child in the care of a state child welfare agency, died as a result of being physically restrained in a psychiatric hospital. His death sparked an outcry against physical restraints and prompted an in-depth report by the state's child advocate and Child Fatality Review Panel. What the report showed was that Andrew had come into care early in his life as a result of parental neglect and abuse. Placed in the care of his grandmother, he continued to suffer maltreatment at the hands of family members, including his mother, who would periodically reenter his life. Among the physical injuries he suffered was a blow to the face that permanently disfigured his eye. His resulting deformity caused him to become an object of teasing and taunts by other children in his neighborhood. Andrew's response to such experiences, and, no doubt to his earlier and ongoing abuse, was to become increasingly violent. He was forced to leave his last foster home before being placed in the psychiatric facility because of death threats made to a foster sibling. His proclivity to violent behavior is most likely to have prompted the staff members' response with physical restraint (Office of the Child Advocate 1998a).

Other lasting effects of the trauma of child abuse, in addition to those mentioned above, include a greater proclivity to abuse one's own children, increased involvement in criminal activity, and psychological problems in adulthood. It should be noted, however, that given the cumulative burden of risks born by some children, separating out the effects of exposure to one source of risk, in this case child maltreatment, is difficult. Some parents who abuse their children were themselves abused, but not all abused children grow up to become abusing parents. The intergenerational transmission of abuse may be tied more closely to the co-occurrence of domestic violence and child abuse (Starr, MacLean, and Keating 1991). Physically abused children are more likely to commit criminal offenses; children exposed to more family violence commit more violent crimes (Starr, MacLean, and Keating 1991). Moreover, a wide number of symptoms appear more frequently among adults who were sexually abused as children, although not all survivors of such abuse exhibit these. They include symptoms ranging from psychosis, suicide, and adult sexual victimization to depression and substance abuse (Starr, MacLean, and Keating 1991).

Health Risks and Vulnerabilities

As reflected in the "Framework of Needs and Resources for Family and Child Well-Being" depicted in chapter 1, health plays a pivotal role in the development and well-being of children. The health of children and their parents depends on a complex set of factors including a healthy lifestyle, a safe environment, adequate nutrition, access to and understanding of health information, and access to appropriate health care (Lewit et al. 1992). Clearly, the risks delineated earlier in this chapter affect health status cumulatively and negatively. Poverty, in particular, increases the likelihood that one or more, and sometimes all, of these conditions for good health are not met. This section discusses some of the additional health risks to already vulnerable children and families.

The first line of defense for good health is preventing disease and illness. A major prevention strategy for children is immunization, yet poor children, mostly those who are uninsured, are the least likely to be fully immunized in a timely way against preventable diseases. They are also least likely to have regular health check-ups. The health status of infants, for the most part predicted by their intrauterine experience and neonatal environment, is greatly dependent on their mothers' behavior. Did she obtain prenatal care? Did she use drugs or alcohol during pregnancy (Lewit et al. 1992)? The risks of substance abuse to both the parent who uses and her children are much greater for poor families. The prevalence of pediatric AIDS is tied directly to the substance abuse and other unsafe behaviors of children's parents; among families affected by AIDS, most are poor and many are families of color. Injuries, the major cause of death for children of all ages except infants (Starfield 1992), are primarily a function of a safe environment and good supervision. Low-income children are more likely to become ill and have more serious injuries than children from wealthier families (Starfield 1992). They are more likely to live in poor, older housing and in neighborhoods where they are exposed to lead poisoning, smoke pollution, and other environmental threats to their well-being and development.

Finally, lack of access to adequate health care is a major problem plaguing poor people. Poor children who live in low-income areas are especially vulnerable. Compared to their counterparts living in high-income areas, their overall health status is poorer. They have less access to preventive and routine care and two to four times as many preventable hospitalizations. When they do receive treatment, it is less likely to be from someone they see on an ongoing basis. And they are less likely to have insurance (Edmunds and Coye 1998). Even poor families with coverage may have difficulty finding health care providers who accept Medicaid. And, in addition to financial barriers to accessing health care, there are numerous nonfinancial barriers, including the family's location and ability to obtain transportation to the service, shortage of providers, disincentives such as immigration rules, rationing mechanisms that complicate access, lack of information about resources or of education about health care, language difficulties, and other problems (Klerman 1992). The following section discusses access to health insurance and its impact on family health, especially that of children. Subsequent sections discuss some of the particular health risks facing vulnerable families and children, including substance abuse, HIV/AIDS, and chronic illness and disability.

Health Insurance

The Committee on Children, Health Insurance, and Access to Care convened by the Robert Wood Johnson Foundation in 1997 found that, according to 1995 data, most children have health insurance (Edmunds and Coye 1998). Nearly 42 of the nation's 71 million children had employer-based coverage. Added to that figure is the 16.5 million children who are covered by the Medicaid program. All told, about 90 percent of children in the U.S.

have some type of health insurance. Although insurance coverage is most often provided by private insurers through a working parent's employer, a recent trend has been for employers to scale back coverage and increase cost sharing with employees (Edmunds and Coye 1998). Poor parents are more likely to work at low-wage jobs that do not provide health insurance. While Medicaid enrollments are increasing as more families lose employer coverage or are forced to trade welfare benefits for entry-level jobs without insurance, most families without any insurance are those in which both parents work (Edmunds and Coye 1998). Moreover, insurance status varies by race. Whereas 69 percent of white children have private insurance, only 40 percent of black children and 35 percent of Hispanic children do. Medicaid insures 45 percent of black children and 37 percent of Hispanic children. Among the 10 percent of children with no insurance, more than one in four Hispanic children and 15 percent of black children are uninsured (Edmunds and Coye 1998).

Medicaid serves more than one in four children in the U.S., with over 22 million enrolled children. Immunization and injury treatment rates for Medicaid-covered children match those of children with private insurance. However, even insured families may not receive needed treatment, especially for special health needs and dental care (Edmunds and Coye 1998; U.S. General Accounting Office [USGAO] 2000). Some states may not include coverage, for example, for dental care, in their Medicaid programs (USGAO 2000). In some communities, low reimbursement rates discourage participation in Medicaid by health care providers. Other communities may have few health care providers available.

Uninsured children have numerous unmet health needs beginning at birth, since they are more likely to be sick as newborns. As preschoolers, they are less likely than other children to receive immunizations. As they age, they are less likely to receive needed medical treatment for injuries or illnesses that are acute or chronic such as asthma, recurrent ear infections, and tooth decay (Edmunds and Coye 1998). Chronic health problems, if untreated, can lead to lasting disabilities such as deafness from ear infections and even death from problems such as asthma, as occurred in the following case.

Four and one half year old Shanice M. died after cardiac arrest during a severe asthma attack despite emergency medical intervention.

Shanice, although in the care of her mother, had been under supervision of the local child welfare agency after medical providers made allegations that her family was not treating her severe asthma properly. Indeed, despite her illness, family members living in her home continued to smoke cigarettes regularly. An official hearing concluded that among the circumstances contributing to her death were the lack of communication between and among health care and child welfare service providers and a general lack of knowledge about the incidence and threats of asthma among child welfare personnel (Office of the Child Advocate 1998b).

Dental care is an important aspect of good health, yet 55 percent of all six to eight year olds have untreated tooth decay (Edmunds and Coye 1998). Poor children have five times more untreated dental disease than do wealthier children (USGAO 2000; Edmund and Coye 1998). Dental problems cause pain and, untreated, can lead to infection, loss of teeth, and other serious problems (USGAO 2000; Edmunds and Coye 1998). In addition, dental problems lead to school absence: an estimated 51 million school hours per year are lost because of children's dental problems (Edmunds and Coye 1998).

The Committee on Children and Health Insurance, mentioned earlier, found that more than 11 million children are uninsured. Moreover, over 3 million children are eligible for Medicaid but are not enrolled (Edmunds and Coye 1998). Children of color are more likely than white children to be uninsured. Among white children, one in ten is uninsured; in contrast, one in six black children and one in four Hispanic children are uninsured (Edmunds and Coye 1998).

Children, whether their families have health insurance or not, depend on their parents to identify their health problems and seek treatment for them. Because of literacy or language problems, parents may not be able to read health information materials or they may lack knowledge about safety, prevention, and health care. Parents may face logistical obstacles to obtaining needed care such as telephoning for an appointment, obtaining transportation to the health care provider, finding child care for other children in the home, or taking time off from work. Other family crises may compete with providing adequate attention to a sick child. Finally, cultural and religious practices may preclude a parent's seeking health care for her child (Klerman 1992; Edmunds and Coye 1998). *(In chapter 3 we describe a number of obstacles facing families with health care needs.)*

Substance Abuse

As Young, Wingfield, and Klempner (2001a:103), among others, have indicated, "Substance abuse is a pervasive, devastating problem — and one of the most serious facing children and families today." Given the scope of substance use in this country, it is highly likely that social workers working with children and families will encounter substance abuse problems in a variety of family service and related settings, including schools, hospitals, mental health centers, and courts. Alcohol and other drug abuse is best viewed along a continuum, from nonproblematic experimental or social use to abuse or dependence. Dependence varies in severity and refers to "compulsive use of a chemical and continued use despite adverse consequences" (Straussner 1993:4). Since it is now recognized that many people abuse more than one type of substance, currently the terms *alcohol and other drug abuse* or *substance use disorders* have replaced the terms *alcoholism* or *drug abuse*.

The *1999 National Household Survey on Drug Abuse* (U.S. Department of Health and Human Services 2000), the primary source of information on the prevalence and incidence of illicit drug, alcohol, and tobacco use in the American population age twelve years and older, reports an estimated 10.3 million people dependent on either alcohol or illicit drugs (4.7 percent). In 1999 an estimated 14.8 million Americans reported use of an illicit drug. One hundred five million Americans age twelve and older report current use of alcohol; about 45 million of this group engaged in binge drinking. Thus, alcohol and other drug abuse is a substantial social problem that affects all family members; in addition, there are significant mental health, physical health, and safety issues when abuse occurs within the context of the family.

Maternal substance abuse, in particular, has sparked an intense debate among service providers, policy makers, and the judicial system. Alcohol use during pregnancy continues to be the leading preventable cause of birth defects (SAMHSA 1991). The Center for Substance Abuse Prevention (as cited in Tracy and Farkas 1994) found that approximately 66 percent of women drink alcohol during pregnancy, placing infants at some level of risk for physical and developmental problems. One study of women seeking prenatal care from a variety of public and private providers showed an overall prevalence rate of 14.8 percent for alcohol and other illicit drugs (Chasnoff, Landress, and Barrett 1990).

In general, members of minority groups are disproportionately represented among drug abusers; it is thought that a number of economic, social, and psychological factors place members of minority groups at higher risk for substance abuse. The same may be true for members of recently immigrated groups. For example, as a group, southeast Asian refugee youths encounter a number of interrelated risk factors; these include economic disadvantage, limited English proficiency, family fragmentation, school failure and post-traumatic stress disorder, all of which place them at high risk for turning to alcohol and drugs as a means to relieve psychological and social stress consequent to culture change (Amodeo 1995).

Children living with a substance abusing parent are at higher risk for physical abuse and neglect (Kelleher et al. 1994; Daro and McCurdy 1991). The National Committee for Prevention of Child Abuse estimates that 9 to 10 million children are affected by substance abusing parents and that 675,000 children are maltreated each year by an alcoholic or drug addicted caretaker (National Committee for Prevention of Child Abuse 1989). Among confirmed cases of child maltreatment nationwide, from forty to 80 percent involve substance abuse problems that interfere with parenting (Child Welfare League of America 1998). Over half of all domestic violence incidents involve substance use either by the perpetrator or the victim (Collins and Messerschmidt 1993).

When children are cared for by substance-abusing parents, they are often exposed to a number of additional related risks:

- chaotic and often dangerous neighborhoods,
- the impact of poverty and homelessness or unstable housing on family life,
- a parent whose addiction is likely to take precedence over the child's basic needs,
- a parent who lacks an extended family and community support system,
- a mother who may have been victimized herself as a child or is currently in a relationship characterized by domestic violence, and
- a parent or parents with poor parenting skills and few or no role models for effective coping (Tracy 1994).

Yet removing children from such homes does not totally reduce the risk. When children from substance-abusing families enter placement, they tend to remain in care and are less frequently reunified with their biological parents or freed for adoption as compared with children placed for reasons unrelated to substance abuse (Besharov 1990; Feig 1990; Walker, Zangrillo, and Smith 1991). After examining records of over one thousand children who entered foster care, the National Black Child Development Institute (1991) concluded that parental substance abuse was a contributing factor in 36 percent of placements, yet only 17 percent of parents were referred to drug treatment prior to the child's placement. Without appropriate intervention the problems that precipitated the need for placement may remain largely unchanged, thus creating a barrier to family reunification following placement of children.

Service needs of the substance-abusing family, particularly those addicted to crack/cocaine, typically extend beyond the traditional domains of substance abuse treatment programs and child welfare services to include housing, early childhood intervention, health, mental health, and vocational services. Outreach is a critical service need, as many addicted mothers avoid prenatal care and treatment for fear of detection and forced removal of their child (Substance Abuse and Mental Health Services Administration 1997). It can be difficult to find a treatment program that can meet the needs of both mother and child. The children may have emotional or behavioral problems as a consequence of being raised in a substance-abusing household (Galanter and Kleber 1999) or have developmental problems related to prenatal exposure to alcohol and drugs (Wetherington, Smeriglio, and Finnegan 1996). Once in treatment, learning to parent again while at the same time learning to adopt a sober lifestyle can be a challenge. Many mothers drop out of treatment, unable to meet the sometimes competing demands of parenting and treatment (Daley and Gorske 2000) or overwhelmed with guilt and shame because of their addiction and past parenting practices (Cox 2000).

Substance abuse among youths is also a significant problem. Among youths age twelve to seventeen, 10.9 percent reported current use of illicit drugs in 1999. And although alcohol use is illegal for those under twenty-one years of age, 10.4 million current drinkers were age twelve to twenty in 1999 (USDHHS 2000). More than two thousand new smokers each day are young people; those who smoke cigarettes are seven times more likely to use illicit drugs than those who do not smoke (USDHHS 2000). One of the most recent surveys of youth alcohol and drug use is the "Monitoring the Future Study" (Johnston, O'Malley, and Bachman 2000), often referred to as the National High School Senior Survey. This survey of a nationally representative sample of eighth, tenth, and twelfth graders tracks trends in drug use and measures student attitudes toward drugs. Data gathered in 1999 show that overall illicit drug use among teens has remained steady, but that the use of certain drugs increased, these being the "club drug" Ecstasy and steroid use among young adolescent boys. The study concludes that substance abuse problems remain widespread among American youth, as reflected in the following statistics:

- more than a third (37 percent) have used inhalants as early as the eighth grade,
- 44 percent of youth have tried cigarettes by the eighth grade,
- 62 percent of twelfth graders and 25 percent of eighth graders report having been drunk at least once.

There are serious and longlasting consequences for youths who use alcohol and other drugs: increased risk of being a victim or perpetrator of violence, engaging in unplanned and unprotected sex, experiencing school failure, and being injured when driving while impaired or with an impaired driver, among others (Center for Substance Abuse Prevention 1996). For these reasons, a number of initiatives supported by the Safe and Drug Free Schools Program seeks to reduce alcohol and tobacco use and violence through education and prevention programs in schools (National Institute on Drug Abuse 1997).[2]

AIDS and HIV Infection

There is no question that substance abuse and HIV/AIDS have been two of the most critical threats to family well-being in the past two decades. Both have become epidemic. While HIV/AIDS was once primarily a disease of gay men, the demographics have shifted to women, who are now the fastest-growing group of those infected. In 1996 at least one in four of those who tested HIV-positive was female (Mason 1998). Women are infected through sexual contact with bisexual or drug-using partners, or through their own use of injected drugs (Taylor-Brown and Garcia 1995).

This virus does not strike all groups in American equally. Most of the women who are infected are African American or Latinas, 57 and 19 percent respectively (Mason 1998), and their children are greatly affected. In fact, 94 percent of the children under thirteen who are living with HIV/AIDS are children of color, and a growing number of children are being orphaned by AIDS. Moreover, the number of cases of pediatric HIV/AIDS is growing (Bok and Morales 1997). For the sixty thousand women who have tested positive for the disease, there is often the dual challenge of being a caregiver while ill. Infected mothers with children have been shown to face many challenges, including dealing with the stigma of the disease, fears about disclosing their illness to their children or of infecting children through casual contact, grief, and finding support and guidance in planning alternative custody arrangements for their children (Faithfull 1997; Hackl et al. 1997; and Mason 1998). Some mothers fail to adequately make these plans for their children (Westpheling 1998). In many families grandparents assume the care of children orphaned by AIDS, although these older adults may be in need of additional financial assistance, which may or may not be available, in order to provide this care (Burnette 1997; Taylor-Brown et al. 1998). Thus HIV/AIDS infection is a terrible risk to which too many American families and children are exposed. It threatens family members' health, well-being, and the integrity of the family unit.[3]

Chronic Illness and Disabilities

According to the Committee on Children, Health Insurance, and Access to Care (Edmunds and Coye 1998), most American children, about 70 percent, are healthy. Approximately 14 million children, 20 percent, suffer from chronic problems such as recurring ear infections, asthma, and other respiratory allergies that require medical interventions and even hospitalizations. About 7 million children, or 10 percent, suffer from one or more severe health conditions, including HIV/AIDS (Edmunds and Coye 1998). Many in this group of children are considered to have a developmental disability, which has been defined as a severe, chronic condition that has its onset in childhood, is expected to continue indefinitely, affects the child ability to learn, move, use language, and requires special services or resources (Developmental Disabilities Assistance and Bill of Rights Act of 2000). These disabilities include mental retardation, cerebral palsy, epilepsy,

autism, learning disabilities, speech and language problems, visual limitations and blindness, hearing limitations and deafness, spina bifida, and con-
genital malformations (Rycus and Hughes 1998).

Rycus and Hughes (1998) point out the wide range of potential causes
of developmental disabilities. A small percentage are genetic. Some disabilities result from perinatal exposure to toxic substances, notably Fetal Alcohol
Syndrome, which is the result of a pregnant woman's consumption of large
amounts of alcohol during pregnancy. Maternal age and health during pregnancy are also a factor. When pregnant women have a chronic illness or are
malnourished, their unborn children may be affected. Viral and bacterial
infections, for example HIV and measles, are also potentially threatening to
fetal health. Complications in pregnancy and birth and premature birth are
additional sources of developmental disabilities in infants. HIV/AIDS is another source of developmental disabilities in children. In many children
who are HIV infected, the virus affects the central nervous system; HIV
infection is the major infectious cause of pediatric mental retardation (Seidel
1991). Finally, trauma caused by accidents and abuse is another possible
cause of developmental disabilities in children. An estimated 25 percent of
all developmental disabilities are the result of child maltreatment (Baladarian
1994). Indeed, developmental disabilities are both a cause and an effect of
child abuse and neglect because children who have disabilities are at a high
risk of being abused or neglected, partly because a child's needs for care
may outstrip a parent's or a community's capacity to meet them (Rycus and
Hughes 1998). In short, when families and children are vulnerable because
of other risks they may face, the addition of a child's serious illness or disability may tax the family's capacity to manage.[4]

Family Separation

Out-of-Home Care[5]

Children and youths in out-of-home care placement, that is, family foster
care or group care, represent another group at risk. In the 1990s there has
been a steady increase in the numbers of such young people. Whereas in
1989 it was estimated there were 360,000 children in placement at any one
time, at the beginning of FY 1996 there were 488,000 children in care;
during 1996 218,260 children left care while 236,998 entered. At the end

of FY 1996 the total number of children in care was 506,708 (Voluntary Cooperative Information Systems 1997). As of March 31, 1998, there were over 520,000 children in out-of-home care (USDHHS 1999). The increase apparently was due to cuts in preventive services, dramatic increases in crack/ cocaine abuse, reduction in public housing and increase in homelessness, continuing unemployment in many geographical areas and among ethnic-minority groups, and other factors.

Although precise data are not available, reports from the field document the changes in the kinds of children entering placement. Most children still enter foster care because of the consequences of parent-related problems, largely child abuse or neglect (Berrick et al. 1998). In addition, there is indication of increasing proportions of children entering care — and remaining there — from these groups: children with special physical or developmental needs, children with HIV infection, crack-addicted or drug-exposed infants, children from poor, multiproblem families, and/or children with emotional problems (see, for example, Dore 1999). Research has also shown that large proportions of children in foster care have major learning problems in school (Blome 1997) and multiple health problems (Simms and Halfon 1994). Also, children entering foster care have a history of difficult birth circumstances: exceptionally high rates of low birth weight, birth abnormality, no prenatal care, and families with three or more young children (Needell and Barth 1998).

The age distribution of children in out-of-home care is also changing. The proportion of adolescents, in particular, increased rapidly in the 1980s, as the permanency planning movement initially resulted in keeping younger children out of care, reuniting them with their biological families following placement, or placing them in adoption or other permanent plans (Maluccio, Krieger, and Pine 1990). Adolescents still constitute a major group in the foster care population, although their proportion is lower as a consequence of the marked rise in the numbers of younger children in foster care. However, in recent years there has also been a dramatic increase in the number of very young children coming to the attention of the child welfare system, including infants placed in foster care, as a result of such societal problems as poverty, homelessness, family violence, child abuse and neglect, and substance abuse (Berrick et al. 1998).

Older youths in placement or transitioning out of care are especially vulnerable and require help. Most of them entered care because of serious histories of abuse, neglect and sexual abuse plus multiple incidents of violence. Many have lived in multiple out-of-home placements or have been returned home and removed repeatedly (Pecora et al. 2000). Moreover, many of them perceive the experience of eventually leaving the child welfare system as yet one more separation or potential rejection.

These young people typically have received little preparation for life after foster care and are unprepared for independent living (Mech and Rycraft 1995). Often, they are largely or completely on their own after discharge, a rare experience for the vast majority of American adolescents. They face similar challenges to employment and education as the general youth population:

> low educational attainment, lack of employment experience, lack of credible references, early parenting, health problems, competition for and location of available jobs, place of residence, influential others and unfair housing and hiring practices. Barriers . . . include the above in addition to housing issues, mental health issues, social support issues, high incidence of disabilities (cognitive, emotional, behavioral and social), and the lack of positive adult role models.
>
> (Annie E. Casey Foundation 1998a:49)

For youths who have been in care for many years, there is, above all, the need to help them to develop a permanent plan for adulthood that respects their developmental needs, emphasizes their safety and well-being, and applies the same principles that it does to children first entering the child welfare system. These include help to maintain ties with the substitute families and/ or reconnect with their families of origin, as we shall discuss in chapter 6.

Finally, those coming to the attention of child welfare services include a disproportionate and expanding number of children, youths, and families of color. There is, moreover, substantial evidence that minority children who enter the child welfare system are at greater risk for poor outcomes than their white counterparts (See Jackson and Brissett-Chapman 1997). In addition, although they are disproportionately represented in foster care and the child welfare system in general, children of color receive inadequate as well as differential treatment and have different outcomes. A review of outcome studies carried out during the past fifteen years suggested that "children of color and their families experience poorer outcomes and receive fewer service than their caucasian counterparts" (Courtney et al. 1996:99). Furthermore, in a study of exit rates among minority children in foster care, Avery

(1998) found that black children returned to their families at only half the rate as white children. The increased recognition of the risks and vulnerabilities of children and adolescents in foster care, including those from families of color, has begun to influence policy, programs, practice, and staff training, particularly in regard to identifying and building on the strengths of minority families and communities (Hill 1997).

Parental Imprisonment

The dramatic rise in the prison population is another serious risk factor for already vulnerable families. Today, there are nearly 3 million incarcerated adults in the United States, the majority of whom are parents (Johnston and Gabel 1995). Increases in incarceration greatly affect children, especially poor children of color. Estimates are that at least 1.5 million children have an incarcerated parent (Bloom and Steinhart 1993; Johnston 1995; Seymour 1998).[6]

The number of women in jails and prison has risen dramatically, up 500 percent between 1980 and 1998 (USGAO 1999b). On any given day in this country an estimated one hundred thousand women are incarcerated (Beaty 1997). Many of these women are substance abusers whose criminal behavior is related to their addiction to drugs and/or alcohol (Seymour 1998). Black women were twice as likely as Hispanic women and eight times as likely as white women to be imprisoned (USGAO 1999b). That same study, conducted by the U.S. General Accounting Office (1999b), showed that two-thirds of the women were mothers of a child under the age of eighteen. Another study of women in New York's Bedford Hills prison found that 80 percent were mothers (Lambert 1999).

A number of studies of incarcerated adults have shown that they share many characteristics of other vulnerable Americans — they have low incomes, limited education and job skills, and are likely to have experienced the childhood traumas of domestic violence, maltreatment, and separation from their parents (Bloom and Steinhart 1993; Johnston and Gabel 1995; Seymour 1998).

Chief among the reasons for the skyrocketing rates of incarceration is the escalation of the war on drugs, with its concomitant mandatory sentencing laws that increase the length of a prison sentence for each prior conviction, and the "three strikes you're out" policies (Beaty 1997; Johnston and Gabel

1995). The median jail sentence is six months, while the median prison sentence is sixty months for women, seventy-two months for men (Johnston and Gabel 1995). Jails are generally local secure facilities housing those either awaiting trial or sentenced to less than a year for misdemeanor crimes; prisons are part of the state or federal correction systems (Johnston and Gabel 1995).

The negative impact of parent's — especially a mother's — incarceration on a child can begin even prior to the infant's birth, since an estimated 8 to 10 percent of women are pregnant upon entering prison (Bloom 1995). Bloom (1995) points to the poor prenatal care incarcerated women receive in prison because of the lack of facilities, lack of medical expertise, especially for dealing with high-risk pregnancies, and the failure of prisons to transport pregnant women to outside facilities. This lack of quality care leads to a high miscarriage rate among incarcerated women, who may already be at risk for problem pregnancies because of their preincarceration substance abuse and resulting lack of self-care.

In most prison systems infants are separated from their mothers following the hospital stay. Only the federal Bureau of Prisons and the prison systems in eleven states allow female inmates to remain with their children after birth, which in the federal system is three months after delivery (USGAO 1999b). Incarceration of a mother affects an entire family, but especially her children. Johnston (1992) cites three major factors in the experience of children with incarcerated mothers in her study: their endurance of traumatic stress, their separation from their mother, and the inadequate quality of the care they received. Traumatic stress may derive from the crime and arrest that preceded the incarceration. Anecdotal evidence suggests that there is little consideration given to children who witness their parent's arrest. And, although there have been no longitudinal studies of the impact on children of parental incarceration, evidence exists that some children experience fear, anxiety, shame, and low self-esteem and depression (Seymour 1998). Children's ability to master the developmental tasks of childhood may be impaired (Johnston 1995). The impact of separation from their mother, who may likely be their sole caregiver and source of financial support, creates additional hardships. These children may experience disrupted and multiple placements and a generally decreased quality of care (Beaty 1997). Many are cared for by their grandparents, who may themselves have limited incomes (Seymour 1998). Moreover, most prison policies give little consideration to the need to maintain parent-child ties (Johnston and Gabel 1995), as the following will show.

According to Bloom and Steinhart (1993), visiting between incarcerated parents and their children has declined from 92 percent in 1978 to less than 50 percent in 1992. In this same study 54 percent of the children had never visited their incarcerated mothers. There are a number of reasons for this lack of visiting and other forms of contact, especially between children and their mothers. The General Accounting Office study cited earlier showed that 30 percent of women in federal prisons were in facilities over five hundred miles from their homes (USGAO 1999b). Bloom and Steinhart (1993) found that 60 percent of the children in their study lived over one hundred miles from the jail or prison where their mother was being held. Increasingly, prisons are being located in rural areas that are inaccessible to family members wanting to visit. Also, women may be placed at greater distances and in more secure facilities that their crimes require because of the lack of closer, more appropriate sites (Bloom and Steinhart 1993). In addition to geographical barriers to contact, there are policy and other types of barriers. For example, Bloom and Steinhart (1993) cite restrictive telephone privileges that allow prisoners to make only collect calls as a barrier to mother-child contact. Children's caregivers may not have sufficient resources to pay for long distance collect calls. Also, visiting and calls may be restricted by the children's current caregiver because she or he is angry at the parent's substance abuse or other behaviors and feels the parent is not fit for contact with the child (Bloom and Steinhart 1993). Women-focused, prison-based services such as drug treatment, parent education, counseling, and job training, which mothers would need in order to be able to assume their children's care after release from prison, are notoriously lacking in women's prisons (Bloom and Steinhart 1993; USGAO 1999b).

Finally, family reunification services are especially lacking. At the same time, new child welfare policies that greatly shorten permanency planning time lines put incarcerated parents at great risk for termination of their parental rights, given that contact is a basic requirement for family reunification (Beaty 1997; Johnston and Gabel 1995). Incarcerated mothers may have little contact with child welfare agencies who have placed their children, because of distance and the lack of collaborative policies between prison and child welfare systems.[7]

In summary, the separation of families because of a parent's — especially a mother's — incarceration places the family at great risk. Children, especially, are hurt by criminal policies that increase the likelihood of parental incarceration and by prison policies that do not attend to the importance of the parent-child bond.

Despite their exposure to one or, most often, a confluence of the risk factors discussed in this chapter, many families are resilient. They find the resources and supports needed to raise their children from both within the family, in their extended kinship network, and in the community. An ecological, competence-centered approach, as outlined in chapter 1, focuses on the strengths a family brings to the tasks of child rearing and the maintenance of family life, the coping mechanisms used to overcome adversity, and the variety of resources required for child and family well-being. In the next chapter we discuss selected institutional supports that are available to families as part of the formal system of care in the United States.

Notes

1. See Chalk and King (1998) for extensive discussion of family violence, including occurrence, policies, programs, and intervention approaches as well as evaluation studies; Gitterman (2001) for a how-to-guide on working with vulnerable populations; Lorion, Brodsky, and Cooley-Quille (1999) for a framework for conceptualizing urban violence; McCardy and Hofford (1998) for description of emerging programs for battered mothers and their children; and Wallace (1996) for description of legal, medical, and social perspectives on family violence. In addition, see the *Future of Children* 9 (1) (1999): 1–144, for a special issue on "Domestic Violence and Children."

2. See Young, Wingfield, and Klempner (2001b) for a special issue of *Child Welfare* on serving children and families with alcohol and other drug-related problems in child welfare.

3. See Anderson et al. (1998) for a series of articles on the impact of HIV/AIDS on families, with discussion of child welfare system responses; Merkel-Holguin (1996b) for guidelines addressing the issues involved in placement of children who lose their parents to HIV/AIDS with adoptive or kinship families; and Stein (1997) for discussion of legal protections, policies, and programs affecting women and children with HIV/AIDS.

4. See Rycus and Hughes (1998) for a compendium of information on developmental disabilities aimed at child welfare professionals.

5. This section draws in part from Pecora et al. (2000:305–314).

6. See Seymour and Hairston (1998) for discussion of research, policies, and programs pertaining to children with parents in prison.

7.   See Beaty (1997) for a review of strategies to improve the child welfare system's response to the needs of incarcerated parents and their children.

Questions for Discussion

1. Consider your current field placement or practice setting. What risk factors are present in the community your agency serves? How and where can you obtain information on the extent of these risk factors in your community, for example, school dropout rates, teen-age pregnancy rates, poverty rates?

2. Choose a family from your caseload and consider the range of risks and vulnerabilities discussed in this chapter. What are the interrelated risks this family faces? How are these impacting on the family's ability to meet the instrumental and expressive needs of its members?

3. Discuss the many ways poverty makes child rearing more difficult for families. Consider, for example, how poverty might influence a family's interaction with their child's school.

4. Visit a homeless shelter in your community. What special programs are available to assist children in keeping up with their schooling — e.g., transportation to own school, tutors? What additional services might the shelter provide to ensure that children's homelessness does not interrupt their educational progress?

5. Is there a women's prison in your community? If so, what arrangements are made by prison authorities to ensure ongoing contact between incarcerated mothers and their children? Does your local public child welfare agency maintain a visiting program at the prison for children in foster care with incarcerated mothers? What efforts does your state's penal system make to ensure that family members can maintain contact with incarcerated men?

6. Many communities have experienced a recent growth in the number of immigrant families. If this is true in your community, from which countries are the new arrivals emigrating? What are the unique needs of these families? What special challenges do they face? If these immigrants are families of color, how are they dealing with the racism they are likely to face?

7. Families in which a parent has HIV/AIDS are especially at risk — of income loss, unmet health care needs, separation, and even death. What special programs and resources are available in your community to help these families, for example, plan for their children's guardianship in the event of a parent's death?

Suggestions for Further Information

Brooks-Gunn, J., G. J. Duncan, and J. L. Aber, eds. 1997a. *Neighborhood Poverty: Context and Consequences for Children*. Vol. 1. New York: Russell Sage Foundation.

————. 1997b. *Neighborhood Poverty: Policy Implications in Studying Neighborhoods*. Vol. 2. New York: Russell Sage Foundation.

Gitterman, A., ed. 2001. *Handbook of Social Work Practice with Vulnerable and Resilient Populations*. 2d ed. New York: Columbia University Press.

Lang, M. H. 1989. *Homelessness Amid Affluence: Structure and Paradox in the American Political Economy*. New York: Praeger.

Reynolds, A. J., H. J. Walberg, and R. P. Weissberg, eds. 1999. *Promoting Positive Outcomes: Issues in Children's and Families' Lives*. Washington, D.C.: CWLA.

Walsh, F. 1998. *Strengthening Family Resilience*. New York: Guilford.

3 Supporting Families and Their Children

A wide range of legislative and social program initiatives have been developed in the United States in the past four decades. These have resulted in a complex network of services aimed at supporting and enhancing family life through health and mental health care, housing, food and nutrition, parent education, early childhood education, special education, child welfare, child care, and a variety of income supports. In chapter 3 we introduce this formal system of family supports and briefly describe some of its key components. These supports are linked to the framework of needs and resources for family and child well-being presented in chapter 1, in particular the bottom of the triangular framework — neighborhood, community, and environmental resources.[1]

In this chapter we build on an understanding of the many risks faced by vulnerable families and their children, as covered in chapter 2, and complement the discussion of formal and informal supports for families and their children that is the focus for chapter 7. We have organized this discussion around the instrumental and expressive family functions introduced in chapter 1. As previously explained, instrumental functions fulfilled by families for their members include provision of basic needs such as food, clothing, and adequate shelter, while expressive functions include helping family members meet their needs for affiliation, belonging, and emotional and intellectual development. Nevertheless, it is important to note that a number of supports defy such a dichotomous classification in their aim at multiple levels of family enhancement. A final section analyzes

approaches to delivering services and discusses some of the issues related
to system reforms.

Supporting Families' Instrumental Functions

Chapter 2 provided details on the devastating effects of poverty on family
life as well as the many correlates of poverty that undermine a family's ability
to meet the basic needs of its members. Insufficient income undermines a
family's ability to fulfill expressive functions as well. Plotnick (1997) has
noted that there are three main antipoverty strategies: preventing poverty
through higher-wage employment programs, reducing poverty by supple-
menting income with cash payments, and mitigating the effects of poverty
through the provision of noncash benefits such as housing and health care.
The focus in this section is on the latter two strategies — reducing poverty
and mitigating its effects. Thus we begin our discussion of the formal system
of services with those generally classified as income supports: income maintenance, child support enforcement, and health care and medical assistance.
Except for the Supplemental Security Income program, each form of assistance was created by federal legislation with benefits provided by public
agencies in each state. The legislative origin of all of them is the Social
Security Act of 1935, which is the framework of the modern welfare state in
the United States (Karger and Stoesz 2002); this act has been amended many
times since its initial passage through legislation, creating new titles corresponding to new programs. Finally, we also discuss two other types of programs aimed at mitigating the effects of poverty: housing supports and food
programs.

Income Maintenance

The major income maintenance programs available to families today are
Supplemental Security Income (SSI) and the Temporary Assistance to
Needy Families program (TANF), which replaced the Aid to Families with
Dependent Children program (AFDC) when welfare reform legislation under the Personal Responsibility and Work Opportunity Reconciliation Act
of 1996 (PRWORA) was passed. Both programs are means-tested, requiring
recipients to meet guidelines for eligibility in order to receive benefits.

TANF provides work-related, temporary assistance to families with dependent children, while SSI provides assistance to the elderly and people with disabilities, including children, who meet income qualifications (Downs et al. 2000).

Temporary Assistance to Needy Families (TANF)

The main function of income supports has been the provision of a "safety net" for our most vulnerable citizens to ensure that none fall below a certain economic level. With the passage of PRWORA in 1996, the safety net created by the AFDC program for poor families was dramatically transformed into a short-term program emphasizing work and financial independence (Downs et al. 2000; Lehman and Danziger 1997). Moreover, states now have much greater latitude in designing their TANF programs. For example, while federal guidelines call for a limit of twenty-four months of receiving benefits, after which a recipient must be employed, states can set shorter time limits, and some have. Connecticut, for example has the shortest — twenty-one months.

This change in income benefits for families was foreshadowed by passage of the Family Support Act of 1988, which also emphasized work and self sufficiency for AFDC recipients. It was under that act that the JOBS program (Jobs Opportunities and Basic Skills), which offered parents education and training as well as employment services, was launched. The act also guaranteed child care and medical insurance for a short period after a family went off welfare, provided benefits to some two-parent families, and strengthened child support enforcement (Downs et al. 2000; Karger and Stoesz 2002).

PRWORA sets limits on the amount of time recipients can receive benefits, including a lifetime limit, requires that recipients exchange work for benefits, forces compliance with child support enforcement, limits benefits for adolescent parents to those who live with adults, and denies assistance to any children a parent might have after becoming eligible for assistance (Abramovitz 1997; Downs et al. 2000). Some benefits to legal immigrants were also eliminated (Balgopal 2000; Fujiwara 1998). The negative impact of the loss of the safety net was hardest on women and children, since they are the primary beneficiaries of income maintenance programs (Balgopal 2000). Moreover, under PRWORA, the huge inequities in state benefit levels that existed in the AFDC program continue. For example, the lifetime limit for a family's receipt of benefits is sixty months, but, as with the term limit before a recipient must be employed, states can set their own terms. Arkansas, for example, set its limit at forty-eight months (Abramovitz 1997; Downs et al. 2000). The largest inequity is found in the benefit levels, which range (as of the year 2002) from a low in Mississippi of $120 per month for a family of three to a high of $923 for the same-sized family in Alaska. A family in Mississippi receiving welfare benefits and food stamps is still at only 44 percent of the federal poverty level, whereas the Alaskan family is at 92 percent (Stoesz 2000). Additionally, benefits are not indexed for inflation, undermining the benefit for all recipients and adding further to the inequity among states.

Because of its removal of the safety net for vulnerable families, in particular families of color, those headed by women, and immigrant families, many have labeled the legislation sexist, racist, and xenophobic (Balgolpal 2000; Keigher 1997; Pelton 1999). Others repudiate use of the term *reform* since it generally implies improvement, which these critics deny has resulted from the recent, radical changes in welfare (Lehman and Danziger 1997; Pelton 1999). Currently there is little evidence of the real impact of these changes. We do not know, for example, what will happen when poor families reach the limits of their eligibility and parents are not yet employed, or when families reach their lifetime limit of eligibility. What happens to a single mother's young children when she is forced to seek employment without adequate help in finding suitable child care or when child care subsidies are unavailable? What will be the impact on the formal child welfare system of so many families losing welfare benefits and having no other source of financial support? The following example starkly illustrates of some of these issues.

A recent television news report's headline story in a large urban city revolved around the challenge of single motherhood and the need for quality child care. In a tragic accident a two-year-old boy fell to his death from an open, seventh-floor window. He had been left alone with his four-year-old brother while the mother went to her job training program. The family had a child care provider paid for with state funds, but on this day the provider was ill. The mother had asked the children's father to stop by and watch the children. She left for work thinking that the children would soon be supervised. The father never appeared, and while the children were home alone the accident occurred, much to the horror of neighbors in the courtyard below.

County commissioners commented that child care resources were available and that no child can or should be left alone. The mother should not have gone to work that day without proper child supervision. The sad and ironic fact was that the mother's commitment to improve her life by participating in a welfare-to-work program resulted in this terrible loss. In the days following this accident, several TV stations and newspapers provided information about child care resources in the community.

One study in Ohio examined the impact of welfare reform on families that were receiving both welfare assistance and child welfare services. The study specifically examined whether a parent's benefit reduction affected the length of time her children remained in foster care. The researchers found that trading welfare benefits for work negatively affected the speed of reunification. When a mother's cash assistance was reduced and she was employed during the quarter following the benefit reduction, she was less likely to be reunified with her children; on the other hand, mothers experiencing a reduction in cash assistance who did not work were reunified at a rate that was 23 percent faster. Moreover, for mothers whose level of assistance was maintained, only 4 percent of their children were still in foster care by the end of an eighteen-month period, as compared to 75 percent of the children whose mothers worked and 65 percent of the children whose mothers did not, with both groups experiencing a loss of assistance (Wells, Guo, and Li 2000).

It is likely that parents involved in the child welfare and general welfare systems have significant problems that make employment difficult. For example, studies have shown that domestic violence keeps women on welfare (Raphael and Tolman 1998–1999). Even when they do find employment, their jobs may be less stable, provide few if any benefits, and require evening or weekend hours with little flexibility, all of which are "conditions that make it difficult for mothers to manage the conflict inherent in working, supervising, education, and nurturing children largely on their own" (Bailey 2000:1). Wells, Guo, and Li (2000) also examined the possible relationship between child maltreatment reports and substantiations and AFDC caseloads in one Ohio county during a three-year period from 1995 to 1998; they found a consistent pattern of increases in substantiated reports and foster care placements that correlated with monthly reductions in the AFDC caseload. *(In chapter 10 we consider these changes in the welfare program and their impact on families in greater depth.)*

Supplemental Security Income (SSI)

Supplemental Security Income (SSI) is a means-tested federal income support program for the elderly poor and the disabled, including children. Unlike TANF, SSI is operated out of the Social Security Administration. Benefit levels are set by the federal government and are adjusted each year for inflation. The SSI program was created in 1972 by combining three federally funded categorical cash assistance programs operated by the states: Old Age Assistance (OAA), Aid to the Blind (AB), and Aid to the Permanently and Totally Disabled (APTD) (Downs et al. 2000; Karger and Stoesz 1990).

Children under eighteen are eligible for benefits if they have a medically certified physical or mental disability (Plotnick 1997). However, the federal government has made eligibility increasingly difficult, and recent legislation has made some groups ineligible for benefits. In the case of children, prior to 1990 eligibility was determined if a child's disability was on a list of severe impairments. Many children were denied benefits, and advocates took the issue to court. In the Supreme Court's 1990 *Sullivan v. Zebley* decision, it was found that the Social Security Administration was using more stringent tests for children's disabilities than for adults, and the agency began to implement a functional limitation assessment to determine eligibility for benefits (Ford and Schwamm 1992). In five years the number of children receiving SSI benefits rose from 332,000 to 975,000 (Plotnick 1997; Schwamm 1996). However, the 1996 PRWORA did away with the functional limitation assessment, defined disability in more limited ways, and required reviews of children every three years. Moreover, because of the fragmentation of mental health and other children's services, there are significant problems in implementing the SSI program for children with mental illness. These children are greatly underrepresented among young beneficiaries (Koyanagi 1994; Ozawa and Hong 1999).

PRWORA also made legal immigrants ineligible for benefits, although these were later restored to some. However, state agencies disbursing federal funds are now responsible to ensure that only qualified immigrants receive benefits and to report anyone known to be unlawfully in the United States to the Immigration and Naturalization Service (Downs et al. 2000; Levenson

1998). This is an issue that will be raised in chapter 4 as an example of a threat to professional responsibility for confidentiality.

Another example of federal attempts to limit SSI benefits is the 1997 repeal of eligibility for substance abusers (Gresenz, Watkins, and Podus 1998). Under a special Drug Addicts and Alcoholics program, substance abusers enrolled in and complying with treatment and those agreeing to have a third party manage their payments were eligible for benefits. The program grew from thirteen thousand cases in 1988 to over one hundred thousand in 1994, with benefit totals of nearly $400 million, prompting concern among federal officials. There also was concern about allegations of fraud, which prompted legislation in 1994 to tighten payment controls (USGAO 1995).[2]

Child Support Enforcement

Since 1975, with the passage of the Child Support Enforcement Act, which established Title IVD of the Social Security Act, the federal government has played a role in establishing paternity and securing financial contributions from noncustodial parents. Although child support enforcement has been tied to welfare benefits, higher-income families can receive collection assistance. In fact, child support policies benefit nonwelfare families more than those receiving welfare benefits (Gaffney and Dubey 1997). The United States General Accounting Office reported that in 1996 13 percent of the 7.4 million AFDC child support cases nationwide received at least one support payment, compared with 28 percent of the 9.3 million non-AFDC child support cases (USGAO 1998). Noncustodial parents with low incomes are less likely to pay child support for a number of reasons: their limited ability to do so, lack of visiting or custody rights, and the fact that their child was born out of wedlock and paternity has not been legally established (Downs et al. 2000; Nichols-Casebolt and Garfinkel 1991; Plotnick 1997). In her study of over two hundred mothers receiving welfare assistance, Edin (1995) found that in trying to balance their families' competing needs for benefits, compliance with requirements, and relationship to (and perhaps support from) the noncustodial parent, the mothers often deliberately hid identifying information from authorities. It is important to note that the government recoups welfare benefits by retaining any past due support that is collected and all but $50 monthly of any current payments (USGAO 1998).

Consistent with the trend to devolve responsibility for policy decisions to the states, the child support provisions of the 1996 PRWORA gave states much greater authority to design their collection and enforcement policies by, for example, letting states decide how much of child support collected would be passed along to families receiving welfare (Downs et al. 2000). The welfare reform legislation also established new requirements for custodial parent cooperation, mandated that benefits be reduced by 25 percent when custodial parents did not cooperate with the child support enforcement agency, and gave that agency the authority to order genetic testing in contested cases (USGAO 1998). Despite these increasingly stringent requirements, the program has failed to secure a stable source of income for poor families, especially those leaving the assistance roles. In the first three states — Connecticut, Florida, and Virginia — where enforced time limits were reached, only 20 to 30 percent of families had any child support collected during the twelve months prior to their leaving assistance. Moreover, the majority of the families (from 47 to 69 percent across the three states) were without any child support order on reaching their termination from welfare; 56 to 81 percent of the cases reviewed needed one or more of the basic child support services — locating the noncustodial parent, establishing paternity, and establishing a support order, all of which must precede collection and enforcement (USGAO 1998).

Experts are calling for reforms in child support that range from restructuring and federalizing the entire program to eliminating the current program and establishing instead an assured child support benefit as a new, federal entitlement program (Garfinkel, Melli, and Robertson 1994; Plotnick 1997; Roberts 1994). Clearly changes are needed if child support enforcement is to have a positive effect on the financial status of poor families and those whose income is reduced because of divorce.

Tax Credits as Income Support

Two additional forms of income support are tax credits on earned income — the Earned Income Tax Credit (EITC) and the Dependent Care Tax Credit. As tax credits, these are wage subsidy programs for working, nonwelfare, poor families. The EITC, which refunds a percent of earned income, is an idea that gained currency in the 1970s. Initially, families with a full-time worker could receive a 10 percent credit (a refund) on earnings up to $8,000 (Abramovitz 1997). In 1993, in a policy environment that increasingly emphasized work and independence, the percent of the credit was increased to 18.5, for a total credit of $1,434 for one child and 19.5 percent for two or more up to $1,511 (Ozawa 1995). The aim was to bring a family with a full-time wage earner above the poverty line when the family received through the EITC and Food Stamps (Abramovitz 1997). There is some evidence that the EITC has been successful in helping some families and, as more parents trade welfare benefits for employment, is likely to be an even more significant poverty reduction strategy in the future (Downs et al. 2000).

The Dependent Care Tax Credit is an income support that is widely used by working families to offset their child care costs. The credit is, in effect, a tax deduction that allows families with an adjusted gross income of $10,000 or less to claim 30 percent of their child care costs up to a maximum of $2,400 per year. The credit is reduced by 1 percent, down to a low of 20 percent, for every $2,000 of income above $10,000 (Ozawa 1995).

Health and Medical Assistance

Poor families and their children are assisted in meeting their health care needs through a range of programs that provide either care directly or insurance coverage so families can obtain care. The two major United States health care assistance programs of the latter type are Medicaid and Medicare. Both programs were enacted in 1965 as part of a series of legislative initiatives called the "Great Society" (O'Looney 1996), amending the Social Security Act by adding Titles XVIII and XIX respectively (Karger and Stoesz 1990). Medicaid is a means-tested medical insurance program for poor children and families that is jointly funded by federal and state governments. States set eligibility guidelines and covered benefits within a set of federal requirements. Medicaid-eligible families seek medical care from providers who agree to accept the Medicaid reimbursement rate that is determined by each state (Karger and Stoesz 1990). Medicaid requires states to provide an array of preventive health care for children as well as diagnostic and treatment of acute and chronic illness as part of its early and periodic screening, diagnosis, and treatment (EPSDT) even when these services may not be covered for other Medicaid recipients (Devaney, Ellwood, and Love 1997).

Medicare provides hospital insurance, Part A, and medical insurance, Part B, for the elderly. Part A is compulsory; Part B is voluntary, with the recipient paying the cost of the insurance that covers doctors' bills and other medical expenses. Recent changes allow spouses to retain some income and assets and still qualify for medicaid coverage for the nursing home care of an ill partner (Karger and Stoesz 1990).

There are a number of problems with the current medical assistance programs. First is participation rate, especially in Medicaid. As noted in chapter 2, one in every four children is enrolled in the program (over 22 million), but millions more are eligible and have not been enrolled (Edmunds and Coye 1998). States in the past were required to qualify all AFDC recipient families for the program. Later Congress severed this tie to welfare and established national Medicaid eligibility levels based on the federal poverty level. While this served to increase the number of eligible children, there were varying participation rates between AFDC families — 90 percent — and poor families not receiving assistance — 69 percent in 1993 (Devaney, Ellwood, and Love 1997). Under the new PRWORA states can require a separate Medicaid application for TANF recipients, which is likely to further reduce participation by the poorest families. Other factors influencing participation is that parents do not know their children can be covered, they may see the application process as too onerous, or they may avoid the program because of the stigma associated with any type of welfare benefit, especially when the same department of social services administers both welfare and medical assistance.

Other problems with Medicaid include low reimbursement rates for providers, which serve as a disincentive to serve Medicaid patients. Also, in some communities there is an extremely limited supply of health care providers and dearth of those willing to accept Medicaid (Devaney, Ellwood, and Love 1997):

> Throughout the country, the value of a Medicaid card is clearly brought into question when so many physicians refuse to accept it as a form of payment. Fear of malpractice liability, dissatisfaction with levels of reimbursement and the inconvenience of claims payment procedures, the belief that Medicaid patients are non-compliant and difficult to serve, and the undying perception that Medicaid is an unresponsive, inflexible system with which to do business continue to dissuade many . . . from participation.
>
> (Hill 1992:152–153).

The problem of obtaining medical assistance is even greater for immigrant families. Under new regulations legal immigrants who entered the United States after August 22, 1996, are not eligible for Medicaid benefits within the first five years of their arrival. Even eligible immigrants may be dissuaded from applying for benefits because they fear that the "public charge" policy will negatively affect their application for citizenship or a work permit, despite the fact that the federal government has clarified that it does not apply to either Medicaid or the State Children's Health Insurance Program (Institute of Medicine 2000).

State Children's Health Insurance Program

As discussed in chapter 2, many poor families and their children — 11 million — are uninsured. A new program — the State Children's Health Insurance Program (SCHIP) — was established to address this problem.[3] SCHIP, enacted as part of the Balanced Budget Act of 1997 and now Title XXI of the Social Security Act, will provide $24 billion in funding by 2002 in block grants to states to expand Medicaid or initiate new health insurance programs for low-income, uninsured children. Funding levels are tied to a state's proportion of uninsured children whose families are at or below 200 percent of the federal poverty level ($32,900 for a family of four) (Institute of Medicine 2000; USGAO 1999a). Under SCHIP, states can help low-income working families by paying the cost of enrollment in family coverage of an individual parent's employer-sponsored insurance plan. Even parents can be insured under SCHIP if a state can show that covering a parent is cost effective (USGAO 1999). SCHIP is the largest federal allocation of funds for children's health since the inception of Medicaid in 1965 (Children's Defense Fund n.d.; Edmunds and Coye 1998).

As illustrated in the editorial summarized below, however, availability of a health insurance program is no guarantee parents will enroll their children. Two years after the program was launched only 1.3 million children had been enrolled; one in seven children still lacks insurance coverage (Institute of Medicine 2000). The tangible and intangible obstacles to obtaining benefits are many; judging from the Medicaid experience, states will need to improve outreach, eligibility determination, and enrollment procedures (Edmunds and Coye 1998). However, one positive outcome of the outreach efforts undertaken by the states to date has been the number of Medicaid-eligible children identified (USGAO 1999a).

A recent editorial appearing in the the *Hartford Courant* (August 28, 2000) criticized those responsible for publicizing the CHIP program, known in Connecticut as the HUSKY plan, because in Connecticut, as in other states, too few eligible children are enrolled. The editorial cited a Robert Wood Johnson Foundation study showing that three of five parents whose children are without health care insurance do not know about the program and that many parents had the misperception that CHIP was only for those on welfare or with very low incomes. In Connecticut officials have spent $3 million on publicity; however, the editorial called for more outreach efforts to eligible families.

Maternal and Child Health Block Grant Program

This program, Title V of the Social Security Act, is a federal block grant to states (usually to public health departments) that match funds on a formula basis aimed at identifying and meeting the health needs of mainly low-income women and children. In most states the program delivers two types of direct health care services — preventive and primary care and long-term care to children with chronic illness and/or disabilities (Hill 1992).

Federally Qualified Health Centers

This program is funded through Section 330 grant funds under the Public Health Service Act. Under this program federal funds directly support community-based health centers providing primary care services to families who lack access to health care because they cannot afford it, they live in isolated areas, or in communities experiencing a shortage of providers (Hill 1992; Institute of Medicine 2000; Morris and Williamson 1986). To be eligible for funding, the health centers must be not-for-profit organizations overseen by a board of directors with community representation, offer free and sliding fee services depending on patients' financial status, and provide culturally competent health care services (Institute of Medicine 2000).

Section 330 funds also support migrant health centers, Health Care for the Homeless Programs, and Public Housing Primary Care Programs (Institute of Medicine 2000). Compared to funding for Medicare and Medicaid, both this program and the Maternal and Child Health programs are small but key health care initiatives that support primary care services to families and children (Hill 1992). The Veterans Health Administration (VA) and the Indian Health Service (IHS) are two additional health services for which some families may be eligible. The VA medical system is one of the nation's largest, with its many hospitals, outpatient clinics, nursing homes, and counseling centers around the country. The IHS provides health care services to members of 547 federally recognized tribes (Institute of Medicine 2000).

School-Based Clinics

Finally, school-based clinics are another way that some children may receive primary health care. First established in the 1970s out of concern that Medicaid was not reaching enough poor children, these centers — over one thousand nationwide — provide physical and behavioral health care using multidisciplinary teams of nurse practitioners, doctors, and social workers (Institute of Medicine 2000). The clinics are funded by a mix of private as well as federal, state, and local sources; they are also reimbursed when Medicaid-eligible children receive services. However, the rapid growth of Medicaid managed care plans has undermined this funding source even though school-based clinics have continued to serve children enrolled in these plans. The new SCHIP program described earlier offers a promising funding source (Grant and Maggio 1997; Institute of Medicine 2000). Although these school-based services are limited, they have potential as preventive and primary health care resources for children (Perloff 1992). *(See chapter 8 for a more complete discussion of meeting children's special developmental needs in school-based settings.)*

Other Health Initiatives

Other health initiatives deal with some of the special problems discussed in chapter 2, such as lead poisoning and asthma. The following is an example of a program designed to address one of these rapidly emerging health problems for children — asthma.

The Centers for Disease Prevention and Control have awarded $2.9 million in funds to twenty-three sites to improve the health of inner-city children with asthma. The program is directed to community-based health organizations that serve mainly children of color in low-income families, because they are known to experience more severe asthma attacks that can result in hospitalization and even death. Through the program professional social workers will serve as asthma counselors to work closely with children and their families, assisting them in dealing with the physical and emotional impact of asthma as well as with the environmental factors that exacerbate asthma. The program is based on findings from the National Cooperative Inner City Asthma Study, which was supported by the National Institute of Allergy and Infectious Diseases (Banks 2001).[4]

Despite the number of strategies for meeting children's health needs, efforts to meet their mental health needs are woefully inadequate. While one in ten children suffers from mental illness, fewer than one in five receives treatment. In January 2001 the United States surgeon general issued a National Action Agenda calling for sweeping reforms of the mental health care system that included, among other strategies, professional training and service integration (O'Neill 2001).[5]

Housing Supports

There are both *supply* and *demand* approaches to assisting vulnerable families meet their needs for housing. Supply approaches provide shelters for the homeless and also use public funds to build new housing or renovate existing housing to meet standards, while demand approaches essentially provide rent and mortgage fund subsidies to low income families to enable them to obtain housing on the open market. In recent years, the federal government's housing policies aimed at increasing the quality and quantity of housing for the poor have emphasized the latter (Morris and Williamson 1986). Details on problems with housing and the current crisis of homelessness were provided in chapter 2. In addition to viewing housing assistance as either supply or demand strategies, housing needs and the solutions to them can be visualized on a continuum, from the provision of shelters for the homeless, to transitional housing with supportive services that are usually time limited, to assistance in securing long-term, affordable, and decent housing (Campbell 2001; Lang 1989). Following a brief discussion of shelter services, this section will describe the two major rental assistance programs —

public housing and Section 8 assistance — and briefly discuss emergency services to the homeless provided by federal law.

In 1987 Congress passed the Steward B. McKinney Homeless Assistance Act providing funds for emergency services to the homeless (Lang 1989; USGAO 2000). Among the services established under this funding are food and shelter as well as programs offering supported housing with other services such as health and mental health care and job training. The rapid expansion of these programs for the homeless could be taken as evidence of the extent of need; in ten years funding grew from $350 million to $1.2 billion (USGAO 2000). Shelters, even those with supported housing services, in no way meet the need for affordable, long-term housing, however.

Housing assistance for low-income families is funded and overseen by the Department of Housing and Urban Development (HUD). HUD's largest programs, public housing and Section 8 tenant-based assistance, benefit over 6 million people (USGAO 2000). Public housing, established by the Housing Act of 1937, is owned and operated by local housing authorities. Tenants pay 30 percent of their monthly income toward the rent (Morris and Williamson 1986). A major problem with public housing is its scarcity, since there has been little new construction in recent years and demand greatly outstrips the current supply (Morris and Williamson 1986; USGAO 2000).

Problems in accessing public housing are compounded for homeless families. In the past local authorities were required to give them preference, but this requirement was eliminated in 1996 along with other provisions that favored local decision making, such as the ability to admit more higher-income families and exclude applicants with criminal convictions and those with a history of drug and alcohol abuse (USGAO 2000).[6] Another criticism of public housing is summed up by Mulroy (1995a:1383): "Many older public housing projects still remain large islands of concentrated poverty that isolate primarily poor black families from the employment and educational opportunities that are offered in more socially and economically mixed neighborhoods."

Partly because of criticisms about segregation, the emphasis in housing policy has shifted to demand strategies. Chief among them is Section 8, which is federally subsidized private housing and was initiated under the Housing and Community Development Act of 1974. Section 8 assistance can be linked to particular housing units or provided through a voucher to eligible tenants who secure open market housing; thus the housing benefit is mobile, staying with the recipient. The subsidy pays the difference between the cost of the rent and the 30 percent of the family's monthly cash income. The housing must meet standards of adequacy and the rent must reflect "fair market" levels determined for the region by HUD (Lang 1989; Mulroy 1995a; USGAO 2000).

Among the problems with this approach are landlord bias against some low-income families, for example, those headed by women, and the greatly diminished supply of affordable housing (Mulroy 1995a). As housing short-ages increase, the market rates for rentals also increase, but federally desig-nated rates may not keep pace, discouraging landlords from participating in the program. And, while housing mobility efforts such as vouchers may be somewhat successful, especially in enabling families to find affordable hous-ing outside the urban areas, market forces such as availability and personal preferences continue to result in communities with high concentrations of lower-income minority families (Harting and Henig 1997). However, for some families who can secure subsidized housing, there is evidence that they are able to move to better communities and secure employment. Par-ticipants in the well-publicized Gautreaux program in Chicago, which helps single-parent black families move from public housing to the suburbs, are more likely to have jobs than their counterparts who remain in the city (Popkin, Rosenbaum, and Meaden 1993). Indeed, housing activists advocate for policies that increase the availability of low-cost housing in low-density, scattered site arrangements that offer residents job opportunities and enable them to participate in neighborhood activities (Lang 1989).[7]

Supports for Food and Nutrition

There are three main national programs that support low-income fami-lies' attainment of adequate food and nutrition, the Food Stamp Program, the Special Supplemental Food Program for Women, Infants, and Children (WIC), the Child and Adult Care Food Program, and the school nutrition programs. The United States Department of Agriculture (USDA) is the fed-eral agency overseeing these programs.

Food Stamp Program

This program originated in the 1930s as part of agricultural policy to deal with the dual problems of the hungry poor and destabilized farm prices (Devaney, Ellwood, and Love 1997). The Food Stamp Act of 1964 created the current entitlement program, which aims to provide an adequate diet to poor people, whether adults or children. Eligible recipients receive stamps (coupons) in dollar amounts that they can then use to purchase food items (DiNitto 1995). The USDA has experimented with other forms of providing benefit, notably electronic systems similar to an automatic teller machine (ATM) card that would be swiped by store clerks and debit the recipient's purchase (DiNitto 1995; Vachon 1985).

The Food Stamp Program is an important income support for low-income families, serving twice as many families as AFDC/TANF. Each month 28 million individuals receive food stamps. For families receiving welfare assistance, these benefits represented 25 to 50 percent of household income (Devaney, Ellwood, and Love 1997). There is an inverse relationship between TANF and Food Stamps for these families; as welfare benefits diminish because a family reaches time limits on benefits or because of earned wages, food stamp benefits rise. Food Stamps also serve somewhat as an equalizer of vast TANF benefit differences among states, because the Food Stamp benefit is higher when income (including welfare income) is lower (DiNitto 1995). There is evidence that the Food Stamp Program achieves its chief aims of increasing both food expenditure and the availability of nutrients in participating households, but not that it directly affects good nutrition. Indeed, one criticism of the program is that, because there are no requirements for the purchase of nutritious food, nor a nutrition education component, the program does not assure improved nutrition (Devaney, Ellwood, and Love 1997). Regardless, "The Food Stamp Program is the cornerstone of the public assistance safety net for low-income individuals" (Devaney, Ellwood, and Love 1997:92).

Special Supplement Food Program for Women, Infants, and Children (WIC)

This program targets low-income pregnant, breast-feeding, or postpartum mothers and their infants and children up to five years old who are at nutritional risk. Eligibility is tied to the federal poverty line; families' incomes cannot exceed 185 percent of this. Similar to the Food Stamp Program, recipients receive coupons that they can exchange for food. However, the coupons must be exchanged for specified nutritious foods such as milk, cereal, infant formula, and juices. Moreover, there is a nutrition education component to the program and participants can also be referred to other health and social services they might need (Devaney, Ellwood, and Love 1997; DiNitto 1995; Hill 1992). The most compelling evidence that the WIC program affects well-being is in studies of pregnancy outcomes in which birth weight is increased and preterm delivery is reduced. There is also evidence that the program has reduced the incidence of iron deficiency anemia in children (Devaney, Ellwood, and Love 1997). The program serves over 1.6 million mothers and 5.3 million infants and children each month, yet only 55 percent of those who are eligible receive the benefit, and there is a waiting list for enrollment (Devaney, Ellwood, and Love 1997; DiNitto 1995).

Two additional programs support adequate food and nutrition for families with low incomes: the Child and Adult Care Food Program and two school nutrition programs — the National School Lunch Program and the School Breakfast Program. The first provides funds for feeding children in child care facilities, both center- and family-based. Centers serving the disabled and elderly may also be eligible (DiNitto 1995). It has been suggested that the Child and Adult Care Food Program is an underutilized resource for the growing numbers of children in families transitioning off welfare who are in informal child care arrangements (Pine 1999).

School Nutrition Programs

The two school nutrition programs together contribute substantially to what children eat since they operate daily in public and nonprofit schools throughout the country. These two federal programs — the National School Lunch Program and the School Breakfast Program — serve 25.6 million children and 6.3 million children per day respectively. The School Lunch Program is the oldest and largest child nutrition program in the country (Morris and Williamson 1986). The two programs provide food and funds at a total cost of $6.4 billion; both are operated by the U.S. Department of Agriculture (Devaney, Ellwood, and Love 1997; DiNitto 1995). Under the programs, schools provide free or reduced-cost meals to students whose family incomes are between 135 and 185 percent of the federal poverty line (DiNitto 1995). While schools offering the breakfast program are much fewer in number, nearly 92 percent of students nationwide have access to the lunch program; 56 percent of them take advantage of it on a typical day. Nearly half of all lunches (47 percent) and most of the breakfasts (85 percent) are served to children whose families are below 185 percent of the poverty line (Devaney,

Ellwood, and Love 1997). This is a clear indication of the programs' significance in supporting the dietary needs of school children, although, as in
other programs, there is concern centering on lack of participation by eligible children.

Supporting Families' Expressive Roles

As depicted in the "Framework of Needs and Resources for Family and
Child Well-Being" in chapter 1, in addition to meeting their members'
basic needs, families play important expressive roles as they nurture, teach,
and socialize their children and care for each other. In fulfilling these
responsibilities, all families regardless of their economic status need supports and services in their communities, as outlined in the above-noted
framework. Working families need child care; parents of children with
exceptionalities need support and services; all families and children need
recreational and educational opportunities. In chapter 7 we discuss the
role of social supports and informal helping in social work practice with
families. In this section we describe selected services available through the
formal system of care, including child day care and Head Start, early intervention services, and child welfare services, all of which serve primarily
low-income families.

Child Care

Child care is care for children when they are not in school or being cared
for by a parent. Day care can be formal care in a licensed center or family
day care home or it can be informal, unlicensed care by a relative or friend
of the child's parent. The former is considered regulated, market care, while
the latter is unregulated, nonmarket care (Morgan 1983). Morgan (1983)
has described child care policy in the United States as being in chaos because of the different origins and purposes of child care programs and the
differing perspectives and interests of their stakeholders — child care, especially that which is publicly funded, has been conceived to address unique
issues or problems. For example, child care provided as a social service for
families offers respite and support to families that may be at risk of maltreat-
ing their children. Child care for these purposes is funded with social ser-

vices dollars and frequently involves social workers in child welfare. In contrast, child care as a support to parents' employment, particularly for those parents leaving welfare to participate in the labor market, is funded through income maintenance programs and involves staff in public welfare agencies.

The principal aim of some child care initiatives is fostering child development. Examples include Head Start, which is described below, kindergarten programs, and school-based parent- child centers. The result is a fragmented system of child care with "no master policy for children and families that could coordinate theory and practice among these funding sources" (Morgan 1983:250). Nationally, the growth of child care coordinating councils and information and referral services has sought to address some of these problems by bringing key stakeholders together to improve quality, availability, and accessibility of child care. And it is important to note that most child care is supported by private funds, paid for by working parents. In 1991 they spent $23.6 billion on care for their children (Stoney and Greenberg 1996).

A national study of the child care choices of working parents found that nearly 50 percent chose formal, market care, 28 percent chose center-based care, and 20 percent chose family day care. About 19 percent preferred care by a relative (other than a child's parent) (Hofferth et al. 1991). However, this survey showed that for families with lower incomes, child care choices differed. Single-parent, female-headed families were much more likely to use relative care — 30 percent. Moreover, there was an inverse correlation between mothers' higher level of education and preference for relative care (Brayfield, Deich, and Hofferth 1993). Another study showed that among low-income working families, 60 percent used relatives as primary child care providers for their children (Collins and Carlson 1998).

Although findings vary, research does suggest a greater likelihood for parents with lower incomes to choose unregulated care. There may be a number of reasons for this, especially for parents transitioning off welfare. As noted earlier in this chapter, parents entering the work force face myriad challenges, one of which is finding suitable care for their children. Some parents may have little time to explore options; others may not have access to information about child care (Kisker and Ross 1997). One study showed that as many as 65 percent of mothers who choose informal, unregulated care had received no information at all about other child care options (Butler, Brigham, and Schultheiss 1992). Another study concluded that while 10 percent of the parents studied found their child care through a formal information and referral service, over two thirds of them learned about their current child care arrangements from friends, neighbors, and relatives (Mitchell, Cooperstein, and Larner 1992).

In addition to access to information about child care options, parents may prefer informal care, especially with relatives, because they trust family members and also because these kin offer care that is culturally consistent with parental values and care giving standards (Butler, Brigham, and Schultheiss 1992). Moreover, parents with low incomes and those newly entering the work force may not be able to obtain formal, licensed care when they need it. Kisker and Ross (1997) point out that many of these parents work weekends (33 percent), on rotating shifts (50 percent), and evenings (10 percent) — work hours when formal care is least likely to be available. Cost is another important factor influencing parental choice. Informal, nonmarket care costs less than formal care, especially center-based child care. Finally, while there is no evidence, but only speculation of this, families faced with reduced income because of welfare benefit caps and who are eligible for child care subsidies may choose care by relatives as a way of stabilizing family income (Pine 1999). Since the focus of this chapter is on public services to vulnerable families and their children, the remainder of the discussion of child care will address subsidized child care as part of recent welfare reform under PRWORA, already discussed.

PRWORA combined earlier child care subsidy programs into the Child Care and Development Fund (CCDF) and disbursed $2.9 billion to the states in 1997 to help low-income families pay for child care (Kisker and Ross 1997). The level of funding to each state is tied to state spending for child care. Consistent with the current policy direction that grants greater autonomy to the states, the CCDF allows states to decide funding levels, the extent of contribution of state funds, reimbursement levels to providers, and quality controls for unlicenced providers (Downs et al. 2000). It is also up to each state to decide how to deal with child care subsidies for low-income working families and those transitioning off welfare. Connecticut, for example, has four different child care subsidy programs in its Child Care Assistance Program; parents qualify for each based on their status, not their income (Pine 1999).

Despite the recent and rapid growth in child care funding, the demand for child care assistance is expected to exceed the available funding. The Congressional Budget Office (CBO) predicted a shortfall of $1.4 billion in funding needed just to support those families leaving welfare (Blank and

Adams 1997). Recently, the U.S. Department of Health and Human Services released statistics showing that, although states had increased their spending by 80 percent since the CBO's predicted shortfall, only 12 percent of eligible children were receiving federal child care subsidies — only 1.8 of the 15 million eligible children (Buzzi 2000).

Subsidized child care as part of welfare reform represents a major policy initiative for families. If parents are to be encouraged to enter the labor market (under the threat of losing income support), they must have adequate child care for their children. Concerns about adequacy (quality), affordability, and accessibility for these parents are issues around which child care and social work professionals can unite. How can parents be helped to be good consumers of child care? What supports and information do they need to make decisions about child care for their children? Are they informed about the benefits of different types of care? How can parents be more involved in policy decisions regarding child care? Do parents know about and have access to child care subsidy programs in their communities? How can access be improved? What can be done to improve the quality of child care across the board from center-based care to informal child care? What should be done to ensure that seamless system of quality care of all types is available for all parents who need it? How can the investment in quality child care become part of a coordinated, neighborhood-based effort to strengthen family life? In short, what is the blueprint for resolving the chaos in child care described earlier (Morgan 1983) and how can that blueprint be operationalized?

Head Start

Project Head Start was part of the legislative "War on Poverty" conducted by the federal government in the 1960s (O'Looney 1996). Head Start was launched in 1965 as a program aimed at helping to meet the developmental needs of preschool children from disadvantaged families, in effect offering them a learning "head start" on elementary school. Federal funds are provided to local governments, nonprofit organizations, and school systems to operate local programs; 90 percent of participating children must come from families with incomes less than or equal to 100 percent of the federal poverty line. Approximately 85 percent of the funding is federal Head Start moneys, with other funding sources such as the Child Care and Development Fund mentioned above, Title XX social services funds, and other state and local dollars providing the balance (Stein 2001; Valentine and Zigler 1985). Over 750,000 children are served annually at a cost of $3.5 billion. However, because of limited funding, only about 38 percent of eligible children are enrolled in a Head Start program (Devaney, Ellwood, and Love 1997).

Since its inception, Head Start has grown to become a family of programs, including family support and social services, medical and dental screening, mental health services, and nutrition. (Downs et al. 2000; Stein 2001; Valentine and Zigler 1985). Head Start's center-based approach has been expanded to include family service centers and a home-based component (Lightburn and Kemp 1994; Lightburn (in press); Stein 2001). There are also special services to children who are bilingual and those with disabilities. Approximately 13 percent of the children served have a disability (Devaney, Ellwood, and Love 1997).

Parent involvement has become a key component in Head Start, reflecting increased knowledge about parents' central role in children's learning at all ages. Parents are involved in the classroom and in policy making in local programs (Devaney, Ellwood, and Love 1997). Employment benefits is one of the positive outcomes in studies of Head Start's effectiveness, especially in a policy environment emphasizing work. In 1992 35 percent of Head Start staff were either parents or former children in the program (Devaney, Ellwood, and Love 1997). As Valentine and Zigler (1985:268) have noted, "Over the years Head Start has developed a focus on family support to enhance child development. The history of the Head Start program itself, then, is a history of the evolution of social policy development for children and families." As it has in the past, the program will likely need to adapt new family needs and realities, for example, the need for full day programs and new ways of involving parents likely to be working.

An early study of Head Start's effectiveness examined increases in children's I.Q. and showed that while there were increases as much as 10 points, these gains were not maintained into the elementary grades. The findings of this well-known study by Westinghouse Learning Corporation (Cicirelli 1969) stunned the program's supporters and prompted calls for examining other program outcomes; many feared the study results would damage the program. Zigler and Muenchow (1992) have proclaimed Head Start to be "America's most successful educational experiment." Since then, other studies have provided evidence of program success. Devaney, Ellwood, and Love (1997), in their review of the research on Head Start's outcomes, cite the positive short-term benefits on children's cognitive and socioemotional development. They note that no comprehensive national evaluation of the Head Start program has been conducted for twenty years, although there have been numerous, rigorous studies of many of the program's demonstration efforts. Barnett (1995), in his review of research on the long-term effects of early childhood care and education in general, noted that the "effects are large enough and persistent enough to make a meaningful difference in the lives of children from low-income families; for many children, preschool programs can mean the difference between failing and passing, regular or special education, staying out of trouble or becoming involved in crime and delinquency, dropping out or graduating from high school" (43).

Child Welfare Services

A vast and intricate range of child welfare services has emerged to help meet the needs of vulnerable children and youths. These services include preventive programs such as child guidance clinics, various outpatient and in-patient psychiatric settings, juvenile delinquency services, day care, and various types of out-of-home care programs. For the purposes of this section we shall focus on public and private child welfare agencies that respond specifically to the needs of children who are abused or neglected, at risk of out-of-home placement, or in some type of out-of-home placement.

As we underscored in chapter 2, at any given time in the U.S. there is over half a million children placed in foster care or kinship care. In addition, there is an untold number who are at risk of such placement because of their families' problems and/or their own difficulties or special needs. In response to the plight of these children and their families, child welfare services are generally seen as having three goals:

- protecting children from harm,
- preserving existing family units, and
- promoting the development of children "into adults who can live independently and contribute to their community" (Pecora et al. 2000:9).

These child welfare services are provided in each state by public agencies. In some states county governments operate the designated child welfare agency. And in most states the public agency, whether at the state or county level, contracts with private agencies to provide some services. Typically, child welfare services include child protection, preventive services, foster care, adoption, and services to adolescents preparing for emancipation. Policies defining services are developed mainly at the federal level, with the United States Department of Health and Human Services providing guidance to the states through regulation and oversight. Federal funds support the majority of child welfare services; funding eligibility is tied to adherence to regulations. Oversight of child welfare services is also provided by each state's juvenile court system; for example, the state agency cannot place a child in foster care without the court's approval (Stein 2001). Currently, as noted earlier in this chapter, four main federal policies guide the states in developing and delivering child welfare services: the Child Abuse Prevention and Treatment Act (CAPTA), the Adoption Assistance and Child Welfare Act (AACWA), the Multiethnic Placement Act, and the Adoption and Safe Families Act (ASFA). CAPTA was passed in 1974 amid intense national attention on the problems of child abuse and neglect. Under this law a national center on child abuse was launched, and a national definition of what constituted child abuse and neglect formulated. Funding to the states was tied to requirements that they develop a state definition of maltreatment and set up reporting mechanisms and regulations (Downs et al. 2000).[8]

The Adoption Assistance and Child Welfare Act was passed in 1980 amidst growing concern about the length of time children were spending in foster care with no attempt made to reunify them with their families. The act resulted from more than a decade of advocacy on behalf of these children and their families, codifying into federal law the concept of a child's right to a permanent family. It emphasized placement prevention, due process for parents and children, family reunification, and accountability through case reviews and judicial hearings. The law amended the Social Security Act, creating a new Title IVE for the funding of foster care and adoption subsidy (Pine 1986; Stein 2001). More recent policy, in the form of two federal laws outlined below, also sought to move children out of foster care and into permanent families.[9]

The Multiethnic Placement Act, passed in 1994, resulted from concern about the number of children of color who are in foster care and remain there longer than white children. It prohibited states from denying or delaying a child's placement on the basis of race or ethnicity alone (Stein 2001).

The Adoption and Safe Families Act, passed in 1997, reflected a shift in emphasis away from family preservation toward child safety and permanency through adoption. For example, in some cases state agencies do not have to make reasonable efforts to reunify families, as had been required under the Adoption Assistance and Child Welfare Act (Social Legislation Information Service 1997). Consequently, hereafter the needs of severely troubled parents are likely to be neglected. Agencies must move quickly to terminate parental rights when children cannot return home — when children have been in care for fifteen of the most recent twenty-two months (Stein 2001). In addition, there are federal adoption incentive funds for states exceeding a baseline number of adoptions — $4000 for each foster child adopted and $6000 for each former child with special needs who is adopted (Social Legislation Information Service 1997). Finally, also to increase the likelihood and speed of a child's adoption, child welfare agencies must undertake concurrent planning, working both to reunify children and to prepare them for adoption if reunification cannot occur (Stein 2001). Taken together, these laws form the policy framework for services to our most vulnerable children and families — those at risk of abuse or neglect and those separated by a foster care placement or at risk of such a separation.

In summary, as considered in further detail by Pecora et al. (2000), child welfare services are guided by the following principles:

- providing a safe and permanent home, preferably with birth family members or, when indicated, another permanent home,
- promoting child well-being and growth and development in families that can care adequately for their children and fulfill their basic needs,
- helping parents in their child-rearing tasks through community supports for families and by providing a safe and nurturing child-rearing environment,
- offering family-centered services that view the family as the center of attention and support it in its child-rearing functions,
- providing culturally competent services that, as noted in chapter 1, respect and build upon the strengths, potentialities, and needs of diverse societal groups, and
- striving for a "cohesive system of family-centered, community-based, culturally competent, timely, and accountable services and supports for children and families" (Pecora et al. 2000:8).[10]

Service Delivery Approaches

As can be seen from their presentation in this chapter, there is a wide range of services aimed at helping vulnerable families care for their members. And those described represent only a selection of the best-known and largest of social services in the United States. There are many other innovative programs that have been undertaken by public and private organizations to meet the specific needs of families and their children that go beyond the scope of this chapter. A key issue in designing social services is defining needs, another is designing the delivery mechanisms for the service so that it reaches its intended recipients. As can be seen from the above services, underutilization remains a problem for many; eligible families and eligible children do not get benefits they need and are entitled to. We turn now to a survey of how services are delivered, considering access, related issues, and attempts at reforming services that address these issues.

Access, Coordination, and Accountability

Access to a social welfare program is a key factor in its utilization by eligible participants. Factors that influence access may be sociological, psychological, economic, or physical (Gates 1980). For example, parents will not use referral services for child care if they are not motivated to do so, especially if they feel that family members and friends are the best and most reliable sources of information. Perception and motivation are powerful sociological factors related to the use of a service (Gates 1980). By the same token, the social worker running the group for young high school–aged women described in chapter 8 ("Sister Sister Let's Talk") would have had no success in recruiting for her group if the initial four members had not told their friends how much fun it was to belong. Family members with substance abuse problems have to admit that they need help, overcoming psychological barriers to seeking it by being labeled as a substance abuser.[11]

Social stigmas associated with a service are powerful disincentives to its use, as noted earlier in the discussion of the SCHIP program. Physical barriers to accessing a service can be numerous (Gates 1980). Anyone who has spent time in a local welfare office can attest to the discomfort of long waits in uncomfortable surroundings accompanied by families and children, many of whom are in dire need and all of whom are required to amass various documents in support of their requests. The latter is an example of selectivity criteria serving as a barrier to obtaining a benefit; eligibility determination can be complicated and time consuming as well as demeaning (Gates 1980). Locating a service away from the people who need it, and even failing to adequately identify an agency with visible signage, are examples of geographic access (or lack of it).

Of course, when resources are limited, agencies may want to ration services by erecting access barriers, for example by not informing all parents about Head Start because there is funding for only a small percentage of eligible children. The special box criticizing Connecticut's outreach for its Husky program presented earlier in this chapter is an example of underutilization of a service (children's health insurance) and an effort to overcome sociological barriers (knowledge of the benefit) to accessing it. Another problem of access is related to who is providing the service and where it is provided; families, especially those from minority groups, must often leave their communities to obtain services from large agencies that they perceive to be "unfriendly" and that are staffed by professionals who may not share their cultural or ethnic experience. Such factors create sociological barriers if they prevent these families from seeking needed services.

Related to the problem of access is the fragmentation of services. A major taproot of this problem is the rapid growth of programs during the 1960s when the federal government declared the "War on Poverty." In the series of legislative initiatives that were a part of the "Great Society," the number of federal categorical programs grew from 160 in 1962 to over 500 in 1970 (O'Looney 1996). While many of these were innovative, they were in most ways not coordinated, particularly in the design of delivery strategies at the state and local levels. The result was the rapid expansion of large bureaucracies that, over time, have mainly resisted reforms. Halpern (1999:207) calls this "problem-specific specialization." When families needing services must find out about and "hunt down" all the agencies providing the services they need, meet eligibility requirements that usually differ from one to the other, and tell their stories to multiple workers, problem specialization erects real barriers to access.

Another issue affecting service delivery is accountability. Increasingly, funders (and in the case of public social services these are policy makers and the public) are calling for social service agencies to demonstrate the effectiveness of their services (Kettner, Moroney, and Martin 1999). Agencies must develop measurable outcomes for the services they provide; baseline data must be collected from clients (Kettner, Moroney, and Martin 1999; Halpern 1999; Mika 1996). The push to accountability, while generally thought to be positive, can create problems in the delivery of service to those who need them. For example, eligibility criteria may be developed to ensure that only the most promising of beneficiaries receives a service, a practice known as "creaming" (Gates 1980). The need for accountability usually results in increased record keeping, the bane of front-line workers, who claim that it takes away valuable time they might otherwise spend with clients. Accountability also means increased policy and practice directives that are contrary to front-line worker autonomy in the provision of services (Halpern 1999). In sum, the issues of access, coordination, and accountability have been at the heart of reforms in the delivery of services, especially those to families and children.

Service Delivery Reforms

Among the most significant of recent attempts to improve the delivery of services have been those aimed at creating friendlier and less formal helping arrangements, which have grown out of the recognition that, as Halpern (1999:255) has said, "The formal social welfare mechanisms used in modern societies to meet the needs of vulnerable families cannot satisfy more subtle human needs — for choice; a sense of belonging, of social membership; a sense of dignity." These reforms have resulted in the organization of services at the community or neighborhood level, which also is aimed at breaking down the categorical walls created by problem-specific services (Halpern 1999).

There has been a renewal of efforts to involve community residents in policy making and the governance of programs as well, similar to the aims of the Community Action Agencies of the 1960s (Gates 1980; Halpern 1999). Moreover, there has been a virtual explosion of guidelines and model components for achieving these program aims (Halpern 1999), which are best captured by Schorr (1997) in her identification of success attributes: programs that are successful in truly supporting families are comprehensive, intensive, flexible, and responsive; they deal with children as part of families and communities; staff members are able to build relationships of trust and respect; and they have a continuing, long-term, and preventive orientation. Moreover, there is evidence of systems thinking in the design of new legislation. Under the Family Preservation and Family Support Act of 1993, state child welfare agencies received funding for a wide range of services to families and were encouraged to work in partnership with local agencies to develop a continuum of community based, family-centered services (Berry 1997).

There is also growing attention to the need for service coordination, particularly between the child welfare and substance abuse systems, as seen in the example below.

With estimates of substance abuse among parents involved in the child welfare system ranging from 40 to 80 percent, the need for coordination between these two service systems is great. And yet, models for coordinated service delivery are few. Young, Gardner, and Dennis (1998) point to the "four clocks" that create timing problems for families with alcohol and drug abuse problems who are involved with child welfare:

- the child welfare clock, with its six-month case reviews, twelve-month permanency hearings, and emphasis on accelerated progress;
- young children's developmental clock, with an emphasis on the importance of the first eighteen months for brain development and attachment;
- the welfare eligibility clock and new timetable for parents to trade benefits for employment; and
- the substance abuse treatment and recovery clock, whose timetable is much slower and likely to be incompatible with the other three.

Two major intervention strategies are prominent in recent developments to improve service delivery — home visiting and family resource centers. Neither is a new idea. Home visiting has its roots, at least in part, in the friendly visitors who provided services to families from charity organization societies at the inception of the social work profession a century ago. Family resource centers are a concept similar to that of the settlement houses, where services were designed and delivered at the community level and were available to all who resided there. The rebirth of both these approaches is credited to the major early childhood intervention and family support effort of the 1980s (Halpern 1999; Weissbourd 1994).

Currently, an estimated 555,000 children are involved in some type of a home visiting program, and these programs now number in the thousands (Gomby, Culross, and Behrman 1999). Programs such as Healthy Families America, Parents As Teachers, and the Comprehensive Child Development Program all seek to help parents to improve their parenting knowledge and skill, promote child development and good health, prevent child abuse and neglect, and generally improve parents' capacity to meet their children's needs (Gomby, Culross, and Behrman 1999).

As considered further in chapter 6, family resource centers, often located in neighborhood schools, aim to make available to families a wide range of services and involve them in planning for services. They aim to be a hub for community development and involve parents as active participants in their child's education (Dupper and Poertner 1997). Not all family resource centers are linked to schools. Some are neighborhood-based in storefronts and churches. Both family resource centers and home visiting programs seek to overcome some of the problems families have in accessing services described earlier.

We have discussed an array of services designed to help families fulfill their instrumental and expressive roles in meeting the needs of family members. How these services are provided and how families are able (or not able) to access them has also been considered. New approaches to service delivery, such as home visiting and family resource centers, attempt to eliminate some of the barriers families face in finding and using services and adhere to some of the guidelines for family-centered social work practice with vulnerable families delineated in chapter 1. As discussed in chapter 10, American attitudes about helping those in need continue to shift, as exemplified in the recent so-called welfare reforms, which are largely punitive for those most affected by them — poor women, their children, and poor immigrants (Abramovitz 1997). Social workers have an enduring commitment to those most in need, however, despite the shifting sands of social welfare policy in an increasingly conservative political climate. In chapter 4 we will review this commitment and the underlying value base of the profession.

Notes

1. For an interesting discussion of the history of the development of supportive services in the United States, see Halpern (1999).

2. For a comprehensive discussion of SSI benefits, see Meyer (1995).

3. To learn more about the State Children's Health Insurance Program (SCHIP) and mental health benefits for children, visit the National Mental Health Association web site: http://www.nmha.org/state/schip /states/index.cfm (October 11, 2001).

4. Readers can find out which sites received grant funds for the Inner City Asthma Intervention Program by visiting the following web site: http:// www.niaid.nih.gov/newsroom/asthmagrants.htm (June 10, 2001).

5. For a comprehensive discussion of innovation in providing mental health services to high risk children and families, see Lindblad-Goldberg, Dore, and Stern (1998); for a copy of the Surgeon General's National Action Agenda on Children's Mental Health, go to http:// www.surgeongeneral.gov/cmh/ (December 13, 2001).

6. For a comprehensive discussion of homelessness and federal, state, and local responses to it, and for interesting case examples, see Lang (1989).

7. It is important to note that federal housing policies greatly favor middle- and upper-income families over those with lower incomes. For wealthier families, the income tax deduction of their mortgage interest represents a much larger housing subsidy than that received by poor families.

8. For the story of how child abuse was "discovered" and became a prominent social welfare issue, see Nelson (1984).

9. For a discussion of the confluent forces leading to the passage of the Adoption Assistance and Child Welfare Act of 1980, see Pine (1986).

10. A number of texts consider child welfare services in depth. See, for example, Downs et al. (2000); Gosson-Tower (2001); Pecora et al., (2000); Petr (1998); and Rycus and Hughes (1998).

11. For a comprehensive discussion of policies and practices for bridging the child welfare and substance abuse service gaps, see Young, Gardner, and Dennis (1998).

Questions for Discussion

1. As part of the interstate compact on child health insurance program, the Center for Budget and Policy Priorities has developed a national campaign called "Start Healthy Stay Healthy" (SHSH). In connection with this cam-

paign, an income eligibility screening tool has been developed. Choose a family you are working with and help them to determine whether their children are eligible for the program by obtaining an SHSH kit on line at <www.cbpp.org> or calling 202-408-1080 to order a screening tool.

2. What are the specific benefit limitations in the Temporary Assistance to Needy Families (TANF) program in your state? What services exist to help families to prepare for a transition from welfare to work?

3. Consider the discussion of barriers to families' accessing services they need. What are some examples of access barriers from your practice? How have you been successful in helping families to overcome them, or in helping them to redesign programs to eliminate access barriers?

4. What organizations in your community provide child care resources and referrals to parents? Do they provide assistance to parents in selecting the right type of care for their child? How do low-income parents receive help in finding and obtaining subsidies for child care in your state? Is there sufficient child care available to the families in the communities in which you work? How well are these information sources reaching families?

5. Visit a Head Start center in your community. What types of programs are offered? Are there links between the center and other programs, for example, home visiting programs, family day care homes, and public schools?

Suggestions for Further Information

Balgopal, P. 2000, ed. *Social Work Practice with Immigrants and Refugees*. New York: Columbia University Press.

Berry, M. 1997. *The Family at Risk: Issues and Trends in Family Preservation Services*. Columbia: University of South Carolina Press.

Devaney, B. L., M. R. Ellwood, and J. M. Love. 1997. Programs that mitigate the effects of poverty on children. *Future of Children* 7 (2): 88–112.

Kagan, S. L. and B. Weissbourd, eds. 1994. *Putting Families First: America's Family Support Movement and the Challenge of Change*. San Francisco: Jossey-Bass.

Karger, H. J. and D. Stoesz. 2002. *Social Welfare Policy: A Pluralistic Approach*. 4th ed. Boston: Allyn and Bacon.

Lang, M. H. 1989. *Homelessness Amid Affluence: Structure and Paradox in the American Political Economy*. New York: Praeger.

Lindblad-Goldberg, M., M. M. Dore, and L. Stern. 1998. *Creating Competence out of Chaos*. New York: Norton.

Stein, T. J. 2001. *Social Policy and Policymaking by the Branches of Government and the Public-At-Large*. New York: Columbia University Press.

Zigler, E., S. L. Kagan, and E. Klugman, eds. 1985. *Children, Families, and Government: Perspectives on American Social Policy*, pp. 249–265. New York: Cambridge University Press.

4 Ethical Issues in Working with Vulnerable Families

Attention to ethics and ethical practice as well as adherence to a code of ethics are all hallmarks of a profession. In the past twenty years, along with rapid changes in contemporary society, there has been increasing attention to ethics in all professions, including social work (Manning 1997), and "social workers' understanding of ethical issues has matured dramatically" (Reamer 1998a:xi). These developments are reflected in the standards for practice embodied in the profession's code of ethics. This chapter briefly reviews the latest social work *Code of Ethics* adopted by the National Association of Social Workers in 1996, defines the ethical practitioner in social work, and then discusses and illustrates selected ethical standards of practice with children and families.

Controversies and Dilemmas

Work with vulnerable children and families is rife with controversies and dilemmas, perhaps more than in any other field of social work practice. There are controversies about a multitude of issues, such as the care of children and who is best suited to provide it, state intervention in family life and how much is acceptable, whether welfare benefits are a right or a privilege,[1] and how much the dominant culture should be imposed on minority cultures. Dilemmas arise from a social worker's multiple and sometimes competing professional obligations to clients, colleagues, the profession, and the agency, as well as from conflicting values about what is good and right. For example, social workers in child protection must balance competing roles of helper and enforcer (Linzer 1999).[2] They also must deal with the controversy about poverty as a chief cause of child maltreatment when they recommend provision of services other than financial assistance (Milner 1994; Pelton 1994) and deal with the tensions inherent in serving essentially involuntary clients (Reamer 1983b). Social workers in adoption services decide who can become a parent and who cannot (Pine 1987) and whether the rights of adopted children to information about the circumstances of their birth trump the rights of their birth parents for privacy (Linzer 1999; Seader 1994; Walsh 1994; Watson 1994).[3] In providing family preservation services, social workers are faced with choosing between the competing goals of child safety and family integrity, both of which are important social values that have been codified into law (Linzer 1999; Maluccio, Pine, and Warsh 1994). Social workers in host settings such as schools may find that fulfilling their professional obligations sometimes causes tensions with other professionals who have different obligations and expectations, especially around issues of confidentiality.

The influence of managed care on social work practice has added to the complexity of ethical decision making and action.[4] Moreover, all social workers whose work involves families and children are painfully aware of the challenges in deciding who is most in need and should receive help, given the reality of limited resources. As these examples illustrate, the ethical aspects of social work practice, especially with children and families, are omnipresent. The challenge is to recognize and deal effectively with them — in short, to become an *ethically competent professional*.[5]

The Social Work Code of Ethics

Understanding the profession's *Code of Ethics* is the first step to becoming an ethical social worker. As Reamer (1998a:xii) has noted, "The Code serves as a lodestar for this remarkably diverse profession." The evolution of the code from the first formal publication in 1960 of its 14 guidelines to the current version with its 155 ethical standards approved in 1996 (Reamer 1998a) reflects the growing complexity of social work practice in an increasingly diverse and complex world.[6] The current code, like none before it, contains four major sections including a preamble, purposes, and ethical principles, in addition to ethical standards.

The preamble articulates the mission of social work as a profession "to enhance human well-being and help meet the basic human needs of all people, with particular attention to the needs and empowerment of people who are vulnerable, oppressed, and living in poverty" (National Association of Social Workers [NASW] 1999:1). It also delineates six core values that reflect what is unique to the profession: service, social justice, dignity and worth of the person, importance of human relationships, integrity, and competence. A second section delineates the six purposes of the code, which are to

- identify the profession's core values,
- summarize its broad ethical principles that reflect these values,
- identify relevant professional obligations,
- provide ethical standards to which the public can hold the profession accountable,
- provide the above information to those entering the profession as part of their socialization to the profession, and
- articulate standards by which the profession can judge whether an individual social worker has engaged in unethical behavior (NASW 1999).

A third section translates the profession's core values into a set of six ethical principles. As Loewenberg, Dolgoff, and Harrington (2000) have noted, "Values deal with what is good and desirable, ethics deal with what is right and correct" (22). Thus, this section provides guidance on how to operationalize the profession's values. For example, in translating the value of the importance of human relationships into action a social worker would need to understand that people's relationships are an important vehicle for achieving change; she or he would seek to partner with people in their interventions and would work to strengthen relationships between people in purposeful ways in order to achieve the goal of improved and enhanced well-being. The value of social justice is operationalized through a social worker's pursuit of social change with or on behalf of oppressed and vulnerable people (Reamer 1998a).

The code's final section delineates a set of ethical standards that concern a professional social worker's obligations to clients, colleagues, practice settings, the profession itself, and the broader society. These standards prescribe the "shoulds" and "should nots" in social work practice. Yet, however well developed the current version is, the code can only provide *guidance* for ethical practice. It cannot make the difficult choices with which social workers are faced daily, because many of these result from conflicting professional obligations (Reamer 1998a). As considered in the next section, the ethically competent social worker needs knowledge and skills that go beyond knowing what the ethical standards are.

Ethical Competence

Nearly every decision in social work includes ethical aspects. Critical thinking skills are essential in recognizing and clarifying these, prioritizing obligations, and making informed and well-reasoned decisions (Loewenberg, Dolgoff, and Harrington 2000). These authors distinguish between two types of issues — ethical problems and ethical dilemmas — that practitioners may face. In a situation involving an ethical problem, the practitioner must make a decision about the right thing to do. For example, a community organizer in a housing project learns that a client who is her partner in an organizing effort and a resident in the facility has an unreported family member illegally living with her.

An ethical dilemma, on the other hand, involves choosing a course of action when the practitioner is faced with two or more competing obligations or a choice involving two or more undesirable outcomes. For example, in working with a group of adolescent girls, what is the practitioner to do when one of them divulges that her stepfather has been sexually abusing her but begs the social worker not to tell anyone of this? Does the social worker adhere to the obligation to protect client confidentiality, or to the laws of her state in which social workers are mandated reporters of sexual abuse? In this dilemma there are both competing obligations and a situation involving two undesirable outcomes, since not reporting fails to protect the young woman from future abuse, while reporting is likely to undermine her, and possibly the rest of the group members', trust in the leader. Thus ethical dilemmas result from competing values — privacy versus lawfulness in the latter case — and competing loyalties — the community organizer's loyalty to her employer, the housing authority, or to her partner/client whose family member has moved in with her in the first case. Loewenberg, Dolgoff, and Harrington (2000) cite competing values and competing loyalties as the two root causes of ethical problems and dilemmas.

With attention to the ethical aspects of social work on the rise, and the demand from the field for guidance in making difficult choices increasing, a number of decision models have been developed for use by practitioners. Reamer (1995) suggests a seven-step process:

1. Identify the relevant ethical issues.
2. Identify the individuals and groups affected by the decision.
3. Identify all possible courses of action and the benefits and harms of each.
4. Examine reasons that support the choice of a course of action.
5. Consult with others — e.g., a supervisor, experts.
6. Decide on an option; document how a decision was arrived at.
7. Monitor the impact of the decision.

Rhodes (1986) has a comparable decision model:

1. What is the problem?
2. What is troubling me about it?
3. What values and standards (social, legal, professional) can help me to deal with it?
4. What are the ethical aspects of this situation?
5. What are the competing obligations in this situation and are any more compelling than others?
6. What possible courses of action might I take and what are the implications of each?

Loewenberg, Dolgoff, and Harrington (2000) have developed a similar "Ethical Assessment Screen" aimed at social work practitioners; it asks them to identify their own personal values that relate to the situation and also which alternative action "protect(s) to the greatest extent possible society's rights and interests" and results in the practitioner doing the "least harm possible" (67). When it is clear that obligations are in direct conflict with one another, these authors offer an "Ethical Principles Screen" that rank orders these ethical obligations. So, for example, the responsibility to protect life takes precedence over a social worker's obligation to protect a client's autonomy or privacy. Finally, Pine (1987) offers a comprehensive model for making decisions in child welfare and applies the model to a challenging case involving permanency planning, custody, and adoption. Users of this model are asked, for example, to consider where rights, needs, or responsibilities of the parties involved may conflict, whether power is distributed equally to those involved and how power might be equalized, and the extent to which limited resources have contributed to the dilemma.

An ethical social worker uses an analytical approach to delineating and resolving ethical dilemmas; ethical acts, then, are *principled* because they can be justified in light of some accepted principles, they are *reasoned* because the decision(s) are based on careful consideration of all aspects of the situation and the relevant ethical principles, and they are *universalizable* because they can be justified and repeated in other similar situation (Haas and Malouf 1995). Another test is that of *impartiality*, or the willingness of the practitioner to act if she or he were in the other person's place (Loewenberg, Dolgoff, and Harrington 2000). Rion (1989) has a simpler test for determining whether someone has acted ethically; he suggests answering the question "Could I comfortably explain my decision to my children?"

The next section of this chapter examines selected ethical principles and the ethical responsibilities of social workers to their clients and to society's welfare and highlights where some of these responsibilities may compete and conflict with one another.

Selected Ethical Principles and Responsibilities

Ethical Responsibilities to Clients

A social worker's primary obligations are to her or his clients, promoting their interests and well-being. This is the first ethical standard in the *Code of Ethics*. This section will discuss some of these obligations and their underlying principles.

Self-Determination and Informed Consent

An important part of the primacy of client interests is the concept of self-determination, which is the basic freedom to make one's own choices and decisions (Freedberg 1989; Haas 1991; Haas and Malouf 1995; Reamer 1983a; Tower 1994). As with all the central ethical principles in social work, self-determination derives from societal values, in this case freedom, the inherent dignity of the individual, and the idea of humans as rational beings (Freedberg 1989). Standard 1.02 of the code requires social workers to "respect and promote the right of clients to self-determination and assist clients in their efforts to identify and clarify their goals" (NASW 1999:4). Freedom to choose and decide implies that a person has options, understands the implications of each option, is not coerced into selecting one of them, and is able to decide (has the mental capacity) from among the options available to him or her. Informed consent is a related concept grounded in the belief in a client's right to self-determination — in this case the right to be supported in making decisions regarding treatment.

Dilemmas often occur because a social worker feels that these tests for freedom to be self-determining are not met, for example, when the client appears not to really understand the implications (and perhaps dangers) of a particular decision he is making, while the social worker is very aware of them, or when the interests of society trump an individual's right to autonomy. An example of this is the requirement to wear seatbelts because of the high cost (to society) of automobile injuries, which can be prevented by wearing seatbelts.

Paternalism is interference with self-determination for the client's own good (Reamer 1983; Freedberg 1989). There are numerous examples in which client autonomy and self-determination are breached in services to families and children. Chief among them are instances where services are mandated, such as in child protection. There, clients whose children have been removed from the home are coerced into services such as parent education for the good of their family and their children, often as a condition for reunification. Other examples include a failure to involve children in decisions about their living arrangements, the argument being made that they are too young to deal with the complexities of decisions.

There is disagreement among professionals about when and how to engage children's participation in decision making. In his study of attitudes about involving children in decision making, Shemmings (2000) found wide variance in the age at which social workers and non–social workers thought children should be able to make certain decisions for themselves, with social workers citing much younger ages for making decisions such as refusing medical treatment. The study also showed that social workers distinguished between a child's involvement in a decision and actually making a decision, whereas non–social workers did not. In short, social workers were more apt to both involve children in decisions and also to feel children had decision-making capacity at an earlier age than non–social workers. Despite these findings in a relatively small sample, the struggle to ensure self-determination and to assess consent issues with children, while at the same time ensuring children's best interest, continues. The following case illustrates this dilemma:

Tyrone is a twelve year old who is a resident of a group home, and has been for about a year, since he was removed from his mother's custody following a court adjudication of child abuse. He is in the custody of the local state child welfare agency. The commitment is about to expire and the agency wants Tyrone to return to live with his mother.

Tyrone has told the social worker at the group home that he wants to remain there and does not want to return to his mother's care. His mother also does not want Tyrone to return to her home, although both would like to continue their schedule of regular visits. Tyrone has threatened to run away if he is returned to his mother's custody and her home.

The child welfare agency social worker is pressing the group home social worker to prepare Tyrone and his mother for reunification. The social worker at the group home is in a dilemma. She feels that Tyrone should have a say in his living arrangements but is aware of the pressure coming from the agency worker, and Tyrone's mother's wishes, as well as the fact that the group home receives most of its funding from the public child welfare agency. How should she proceed?

The issue of sexual abuse provides a different perspective on the principle of informed consent. As Finkelhor (1979) points out, arguments about what is wrong with involving children in sexual acts for an adult's pleasure have been widely made but remain inadequate. These include the position that involving children in sexual acts is intrinsically wrong, against social mores, that they entail premature sexualizing of a child, and, finally, that sexual encounters are dangerous both physically and psychologically to children. While there is some evidence in support of each argument, Finkelhor notes that the most compelling reason that sex with children is wrong is that children are unable to consent, meaning that the tests for informed consent — knowledge, competence, and freedom — cannot be fully met since children have no way of understanding all the ramifications of a sexual relationship. Moreover, as is well documented, coercion, whether in a threat about keeping the abuse secret or in denying a child other forms of needed attention, is almost always a feature of child sexual abuse (MacFarlane et al. 1986).

The issue of when a child or adult is capable of consenting to a sexual relationship finds frequent expression in social work practice with adolescents and young people who have developmental disabilities. Increased normalization of people with all types of disabilities, including cognitive disabilities, has been a major force in promoting their self-determination wherever possible, sometimes to the dismay of their families, as in the following case example:

A social worker in a day treatment program for people with cognitive disabilities has been working with a young woman, Cheryl, age twenty-six, for some time. Cheryl is very interested in a young man who also attends the program. At one point during a family conference, the social worker suggests to Cheryl's parents that a sexual relationship would likely be in the natural progression of this attraction and that they should consider helping their daughter to obtain contraceptives. The parents are adamantly opposed to this. How should the social worker proceed?

The AIDS epidemic has brought a number of ethical issues into sharp focus, especially informed consent and confidentiality, as well as concerns about equity and distributive justice. One example is New York state's decision to mandate HIV testing for all children entering foster care. The policy has been hotly debated, particularly in the case of adolescents (Frisino and Pollack 1997). Defenders of the policy point to the benefits of early identification and intervention, the fact that the highest rate of increase in the disease is among young people in their twenties who were infected as adolescents, and that adolescents often engage in risky behaviors that increase their chances of both getting and giving infection. Youth advocates concerned about the rights of adolescents were successful in getting the policy amended to require child serving agencies to assess youth's risk factors *and* capacity to consent to the test. Consenting adolescents must be offered information and counseling on the testing options and on confidentiality provisions (Frisino and Pollack 1997). This example shows the importance of understanding the underlying ethical issues in policy decisions and the role of social workers in advocating for clients' rights.

The law in this country generally regards children as incompetent to consent, providing parents and guardians a kind of proxy consent on their behalf. Known as the *exercise of substituted judgment*, the adult is expected to act in the child's best interests, standing in the shoes of the child to make the decision the child would have made had she or he been competent to do so (Koocher and Keith-Spiegel 1990). What happens when parents' interests conflict with those of a child? Such is the case when a child, whose parents' religious belief forbids medical intervention, is gravely ill.[7] Another example is illustrated in the case below.

Sarah Jones is a school social worker in a middle school. She is running a group for seventh graders on dealing with alcohol abuse in the family, and Tabitha has been referred by her teacher to join the group. Both the teacher and the social worker are aware that Tabitha struggles with her parents' alcoholism and that sometimes their incapacity makes heavy demands on their daughter to keep the household running and her younger siblings cared for. She sometimes misses school because of these demands.

Tabitha very much wants to join the group, but she is sure that neither of her parents will sign the consent form because that would mean they would be admitting their problems. Currently they go to great lengths to keep their family secret. The school policy is very clear about requiring parental permission for all activities involving students. What should the social worker do?

The above situation illustrates also how children can and should be involved in the helping process. How can Sarah Jones empower Tabitha by creating conditions whereby she is helped to decide what to do? What if Tabitha decides she would like to join the group without her parents' permission? Should the worker ignore her obligation to the school's policy?

Minor children do have some rights to make decisions about their medical care, however. They can seek treatment for drug and alcohol abuse without parental consent. Moreover, they can be treated for sexually transmitted diseases and secure contraceptive devices without parents' knowledge or consent. And, the U.S. Supreme Court held, in *Planned Parenthood v. Danforth*, that a Missouri law requiring a minor seeking an abortion to have parental consent was unconstitutional (Dickson 1998).

Privacy, Confidentiality, and Privilege

The ethical principle of confidentiality derives from societal values of privacy. Confidentiality and privilege are often used interchangeably, but they do not mean the same thing. Confidentiality is the adherence to an understanding that information shared by a client in the context of a professional relationship will not be shared outside that relationship; privilege protects confidential communication from being disclosed in a legal proceeding (Downs et al. 2000; Loewenberg, Dolgoff, and Harrington 2000; Parsons 2001; Rhodes 1986). Standard 1.07 in the *Code of Ethics* requires social workers to "respect clients' right to privacy" by seeking only that information necessary to work with the client (NASW 1999:6). The code further specifies that confidential information is not to be disclosed without the consent of the client and that a social worker must make known to clients any limits to maintaining confidentiality (NASW 1999). Taken together, privacy, confidentiality, and privilege represent a moral, professional, and legal guarantee to the client that she can trust the social worker to use information gained in their relationship only for the client's benefit, revealing it to others only with permission. Without this trust, there is a risk that people who need help might not seek it; those in a professional relationship may withhold information important to the success of the intervention, and those whose information was revealed without their consent will feel betrayed by the social worker (Loewenberg, Dolgoff, and Harrington 2000).

There is, however, a number of limits and challenges to confidentiality. First, despite the protection of privilege, confidential information may be legally required, as in the cases of mandated reporting of child abuse or immigration policy requirements regarding undocumented immigrants (Levenson 1998; Parsons 2001). Second, privilege as applied to client records is not a guaranteed right to privacy but one governed by state and case law. An important ruling in *Jaffe v. Remond*, which involved the subpoena of a social worker's records in her treatment of a police officer who had shot and killed a suspect, upheld confidentiality but provided protection only in the federal court system (NASW 1996a, b; Parsons 2001). Third, a social worker may be compelled to breach confidentiality if he or she feels that the client is a danger to either herself or others. Since suicide has become a major cause of death among high school students, many schools now have policies about how social workers and counselors must treat teenagers' suicide threats

(Dickson 1998). In the case of threats of harm to others, the "duty to warn" derives from a famous California case, *Tarasoff v. the Regents of the University of California,* in which a man killed his former girlfriend after telling his therapist about his intent to do so. The therapist failed to notify Tatiana Tarasoff of the potential danger (Parsons 2001; Weil and Sanchez 1983). Given the recent rise of school violence as discussed in chapter 2, school social workers working with troubled youths are likely to confront increasing tensions around confidentiality issues and school policies aimed at safety.

Fourth, parents' requests for information about their children's treatment can also challenge confidentiality. Here legal rights of parents of minor children and ethical responsibilities of social workers may collide. However, children's rights to confidentiality are protected by the Family Education Rights and Privacy Act of 1974. Also known as the Buckley Amendment, this law provides for parents' access to records, but a counselor's notes need not be considered a part of the official school record (Allen-Meares, Washington, and Welshe 2000; Parsons 2001; School Social Work Association of America 2001). Fifth, the prevalence of managed care in the social services has challenged social workers on many fronts. Managed care companies' need for and use of data pose serious threats to confidentiality (Davidson and Davidson 1998).

Finally there are other ways that confidentiality can be undermined, for example in case conferences, when cases are discussed for training and learning purposes, in group treatment, in evaluation and research, and in the ways that records are used and maintained. The latter is an especially important issue with the increased use of technology for recording and managing information (Davidson and Davidson 1998; Parsons 2001; Rothman 1998).

The following case example illustrates some of the challenges faced by a social worker balancing legal requirements, a client's best interests, and confidentiality.

_____

Tim Mahoney is a social worker in a family serving agency working with a family from Guatemala. The family consists of a father and his four children. Although the father is employed in a lawn maintenance firm, he earns minimum wage and only on a per diem basis; family income is insufficient to meet their basic needs. The children were born in the U.S., but Mr. Mahoney is fairly certain that the father is an undocumented immigrant. He wants to refer the family to the county's department of social services for welfare assistance, but he is aware that under recent welfare reform, which created the Temporary Assistance to Needy Families (TANF), there are now provisions requiring citizen verification and the reporting of known illegal immigrants. How should he advise this father on getting the family needed help? What does Tim Mahoney need to know about immigration law, welfare law, and their potential conflicts with professional obligations?[8]

Ethical Responsibilities to the Broader Society

Social work is unique among professions for its commitment to vulnerable and oppressed people and its goal of improving their access to basic social goods such as food, shelter, work and income, education and health care (Reamer 1998b; Wakefield 1988). Thus social justice is a core value of social work (Abramovitz 1993; Figueira-McDonough 1993; Schneider and Netting 1999). The new *Code of Ethics* pays much more attention to social justice than earlier versions did (Swenson 1998). Standard 6.01 says that "social workers should promote the general welfare of society, from local to global levels, and the development of people, their communities, and their environments" (NASW 1999:20).[9] Other standards in this section of the code call on social workers to "engage in social and political action that seeks to ensure that all people have equal access to the resources, employment, services, and opportunities they require to meet their basic human needs and to develop fully" (NASW 1999:20), "promote conditions that encourage respect for cultural and social diversity within the United States and globally" (NASW 1999:21), and "act to prevent and eliminate domination of, exploitation of, and discrimination against any person, group, or class" (NASW 1999:21).

How is the ethical practitioner to proceed, given these broad but essential responsibilities? First, it is important to recognize the ethical aspects of social (and economic) policy and program planning. This is important whether these "linger below the surface or float more visibly on top" (Reamer 1990:177). Reamer (1990) has pointed out that there are ethical aspects involved in decisions to develop programs, such as a belief in society's obligation to help a group of people in need, in program design, such as how the benefits of a program will be allocated in a fair and equitable way since these are likely to be limited, and in how a program is operated, such as whether recipients and program staff are treated with dignity and respect.[10] An example of a less visible ethical issue in program design follows.

Mary Clarke is a social worker in the local county department of social services. One of her responsibilities is counseling welfare recipients about time limits on their eligibility for assistance and the need to seek employment. She also refers her clients to the agency's child care division where staff members help parents to apply for child care subsidy and seek appropriate child care arrangements for their children.

Mary Clarke feels fairly certain that her agency provides appropriate services to parents who have reached their time limit of eligibility for assistance; however, she is a subscriber to an e-mail newsletter published by a national child advocacy organization. A recent bulletin pointed out that of 15 million eligible children in the U.S., only 1.8 received federal child care subsidies (Child Welfare League of America 2000a). What, if any, connection exists between Mary Clarke's professional responsibilities and those in her work setting? How should she respond to this information? What does she need to know about her own agency's program to provide subsidized child care? What are the ethical issues that "linger below the surface" here?

Second, it is essential to develop knowledge and skills for ethical practice. Figueira-McDonough (1993) claims that carrying out the profession's social justice obligations requires that a social worker engage in a "policy practice" whose methods include legislative advocacy, reform through the courts, social action, and social policy analysis. Two examples of policy practice follow.

James Woods is a family preservation specialist in a nonprofit child welfare agency that is under contract with the state to provide intensive, in-home services to families who are at risk of separation. In its two years of operation the agency's program has been very successful in helping families remain together. Funding for the second year was increased, reflecting an increase in the number of families the staff was able to serve.

Now, however, there is a proposal in the state legislature to reduce the state budget for this program. James and his colleagues learn when hearings on this part of the budget are to take place and develop written and verbal testimony on the merits of the program and why funds should be increased, not decreased. In addition, they recruit two parents whose families were successful in staying together as a result of their involvement in the program who will be part of their testimony.

As the above example shows, legislative advocacy is a critical skill in maintaining funding for successful programs, particularly at the state level, as responsibility for social welfare has shifted there from the federal level (Schneider and Netting 1995). Social action is another.[11]

Mary Clarke, the social worker in the department of social services, has learned that the child care division of her agency has reported success in helping parents transitioning off welfare to find child care and receive subsidies. She also learned that over three-fourths of these parents are using informal child care with relatives and neighbors rather than licensed child care centers or family day care homes.

Ms. Clarke is aware of some of the research questioning the quality of such informal arrangements. She is also concerned about the lack of formal supports such as training for informal caregivers. She decides to do something about this situation and contacts the local child care council to learn more about what can be done in her county. With her help a task force on informal child care is organized, and after a year of work there is a comprehensive program of support for informal child care providers including group training programs, lending libraries for toys and books located at various places in the community, and a special "read and learn" program begun by the local library for informal caregivers and the children they care for.

As illustrated above, social action can be an effective method of intervention for attaining social justice goals. Underpinning both legislative advocacy and social action is an understanding of principles such as distributive justice, which "involves the use of ethical concepts and criteria to determine how scarce resources should be divided among people, communities, groups and organizations" (Reamer 1995:119). For example, should publicly funded health care benefits go to the youngest recipients, who will have longer to enjoy their health and contribute more to society? To the sickest people, as they are most in need? To the first people on line to sign up? Should they be denied to those who are ill because of personal choices they have made, for example, to smoke or drink excessively? Social workers make difficult distributive justice decisions when they choose whether or not to refer a family to a special intervention service on the basis of the family's likelihood of success in the program or on the basis of eligibility criteria that seek to ensure high rates of success. This rationing of services to those most likely to succeed is just one of the many ways that the concept of distributive justice is reflected in family and children's services and must be understood by ethically competent social workers.

As this chapter has shown, and as reflected in the "Framework of Needs and Resources for Family and Child Well-Being," ethics are at the heart of social work practice whether the social worker is working directly with children and their families, is engaged in macro-level administration and policy practice, or is undertaking research.[12] It is adherence to a code of ethics, with its dual goals of commitment to human dignity and client self-determination and facilitating access of deprived groups to basic social goods, that distinguishes the profession (Wakefield 1988). Although we can be proud of our "increasingly mature understanding of the complex ethical issues practitioners face" (Reamer 1998b:497), social workers must continuously strive for ethical competence through education and training and by being alert to new and emerging developments and their concomitant ethical issues.[13] Careful attention to ethical principles and issues should be incorporated in the practice and service delivery decisions that we shall discuss in subsequent chapters.

Notes

1. For a comprehensive discussion of welfare reform and the ethical issues inherent in social welfare policies, see Linzer (1999).
2. See Webb (1996) for discussion of ethical issues faced by child welfare practitioners working with substance abusing parents.
3. See Babb (1999) and Loewenberg, Dolgoff, and Harrington (2000) for discussion of ethical issues in social work practice.

4. See Davidson and Davidson (1998) for delineation of a complex set of ethical questions about managed care that social workers should consider.
5. See Pine (1987) for a decision-making model useful in dealing with difficult ethical dilemmas in child welfare.
6. See Reamer (1998a) for the most comprehensive published discussion of the NASW *Code of Ethics*, with illustrations of key professional standards.
7. See Fraser (1995) for a thought-provoking article on the rights of and health risks to children in Christian Science families.
8. See Levenson (1998) for a discussion of how some provisions of recent welfare and immigration policies impact ethical social work practice.
9. See Wronka's (1995) discussion of human rights as mandates to fulfill basic human needs.
10. Reamer (2001a) has developed an audit instrument to guide a comprehensive review of an agency's ethical policies and practices.
11. See Koch (2000) for a concise discussion of key policy issues and debates.
12. See Putnam, Liss, and Landsverk (1996) for a comprehensive discussion of ethical issues involving maltreated children and adolescents.
13. See Reamer (2001b) for guidance on developing course content on ethical dilemmas in social work practice and Congress (2002) for resources on teaching social work values and ethics.

Questions for Discussion

1. Consider a dilemma you have faced in your work. Do you think it had ethical dimensions? Did the situation involve competing values or competing loyalties, as discussed in this chapter? How did you resolve the dilemma?
2. Take a dilemma you encountered in your practice or personal life, perhaps the issue you have considered above. Use one of the decision models delineated in this chapter to sort out the ethical aspects of the situation and determine a course of action.
3. Read the NASW *Code of Ethics*. If you currently work in a human service organization, how aware do you think your colleagues are of the practice standards outlined in the code? How does your agency's administration ensure that staff members are aware of the profession's ethical obligations? For

example, do you have an ethics committee in your agency? Are training workshops on ethics and ethical decision making available to staff?

4. Sometimes ethical dilemmas result from cultural differences. For example, in investigating a child maltreatment case, a social worker may discover that a parent's view of child discipline is culturally determined — acceptable in the parent's culture, but inconsistent with the expectations of the majority culture. Have you faced a situation in your practice in which cultural differences presented such a conflict or dilemma? How did you resolve it?

5. As described in this chapter, a social worker's legal obligation to report abuse, or his or her obligation to protect a third party, may undermine the professional obligation to confidentiality. How might a social worker fulfil the responsibility to either report a client's behavior or warn another person of potential danger and still maintain a positive relationship with that client? How and when should clients be helped to understand these professional obligations?

6. Compare the NASW *Code of Ethics* with other ethical codes for social workers, for example, the National Association of Black Social Workers' (NABSW) code of ethics and a code of ethics from another country. What are the main values expressed in these codes? How do these codes differ from the NASW *Code of Ethics*? Could you imagine that these differences might lead to practice and ethical differences among social workers? For example, what dilemmas in child welfare practice might a social worker trying to adhere to the NABSW code of ethics face in dealing with a transracial adoption placement?

Suggestions for Further Information

Gambrill, E. and R. Pruger, eds. 1997. *Controversial Issues in Social Work Ethics, Values, and Obligations*. Boston: Allyn and Bacon.

Haas, L. J. and J. L. Malouf. 1989. *Keeping Up the Good Work: A Practitioner's Guide to Mental Health Ethics*. Sarasota, Fla.: Professional Resource Exchange.

Koocher, G. P. and P. C. Keith-Spiegel. 1990. *Children, Ethics, and the Law: Professional Issues and Cases*. Lincoln: University of Nebraska Press.

Linzer, N. 1999. *Resolving Ethical Dilemmas in Social Work Practice*. Boston: Allyn and Bacon.

Loewenberg, F. M., R. Dolgoff, and D. Harrington. 2000. *Ethical Decisions for Social Work Practice*. 6th ed. Itasca, Ill.: Peacock.

Parsons, R. D. 2001. *The Ethics of Professional Practice*. Boston: Allyn and Bacon.

Reamer, F. G. 1998a. *Ethical Standards in Social Work: A Critical Review of the "NASW Code of Ethics."* Washington, D.C.: NASW.

————. 2001. *Ethics Education in Social Work.* Washington, D.C: Council on Social Work Education.

Rothman, J. C. 1998. *From the Front Lines: Student Cases in Social Work Ethics.* Boston: Allyn and Bacon.

Part 2

Practice Base

5 Engagement, Assessment, Case Planning, and Goal Setting

We now consider the central features of the processes of engagement, assessment, case planning, and goal setting as they apply in the early phases of working with families and children, using the framework described in chapter 1. We show the application of concepts and principles introduced in previous chapters to these processes and illustrate them with case examples in diverse agency settings, giving appropriate attention to dimensions of race, ethnicity, and culture.

Engagement

Engaging prospective clients in competence-oriented and family-centered work requires particular ways of viewing the roles of clients and workers and their relationship with each other. To begin with, the worker seeks to create a welcoming environment that respects and values the prospective client and her or his concerns, capacities, and potentialities. In addition, the client-worker relationship is "redefined as one in which two or more persons are working on a shared project. Each brings a special expertise to the task" (Hartman 1979:264). The worker reduces her or his authority and encourages client autonomy and participation in the helping process. He or she seeks to decrease social distance from the client and develop a relationship in which openness, authenticity, and human caring are nurtured (Germain and Gitterman 1996). Moreover, the worker uses the client-worker relationship to help foster the client's sense of identity and self-image and mobilize her or his coping and adaptive strivings.

Above all, clients are explicitly regarded as partners in the helping process, as persons with assets and potentialities, as resources rather than carriers and/ or sources of pathology. As emphasized in a classic article by Studt (1968) over three decades ago, social workers are defined primarily as catalysts or change agents who play diverse roles and use varying approaches in order to help clients to identify and use appropriate experiences or create new experiences and resources. The worker uses a variety of approaches to help provide the conditions necessary for clients to achieve their purposes. In addition to the role of clinician, a worker may need to serve as a guide, strategist, teacher, broker, or advocate, while being attuned to ways of helping that can empower each member of the client system.

Regarding clients as resources does not mean, however, that the burden of change or problem solving is placed on their shoulders. It would be too simplistic to equate this formulation with the formerly popular, and recently revived, American notion of "pulling oneself up by one's bootstraps." On the contrary, an essential corollary is that appropriate environmental supports must be provided to enable people to develop their potentialities and to function as resources on their behalf and/or in the interest of others. These supports are needed to help people cope with the excessive stress created by social systems and institutions.

As a central feature of the process of engagement, early on the practitioner needs to consider the readiness of the clients to become constructively involved in the helping process. In addition to the capacity to perform a given action, readiness implies some tension that needs release and some motivation toward an objective. The tension and motivation can be expressed in different forms, such as anxiety, dissatisfaction, guilt, or even a hopeless dream or a fanciful ambition. The quantity and quality of the client's tension influence the timing of the activity, which should be geared to the person's readiness and spontaneity. In some situations, however, an impulse-ridden person may need help to delay action.

The traditional view of motivation as a client trait is less valuable than "a transactional model dealing with motivation as a process that takes into account the interactions among client, worker, and the environment" (Moore-Kirkland 1981:33). Such a model builds on the original formulation of the dynamic interaction among motivation, capacity, and opportunity by Ripple,

Alexander and Polemis (1964), especially their emphasis on the pivotal role of motivation in social work intervention.

Following such an orientation, the worker redefines resistive behavior as motivation and considers questions such as the following in formulating the assessment and service goals (Moore-Kirkland 1981):

- What is the level of anxiety regarding the problem(s), the services, or the relationship with the worker, and what are the specific sources of anxiety or lack of anxiety?
- How does the client perceive the consequences of achieving the goals of the change effort?
- What are the effective motivators in the client's life at this time?
- What practical factors might impede change?

Mobilizing motivation during the engagement phase — as throughout the helping process — is especially critical with involuntary clients, that is, those who come to the attention of agencies and social workers because of pressure from others. "Involuntary" status probably defines the overwhelming majority of clients involved with family and children's agencies; many of them are "mandated" clients, as in protective service agencies. Initiating and maintaining contact with these persons can be facilitated through guidelines such as the following (Rooney 1992:161–174):

- assessing the client's response to pressured contact, such as anger, indifference, or blaming others,
- expressing empathy for the client's feelings by appreciating her or his response to being pressured to seek service, and
- noting the values and strengths expressed by the client in response to pressured contact and viewing these reactions as potential assets to promote the client's positive motivation.[1]

Engaging clients who are described as "involuntary," "hard to reach," or "unmotivated," such as parents with substance abuse problems, need not be frustrating or hopeless. To involve these parents effectively, practitioners need to move toward *congruence*, that is, to the point where each has the same or comparable understanding of each other's roles. As considered further in subsequent chapters, in many such cases "much . . . could be accomplished through reduction of social distance between client and practitioner, provision of needed tangible services and supports, opportunities to enhance the person's hope and motivation, and teaching of interpersonal skills and coping patterns" (Maluccio 1979:194).

To engage prospective clients effectively and in line with the above guidelines, practitioners can use strategies such as the following:

1. *Establishing an emotional connection and building a relationship with the client system*:

- clarifying who the worker is and why he or she is there,
- starting where the client is — and listening to the client,
- nurturing an authentic and caring relationship,
- reducing worker's authority and encouraging client autonomy and participation in the helping process,
- regarding clients as partners and resources in the helping process,
- fostering the client's sense of identity and self-esteem, and
- being sensitive to the feelings and values of clients from diverse ethnic or racial groups.

2. *Mobilizing the client's motivation*:

- redefining resistive behavior as motivation for change,
- identifying the sources and impact of the client's anxiety regarding potential change,
- delineating sources of motivation for change, and
- considering factors that may impede change.

3. *Exploring and interviewing*:

- involving children, parents, and other family members in presenting, exploring, or clarifying the "presenting problem" or need,
- encouraging child and family members to generate information relevant to the child's and family's functioning,
- gathering pertinent information on the child's development and medical history,
- obtaining the child's perceptions as well as the perceptions of parents and others regarding their situation,

- understanding the diverse views of different members of the client system, with sensitivity to their race and ethnicity,
- obtaining the perspectives of others in the family's network and ecology,
- paying special attention to potentialities or strengths in the child, family, network, and community, and
- offering concrete services if needed.

In line with the above concepts, the following example illustrates how the client-worker relationship can be redefined so that the practitioner can understand members of the client system, successfully engage them, and help promote their growth.

A social worker in a day care center became acquainted with Mrs. J, a mother who had recently immigrated from Eastern Europe, when she dropped off and picked up her child each day. Mrs. J began to linger for short conversations with the worker. Eventually, she asked the worker to visit her at home so that they could talk further about some of her concerns.

Mrs. J expressed much dissatisfaction with her life; she felt lonely, unfulfilled, and unhappy over the lack of contact with other adults other than her husband, who worked long hours in a nearby city. People in her neighborhood tended to keep to themselves, and she was fearful that they "didn't like" her because she was a foreigner. Although she yearned for opportunities to develop her interests and form close relationships with others, her environment provided little challenge or inspiration.

As the worker became aware of Mrs. J's needs and qualities, she encouraged her to try to create an informal support system in the neighborhood, thus making the environment more nurturing. Mrs. J brought considerable knowledge and skills to this task. Even though she was a newcomer, she had a good understanding of the needs and characteristics of the community and also had skills in arts and crafts. The worker, on the other hand, had information about — and access to — formal agencies in the city. Mrs. J and the worker began to hold informal arts and crafts events at the day care center for parents and children in the neighborhood. This not only provided an opportunity for families to have fun together but also began to produce the kind of informal support that Mrs. J had wanted.

While playing the role of enabler and community organizer, the worker respected and supported Mrs. J and helped her to create opportunities that were responsive to her needs and talents. In turn, Mrs. J, as an effective leader, attained satisfaction through her participation in meaningful activities that enhanced her sense of competence. At the same time, with the worker's encouragement, she created an environment that was more supportive and challenging for herself as well as for other mothers in the area.

The following case example of another family illustrates the social worker's efforts to engage the client system and build relationships by mobilizing the potentialities of clients and their motivation for change, as well as resources in their network, in a situation involving child abuse, family breakdown, and mother-child separation and eventual reunion. The techniques used by the worker reflected understanding of the diverse views of members of the family and appreciation of the mother's motivation for changing her behavior and resuming care of her child.

Marie W, now divorced, had been married to Tom W for ten years. They have a nine-year-old son, Kevin. Mr. W was physically abusive to both his wife and child. When Kevin was five, his day care provider reported to the state child welfare agency her concerns that Kevin might have been sexually abused. The evaluation, though inconclusive, suggested that the child might have been victimized by someone. At the same time, Mrs. W, distraught over the breakup of her marriage and ensuing financial difficulties, asked her sister and brother-in-law to provide temporary care for Kevin in their home. The agency then required that Mrs. W participate in a sexual abuse evaluation prior to Kevin's return to her care. Following a long series of delays in initiating the evaluation, which the agency viewed as evidence of Mrs. W's noncompliance, the court awarded Kevin's aunt and uncle temporary guardianship and required that visits with the parents be supervised.

Mrs. W participated in supervised visits at an agency-based visitation center for six months. Each of the visits between Kevin and his mother went very well. However, when a new job took her to a distant part of the state, Mrs. W did not contact her son for seven months. Mrs. W then relocated nearer to Kevin and petitioned the court for his return. The judge appointed a social worker to help improve the relationship between Kevin and his mother. Several months into the therapy, Mrs. W disclosed her alcohol abuse. She explained that the trauma of losing her husband and son was overwhelming; she could not tolerate the pain of just visiting with her son, and for that reason she could not participate in parent-teacher conferences, watch Kevin's softball games, or involve herself in other parenting tasks. She indicated that alcohol helped ease the pain but that, more than anything, she wanted her son back.

The social worker recognized Mrs. W's disclosure as evidence of the client's trust in her, willingness to confront her problems, and motivation to become a better parent. She used the disclosure to point to Mrs. W's courage and newly found hope that the future might be brighter than she had once thought. With the social worker's support and encouragement, Mrs. W began to attend meetings of Alcoholics Anonymous. After a period of proven sobriety, Mrs. W began weekly unsupervised visits with Kevin that were gradually lengthened to a full day, and then overnight. She began to feel motivated and confident enough to become more integrated in her son's life.

Mrs. W's sister objected to the social worker's recommendations to increase Mrs. W's time with Kevin. The sister's attitude initially prompted despair, but, helped by the social worker's encouragement, Mrs. W developed a new set of strategies to control her anger and maintain her focus on the goal of reunifying with her son. At the same time, the worker also discovered that, early in her marriage, Mrs. W had had a positive relation with Mr. W's family, but they had become estranged during the separation and divorce. Mrs. W expressed a desire to reconnect with her former in-laws and Kevin's grandparents. The worker then focused on strengthening ties in the kinship network, and her former in-laws became available to support this single-parent family in the future. After two years of continued growth and change by Mrs. W, along with continued support from her former in-laws, Kevin returned to his mother's care on a full-time basis. In this case the worker showed particular sensitivity to the theme of human diversity, as reflected in her attention to the role and value of the extended kinship system.

The above case examples illustrate engagement primarily of adults. It is equally important to engage children and adolescents. Children and youths can themselves be actively involved in the helping process, including such aspects as reaching decisions regarding ways to help with the family's problems and the best living arrangements for them. As practitioners become more comfortable asking for their views, they find that children and youths have a lot to say that should be taken into account in planning services on their behalf. In child welfare agency settings some older children make it clear that they prefer to be in a long-term foster home with continuing contacts with their parents rather than being adopted or placed in an institution (Barth and Berry 1994). Moreover, the contract or written agreement can be profitably used as a means of helping children to make decisions, assume responsibility for their own behavior, and take some control over their lives. For example, with adolescents in foster care, agreements can be used to clarify the tasks to be performed by the young person, the foster parents, and the social worker so as to facilitate the process of preparation for emancipation and independent living (Maluccio, Krieger, and Pine 1990).

Assessment

Intervention with children and families, as with other client groups, is based on careful understanding of the client system — that is, the special needs, qualities, problems, goals, and behaviors of the person, family, or group. A major purpose of the assessment phase is to understand the client's readiness and competence for change. To do so effectively, the worker needs to complement clinically based assessment procedures with other methods, such as participant observation. As much as feasible and appropriate, the worker should become involved in the client's life situation and seek to appreciate, through direct experience, what is going on with the client in relevant contexts, such as the family, neighborhood, or school.

Workers should understand, as clearly as possible, each client's competence and the multiple factors affecting it, in order to make professional use of life experiences and strengths as resources for change in the situations of their clients. Accordingly, the following guidelines can be helpful in assessment, in line with the "Framework of Needs and Resources for Family and Child Well-Being as well as the competence- and strength-oriented perspectives presented in chapter 1.[2]

1. *Clarify the Competence of the Client System*

It is useful in each case situation to ask the following questions to clarify the competence of the client system. What are the unique capacities, skills, attitudes, motivations, strengths, and potentialities of the client? What are the particular areas of coping strengths? What are indicators of resilience in the person? Which areas of competence need to be reinforced or supported? Which life experiences may be mobilized to stimulate or support the process of change?

2. *Clarify the Environmental Characteristics That Influence the Coping and Adaptive Patterns of the Client System*

The case example of the W family illustrates the positive as well as negative impact of the client's environment. What are the critical environmental challenges confronting the client? What actual or potential supports are available in the environment? What are the special potentialities or strengths in the particular racial or ethnic group? Are there mutual aid groups that can be mobilized? What are the risks and vulnerabilities in the client system? What blocks, obstacles, and deficits interfere with each person's life processes and adaptive strivings?

3. *Clarify the "Goodness of Fit" Between the Client System and Its Environment*

As illustrated by the case example of Mrs. J, it is useful to focus on such questions as the following: Does the environment contain the elements necessary to support, nourish, and challenge each person? What needs to be changed to make the transaction more mutually rewarding, to achieve a better adaptive fit, and to help the person to build on her or his life experiences? What new experiences or activities should be planned?

As reflected in the ecological perspective presented in chapter 1, assessment also requires that human difficulties be viewed as problems in living or as manifestations of the poor fit between people and their environments. These problems include developmental crises such as adolescence, life transitions such as marriage or divorce, and discrepancies between a person's needs and environmental resources such as lack of supports for gay and lesbian adolescents, inadequate day care services near a single mother's home, or services for persons with disabilities. Problems, needs, or conflicts are not seen as specific weaknesses or properties of the person. They are redefined in transactional terms so as to suggest ways of intervening in the person-environment transaction. In particular, problems are translated into adaptive tasks or meaningful life experiences, which provide the client with opportunities for action and for mastery, as seen above in the case of Mrs. J.

Change efforts can then be directed toward supporting the client's resilience and coping strategies, learning necessary skills, and, in many situations, rising above adversity (Wolin and Wolin 1993), as suggested in the following brief examples. A parent referred for child neglect is viewed as needing to learn skills in child care and is provided with a homemaker and a parent aide who offer concrete help and also serve as role models. A couple experiencing marital discord is encouraged to clarify factors that lead to their persistent arguments. A young unmarried mother is seen as having a problem in role transition rather than an underlying personality conflict and is provided with activities that help her to gain competence as a new parent.

In another example the recurring violence that is common in many urban, suburban, and rural communities is examined for its impact on young people who are its direct victims or witnesses, as noted in chapter 2. (Also see Guterman and Cameron 1997.) As extensively discussed in various child welfare texts (see Dubowitz and DePanfilis 2000; Pecora et al. 2000), it is also essential to assess the risk to the child and other family members in each case, taking into account racial, cultural, and ethnic factors. Assessing safety is especially crucial in light of the frequency and extent of violence in many family situations coming to the attention of child and family service agencies.[3] As noted by Holder (2000a:230):

> A child may be unsafe when a family situation involves family conditions that are out of control, can be expected to occur (be displayed) immediately, and likely will have severe effects for a child. A safety assessment refers to the application of a method to identify the presence of threats to a child's safety within the family or home.

As the following example illustrates, and as discussed in chapter 1, there is frequently an overlap between domestic violence and child abuse, further underlining the importance of addressing safety for children, mothers, and other family members along with close collaboration between child protective agencies and domestic violence programs.

Sarah, a young mother in a physically abusive marriage, is frightened and worried. Three months ago her four-year-old son was hit with an ashtray thrown at her by her husband during an episode of domestic violence. Trying to protect her son from harm, she instructed him in the future to go outside whenever his father becomes violent and hide in the toolshed until it is safe to come in. Child Protective Services (CPS) pays her a visit when a neighbor reports seeing the child cowering shoeless in the shed one freezing winter night. Fearing that she would be charged with neglect or abuse and that her son would be taken away from her, Sarah denies that there is violence in her home.

The worker makes a strength-based assessment of the situation instead of a deficit-based one. She asks Sarah about domestic violence, telling her that CPS is "here to help." Because Sarah has heard from her neighbors that CPS is indeed a resource that can help her with family problems, she confides in the worker about the abuse from her husband. Together, they discuss ways through which she can protect herself and her kids from the batterer, explore her options, make a safety plan for her and her child, and work with partnering domestic violence and social service agencies that can support her. Her batterer is held accountable for the violence, and Sarah is not charged. (Adapted with permission of the Family Violence Prevention Fund from its website [http://www.fvp.org]).[4]

As indicated in chapter 2, children who live with families where domestic violence occurs face numerous risks even if they are not physically harmed, including risk for substance abuse, violence, and delinquency. However, as the above example illustrates, often an effective and essential way to protect these children is by protecting their mothers through forceful and timely intervention.

An additional safety issue concerns the ability to identify and document the impact of substance abuse on parenting skills, the consequences of substance abuse for the child, and the determination of the level of overall safety in the family. In cases of substance abuse, comprehensive assessment information is needed in such areas as extended family support that could reinforce sobriety and provide safety for the child, housing and neighborhood influences, parenting skills, history of domestic violence, and previous and concurrent victimization of the parent (Tracy 1994). Some key skills for assisting in such assessments include worker use of support rather than confrontation, ability to form decision-making partnerships, ability to identify strengths, ability to keep people safe, and ability to enhance and facilitate motivation (Annie E. Casey Foundation n.d.f; Hohman 1998).

Along with considering safety issues, in many case situations there is a need to restructure the environment of the family. The functioning of each child and other family members can also flourish through a nutritive environment that is suited to their needs and qualities and supports their life processes. Consequently, the worker needs to understand the environment in all of complexities and find ways of enriching or restructuring it in a systematic fashion. In many situations the client environment needs to be modified so as to facilitate coping efforts and adaptive strivings as considered in chapter 7; social networks are especially important in this regard. Indeed, a key characteristic of competent persons is that they are able to identify and use natural helping networks. Some people, however, need help to make effective use of resources within their own actual or potential networks. The earlier case example of Mrs. W illustrates the application of the "Framework of Needs and Resources" presented in chapter 1. This mother was helped to assess the potential strengths of her kinship network and find ways of enhancing family ties so that they might to support her in becoming successfully reunited with her son.

Emphasis on the environment of the client system is not new in social work, as noted by such theorists as Germain and Gitterman (1996). We need to regard environmental resources and supports as potentially valuable instruments of help and appreciate the environment's potential to release or inhibit human potentialities for growth, adaptation, and competence. Doing so can lead to more accurate environmental assessment and more effective environmental intervention.

Much can be accomplished by identifying and using environmental instruments — that is, people, resources, social networks or supports, and facilities that exist in the environment or can be added to it. These instruments are integral to intervention (Germain and Gitterman 1996; Saleebey 2002). In the area of child welfare, for instance, homemakers or parent aides are found to be effective instruments of help in working with parents who abuse or neglect their children. In short, emphasis on changing the environment is as important as — if not more important than — attention to changing people themselves. In this regard, it is necessary early on to complete a comprehensive assessment of resources in the family's social networks, which we shall describe in chapter 7.

As reflected above, in the assessment phase practitioners use strategies such as the following:

- organizing the data that are gathered in each case, on the basis of the assessment framework described in chapter 1, which focuses on needs and resources in the interrelated areas of child and family well-being: children's optimal development, family survival and functioning, and neighborhood and community resources;
- analyzing the "problems" and "needs" in transactional terms, that is, following the competence-centered perspective outlined in chapter 1 and reflected in the above-noted framework;
- taking into account the race, ethnicity, and culture of the client system and the impact on parent-child and family relationships;
- paying special attention to assessment of risks and vulnerabilities in such areas as poverty, family violence, and health, as delineated in chapter 2; and
- clarifying the competence of the client system, the qualities of the impinging environment, and the "goodness of fit" between the client system and its environment.

In addition, as emphasized by Gambrill (1997:209–210), practitioners need to avoid common errors that occur in the assessment phase. These include emphasis on irrelevant outcomes, formulation of inaccurate and incomplete causal analysis, and selection of ineffective or harmful service plans. Examples of such errors follow:

- Problem-related behaviors are not clearly described.
- Cultural factors are overlooked.
- The functions of behaviors of interest are unknown (e.g., related environmental consequences such as reactions by significant others are not identified).
- Related setting events and antecedents are not identified.
- The client's strengths are ignored.
- Positive alternatives to undesired behaviors are not identified.
- Baseline data are not available (e.g., description of the severity of behaviors, thoughts, or feelings prior to intervention).
- Related physical characteristics of the environment are overlooked.
- Higher-level contingencies (e.g., loss of financial aid) are overlooked. (Gambrill 1997:209)

Practitioners can guard against such errors by testing and retesting their formulations on the basis of the evidence gathered in a given case and through checking with the clients, as we recommend in the discussion regarding client feedback in chapter 9. As Gambrill (1997:212) stresses, "Assessment should offer clients a more helpful vocabulary for describing problems and options, and a model of how to break down a problem into manageable parts." Toward these ends, assessment requires critical thinking, that is, "the careful examination and evaluation of beliefs and actions in order to arrive at well reasoned ones" (Gambrill 1997:125).[5]

Various tools and guides are available to carry out the assessment in each case situation. A representative model is the "Integrative Skills Assessment Protocol" proposed by Jordan and Franklin (1995) on the basis of their critical examination of the assessment techniques employed in several social work practice approaches. Their framework, which can cover a number of situations and agencies, incorporates typical areas that should be considered by the worker in the process of formulating the assessment:

- identifying information, including a brief description of the presenting problem(s) or symptom(s),
- presenting problem(s), listing those identified by client and worker, specifying each problem, and prioritizing the various problems,
- client system, including description of intrapersonal issues, interpersonal dimensions (family, work or school, and peers),
- health status of family members *(also see appendix 7 for electronic resources on health of children and adults),*
- social context and social support networks, including agency characteristics and client's environmental context,
- measurement of individual, marital and family functioning, along with social supports; and
- summary, including practitioner impressions, diagnosis, target problems, and progress indicators.

Kemp, Whittaker, and Tracy (1997:123–128) delineate a number of tools and methods for assessment of the perceived physical, social/interactional, institutional/organizational, and social/political/ cultural environments in which clients function. Webb (1996:74–97) describes newer instruments such as the genogram and ecomap as well as traditional tools such as developmental history forms, projective techniques, and assessment forms. She also provides a useful and comprehensive "sample biopsychosocial assessment summary" (Webb 1996:91–95). In addition, Day, Robison, and Sheikh (1998) examine the purposes as well as strengths and limitations of a range of assessment tools that can be used in child protection cases and cases in other family and children's service settings; they also offer guidelines for building a comprehensive assessment strategy for a community-based child protection system. The tools and instruments considered by the above authors are described, among others, in appendix 1. (In addition, see, for example, LeProhn et al. 2001.)

We also suggest consideration of the "culturagram" originally devised by Congress (1994) and more recently revised by her (Congress 2002b), for use in assessment and intervention with new immigrant families and other culturally diverse families. The author has developed this tool as a structured method of assessment that is responsive to the cultural diversity of families coming to the attention of social agencies and the corresponding need for social work practice that reflects attention to human diversity. It covers a range of aspects pertaining to the family's transition into a new culture, including reasons for immigration, language spoken at home and in the community; values about family, education, and work, and the meaning of holidays and special events.

As Congress (1994:531) indicates: "With the culturagram, social workers are able to assess the impact of culture on the family, individualize ethnically similar families, become more empathic with regard to cultural differences, and empower culturally diverse clients and their families."

The culturagram is helpful as a tool that students and practitioners can use to organize the assessment information in a particular case and to develop a better understanding of the family. It not only reminds them of areas to consider in the process of formulating an assessment but also helps to enhance their cultural awareness and sensitivity. In this regard, it is similar to the "cultural genogram" described by Hardy and Laszloffy (1995), who challenge family therapy trainees to analyze their cultural background and its impact on their cultural identity as well as their roles as therapists.

The culturagram and similar tools have great potential for use with new immigrant families, especially those with children enrolled in public schools. The tools are grounded in knowledge areas presented in chapter 1 regarding new immigrants from developing countries, particularly the tasks of becoming integrated into schools and other institutions in the new culture, and thus can help promote culturally competent practice.[6]

Case Planning and Goal Setting

In the case-planning and goal-setting phases of the helping process, practitioners seek to provide opportunities for clients to consider and choose among alternative courses of action — to evaluate various possibilities, test readiness of clients, and select the most appropriate alternative. Furthermore, the deliberative process can stimulate clients' cognitive growth and mastery, mobilize their decision-making function, and reinforce the sense of autonomy that comes from involvement in purposive activities consonant with their needs as well as societal requirements.

Through the provision of information concerning the potential effects of the action, feedback to heighten clients' awareness of their reality, and support in taking a risk, the worker plays an important role. Client-worker interaction becomes more meaningful and productive as both parties go through the process of reaching agreement on specific goals, tasks, and procedures. In this connection it is useful to keep in mind the systems theory principle of equifinality — the notion that the same result can be achieved in different ways. If diverse opportunities for action are identified, the individual is able to look at the world in novel ways and select the activity most suited to her or his personal style of coping and drive for competence. This is crucial, as people cope differently with similar life crises.

In case planning and goal setting, as in the engagement and assessment phases, social work practitioners need to view their clients more explicitly as resources — human beings with assets and potentialities that can be mobilized on their own behalf — and help clients to see *themselves* as resources. Mobilizing the potentialities and motivation of clients requires practitioners to select actions that provide opportunities for clients to build on their strengths (Saleebey 1997a, 2002). This involves identifying issues of primary concern around which motivation can be awakened and taking into consideration the person's strengths and potentialities and ethnic and racial characteristics, as well as environmental resources and deficits (Iglehart and Becerra 1995). Above all, it means emphasizing interventions that empower human beings to take action on their own behalf (Parsons and Cox 1994; Pinderhughes 1997).

Case planning and goal setting culminate in a contract or service agreement between the social worker(s) and the client system that serves as a guide to intervention in each case. Such an agreement is a written statement of concurrence among the family, social worker, and other collaborating professionals. It is an integral part of the helping process in child and family services and it serves a variety of purposes, including, in particular:

- facilitating decision making on the part of parents, social workers, children, and collaterals,
- specifying time frames for decision making,
- encouraging participation of parents and thereby promoting their sense of competence and control,
- maintaining a focus on the child's need for safety and permanency as central issues,
- ensuring clarity of tasks, goals, and purpose for clients, workers, and collaterals, and
- providing for periodic review and assessment of progress.

The agreement should spell out the roles and tasks of all participants and be directly related to the family's referral to the agency. In particular, it should include to the extent possible:

- goals and expectations,
- the roles each party will play in achieving the plan,
- the tasks each party must complete to provide for the child's growth, health, and safety and the family's integrity,
- small, concrete tasks that can be readily achieved,
- support for children, parents, and other family members as they are involved in decision making regarding the child, and
- a plan for regularly convening formal and informal reviews of progress toward the goals delineated in the service agreement, revising or amending the goals as needed.

As illustrated in the example in the next section, formulating and reviewing the service agreement should be planned and implemented with the active involvement of family members, caregivers, and service providers; it should also include recognition that parents often feel intimidated and overwhelmed by a group of experts and may not feel free to express their own opinions. In sum, use of the contract or working agreement with children and families can stimulate the person's cognitive growth and mastery, broaden her or his knowledge of different alternatives and their consequences, and mobilize her or his decision-making function.[7] Also, as explained by Rooney (1992:175–200), practice with involuntary clients requires emphasis on a number of strategies, including extensive exploration of the client's view of existing problems, reframing the problem in line with the client's concerns and values, and offering incentives to make mandated services more attractive.

Parent-Child Visiting in Out-of-Home Care

There are various components of service agreements in family and children's services. An example is the "visiting plan," which is formulated and agreed upon among practitioners, birth parents, and children in cases involving reunification of a child in foster care with the family.

Planning for visits can be complicated and time consuming, and the visit itself may be emotionally depleting for all involved. However, as Warsh, Maluccio, and Pine (1994) indicate, parent-child or family-child visiting is the *"heart of reunification"* because it is the forum in which parents and children learn to be together again. To promote visiting that is tied to case goals, and thus facilitates successful reunification, a visiting plan is designed with full participation of children and their parents and caregivers. The plan, which is an integral feature of the service, includes clarification of the purposes of visiting, along with description of specific visiting arrangements in relation to case goals and the roles of all participants in the planned visit.[8]

In addition, we should consider the model of *concurrent planning* — a recent innovation in the family and child welfare field that is used specifically in cases involving young children in out-of-home care. As indicated by Katz (1999:72), concurrent planning involves working "towards family reunification while, at the same time, developing an alternative permanent plan" for the child.[9] This approach, which has been found to be particularly effective with "difficult-to-treat" families, combines the following strategies: "vigorous family outreach, expedited timelines, and potentially permanent family foster care placements to improve the odds of timely permanency for very young children" (Katz 1999:72).

There are, of course, many situations in which concurrent planning is not appropriate or effective, such as cases involving extreme physical abuse of the child and/or excessive family violence. However, following careful assessment, it is a concept well worth considering:

At its best, concurrent planning represents team decision making involving professionals as well as the child, the child's caregivers, birth parents, and extended family members. Its central purpose is accomplished through comprehensive assessment of the parent-child relationship, parental functioning and support systems.

(Pecora et al. 2000:77)

The following example illustrates involving clients in case planning and goal setting in line with the principles described in this section.

Ryan, a shy fifteen-year-old, had been diagnosed with attention deficit disorder and a learning disability that resulted in poor language comprehension and production. He was doing very poorly in school, which compounded his already low self-esteem. To make matters worse, his older brother, Charley, was an outstanding college freshman, excelling both academically and on the football field. With the school year coming to a close, Ryan told his social worker that he was preparing to quit his part-time job so that he could take the summer off and "just sleep."

The social worker noted that the only time Ryan seemed to talk with any passion and sense of hopefulness was when he described his guitar playing. He played frequently with a group of his friends with whom he had formed a band and wished that someday he might earn his living as a musician. She explored with Ryan the possibility of his using the summer to work toward this goal. Together they created a list of action steps that he would need to take, such as establishing a regular practice schedule for the band, creating a two-hour show, identifying venues, purchasing a new amplifier, and developing a publicity campaign.

By the end of the summer Ryan and his friends had accomplished all their goals and were scheduled to play at a host of school dances through the end of the year. Even Ryan's parents, who earlier had been seeing Ryan as a failure or "just plain lazy," had to admire the energy and drive their son demonstrated once he was helped to focus on an aspect of his life that was a strength and really mattered to him.

As illustrated in part through the above example, in the case-planning and goal-setting phases practitioners use strategies such as the following:

- consider with the clients different alternatives and their consequences,
- construct case plans that are explicitly geared toward promoting the client's competence as well as child and family functioning,
- examine ways of mobilizing actual or potential resources in the environment of the client system or creating new ones if necessary,
- elicit opinions from clients on the various action plans being considered, what the clients need, and what might work best for them,
- delineate with the clients what constitutes competent solutions and the tasks they must be able to perform to accomplish their plans and goals,
- specify goals of their work together and formulate a working agreement or contract regarding the work that is to be carried out, including attainable and clearly stated objectives and tasks that become the focus of client-worker activities,
- help the child, parents, and other members to form a partnership that works to establish agreed-upon goals,
- assist the client to be in control as much as possible, and
- convene formal and informal reviews of progress toward the agreed upon goals, revising or amending them as required.

In addition, as we have indicated in preceding sections, intervention planning is best viewed in the context of a comprehensive assessment process with the child and family. Often a clear demarcation between assessment and intervention is difficult to detect. Beginning practitioners appropriately wonder where assessment ends and intervention begins, or, in their eagerness to help, they may offer specific interventions too early in the process, before sufficient assessment data have been gathered and the worker and client have become properly engaged. Furthermore, many times the gathering of assessment data represents a major intervention in and of itself; for example, parents may complain about a child's behavior but, after collecting baseline data on its frequency of occurrence, decide that it does not warrant intervention.

Assessment is, therefore, an ongoing and continuous process, and the best practitioner continues gathering assessment data during the process of intervention. Yet there does come a point in time when explicit interventive action needs to occur. In general, such intervention should begin when the following conditions have been met: a working relationship has been established, an assessment has been completed, mutually agreed upon goals have been developed, the priorities are right (e.g., crisis and safety issues are addressed first), and the skills and resources to mount the intervention are available (Cormier and Cormier 1985). Also it is important that objectives for family centered service be clear, measurable, and directly related to primary risk factors, so that both family members and workers can determine when a goal has been met. Given current mandates for assuring stability and permanency for children, time limits to goal completion are vitally important; there should be reasonable but not excessive time limits placed on goal achievement, with clear indicators specified that would warrant extensions to those time limits.[10]

Engagement and assessment that actively involve the family as well as other significant members of its network are critical to adequate case planning and goal setting. As we have illustrated in this chapter, adults as well as children can be thoughtfully and extensively engaged in these processes — and in ways that help promote their functioning and competence. Such engagement should be carried out on the basis of our understanding of vulnerable families (as considered in chapter 1) and with sensitivity to the potential risks delineated in chapter 2. In the following chapter we consider intervention approaches within a family-centered framework, building on the principles and guidelines for engagement and assessment that have been presented here.

Notes

1. For in-depth treatment of social work practice with involuntary clients, see Rooney (1992). Also see Berg (1994) and Franklin et al. (2001) for solution-focused techniques for engaging clients in goal setting; Littell, Alexander, and Reynolds (2001) for a review of research on client participation in psychosocial intervention; and Hohman (1998) for description of motivational techniques particularly useful in engaging clients in discussion around substance abuse issues.
2. See Maluccio (1981 and 1999); Norman (2000); and Saleebey (1997a and 2002) for elaboration on the competence and strength perspectives,

and Early (2001) and Graybeal (2001) for discussion of assessment tools from a strength perspective.

3. The literature includes extensive treatment of various aspects of risk assessment. See the following: Pecora et al. (2000), for a comprehensive discussion of concepts and issues in risk assessment; Pecora (1991), for consideration of the advantages and limitations of risk assessment tools; Holder and Corey (1987), for guidelines on decision-making in cases involving risk; Holder (2000a, b), for discussion of risk and safety issues; Brissett-Chapman (2000), for consideration of cultural factors in risk assessment; Zuskin (2000), for assessment of domestic violence in families with children; McCroskey and Meezan (1997), for guidelines on assessment of family functioning; and Turnell and Edwards (1999) for guidelines on safety assessment.

4. This material was adapted with permission from the website of the Family Violence Prevention Fund: http://www.fvpf.org (June 10, 2001).

5. See Gambrill (1997:125–150) for a rich discussion of critical thinking as a guide to practice decisions.

6. See Johnson-Powell and Yamamoto (1997) for other culture-specific assessment tools and guidelines and Webb (2001) for assessment of culturally diverse parent-child and family relationships

7. For further discussion of service agreements and guidelines for its implementation in family and child welfare, see Pecora et al. (2000); Rykus and Hughes (1998); and Warsh, Maluccio, and Pine (1994). For application of contracting to work with involuntary clients, see Rooney (1992:174–230).

8. See Warsh, Maluccio, and Pine (1994:51–89) for extensive discussion of the philosophy, principles, and phases of parent-child visiting as a central feature of practice with children in out-of-home care and their families.

9. Katz (1999) delineates strategies for implementing the model of concurrent planning, along with description of potential pitfalls in its implementation.

10. See Webb (1996) for application of assessment, case planning, and goal setting principles to children in out-of-home placement, nontraditional families, substance-abusing families, and families affected by illness and death. Also, Hohman and Butt (2001) discuss the issues of time limits and case planning in relation to substance abuse and treatment and recovery.

Questions for Discussion

1. Choosing a family with which you are working or have worked, discuss how you applied or could have applied the principles of engagement in the helping process that were described in this chapter.

2. We have presented in this chapter a competence-centered perspective on assessment in case situations involving families and children. Discuss how this perspective may or may not be applicable to cases with which you are currently working.

3. Gambrill (1997) describes a variety of errors that commonly occur in the assessment phase. Which of these errors have you found in your practice with families and children, and how could you guard against such errors in the future?

4. Based upon your knowledge of a client family or your own family background, complete the culturagram described in this chapter, or the ecomap, social network map, or genogram described in appendix 1. If you do not have all the information needed, consider where and how you might obtain that information. Finally, discuss how the information contained in the culturagram, ecomap, or genogram might be applicable in your own practice setting.

5. Provide a case example in which you sought to involve a family unit or its members in case planning and goal setting. What worked, and what would you do differently to maximize the family's participation in this process?

Suggestions for Further Information

Anderson, G. R., A. S. Ryan, and B. R. Leashore, eds. 1997. *The Challenge of Permanency Planning in a Multicultural Society*. New York: Haworth.

Congress, E. 1994. The use of culturagrams to assess and empower culturally diverse families. *Families in Society: The Journal of Contemporary Social Work* 75:531–540.

Compton, B. R. and B. Galaway, eds. 1999. *Social Work Processes*. 6th ed. Pacific Grove, Cal.: Brooks/Cole.

Gambrill, E. 1997. *Social Work Practice: A Critical Thinker's Guide*. New York: Oxford University Press.

Kemp, S., J. K. Whittaker, and E. M. Tracy. 1997. *Person-Environment Practice: The Social Ecology of Interpersonal Helping*. New York: de Gruyter.

Littell, J. H., L. B. Alexander, and W. H. Reynolds. 2001. Client participation: Central and under-investigated elements of intervention. *Social Service Review* 75:1–28.

Webb, N. B. 1996. *Social Work Practice with Children*. New York: Guilford.

6   Family-Centered Intervention

In this chapter we build upon the engagement and assessment processes and return to and expand upon the guidelines for implementing child-focused and family-centered practice that we delineated in chapter 1. We begin with a description of family-centered practice: its focus, goals, and major principles. We then discuss each guideline, using case examples and program examples to illustrate worker skills and the knowledge required for implementing child-focused and family-centered intervention.

What Is Meant by Family-Centered Intervention?

The Child Welfare League of America describes family-centered services as encompassing "a range of activities for families with problems that threaten their stability: case management, counseling/therapy, education/ skill building, advocacy, and/or the provision of concrete services such as food, housing, or health care" (Child Welfare League of America 1989:29).

The goals of such services are to promote the protection and well-being of children, to increase parenting abilities and to nurture a stable family environment. Following an ecological perspective and the "Framework of Needs and Resources for Family and Child Well-Being" presented in chapter 1, specific objectives of service might include provision of information, skills, or resources to help families better cope with their situation while simultaneously working with family members to alleviate environmental, discriminatory, or social conditions that are stressful for them. There is a broad array of family situations that may benefit from family-centered services (Child Welfare League of America 1989):

- emergencies such as eviction, lack of food, shutoff of utilities,
- cases of family violence (child or parent),
- cases of child neglect,
- substance affected families,
- families with parent-child conflict and acting out behavior,
- incarcerated parents,
- foster and adoptive families in need of support,
- teenage parents, and
- caregivers with physical or mental disabilities.

As discussed in the preceding chapter, intervention planning is best viewed in the context of a comprehensive assessment process with the child and family. Clear goals are important not only at the outset of intervention but also in determining when interventions can be safely concluded. To this end, the Child Welfare League of America (1989) suggests that a family should meet one or more of the following goals to achieve successful case closure:

- basic child and family needs are met,
- children are no longer in danger,
- family members have acquired new skills to adopt safe and healthy family lifestyles,
- family communication is effective, and
- emotional problems that contributed to the initial need for service have been reduced.

Intervention Strategies

The major interventions utilized by the family-centered practitioner consist of those strategies designed to safeguard the child and family unit and to promote the well-being of children and families. This goal is achieved through activities that address the child's developmental needs, the family's survival and developmental needs, and the availability and quality of neighborhood, community, and environmental resources, as reflected in the previously described "Framework of Needs and Resources for Family and Child Well-Being." Although family-centered interventions may take on many forms, they are based upon several common principles and values: the family as the unit of attention, strengthening or empowering the family to function at its best, engaging families in designing all aspects of service, and linking families to community-based networks of supports and services (National Child Welfare Resource Center for Family-Centered Practice 2000).

A number of guidelines were proposed in chapter 1 to help practitioners choose from among the many helping strategies and interventions that exist. This section reviews a range of practice strategies in accordance with those guidelines. Choice of strategy is dependent upon the service setting, the worker's defined role, discussion with the family, and the client-worker agreement, as described in chapter 5. Overriding any specific intervention skill or technique is the case management function; that is, creating the service plan, coordinating an array of services, periodic review of delivery and outcome, arranging for follow-up services, and terminating the service when goals have been met (Child Welfare League of America 1989).

Prevention and Intervention Strategies That Reduce Stress and Risk

Intervention techniques useful in reducing stress and risk include skill building, family support, and provision of concrete services. Each of these is presented below.

Skill Building

Information is power. When family members learn how to handle stress, risk within the household may be reduced. Family-centered practice involves helping family members acquire new knowledge and skills in such areas as parenting, family communication, relapse prevention, and household management.[1] Each family's learning needs are unique. Likewise, individual family members, depending on their experience and developmental level, may have a different learning style. Family-centered practitioners must be good teachers, with the ability to

- be responsive to the styles and values of families from communities of color, immigrants, and other special populations;

- break complex tasks into smaller specific steps (e.g., how to look for housing; how to talk with your child's teacher);
- conduct a contextual assessment of problematic family interactions (e.g., what contingencies trigger and maintain problem behaviors within the family);
- assess the key skills needed for less stressful family interactions (e.g., accepting "no," giving direct commands, handling anger);
- explain and model appropriate skills, using techniques such as role play, modeling, or videotaped practice;
- assess individual learning styles and ways to teach adults as well as children;
- establish homework and other means of ensuring generalization of skills from one setting to another;
- promote and reward skill acquisition;
- emphasize strategies that help develop the strengths of family members; and
- motivate the family to stay involved even when faced with challenges and setbacks.

Family-centered approaches teach skills as an integral part of their services. For example, multisystemic family treatment approaches with delinquent youth (Henggeler et al. 1998:91) stress the importance of helping parents make and enforce rules as well as offer parents a set of guidelines for rule development:

- defining the expected behavior clearly and specifically so that the caretaker can tell whether it has occurred,
- stating rules in terms of positive behaviors, making clear, for example, that the youth should return home by *[specific time]*,
- listing the privilege that will be given or withheld if the rule is kept or broken,
- enforcing rules 100 percent of the time,
- enforcing rules in an "unemotional manner," and
- having parents agree on — and enforce — the rules (if both parents are involved).

Additionally, the Homebuilders model (Kinney, Haapala, and Booth 1991) teaches families the use of consequences, behavior charts, motivation systems, and contracts to change behavior; cognitive intervention skills and basic communication methods such as active listening and using "I" messages are also taught. While some family members are able to learn new skills through didactic training sessions, either conducted in groups or individually, many parents find the opportunity to practice new parenting skills within their home more conducive to learning.

Family Support

The Child Welfare League of America and the Family Resource Coalition use the term *family resource, support, and education services* to refer to the wide variety of community-based services that assist and support adults in their roles as parents (Child Welfare League of America 1989; Family Resource Coalition of America 1996). Core family support services include home visiting, child developmental screening, parent education and social, emotional, and educational support for parents (Comer and Fraser 1998). Many family support programs also address family self-sufficiency by offering services such as job training, English as a second language, and literacy classes; follow-up studies of those aspects of the program, among others, suggest that these services contribute to long term positive outcomes for the family (Tracy 2001).

Family support programs serve diverse families in all forms: adoptive, parents, foster parents, kinship care providers and extended family members. Among the lessons learned from family support programs are the following:

- programs must recognize cultural differences in child-rearing values and methods and understand what families consider desirable for their children to learn,[2]
- barriers to participation must be addressed (cultural, linguistic, logistic),
- programs must focus on content and deliver it in a format acceptable to the families,
- programs must focus on content and deliver it in a format acceptable to the families,
- programs must stress that every family is unique,
- programs must rely on the definition of *family* as used and practiced by the families served, and
- programs must recognize the need for advocacy, empowerment

and political action to remedy the underlying social and economic conditions that add stress to family life (Shartrand 1996).

The Family Resource Coalition (1996) provides the following set of principles for family support practice:

- Staff and families work together in relationships based on equality and respect.
- Staff enhance families' capacity to support the growth and development of all family members — adults, youths, and children.
- Families are resources to their own members, to other families, to programs, and to communities.
- Programs affirm and strengthen families' cultural, racial, and linguistic identities and enhance their ability to function in a multicultural society.
- Programs are embedded in their communities and contribute to the community-building process.
- Programs advocate with families for services and systems that are fair, responsive, and accountable to the families served.
- Practitioners work with families to mobilize formal and informal resources to support family development.
- Programs are flexible and continually responsive to emerging family and community issues.
- Principles of family support are modeled in all program activities, including planning, governance, and administration.

While specific services vary depending on the location and population served, they should be consistent with — and guided by — the principles listed above.

Concrete Services

One of the hallmarks of family-centered practice approaches is the creative mixing of concrete (or hard) and clinical (or soft) services, in order to strengthen families and promote the competent functioning of its members. Concrete services include the provision of material goods or financial assistance to acquire material goods. Providing transportation for a family, paying for a summer recreation program for a youth, and helping with household chores and home repair are some examples. Clinical services include assessment, counseling, family education, and the like. "Enabling" services are closely related to clinical services, in that they link a family with needed formal and informal supportive services.

Concrete services serve important functions. First of all, they directly address and ameliorate the types of environmental problems many families face — for example, not being able to visit an incarcerated parent because of a lack of transportation, living in a house that poses safety risks to children but being unable to pay for needed repairs, and not having the financial resources to provide concrete reinforcement (stickers or small rewards) as part of a child behavior management program. Traditional agencies, which tend to focus exclusively on clinical service provision, may be unwilling or unable to provide such concrete services (Tracy, Green, and Bremseth 1993).

Second, concrete services serve important functions depending on the stage of help. Early on in the helping process, such services can reduce the immediate crisis situation facing a family, as in securing equipment needed to enable a child with a disability to remain in the home. For instance, families are not ready to deal with interpersonal and behavioral difficulties if they do not have heat or electricity; some service programs have access to emergency funds to deal with such environmental problems (Tracy et al. 1999). In some cases, when environmental concerns are addressed early on, the situation may not develop into a crisis or safety risk.

Concrete services also help solidify and establish a good working relationship between the family and service provider. The following example from a rural mental health agency illustrates the important caring message that concrete services can convey.

When the agency's three-member home-based team brought toys to a family on Christmas Eve, the mother's attitude toward accepting help from outsiders, especially "city folk," changed dramatically because she knew that the workers really cared about her and her family and that the gifts symbolized their caring (Tracy et al. 1999).

In the example above, concrete services demonstrated tangible support for the family and were viewed as offering a different type of help, in comparison with the traditional "talk" therapies. Perhaps for this reason, provision of concrete services has been highly correlated with "success" in service outcome, including accomplishment of treatment goals and preservation of families (Berry 1997).

Concrete services help to secure the family's active involvement in the change effort, and they may also support maintenance of change after service is completed. Concrete service provision near the termination of services may help to maintain the changes made by the family and thereby ensure more family stability. An example might be helping a mother to find new housing and connect with nonusing members of her social network to maintain sobriety and prevent relapse following substance abuse treatment.

Concrete services also are an important component of consumer-driven service approaches. Often, when families are asked what type of help they need, the answer is some type of concrete service, and when the worker is unable to help in this way, because of agency policy, funding, or eligibility requirements, a key opportunity to begin the change process may be lost. A balance between concrete and clinical services, designed with the needs of the individual family involved, should be sought.[3]

Some examples of combinations of clinical and concrete services include parent training in physical therapy techniques combined with the provision of adaptive equipment for the home, family therapy sessions revolving around communication and "fair fighting," in combination with supplying a "board" game so that the family can practice their new skills, and referral to a substance abuse treatment group in combination with flexible funds for car repairs so that reliable transportation to the group sessions is possible. Clinical services help people acquire more adaptive behaviors, thoughts, and feelings; concrete services often allow people an opportunity to put their new clinical skills into real-life application.

Focus on the Family's Transactions with Other Systems

In family-centered intervention there is a focus on the family's transaction with other systems. This includes those interventions that help family members obtain needed services and community resources through activities such as case advocacy (Ezell 2001), empowerment, social network interventions, and community liaison work. Family-centered social workers help family members improve relationships within the family as well as with people and organizations, both formal and informal, outside of the family. For example, a couple may benefit from learning fair fighting techniques; at the same time, they may need to learn how to communicate more effectively in the workplace.

Group approaches are often helpful in changing transactions within the family as well as between the family and other systems. As described in chapter 8, self-help group approaches often focus on changing the environment; an example would be a community disability rights education program initiated by parents of children with special needs to improve attitudes toward disabilities. Group approaches also bridge the gap between personal definitions of problems and the social context in which they occur. For example, girls participating in a group for people who have been sexually abused wrote poems about their experiences as victims; while the writing of poems was itself a therapeutic experience, the fact that the poems were sent for publication in a professional journal made the experience an empowering one.

We are beginning to identify some key skills and techniques for negotiating relationships with larger social systems. For instance, parents who make the school system work for them, rather than attempting to solve their child's school problem on their own, are often more successful in helping their child succeed academically (Patten 2000). Family-centered practitioners often teach family members how best to interact with formal and informal service systems. This might involve learning whom to contact, how to establish a relationship with a key informant, what to know about client rights and responsibilities, and how best to state one's case in a nonthreatening manner. Typically, as the following example illustrates, when a family is referred for services there are multiple relationship problems to be addressed: problems within the family, problems the family has in dealing with outside systems and groups, and dealing with systems and groups that view the family as the problem.

Sally and Ralph Johnson were involved in a postadoption support service, having formed their family through international adoption of four children from India. All the children experienced multiple placements prior to the adoption, which was finalized several years ago. Two of the children had polio and now wear leg braces. The parents outlined the following concerns: arguments between the parents, no time for the parents as a couple, behavior management issues with all four children, especially around home chores, work-related problems of the father due to a recent lay-off, mental health issues for the mother, and problems with the local school district.

The parents questioned the appropriateness of the special educational assessment of one of the children; they did not feel the testing accurately captured their child's learning style and needs, especially given her complex history. At the same time, the school district viewed the family as "difficult" and "hard to please." The teacher thought the children were not dressed appropriately for school, citing torn pants as an example. The parents said the leg braces constantly ripped pants and pointed to an enormous pile of mending that needed to be done.

An ecomap (Hartman and Laird 1983), as introduced in chapter 5, helped identify stressful and conflicted relationships as well as connections that were needed but currently missing or underutilized. In addition, a placement genogram (McMillen and Groze 1994) provided insight and understanding of the children's behavior and its impact on the family; the worker began to understand that the children had no real sense that this was their permanent home.

In the example above, a combination of skills training approaches with the family, direct advocacy on their behalf with the school, and provision of concrete services in the form of volunteer mending was effective in reducing stress levels.

Family Approaches as Alternatives to Placement

Family Preservation Services

Family preservation or family-centered services are more or less intensive services delivered in the client's home over a relatively brief time-limited period. The presenting problems of referred families are often multiple and complex: child abuse, child neglect, sexual abuse, alcohol and other drug abuse, and oppositional behavior in the home, school, and community that include status offenses and delinquency, among others.

The primary goals of family preservation services are to

- allow children to remain safely in their own homes,

- maintain and strengthen family bonds,
- stabilize the crisis situation precipitating the need for placement,
- increase the family's coping skills and competencies, and
- facilitate the family's use of appropriate formal and informal helping resources (Nelson and Landsman 1992).

In short, family preservation services are intended to "remove the risk of harm to the child instead of removing the child from the home" (Edna McConnell Clark Foundation 1993:1).

According to the Child Welfare League of America (1989) standards outlined earlier, intensive family-centered crisis services should consist of low caseloads (two to six families), intense service delivery (an average of eight to ten hours per week), and brief duration of service (four to twelve weeks). Approximately 60 percent of worker time should be spent on direct face-to-face contact with the family, with an emphasis on providing counseling, education, and supporting services. Regardless of their theoretical orientation, family preservation programs typically share a number of common features:

- Only families at imminent risk of placement are accepted.
- Services are crisis oriented, and families are seen as soon as possible after a referral is made.
- Staff is accessible, maintaining flexible hours seven days a week.
- Intake and assessment procedures ensure that no child is left in danger.
- Although problems of individuals may be addressed, the focus of service is on the family as unit.
- Workers see families in the families' homes, making frequent visits convenient to each family's schedule. Other services are also provided in school and neighborhood settings.
- The service approach offers a mix of clinical and concrete interventions — such as counseling, education, skills training, information and referral, and advocacy.
- Services are based on identified family needs rather than strict categorical eligibility.
- Each worker carries a small caseload at any given time. A limited number of programs make use of teams.
- Programs limit the length of involvement with the family to a short period, typically be between one to six months.

- Depending on the program model, interventions drawn from social learning theory, cognitive-behavior theory, or family systems
  theory may be employed. (Whittaker and Tracy 1989; Cole and
  Duva 1990).

An important service component of all intensive family preservation services models is the provision of concrete or hard services, as in helping the
family obtain housing or advocating for medical or financial benefits (Tracy
2001). In one evaluation of the Homebuilders model, about three fourths
of all families received some form of concrete service (Fraser, Pecora, and
Haapala 1991). In some programs flexible funding is available to purchase
needed goods and services or to reduce barriers to service utilization (e.g.,
getting a car fixed to ensure reliable transportation to a drug treatment
program).

In recent years home-based family preservation programs, especially those
offering intensive short-term services, have come under public scrutiny;
communities have become concerned with what they perceive to be family
preservation with disregard for — or insufficient attention to — child safety
(Weisman 1994). In addition, professionals have questioned the effectiveness
of family preservation, as various studies have found mixed results (Littell
and Schuerman 1995; Gelles 1996; McKenzie 1998; Westat et al. 2001).
These and other studies have cast doubt on the earlier claims of success of
intensive family preservation services. For example, widely cited studies such
as those by McCroskey and Meezan (1997) in California, Schuerman,
Rzepnicki, and Littell (1994) in Illinois, and Feldman (1991) in New Jersey,
found either no placement prevention effects or short-term effects that dis-
sipated with time. In a more recent study of the Homebuilders model in
three states, it was found that there were no significant differences between
the experimental and control groups on rates of placement, case closings,
or subsequent maltreatment, and only a few areas of child and family functioning "in which the experimental group displayed better outcomes than
the control group in at least one of the states" (U.S. Department of Health
and Human Services 2001:xxv).

In their review of brief intensive family preservation services, Blythe,
Salley and Jayaratne (1994) examined twelve studies, including program
evaluation efforts as well as quasi-experimental and experimental designs.
They concluded that, with some notable exceptions, these studies "as a whole
provide some support for the effectiveness of family preservation services"

(223). However, they also identified a number of recurring concerns that include

- the indication that the subjects were not at "imminent risk" of out-of-home placement, thus raising the question about adequacy of targeting of services;
- the unclear nature of the interventions provided to the experimental and control groups (the interventions varied across the participants); and
- the inability to make comparisons across diverse studies, resulting from the lack of uniformity in relation to the definition of such variables as child placement, intensity and nature of services, and follow-up intervals.

On the basis of the above review Blythe, Salley and Jayaratne (1994:223) concluded as follows:

Clearly, intensive family preservation programs have the potential to help many families avoid unnecessary placement of children, especially when the programs reach the appropriate population. In a short period, several studies have been produced that advance the knowledge of family preservation practice and point to challenges for the next round of research. Although family preservation programs have been evaluated more frequently than other programs for this population, lingering scepticism regarding their effectiveness calls for additional and more rigorous research.

Berry (1997) also advocates further research on the effectiveness of services and presents a cogent, comprehensive, and authoritative examination of the family preservation movement and related evaluative research. In particular, she analyzes the policy framework of permanency planning for children and its significance for family preservation, examines family preservation practice methods and service models and their effectiveness, and discusses pertinent program, policy, and research issues. In so doing she sheds considerable light in a crucial area of child and family welfare theory and practice and stimulates others in the field to engage in a more balanced discourse regarding such a complex topic. Above all, Berry demonstrates that family preservation services need to be clearly de-

lineated, tested, and refined before programs can be replicated and compared to one another in a systematic fashion. Her overall conclusion is
noteworthy:

> While controlled studies of the effectiveness of these programs have
> found mixed rates of placement prevention, many researchers and
> scholars in the field agree that family preservation is an appropriate
> service model for many families, particularly those in acute — not
> chronic — crisis and when used discriminately as one element in an
> array of child welfare services. (Berry 1997:193).

In the future, research must continue to focus on outcomes beyond placement prevention alone (McCroskey and Meezan 1997), methods of determining what services are effective for which presenting problems (Littell,
Schuerman, and Chak 1994), and the proper role of these services within
the continuum of child and family services (Wells and Tracy 1996).[4]

Preservation of Family Ties

Preserving family ties when children or youths are placed in out-of-home
care is an ongoing challenge in family and children's services. This is a
challenge that practitioners need to address actively and consistently, as the
natural bonds between these youngsters and their families are still important
even after they are separated from each other.

Consistent parental visiting between parents and other family members
and youngsters in out-of-home care represents an effective means of preserving family ties. Indeed, "the findings of various studies have highlighted
the crucial role played by parental visiting or other parent-child contact in
the outcome of the placement as well as the child's functioning and development" (Pecora et al. 2000:79).[5] Davis et al. (1996), for example, found
that the majority of children and youths who had regular visits with their
parents at the level recommended by the courts were eventually reunified.
On the basis of findings such as these, various researchers and practitioners
have emphasized the importance of parent-child and family child visiting
in foster care. As Pecora et al. (2000:80) observe:

> In addition to promoting family reunification, parent-child contact can
> enhance social functioning by assuring the child that he or she has

not been rejected, helping the child and parents to understand why he or she cannot live at home, preventing the child's idealization or villainization of the parent, and helping parents maintain their relationships with their children.

Utilizing the Help of the Family's Extended Kinship System to Avert or Reduce Duration of Placement

Two methods of involving the extended family system are described below: kinship care and family group conferencing.

Kinship Care

Kinship care, also described as relative foster care or family foster care, is an ancient phenomenon; it consists of care by related members of the extended family network. When children need to be placed in out-of-home care, kinship care is increasingly the first option considered.

As explicated by Wilson and Chipungu (1996:387), kinship care is favored by practitioners and families, since it

- enables children to live with persons whom they know and trust,
- reduces the trauma children may experience when they are placed with persons who are initially unknown to them,
- reinforces children's sense of identity and self-esteem, which flows from their family history and culture,
- facilitates children's connections to their siblings, and
- strengthens the ability of families to give children the support they need.

In recent years there has been an enormous increase in the use of kinship care by public child welfare agencies throughout the country, particularly with families of color. As Crumbley and Little (1997:xiii) explain, this increase "has been attributed to parallel increases in divorce, marital separation, alcohol and other drug abuse, parental incarceration, child abuse, and AIDS-related parental incapacity or morality." In response to such an increase, various authors have formulated practice principles and strategies that are useful for practitioners as well as administrators. These focus on such areas as the following:

- principles and strategies for enhancing staff relationships with kin-ship parents and facilitating the empowerment of families (Nisi-voccia 1996),
- clinical issues, assessment and intervention strategies, and case management approaches (Crumbley and Little 1997),
- practice models that build on research (Hegar and Scannapieco 1999),
- culturally sensitive, strength-based, and family-centered service de-livery models (Jackson, Mathews, and Zuskin (1998),
- improving practice through application of research findings (Glee-son and Hairston 1999), and
- practice standards in the areas of assessment of kinship families, services for children, birth parents, and kinship parents, monitor-ing, supervision, and training, and program coordination (Child Welfare League of America 1994).

The rapid and extensive growth in kinship care raises numerous issues that should be considered. In particular, as noted in a report of the National Commission on Family Foster Care (1991:92), there is considerable con-fusion and controversy in this practice area:

Of concern are the complex dynamics that lead to placement (in kin-ship care); internal family relationships; family-agency relationships; legal and child welfare factors concerning both protection and nur-turing, permanency planning, monitoring and supervision; and equity and financial costs.

On the whole, however, kinship care is a valuable approach to providing services to many children who must be separated from their parents. In particular, "if provided in a high quality manner with adequate parent sup-ports, it can offer stable placements that maintain family continuity and promote child well-being" (Pecora et al. 2000:355).[6] The following case illustrates some of the practice issues involved in work with kinship care families.[7]

Jack is a nine-year-old Caucasian boy living with his maternal grand-mother, who has assumed kinship foster care. He has been diagnosed with pervasive developmental disorder, fetal alcohol syndrome, and mild mental retardation. His biological mother abused drugs and alcohol during her pregnancy with Jack; she drops by a few times a year and causes "havoc" for the grandmother because she finds fault with how her mother is raising Jack. The grandmother feels torn; she has a sense of loss over her own daughter and deep concern for Jack, but she also has a sense of deprivation and resentment over what will most surely become a permanent placement.

Jack is enrolled in a public school classroom for children with severe emotional disturbances. He attends regular education, art, music, and gym classes. He is sent to the principal's office several times a week because of disruptive classroom behavior. He is absent from school several days each week because the grandmother has difficulty getting him ready for school.

The grandmother lives in a small rural community in a trailer that is cluttered with "happy meal" containers and trash, such that there is little living space left. The trailer also has a distinct odor. The family lives on Supplemental Social Security and Social Security benefits, but the mother has a habit of bailing friends and neighbors out, and her own bills thus accumulate. Utility shut-offs are imminent. Jack's clothes are too small for his body size and he is in need of a haircut, which the grandmother says she cannot afford. His schoolmates tease him by calling him a girl.

The mother wants to gain control of Jack's behavior and improve her relationship with him. Jack has few verbal communication skills and does not know how to complete self-care skills on his own. The mother finds bathing and bathroom tasks too much for her now. She also does not know how to play with Jack.

In the above situation the family needs skills and resources in order to provide for Jack's care and safeguard as well as promote his well-being. Advocacy with the school system is an essential component, since the school is a major source of support and respite for the grandmother. Short and long term goals are needed around school attendance. The grandmother needs assistance to request additional accommodations for Jack's education based on his disabilities. Another focus is on behavior management at home. Finally, helping all family members decide on a workable plan for the future while maintaining some sense of connection for the child is an important focus as well.

Family Group Conferencing

A Family Group Conference is a meeting between a family and members of their extended kinship group in which the family members and significant support persons decide on a plan to ensure safety within the family (Pennell and Burford 2000). Family group conferences are consistent with several other practice trends in child welfare, including kinship care, strengths perspective, empowerment, and partnerships with families (Merkel-Holguin 1996a). Family group conferencing has been applied and adapted for use in the United Kingdom (Marsh and Crow 1997), Canada (Pennell and Burford 2000), and in several states in the United States, such as Illinois and North Carolina (Connolly and McKenzie 1999).

The family group conference process is derived from two primary models of family decision making: the Family Group Conference model, which was developed and legislated in 1989 in New Zealand (Hassall 1996), and the Family Unity Meeting model developed by the American Bar Association's Center on Children and the Law (Hardin et al. 1996). Both models actively involve family members in making decisions for themselves; however, the models differ in terms of the professional role and composition of the family members during the actual meeting. For example, one of the key principles of the Family Group Conference model, in contrast to the Family Unity model, is for the entire family, with no one excluded, to have a private meeting without professionals being present when plans are developed.

Regardless of the model adopted, the process of holding a family group conference generally proceeds in the following stages: referral to hold a meeting, preparation and planning, holding the meeting, and activities and follow-up subsequent to the meeting, including approval and implementation of the plan. The preparation phase is the most active and critical time for social work involvement and can take several weeks or more to complete. Among the issues that must be addressed are ensuring safety, defining what is meant by family, inviting family members and other relevant participants, involving offenders, communicating participants' roles, managing unresolved family issues, and coordinating logistics of travel and meeting place (Merkel-Holguin 1996a).

As Pennell and Burford (2000:131) note, "Family group conferencing integrates efforts to advance child and adult safety and strengthens family unity while expanding its meaning." The planning phase is very important for identifying family members, getting the right people to the meeting, and fostering a safe atmosphere for decision making. One family conference project uses an adaptation of the Social Network Map (Tracy and Whittaker 1990) to identify key participants. Measures to ensure safety are often required and include involving in the meeting support persons for victims of abuse, enlisting the help of a family member who carries authority to take responsibility for keeping violent family members in control during the meeting, excluding the participation of offenders if safety cannot be assured, and planning regular follow-up and monitoring of the approved plan.

Family group conferences may involve many (ten to thirteen) participants (including family members, extended family, and formal or informal support persons) and may last several hours. Such meetings typically begin with an opening ritual meaningful to the culture of the family and the sharing of ground rules, followed by information shared by service providers and family members.[8] The following case examples illustrate family group conferences in action.

Members of an extended family network agree to attend a family group conference to create a plan for two of their preschool age children, both members of a Native American tribe, who are in the custody of the child welfare agency. The children came into care because of domestic violence and prenatal drug use. The family meeting included eleven family members; other tribal members participated via telephone conference calling. The family discussed who might be available to raise the children and then developed three plans in rank order of preference. The court approved the plan that had the children remain in the home of the maternal aunt and uncle, which became a stable home for them.[9]

In another case situation, the family and extended family members met together on behalf of a fifteen-year-old girl, Wendy, who had been referred to the child welfare agency after showing up at school with a black eye. The girl said that her father had hit her because she had tried to sell some drugs. Ultimately, the police were involved, but no charges were brought against either Wendy or her father. During the investigation the father's violent behavior, past criminal record, and alcoholism were uncovered.

Wendy took notes during the family's private deliberation time. The family developed a plan that included counseling for the children and for the parents in the family, curfews for the children, regular family outings, separate housing for the father until he completed treatment, and a safety plan. This family had no further allegations or incidents of abuse in the twelve-month follow-up period (Adapted from Burford, Pennell, and MacLeod 1999:279–280).[10]

As the above examples illustrate, the decisions made by participants in family group conferences revolve both around service provision (child care, addictions treatment, transportation) and child placement (kinship care). Key elements to success include the use of written plans, adequate funding and availability of services, and regular monitoring of implementation. While definitive outcome data using strong research designs are just emerging, one study of family group conferencing demonstrated that both family unity and safety for all family members (women and children) were enhanced for conference participants, as opposed to a comparison group of families not receiving family group conferences (Pennell and Burford 2000).

Involving Children and Youths in Service Planning

Family friendly service delivery approaches must also be child friendly, meaning that services are acceptable and understandable to the child as well as the adult caregivers. The involvement of children and youths in the development of service plans must always be based upon an accurate assessment of the child's developmental and chronological age, any special learning needs of the child, and the cultural context in which the child is being raised. Many of the approaches to promoting family involvement are also applicable to children and youths; these include a focus on strengths, home-based service delivery, use of family conferencing techniques, skills-building approaches, and clearly written service contracts. Several assessment instruments described in appendix 1, such as the placement genogram (McMillen and Groze 1994) and the child's ecomap (Fahlberg 1991), allow children to express their perspectives and reactions to events.

Children and youths can express their preferred plan for permanency.[11] Some older youths would prefer a long-term foster care or kinship guardianship care option as opposed to adoption or living in a group setting. In addition, allowing sibling groups to remain together should be given preference over plans that separate brothers and sisters unnecessarily, unless there are valid reasons to do the latter. Children and youths can also be involved in making service decisions, such as establishing change goals for themselves and their family. For example, home-based family intervention programs typically require older children and youths to sign the family's consent for service and the service plan, thereby engaging them in the helping process and promoting their commitment to the outcome. Such practices are consistent with the profession's ethical standards on self-determination and informed consent. Moreover, older youths can help assess their self-sufficiency and life skills (Nollan et al. 2000) and participate in the development of written service contracts to ready themselves for emancipation and interdependent living (Maluccio, Krieger, and Pine 1990). A major aspect of such preparation is developing and maintaining the essential connections and relationships with others that are helpful as well as necessary in meeting their common human needs.

Child and Family Safety Planning

Assessment and intervention to promote family and child safety are typically addressed in the early stages of family-centered service plans. Many service programs require a signed safety contract before beginning work with the family; this contract would include issues relating to use of physical violence and the presence of weapons or firearms in the home. Written contracts regarding how to respond to suicide ideation or threats are also commonly used. Many of the techniques described in this section are intended to establish a safe working environment both for the family and the social worker.

During family visits or sessions there are many clinical strategies or practical tips that can be used to reduce the potential for violence and prevent feelings from escalating out of control. Clinical strategies represent "good" practice techniques, such as

- ensuring that the engagement process has been successful before change efforts are initiated,
- ensuring that the change goals established are important to the family,
- making sure that each family member's perspective has been heard and understood equally,
- identifying and focusing on strengths in addition to problem areas,
- obtaining an accurate assessment of how the family responds to stress, including use of violence and alcohol and drug use,
- obtaining accurate and current referral information to determine the level of risk at the outset,
- using active listening and "I" messages (versus confrontation) to defuse stressful situations,
- teaching family members specific skills that will help to reduce stress, such as anger management techniques,
- knowing when to take short breaks or otherwise change the pace when feelings run high,
- being able to assess verbal and nonverbal cues that anger is escalating (e.g., pacing, clenched mouth, yelling) and reacting appropriately, and
- consulting one's supervisor when safety issues interfere with the work.[12]

Additionally, some of the practical tips that workers can use in dealing with a highly volatile situation include

- familiarizing yourself with the area to be visited,
- positioning yourself so you can see what is happening and can leave easily if necessary,
- limiting carrying personal or valuable possessions with you during family sessions,
- maintaining your automobile in good condition and learning the safest route to and from the neighborhood if you make home visits,
- learning how to decline offers of food if you assess that it is not safe to accept refreshments,

- using neutral settings for family settings, and
- following your instincts if you feel unsafe and take the appropriate action (e.g., leave, call police, call supervisor) (adapted from the National Resource Center on Child Abuse and Neglect [1997] and the Annie E. Casey Foundation [n.d.a]).

A wide range of clinical interventions are also helpful to prevent the likelihood of violence in between sessions with the family. These include helping the family to establish a daily routine, changing the environment so as to eliminate triggers for violence, monitoring the family via phone calls, homework assignments, and written contracts (Annie E. Casey Foundation n.d.a). A specific type of contract to deal with crisis events, called a *crisis card*, may maintain safety and stability in between planned sessions or visits with the family. Crisis cards are similar to contracts, but they enable people to become more aware of and change their response to their emotions (Annie E. Casey Foundation n.d.b; Kinney, Haapala, and Booth 1991). Following is a brief description of how to construct a crisis card.

The first step is to identify situations and feelings on a scale of 1 *(worst)* to 10 *(best)*. For example, a parent may identify 4 as the "cutting" point at which she is so angry that she is likely to physically abuse her child. She knows that if she gets below a 4 it is very difficult for her to regain control of her emotions. At that point she looks at her crisis card and sees a number of alternative behaviors that she has previously brainstormed with her worker:

- call my friend Mary,
- call my case worker,
- ask my neighbor to come over,
- count to ten and take a deep breath, and
- listen to calm music.

The alternative coping behaviors listed on the crisis card, as illustrated above, should be easy for the family member to accomplish, given the fact that they are not at their best when they will be beginning these activities. Usually, when a crisis card is used, the family member is asked to rate herself or himself at several points during the course of a day. In this way the worker is able to monitor the situation over time. As the family member gains more practice in the use of this technique, adjustments can be made as needed to maintain safety. An alternate method of using the crisis card is in a group.

As an example, teen mothers could complete individual crisis cards as a support group activity and could then check in between sessions with a "support buddy" from the group. In such an example, members of the group as well as the group facilitator would be able to monitor implementation.

Termination

Closing a case can be a valuable and productive phase of the helping process, if its particular challenges are recognized and met by worker and client. As suggested earlier, some examples of indicators for considering case closure are

- problems or needs that contributed to the initial need for service have been reduced or ameliorated,
- basic needs are met,
- children are no longer in danger,
- family members have learned new skills conducive to safe and healthy family functioning, and
- family communication is effective.

In addition, client-worker contact can be brought to a close in a way that serves to promote each person's competence. It is not uncommon for clients, especially children, to regress right before termination. Just at the point when goals are being met, the client presents a new problem. These are often natural reactions to endings and to loss of attachment. In such situations workers should strive to help clients appreciate the progress that they have made, solidify their gains, and strengthen skills for anticipating and coping with future life challenges and crises. Workers can assist clients in identifying the skills and coping patterns that they have effectively employed in their efforts to solve problems or achieve their goals; they can also help clients to understand how they may call on these skills in the future.

At termination clients should also have established connections to needed formal and informal support services and should know how to access additional help if needed. Most families are not totally independent, but rather are interdependent, with a system of support in place to help them meet their needs. To this end family-centered practitioners typically establish termination plans that include planned follow-up or booster sessions, referrals to other needed services, and opportunities for families and older youths to be more involved in their neighborhoods and communities. For example, a family member who has completed alcohol or drug treatment might be in need of resources, connections, and supports to maintain a sober lifestyle. In the termination phase as well as throughout the helping process, workers should incorporate as much as possible *youth development services*, that is, services that help build skills and competencies for meeting their personal and social needs. A critical aspect of such services is collaboration with youths to strengthen or regain their connection to community; also important is working with communities to encourage their support for young people. These approaches are discussed more fully in the next chapter on social network interventions.

The termination phase can also serve as a vehicle for workers to assess their own performance as well as the agency's services. Such assessment, of course, is an ongoing part of the intervention. As we shall discuss further in chapter 9 in connection with the theme of evaluation of outcomes, the termination phase provides an opportunity for family members as well as practitioners to engage in the process of evaluation in a more purposive and systematic fashion. In the above-noted chapter, we shall present various tools that may be used to measure changes in the family's functioning and situation. The ecomap, for example, can serve to show graphically the changes that have occurred and/or the challenges that still lie ahead.

We have described intervention approaches that are consistent with the basic guidelines for child-focused and family-centered practice presented earlier in the text. These intervention approaches and techniques are intended to promote child and family safety, stability, and well-being though direct work with families and children. In chapter 7 we turn our attention to intervention into the child and family's broader social environment, drawing upon our knowledge of the powerful role of social support networks in family interactions and relationships.[13]

Notes

1.   See Henggeler et al. (1998) and Kinney, Haapala, and Booth (1991) for specific parent training curricula and techniques to overcome barriers that make skill acquisition particularly difficult for some families.

2. For example, the concept of "education" among many Latino families refers to bringing up a moral and responsible child, teaching children manners, respect for elders, and the difference between right and wrong (Shartrand 1996).
3. See Fraser, Pecora, and Haapala (1991) for detailed information on the wide range of clinical and concrete services that can be provided. Berry (1997) also has an excellent chapter on the use of concrete services within home-based services. In addition, Tracy (2001) reviews the role of concrete services, with several detailed examples.
4. See Walton, Sandau-Beckler, and Mannes (2001) for discussion of balancing family-centered services and child well-being. Also see Berry (1997); Berry, Cash, and Brook (2000); Littell and Schuerman (1995); Maluccio, Ainsworth, and Thoburn (2000); Pecora et al. (2000); and Westat et al. (2001) for reviews and discussion of recent family preservation research and evaluation.
5. Practice principles and strategies for using parent-child visiting planfully in family reunification services are extensively considered by Aldgate (1980), Hess and Proch (1988, 1993), Palmer (1995), and Warsh, Maluccio, and Pine (1994). Wright (2001) describes "best practice" in planning and implementing parent-child visiting in out-of-home care.
6. For extensive discussion of kinship care, including reviews of research studies, see Hegar and Scannapieco (1999) and Gleeson and Hairston (1999). For a comprehensive look at the key elements in providing quality of care in kinship and nonrelated foster homes, see Shlonsky and Berrick (2001). In addition, the CWLA *Standards of Excellence for Kinship Care Services* (Child Welfare League of America 2000b) outline goals for achieving quality supports and services for children and families in kinship care. Agathen, O'Donnell, and Wells (1999) describe various instruments for measuring the quality of care in kinship foster homes.
7. We thank Jennifer A. Crisman Morrison for preparing the case vignette used for discussion purposes.
8. As an example, see the Family Group Decision Making Project Manual available online at http://social.chass.ncsu.edu/jpennell/fgdm /manual/ApndxC.htm (May 15, 2001).
9. We thank Kellie Steele Adams for providing this example.
10. We thank Gale Burford, Joan Pennell, and Susan MacLeod for permission to include this example.

11. Guardian ad litems and court appointed special advocates (CASAs) represent the child's point of view and interest in judicial proceedings. See Litzelfelner (2000) for a recent evaluation of the impact of these programs on placement and permanency.
12. See Turnell and Edwards (1999) for discussion of a safety-oriented approach to child protection services.
13. See appendix 4 for description of electronic resources in the area of family and children's services.

Questions for Discussion

1. Using the guidelines for child-focused family-centered practice, select a case example from this chapter (or from your own practice or field setting) and consider the major priorities for the family. How is the service plan addressing each of the guidelines?

2. Contact an agency in your community (such as a child guidance clinic, domestic violence service, or family service agency). Inquire how the agency views family preservation and what family-based services it offers. How does the agency balance child safety and family preservation? On the basis of the information that you gather, how would you respond to the question "Do services to avert placement pose a safety risk for the child?"

3. How adequate are your agency's policies and services in the area of birth family–children visiting? What suggestions or recommendations would you offer to the agency for improvement in this area of practice?

4. Plan a focus group with kinship care providers in your agency or community, for the purpose of obtaining their suggestions and recommendations on improving kinship care services. Present these at a staff meeting for consideration and action.

5. Discuss the role of concrete services in your agency or field setting, including factors that act as facilitators or barriers to the use of concrete services. What recommendations might you make to improve the use and effectiveness of concrete services?

Suggestions for Further Information

Berry, M. 1997. *The Family at Risk: Issues and Trends in Family Preservation Services.* Columbia: University of South Carolina Press.

Child Welfare League of America. 1994. *Kinship Care: A Natural Bridge*. Washington, D.C.: CWLA.

Corcoran, J. 2000. Family interventions with child physical abuse and neglect: A critical review. *Children and Youth Services Review* 22 (7): 563–591.

Hegar, R. L. and M. Scannapieco, eds. 1999. *Kinship Foster Care: Policy, Practice, and Research*. New York: Oxford University Press.

Lindblad-Goldberg, M., M. M. Dore, and L. Stern. 1998. *Creating Competence from Chaos: A Comprehensive Guide to Home-Based Services*. New York: Norton.

Pecora, P. J., J. K. Whittaker, A. N. Maluccio, and R. P. Barth. 2000. *The Child Welfare Challenge: Policy, Practice, and Research*. 2d ed. New York: de Gruyter.

Rycus, J. S. and R. C. Hughes, 1998. *Field Guide to Child Welfare*. Vols. 1–4. Washington, D.C.: CWLA.

7 Social Network Intervention

We now turn to the role of social support as an integral component of social work practice with children, youths, and families. Social support can occur spontaneously, as in one neighbor bringing meals to another, or it can occur in professionally arranged helping networks, such as Meals on Wheels. Formal social services staffed by paid human service professionals, as described in chapter 3, often provide social support as either the sole or partial focus of their service; for example, a social worker facilitating a parent education group may provide information, resource referrals, skills training, and emotional support for the participants. Informal support, which is the primary focus of this chapter, can be delivered by kinship networks, volunteers, or local community groups. A social support network is that subset of a network that provides support on a regular basis (Whittaker and Garbarino 1983). In many cases social workers can be the catalysts that mobilize and enhance various forms of informal helping to benefit individual clients, family members, and communities.

After briefly considering the rationale and values pertaining to social support intervention with children and families, in this chapter we discuss how social support is conceptualized and defined and then present guidelines for assessing social support, establishing support goals, choosing a strategy to mobilize support, and balancing child and family support needs with attention to cultural context. We examine four broad categories of social support interventions — from placement prevention to postplacement services — and offer relevant examples. We conclude with suggestions for supporting social workers in child and family practice.

Rationale and Values

Social support interventions can address the child's needs for optimal development, the family's survival and developmental needs, and neighborhood, community, and environmental needs. As noted in chapter 1, recent studies of stress, coping, and resiliency in childhood indicate that family support, parental monitoring and involvement, a caring neighborhood, and a caring school environment are among the key protective factors for healthy child development (Search Institute 1996; Smith and Carlson 1997). Social support interventions play an important role in helping families carry out the child-rearing task, especially when it is complicated by other child, family, or environmental stressors. Informal helping networks provide emotional and material supports to families, serve as role models for parenting, and often link parents with outside sources of help and advice (Powell 1979). If the family is formed through adoption, greater additional support has been associated with more favorable adoption outcomes, including closer and more positive parent-child relationships (Groze 1996).

For families that lack the needed skills or resources to parent successfully and safely, social support networks can provide child-rearing advice and monitoring of parental behavior (DiLeonardi 1993; Thompson 1995; Thompson, Laible, and Robbennolt 1997). Last, social support interventions can be a key feature of community development efforts, improving relationships between formal organizations and community members, offering an alternative method to reach out to those in need, and providing an outlet and means for people to feel a sense of community involvement and attachment. Social support, especially from kinship networks, is a vital resource particularly for immigrant families.

Social support serves both to prevent stress and to buffer the impact of stressful events. A wide range of studies document that people with more social and environmental resources are in better physical and mental health and are better able to adapt to and cope with life changes (Barrera 1986; Cohen and Wills 1985; Thompson 1995). The values underpinning social support interventions with children and families include the recognition that

- all families need support,
- child development is enhanced through healthy parent-child relationships and a strong family unit,

- most parents want to be successful parents,
- families are influenced by cultural and ethnic values that are reflected in culturally specific patterns of giving and receiving help, and
- parenting is influenced by the parents' ability to deal with the environment in such areas as work, school, and social networks (Child Welfare League of America 1989).

Conceptualizing Social Support Practice

Social support is best thought of as "a multidimensional construct with both functional and structural components" (DePanfilis 1996:38). There are several types or forms of social support: emotional support, such as having someone offer encouragement, informational support, such as having someone offer advice, and concrete or tangible support, such as having someone help with a chore (Tracy and Whittaker 1990). The functions that social support may perform within families include the following, as identified by Thompson (1995):

- emotional sustenance and a sense that you are not alone,
- counseling advice and guidance in dealing with challenging life events,
- access to information, services, material resources, and tangible assistance,
- skills acquisition and training,
- social control and monitoring of family behavior, and
- developmental remediation of the victims of child abuse and neglect.

Social networks provide the structure through which support is made available to families and can be described in terms of the nature and qualities of network relationships. As delineated by Thompson (1995), these include

Network size — the total number of people and groups in the network.
Composition — the variety of groups or clusters in the network, such as household members, relatives, friends, neighbors, and work associates.

Frequency of contact — how often network members interact with one another.

Dispersion — the ease with which network members can contact each other and communicate.

Stability — how long people have known one another, consistency of network composition over time.

Valence — the emotional quality of network relationships (positive or negative).

Reciprocity — extent to which the social support provided is balanced by support received (mutually supportive or unidirectional).

Multiplexity (Multidimensionality) — the number of different supportive functions assumed by individuals within a social network.

Homogeneity — extent to which network members share common attributes.

Density — extent to which network members are associated with each other.

Several other concepts are important to note. *Perceived* support refers to the extent to which people subjectively experience support from network relationships. *Enacted* support refers to the actual utilization of support resources. Enacted support may not be perceived as supportive, depending on the support provider, the timing of support, or the type of support delivered. *Network orientation* refers to beliefs, attitudes, or expectations regarding the use of network relationships to cope with a problem (Vaux, Burda, and Stewart 1986). Some people have adequate networks in terms of size and composition, but they do not use them because of a negative network orientation. Another barrier to use of social network resources is inadequate social skills — difficulty in requesting help, developing relationships, and maintaining supportive social ties. As Beeman (1997) and Crittenden (1985) have demonstrated, the most vulnerable of families may lack social skills and have significant difficulties in interacting with their personal social networks.[1]

Assessing Social Support and Social Networks

Given the significance of social support, and its complexity, a necessary first task in practice with children and families is to complete an accurate assessment of social network resources, building on the framework for assessment presented in chapter 1, which reflects special attention to resources in the family's neighborhood, community, and broader environment. All too often important social resources are not identified at all or are identified too late to be of any help in implementing a case plan. As the following example illustrates, network members who remain uninvolved may sabotage the best of intervention plans:

A single mother raising a toddler was referred to the child welfare agency because of child neglect issues. The safety of the home environment was a high priority, and an initial safety plan was developed. One change made to the physical environment was the installation of safety plugs to all electric outlets in the home. However, a few days later all the safety plugs had been removed. The mother told the worker, "My sister read that kids pull the plugs out and swallow them, so I took them all out."

It is important, then, to establish early on a working knowledge of key network resources in a particular case.[2] The need for social network interventions should be considered part of the overall plan made with the family. The following questions serve as guidelines for assessment of social networks and social supports:[3]

• *Who is in the network, how are they related to the client, and who could be potential members?* It is important to point out that more social network resources do not necessarily imply more social support. People may be surrounded by large social networks but may not feel supported or may not be receiving the supports they need. Findings from a descriptive study of social networks with high-risk families revealed that the functional properties of social networks were more critical to assess than the structural features alone. Social network size was a poor indicator of support, because the majority of respondents had people in their network who were almost always critical of them. The proportion of critical network members was negatively related to emotional support. Reciprocity was also positively related to some types of support, particularly concrete support (Tracy and Whittaker 1990).
• *What are the strengths and capabilities of the social network?* The strengths that might be examined include the number of supportive rela-

tionships, the variety of supportive relationships, the types of support available (emotional, concrete, and informational), and the reciprocity among helping relationships. There is no one perfect network, rather, there are networks that meet individual or family needs to a greater or lesser extent.

• *What are the gaps in social support needs?* Is there a lack of fit between the types of support network members are willing or capable of providing and the types of support the client needs or desires? Different social ties may provide different supports. Relationships with a wide variety of people ensures provision of all types of needed support (Walker, Wasserman, and Wellman 1993).

• *What relationships in the network are based on mutual exchange? Does reciprocity seem to be an issue for the client?* Is the client always giving to others and thereby experiencing stress and drain? Or is the client always a recipient of help, appearing to be a drain on the network, with the result that network members are stressed and overburdened? Some networks may be a source of excessive demands and caregiving responsibilities, particularly for women (Fischer 1982; Belle 1982). Or the network may involve intense close reciprocal relationships, as described in a classic study by Stack (1974). Neglecting families, for example, are less likely to be reciprocal to their neighbors, less likely to help their neighbors or be viewed as able to help others, and thereby more likely to be stigmatized and excluded from local networks of support (Polansky, Gaudin, and Ammons 1985).

• *What network members are identified as responsive to requests for help, effective in their helping, accessible, and dependable?* Do sufficient numbers of network members meet these conditions? These are the people and resources that would most likely be an asset to any intervention plan. Some clients do not have a social network that supports their efforts for change; they may be receiving conflicting advice from network members or outright discouragement for their pursuit of change.

• *What network members are critical of the client in a negative or demanding way?* Is the client surrounded by a network that is perceived as negative, nonsupportive, and/or stress producing? Some existing social networks may be negative in the sense that they are critical or encourage harmful or antisocial behaviors such as drug abuse (Dunlap 1992).

• *What obstacles or barriers limit effective use of social network resources?* Does the client lack supportive resources or skills in accessing resources? For example, he or she may lack some key social and communication skills, such as initiating conversations, offering feedback, asking for help, saying thank you when appropriate, and reciprocating to others. Are network members unable to provide more help because of a lack of skills or knowledge? Have they provided so much support in the past that they are now unwilling or unable to continue to do so? Or, as Thompson (1995) has suggested, are neighborhood network resources also "needy," limited and strained so as to be unable to provide the types of supports and resources most useful for families?

• *How are social support needs prioritized in relation to other presenting problems and needs?* Does the physical environment need further examination? For example, a dangerous neighborhood may be a contributing factor to a family's isolation and distrust of others (Kemp, Whittaker, and Tracy 1997). Poor families, often lacking cars and telephones, may have fewer contacts with network members (Coohey 1996), but may still be emotionally involved with distant network members (Garbarino and Kostelny 1994). Families that have many changes in residence may have less stable networks, with consequences for the types of support upon which they can rely (Gaudin, Polansky, and Kilpatrick 1996).

Mobilizing Support Systems

Following are guidelines that we have found useful in mobilizing support systems within family and children's services.

Setting Goals

Social network interventions are typically directed toward either structural changes in the network itself or functional changes in the nature or quality of social network relationships. Sometimes a structural change is required in order to achieve a functional change (as in changing the composition of a social network through linking with a community resource); at other times, network members must learn new skills in order to provide needed types of support (as in teaching a family member how to respond to psychiatric symptoms) or people must learn how to ask for and respond to supportive behaviors. Some examples of structural changes in setting intervention goals include

- increasing or decreasing the size of the network, as through increasing the number of friends,
- changing the composition of the social network, as in adding new child care resources or reestablishing old network connections, and
- increasing or decreasing frequency of contact with particular social network members.

Functional changes might include increasing or mobilizing various types of support such as concrete emotional or informational support in respite care services for a family, and teaching network members new skills for interaction, as in how to respond to memory losses of an older family member. Some examples of skill-enhancing interventions to facilitate more social support within a particular social network include

- teaching friendship building skills,
- decreasing negative or self-defeating statements,
- increasing positive self-statements and the ability to identify personal strengths,
- developing strategies for handling criticism from others,
- increasing assertive skills,
- increasing communication skills,
- teaching reciprocity skills, and
- developing a plan to ask for help during a crisis period (Kemp, Whittaker, and Tracy 1997).

Balancing Child, Parent, and Family Support Needs

The choice of a social support intervention must also consider balancing the support needs of the child, the parent, and the family as a whole. Some support interventions are directed primarily to parents, as a means of sustaining their role as child caregivers, e.g., a support group for parents of children with chronic illnesses (Mayers and Spiegel 1992; Dreier and Lewis 1991) or a parent group for incarcerated fathers. Other support interventions seek to help the family as a whole, as in a family resource center located in an early childhood care program where literacy training, resource information, and parent-child activities might be offered (Larner 1995). Often neglected are the support needs of the child[4] and the role that social support may play for the child at various developmental stages, as Thompson (1995:62–63) indicates:

> For infants and toddlers social support might be enlisted to provide alternative attachment figures . . . with whom children can develop secure emotional bonds. For preschoolers and grade school children, social support might be oriented toward strengthening peer social skills and integrating children in the positive social networks of age-mates in day care, school, and after school programs. For grade school children, social support to strengthen academic and intellectual competence should also be considered, as well as using supportive interventions to enhance self-esteem and reduce anxiety and depression through a variety of counseling and peer-oriented interventions. In adolescence . . . a broader concern for strengthening extrafamilial peer and adult social support systems is warranted both to provide emotional sustenance and to monitor for self-destructive behavior.

Let us consider, for example, the support needs of older youths transitioning out of care, a theme examined by researchers and practitioners in Maluccio, Krieger, and Pine (1990). Most entered care because of serious histories of maltreatment plus multiple incidents of domestic and community violence. Many have lived in multiple out-of-home placements or have experienced one or more failed reunifications with their families. These youths are ill prepared for independent living. They are often emotionally, intellectually and physically delayed, have support needs in such areas as housing, mental health, social support, and disabilities (cognitive, emotional, behavioral, and social), and lack positive adult role models (Annie E. Casey Foundation 1998a:49). Also, those emancipated from foster care are overrepresented among the homeless population, suggesting that the consequences are high for failure to adapt to community living (Roman and Wolfe 1997).

Youth development services support the acquisition of competencies that lead to a healthy and productive adulthood.[5] These include "access to safe places, challenging experiences, and caring people on a daily basis" (Roth et al. 1999:269). Recent research suggests that young people need "opportunities for physical activity, development of competence and achievement, self-definition, creative expression, positive social interaction with peers and adults, a sense of structure and clear limits, and meaningful participation in authentic work" (Quinn 1999:103). Social support interventions become an important component of youth development and independent living services; interventions may include, among others, maintaining supportive services for longer time periods, facilitating family ties where feasible, and providing social skills and life skills training (Fein, Maluccio, and Kluger 1990). Child and family care is a unique opportunity as well to provide training, mentoring, and support both to the parent and the child (Abandoned Infants Assistance Resource Center 2000).

While there is still much to be learned about children's and youth's social networks, relevant social support interventions might include

- support groups for children experiencing life transitions or losses as in children of divorce, teenage parents, or children of battered women (Farmer and Galaris 1993; Gruszniski, Brink, and Edleson 1988; Thompson and Peebles-Wilkins 1992; Zambelli and De-Rosa 1992);
- peer support groups to promote positive behaviors for runaway youth (Bradley 1997);
- mentoring programs to expose children and youths to positive and credible adult models and lifestyles (Weinreb 1997);
- support services to grandparents, siblings, and extended family members, particularly for children of color (Hirsch et al. 1994; Taylor, Chatters, and Mays 1988);
- peer tutoring and teacher support to enhance school outcomes (Rosenfeld, Richman, and Bowen 2000);
- supervised after-school care and recreation services for "latch-key" children (Belle 1994; Coohey 1998); and
- opportunities for youth to become involved in community service projects and school decision making as a way of "giving back" to others (Weinreb 1997).

A Continuum of Support Interventions

Social network interventions serve different functions, depending on the timing of their delivery. Support needs may vary according to whether an event is anticipated, experienced, or concluded (Jacobson 1986). For example, the support needs of a family receiving placement prevention services may be different from those of a family working toward reunification. Similarly, families at different points in the adoption process face different support challenges. Concurrent case planning dictates that workers in many cases simultaneously consider and balance support needs for different outcomes and services. Kinship care providers must assess their need for support over the life of the child in considering adoption or guardianship options (Gleeson and Hairston 1999). Shared family care, as discussed in chapter 5, is another child welfare service with implications for social support delivery for both the parent and the child.

As just one example of delivery of social support through different points in a continuum of services, below we describe social support interventions as they might apply in work with a family involved in a child protection case (adapted from Tracy et al. 1995):

- *Placement prevention*: Consider supports available to help defuse stress and crisis situations. Work to increase the quality and quantity of social network ties. Utilize positive social support ties as part of safety planning. Link families and youths with prosocial networks, if none currently exists. Typical social support interventions might include parent-to-parent outreach, peer counseling, concrete support, and volunteer linking.
- *Preplacement services*: Consider what supports are available to facilitate the transition to an alternate setting. In the case of kinship care, also consider what types of supports are needed by the kin caregivers. Provide informational support about placement to all parties — biological parents, children, and caregivers (foster or kin). Convene the child's social network for a family group conference to make a plan for the care and protection of the child. Connect caregivers with forms of support needed to care for the child, including resources to support the child's religious, racial, and cultural identity and connections.
- *During placement*: Consider what supports are available to facilitate needed change in the family situation (and what supports or network members are not facilitative of change or have the potential to sabotage change efforts). Provide needed informational, concrete, and emotional supports. Connect the biological family with informal and formal support systems. Continue to support the child and those who care for the child — foster parents, kinship care providers, or group home/residential care staff. Identify supportive resources for concurrent case plans, such as resources for reunification or resources for kinship care or adoption. Mobilize change efforts

and find help or resources that will maintain and monitor the change over time, such as Alcoholics Anonymous as support for sobriety.

• *After-care services/postplacement*: Consider what supports are available to maintain changes over time and through various developmental stages of the child. Work to increase the quantity and quality of social network ties (for the child and parents) and ensure that families (biological families, kinship care providers who have assumed guardianship, and adoptive families) have the skills, information, and connections to mobilize support in the future. Mobilize a prosocial network for the child with appropriate educational and recreational supports. Provide booster sessions for the family (as in postlegalization services), peer counseling (as in parent-to-parent support), and/or ongoing support groups (as in services to adoptive families or families working toward reunification).

Social Support Intervention Strategies

The remaining sections of this chapter describe four major strategies of social network intervention: network facilitation, mutual aid/self-help, natural helper intervention, and volunteer linking and network facilitation.[6]

Network Facilitation

Network facilitation is typically individually tailored, based on identifying the family's use of formal and informal social support resources. Assessment of the strengths and capabilities of the social network is often valuable in deciding whether the family would benefit from changes in their existing social network or whether the family's network should be supplemented with additional members. It is important to assess the following factors:

• network members currently providing little or no support,
• stress-producing network member involvement,
• network members unable to be more supportive because of a lack knowledge or skills,
• network members burned out or overwhelmed with caregiving demands,

- client unable to ask for help appropriately,
- client philosophically or emotionally opposed to accepting help from others, and
- client physically isolated from social network contacts, without the means to meet new network members (adapted from Kemp, Whittaker, and Tracy 1997).

The following case example, set within the context of multisystemic treatment, illustrates network facilitation to prevent placement of a delinquent adolescent.[7] The social support strategies employed enlarged the resources available to the family, balanced child and parent needs, and served to monitor for safety.

Joe Smith was a thirteen-year-old boy living with his mother and older sister in government-subsidized housing in a low-income neighborhood. Joe was referred by juvenile court because he was at imminent risk of incarceration as a result of chronic delinquent behavior. Joe's delinquent behavior was linked primarily with lack of parental monitoring, which, in turn, allowed him to associate with deviant peers.

The worker helped Ms. Smith to find ways of dealing with this problem. As a result, Ms. Smith agreed to allow her son to play football, where Joe knew several prosocial peers. Social network interventions, such as linking Joe with the football coach, were needed to implement this plan. The mother also wanted help to monitor Joe's whereabouts after school hours. Ultimately, her brother helped Joe get to football practice. The family's church helped finance the costs involved in being a part of the team. Joe attended an after-school program on days when there was no football practice (adapted from Henggeler et al. 1998:223).

Network meetings are frequently used to solidify new relationships as well as to enhance the functioning of or reconnect to old relationships. During a network meeting, participants discuss the client's situation, develop a plan of action and support, and learn new information or skills to assist in helping. Network meetings can be useful in reconnecting past network members; some network members may have dropped out of a client's network because they were not able to respond appropriately to the client's level of need (Morin and Seidman 1986).

In addition, as described in chapter 6, family group conferencing can be thought of as a specialized form of network meeting in which members of the extended family and neighborhood are drawn together to discuss the situation affecting the child's safety and develop a plan to address family needs (Fuchs 2000). Family group conferences are generally held in three stages: preparing for the conference, holding the conference so as to ensure that the family is the decision-making body, and approving and implementing the plan. It is during the planning stage that social network resources are accessed and mobilized. Some family group conferencing projects have used social network mapping tools to identify key network members (Pennell and Burford 1995; Burford and Hudson 2000). Linkage skills are most important here and generally proceed in three stages: identifying, engaging and accessing resources, developing a plan to make the linkage, and ensuring that the linkage maintains over time (Kemp, Whittaker, and Tracy 1997).

Mutual Aid/Self-Help

Mutual aid, or self-help, mobilizes relationships between people who share common tasks, goals, or problems (Gitterman and Shulman 1994). Programs based on mutual aid/self-help may take several forms: a support group for a specific client population or locale, consumer-run programs or drop-in centers, and/or peer matching of one client to another. There are various advantages to self-help approaches:

- recognition and respect for clients as collaborative partners,
- ongoing extension of support to clients,
- support for recovery and maintenance of change
- congruence with client expectations and needs, and
- ability to focus attention and social action on solutions to problems (Whittaker and Tracy 1989).

Self-help groups allow members to learn from one another and to expand their vision of their experience. Four broad types of mutual aid groups have been identified:

- for physical or mental illness,
- for addictive behavior,
- for coping with crisis of transition, and
- for friends and relatives.

There are literally hundreds of self-help organizations, many organized nationwide and with chapters in every state. Participants in a self-help group may realize for the first time that they are not alone and not fully responsible for their situation. These groups reach out to consumers of services (e.g., Recovery Incorporated) and in some cases family members or concerned others (e.g., Alliance of the Mentally Ill, Alzheimer's Association). There are also various self-help clearinghouses and research centers (Powell 1995). (*See appendix 9 for examples of self-help clearinghouses*).

Cameron and Vanderwoerd (1997) describe practice principles for mutual aid organizations within protective services:

- high levels of direct contact among participants (two to five times per week);
- access to a wide variety of helping strategies (e.g., respite, information, concrete services),
- access to a safe and positive network of peers,
- members become friends with one another,
- members become helpers as well as receivers of assistance, and
- support for a broad range of new social roles (e.g., volunteer, student leader).

Starting a self-help group for children and/or families can be a labor-intensive project. Connecting people, establishing a safe meeting place, and providing child care are practical matters for consideration. Yet, there is empirical evidence that such groups can yield positive outcomes for children and families in such areas as independence from formal service providers, integration in the community, and levels of support, stress, and self-esteem (Cameron 2000).

Natural Helper Interventions

Natural helpers are people whom others view as particularly resourceful and understanding, possessing the time and energy to help others; often they are people who have "been there," having faced and overcome life challenges (Pancoast, Parker, and Froland 1983). Natural helpers provide various types of support, link people with professional and other needed services, and in some cases substitute for or supplement professional helping services. A wide range of informal resources, strengths, and assets that might otherwise remain separate from the formal service system can be enlisted in the helping process through natural helper interventions, in such areas as skill building, emotional support, community leadership and networking, resource acquisition, and concrete help. Some examples of activities involving natural helpers are outlined below.

SOME ACTIVITIES OF NATURAL HELPERS[8]

Skill Building:

Helping others learn to get and keep transportation
Helping others learn to get and keep child care/babysitting
Helping others learn to obtain housing
Helping others learn to get and keep clothing
Helping others get repair services
Helping others manage money

Providing Emotional Support:

Listening
Being available, spending time
Mentoring
Providing positive regards

Community Leadership and Networking:

Skills/Resource Exchanges
Developing job clubs
Starting a child care co-op
Organizing family activities
Organizing tutoring
Starting support groups
Joining boards coalitions

Resource Acquisition:

Participation in focus groups
Knowing where to find resources
Attending training workshops

Concrete Help:

Child care
Fixing things
Braiding hair
Gardening

There are several categories of natural helpers. *Gatekeepers* are those people in a position to know how others are doing or to offer help. *Bridge people* are individuals who can introduce professional helpers to members of the community who hold substantial influence over other community members (Annie E. Casey Foundation n.d.c). *Indigenous helpers* are people who perform culturally defined and sanctioned folk remedies. Also, Germain and Gitterman (1996) point out that natural helpers may be children or teenagers and can be found, in addition to neighborhoods and communities, in housing projects, workplaces, and churches. Gilligan (2001) describes the roles of adult mentors in promoting the resilience of children in out-of-home care.

Natural helpers extend the services of formal agencies, reach out to hard-to-reach clients, foster prevention and early intervention services, serve as role models, and remain available for long-term support. Within child and family practice natural helper interventions serve to prevent family stress from building to the point of maltreatment; helpers may hear about situations before they reach crisis proportions and may be better able to support families reluctant to participate in formal services. Natural helpers can also provide monitoring of parental behavior. The Annie E. Casey Foundation program, "People Helping People," is an example of a natural helper/professional partnership as part of a neighborhood approach to drug abuse. The program recruits neighborhood-based foster families and identifies others who wish to provide support and ensure safety to children and families. Direct and supportive family services are planned and coordinated between the child protective agency, the professional team, natural helpers, and extended family. As the team reports: "The idea is that the more everyone feels connected, supported, involved and responded to, the less likely they will be to get angry, lose control, or hurt one another" (Annie E Casey Foundation n.d.c:22). (*See appendix 10 for informational and training materials on alcohol and substance abuse.*)

Natural helpers understand the community's culture and the ways in which problems are defined in the community. Natural helpers may act as cultural consultants and guides (Green and Leigh 1989); for example, they may be able to help nonminority social workers understand traditional helping practices, such as where traditional healing ceremonies can be found among an urban native American population. They may also serve to dispel some of the negative myths and stereotypes surrounding formal social services that may exist in cross-cultural service settings. Gaudin et al. (1990/1991) describe the use of natural helper interventions with a rural child protective population. Clients in rural areas may be miles away from formal treatment services; they and their social workers may need to rely on the help and support provided by natural helpers in the community.[9]

Natural helper intervention strategies may be particularly useful in reaching out to a more diverse group of foster and adoptive families. For example, several reports on the challenges of recruiting African American foster and adoptive families recommend a variety of informal network interventions in combination with culturally sensitive and competent service approaches (Brissett-Chapman and Issacs-Shockley 1997; W. K. Kellogg Foundation n.d.; McRoy, Oglesby, and Grape 1997).

Volunteer Linking and Network Facilitation

Volunteer linking provides yet another means to increase social network size, enhance social network composition, and facilitate supportive exchanges. Examples include Big/Little Brothers and Sisters programs, mentoring for students at risk for school dropout, and volunteer visiting programs for children born with a handicapping condition or hospitalized with a chronic illness. Germain and Gittermain (1996) found that successful volunteer programs provide opportunities for useful and personally rewarding service and have the potential to lead to experiences relevant for future career advancement.

A variant of the volunteer program is self-help, that of matching one or more consumers with one another, as in a buddy system for parents learning behavior management techniques or an alumni group for children in residential treatment programs. Often, consumers of services are in the best position to show others how to negotiate complex service delivery systems. In addition, groups of consumers can advocate for needed system changes, as in parents of children with developmental disabilities advocating for their childrens' educational rights.[10] In this connection it should be noted that the use of computer technology to connect people to one another and provide support is a growing trend in the self-help movement.[11]

Social Support and Culture and Ethnicity

In planning and implementing social support intervention strategies, there should be special attention to the role and significance of culture and ethnicity. Families of color, and many majority families as well, have special concerns about raising children in a multicultural society that does not always ensure an equitable distribution of resources and an appreciation for diversity. It can be difficult and painful to explain the facts of the world to children: "Why are there no women presidents?" "Why is that man on the street asking us for money?" It is even more difficult to see children experience discrimination and oppression in their young lives. Some specific concerns of parents in relation to multicultural issues include

- an acknowledgment of living outside the mainstream and being vulnerable to discrimination and maltreatment,
- ambivalence between passivity and belligerence in situations that may or may not be tainted with discrimination,
- ongoing and vocalized concerns about the child's culture being respected and included in the learning environment,
- questioning if the environment is psychologically safe for any African American, Native American, immigrant child, etc., and
- strategies to impact and influence the child's environment toward the child's success (Ferguson, Tracy, and Simonelli 1993:51).

Moreover, as indicated in chapter 1, immigrant families experience a number of disruptions in family life. One of the basic tasks facing these families is connecting with and integrating into a new culture. They must do this in the face of several stressors: language barriers, homesickness, lack of ethnic contacts, and adjusting to American lifestyles. For most of the immigrant families in contact with social service agencies, issues of poverty, joblessness or underemployment, and discrimination are present. Some refugees have experienced severe hardships in their country of origin: forced relocation, threats, imprisonment, or deaths of family members. These fears are brought with them and may be reflected in fear and distrust of "government " or the "system."

Establishing a social network in the new culture is important in reducing psychological distress — having relatives nearby, friends with whom one can talk, and a large close-knit network can be protective factors (Franks and Faux 1990; Kuo and Tsai 1986; Lynm 1985). The answer for many newcomers is to depend on social networks for vital and useful information: jobs, housing, language classes, child care, and emergency aid. Some immigrants enter this country with the aid of a sponsor or sponsoring organization such as a church or synagogue, which then performs these functions. Other immigrants rely upon their ethnic community to meet these needs before venturing into more mainstream culture. As discussed in chapter 5, the culturagram (Congress 1994) and other similar tools are useful in determining cultural connections that have been maintained by the immigrant family: those that can be utilized as helping resources and those that need strengthening.[12]

Social support intervention strategies, as described in the preceding section, are congruent with culturally sensitive practice, but the following guidelines should be kept in mind in working with diverse client populations:

- understand the family's network as they define it, making sure that culturally significant social support resources, such as grandmothers, maternal aunts/uncles, or elders are included;
- utilize culturally significant helping strategies, as in valuing reciprocity: "What goes around comes around" (Stack 1974);
- include culturally relevant decision-making styles, such as family group conferencing, as discussed in previous chapters;
- respect the natural helper role of religious institutions within the cultural community;
- recognize support that may extend across generations in a family and across geographic distances, as in the base household of an African American family (Hodges 1991);
- learn about culturally relevant agencies, societies, and civic and fraternal organizations, as these may be sources of connection and support, particularly for immigrant families; and

- ensure that the agency or organization is representative of the clientele and provides culturally competent services.

Meeting the Support Needs of Social Workers

We end this chapter with some thoughts on supporting social workers who work with children and families. Workers who themselves are supported and sustained by the organizations for which they work are often better able to meet the support needs of families. Social work with children, youths, and families may involve highly intense personal contact with clients undergoing stressful and sometimes dangerous situations. Work days may be long or unpredictable. Workers need to be highly flexible in the approaches and skills used. Reasonable caseloads and high-quality, ongoing, and dependable supervision support and prepare the worker for these situations. In addition, team supervision and backup, in-service training, and consultation are factors that help practitioners feel confident and prepared for the work ahead. Concrete supports in the form of professional-level salaries and benefits, adequate mileage reimbursement, travel time, car phones, access to books and training materials for use with clients, and copy machines make the task more manageable.

Flexible funding and easy and reliable access to community resources support the worker and family; it is difficult to help troubled families when you are the only game in town — a continuum of services is needed. While some workers personally benefit from time- and stress-management training,[13] it should not be assumed that self-change strategies alone are always effective in reducing stress. Organizational changes may be needed as well. One personal attitude for staff members to adopt is a strengths perspective, while at the same time keeping expectations realistic and attainable; expectations that are unrealistic create additional stress on families as well as workers (Blythe, Tracy, and Kotovsky 1992).

Social workers need to build a collaborative informal professional support network, consisting of key contacts in their own and related agencies. Sometimes formal collaborative relationships exist administratively between two or more service systems; in other cases strong professional relationships begin from the direct service level and work up. Also, most human service professionals will benefit from cross-disciplinary training, in order to better understand their own and other service systems. Last, membership in formal professional organizations and involvement in advocacy or policy related initiatives help social workers feel connected to larger service systems and ultimately more empowered to work on behalf of their clients.

We have explored a range of intervention strategies that draw strength from the family's social environment and emphasize social networks. In particular, we have described the role of network facilitation, mutual aid/self-help, natural helper intervention, and volunteer linking and network facilitation. In the next chapter we focus exclusively on school-based interventions because of the important role of school in the lives of both children and families.

Notes

1. See appendix 9 for a description of electronic resources on support groups and on mentoring.
2. A number of tools are available for identifying social networks and measuring social support; see Streeter and Franklin 1992 for reviews of social support and social network measures. An ecomap indicates supportive and stressful relationships surrounding a family (Hartman 1994). A social network map (Tracy and Whittaker 1990) collects information on the total size and composition of the network and the nature of relationships within the network. Some social network mapping tools have been adapted for use with children (Rosenfield, Richman, and Bowen 2000), while others are focused on understanding support available to the family as a unit (Dunst, Trivette, and Deal 1988).

   Child welfare risk assessment models typically assess or rate the type and amount of social support available to the family as well as the family's willingness and ability to make use of supportive relationships. Increasingly, social support resources are identified in preparations for family group conferencing (Pennell and Burford 1995), team decision-making meetings (Annie E. Casey Foundation n.d.b), and planning for kinship care (Hegar and Scannapieco 1999).
3. These assessment guidelines are drawn from one of the authors' earlier work on social support assessment. See, for example, Kemp, Whittaker, and Tracy (1997) and Tracy and Whittaker (1990).
4. See Nestman and Hurrelmann (1994) for information on social networks and social support in childhood and adolescence and Appendix 4 for tools and instruments on child developmental needs.

5. We thank Martha Roditti for help in reviewing the literature on youth development.
6. Kemp, Whittaker, and Tracy (1997) provide further information on the implementation of these strategies. Our focus here is on selected examples of support interventions with children, youths and families served by a variety of service systems: schools, hospitals, child welfare, mental health, juvenile justice.
7. See Henggeler, Schoenwald, Borduin, Rowland, and Cunningham 1998:223–225 for a complete description of the family assessment and service delivery in this case.
8. Adapted from the Annie E. Casey Foundation (n.d.b).
9. See Gaudin (1993) and Gaudin and Dubowitz (1997) for further information on social support and child neglect.
10. See appendix 5 for description of electronic resources on children's special needs and exceptionalities.
11. A National Self-Help Clearinghouse, http://www.selfhelpweb.org (April 5, 2001), helps people access self-help groups, publishes an online newsletter, and links people to online support groups and chat rooms.
12. Balgopal (2000) focuses extensively on the role of social supports and kinship networks in shaping the experiences of new immigrant groups in the U.S.
13. For a detailed training program to lessen burnout in child welfare, see "The Resiliency Workshop" (Annie E. Casey Foundation n.d.d).

Questions for Discussion

1. From the tools listed in note 2 of this chapter, select one to identify and measure social support and complete an assessment of your own social network. What did you learn about the types of support available to you? If you were to adopt a social support change goal, what would it be?
2. What might be the social support needs and resources of teenage parents?
3. In what ways might a social worker build a more supportive network for a single-parent family raising a child with a developmental disability?
4. How might a social worker rebuild a supportive network for a parent (mother or father) recently discharged from prison?
5. You are providing a parent training program within a child welfare agency. The participants are parents who have abused or neglected their children.

What skills and/or knowledge of social support might you add to the curriculum provided by the agency?

Suggestions for Further Information

Adams, P. and K. Nelson, eds. 1995. *Reinventing Human Services: Community- and Family-Centered Practice*. New York: Aldine de Gruyter.

Cameron, G. and J. Vanderwoerd. 1997. *Protecting Children and Supporting Families: Promising Programs and Organizational Realities*. New York: Aldine de Gruyter.

Gilligan, R. 2001. *Promoting Resilience: A Resource Guide on Working with Children in the Care System*. London: British Agencies for Adoption and Fostering.

Gottlieb, B. H. 1983. *Social Support Strategies*. Beverly Hills: Sage.

Kemp, S., J. K. Whittaker, and E. M. Tracy. 1997. *Person-Environment Practice: The Social Ecology of Interpersonal Helping*. New York: Aldine de Gruyter.

Thompson, R. A. 1995. *Preventing Child Maltreatment Through Social Support*. Thousand Oaks, Cal.: Sage.

Whittaker, J. K., and J. Garbarino. 1983. *Social Support Networks: Informal Helping in the Human Services*. New York: Aldine de Gruyter.

8 School-Based Intervention

Because children spend a significant portion of their day in school, the school environment can have a critical impact on child functioning and is therefore an essential factor to be considered in all phases of social work with children. Following consideration of the rationale for social work involvement in schools, in this chapter we focus on the role and function of social work services for school-age children and their families. Although much applies to independent schools as well, we deal primarily with those social services provided as part of a publicly funded school program. We also discuss the school as a particular assessment and intervention focus for those social workers working with children involved with other service systems such as child welfare, mental health, health, juvenile justice, or in private practice.

Our underlying belief is that interventions that address multiple levels of the child's environment are likely to be more effective and long lasting. As Webb (1996:14) states, "No longer can a practitioner focus primarily on a child's inner world; nor will it suffice to intervene exclusively with the child's family or social environment." As we explore in this chapter, comprehensive school-based interventions provide an excellent opportunity to effect changes and/or prevent problems in multiple levels of the child's environment. Thus school-based interventions can serve wide-reaching purposes, promoting changes to address the child's developmental needs, the family's survival and developmental needs, and neighborhood, community, and environmental needs. In short, school-based interventions take into account the three interrelated aspects of well-being delineated in the conceptual framework of needs and resources to which we have ben referring through-out this text.

Rationale for Social Worker Involvement with Schools

There is a strong tradition in the United States of providing noneduca-tional services in schools. Early in this century universal health and dental services were commonly delivered via schools (Tyack 1992). Settlement workers and philanthropic groups also provided a wide range of social and recreational services to help immigrant children "adapt" to American culture.

The current need for services to meet the nonacademic needs of students remains essentially the same, although the number and types of students in need, and perhaps the needs, have increased dramatically. In chapter 2 we outlined the many risks and vulnerabilities facing children and families in today's world. These same risks are literally brought into the classroom (U.S. Department of Education 1994), making it difficult for even the best teach-ers to teach or students to learn. Schools both reflect, and must adapt to, the social and economic conditions of the communities in which they reside. As Dryfoos (1994:5) argues:

> Today's schools feel pressured to feed children; provide psychological support services; offer health screening; establish referral networks related to substance abuse, child welfare and sexual abuse; cooperate with local police and probation officers; add curricula for preven-tion of substance abuse, teen pregnancy, suicide, and violence; and actively promote social skills, good nutrition, safety, and general health.

Obviously, schools, or for that matter any single service system, cannot meet all these needs. But many see the school as an organizing force for comprehensive, coordinated services. As Gilligan (1998:13) asserts, the school has "potential as an ally for children, a guarantor of basic protection, a capacity builder, a secure base from which to explore the self and the world, an integrator into community and culture, a gateway to adult oppor-tunity, and a resource for parents and communities."

A number of legislative and reform initiatives also support an increased role of schools in addressing nonacademic student needs, as summarized in table 8.1.

Beginning with the National Commission on Excellence in Education's (1983) report, which referred to the United States as "a nation at risk," educators have recognized the need for schools to keep up with changes in society. Federal legislation lays the groundwork for social work services in schools. These include the Vocational Rehabilitation Act of 1973, as amended through 1998 (PL 105–220), the Education for All Handicapped Children Act of 1975 (PL 94–142) and subsequent Individuals with Disabilities Education Act of 1990 (PL 101–476), the IDEA Amendments of 1991 (PL 102–119), and the Augustus Hawkins–Robert Stafford Elementary and Secondary School Improvement Amendments of 1988. In particular, the Educate America Act of 1994 (PL 103–227) underscored the changing needs of students and the necessity for schools to address underlying community and family problems that impact student learning. As outlined in table 8.2, the act identified eight "National Goals for Education" in such areas as school readiness, achievement, graduation rate, and school environment.

The eighth and final goal on parental involvement in schools explicitly recognized the joint responsibility of the school and the home in promoting the social and emotional as well as the academic growth of children.

Social Work Services in Schools

School social workers serve as a link between the school, home, and community. As such, social workers in schools deal with all aspects of the child's environment — classroom, home, or neighborhood — that may negatively impact the child's functioning and performance in school. In line with the previously noted "Framework of Needs and Resources for Family and Child Well-Being," social workers in schools generally approach their work from an ecological perspective, focusing both on the person and the environment. No other discipline within the school adopts this dual perspective (Allen-Meares 1996). In accordance with this perspective, social work interventions within schools may focus on changing the student, the environment, or both. The school social worker recognizes that what occurs during the school day as well as what happens to the child before and after the school day (in their home, en route to school, in their community) are vitally important factors in assessment and intervention within the school setting.

TABLE 8.1 Selected Federal Legislation Influencing
Social Work Services in Schools: Major Principles

Elementary and Secondary Education Act of 1965 (ESEA) (20 U.S.C. 2701 et seq.)

- Authorized Title I Funds, which provided aid to economically disadvantaged students

Vocational Rehabilitation Act of 1973 as amended through 1998 (PL 105–220)

- Section 504 of this act provides that no otherwise qualified disabled person shall, solely by reason of disability, be excluded from participation, be denied the benefits of or be subject to discrimination in any program or activity receiving federal financial assistance (29 U.S.C. 794)
- School districts that receive federal funds are required to make reasonable accommodations for students with physical or mental conditions that limit one or more of the student's major life activities
- Examples of qualifying conditions include communicable diseases (HIV, TB), medical conditions (asthma, diabetes), temporary medical conditions due to illness or accident, attention deficit disorder, drug/alcohol addiction

Family Educational Rights and Privacy Act of 1974 (Buckley Amendment) (PL 103–382)

- Parents have access to and right to challenge school records of children under eighteen years of age
- Pupils eighteen years old or older have right to examine their own school records
- Safeguards confidentiality of school records

Education for All Handicapped (EHA) Children Act of 1975 (PL 94–142)

- Required free, appropriate public education (FAPE) for children with handicapping conditions
- Major principles and provisions include child find, nondiscriminatory testing, individualized educational program (IEP), least restrictive environment, procedural due process, parent participation
- Defined social work services as a related service, not mandated but required if identified in an IEP
- Defined eleven disabilities as eligible for special education: mentally retarded, hard of hearing, deaf, speech impaired, visually handicapped, seriously emotionally disturbed, orthopedically handicapped, other health impaired, deaf-blind, multihandicapped, specific learning disabilities

EHA Amendments of 1986 (PL 99–457)

- Provided for coordinated early intervention services, birth to three years old
- Mandated free, appropriate public education (FAPE) for all handicapped children beginning at age three
- Provided for family-focused Individual Family Services Plan to be developed
- Eligible population includes those with developmental delays, those with physical or mental conditions that have high probability of resulting in a delay, and those "at risk" for future developmental problems

Augustus Hawkins–Robert Stafford Elementary and Secondary School Improvements Amendments of 1988 (PL 100–297)

- Reauthorized existing federal programs
- Included school social workers in the definition of pupil personnel services
- Created new programs (e.g., drug abuse education and prevention, dropout prevention and reentry)

Americans with Disabilities Act of 1990 (ADA) (PL 101–336)

- Defined disabled person as one who has a physical or mental impairment that substantially limits a major life activity, a person who has a past record of such an impairment, or a person who is regarded by other people as having such an impairment
- Required that a school district make reasonable accommodation for the known disabilities of job applicants and employees

Individuals with Disabilities Education Act (IDEA) of 1990 (PL101–476)

- Replaced PL 94–142
- Provided for early intervention services and education for all children with disabilities (birth to age twenty-one)
- Added two additional disability categories, autism and traumatic brain injury, to eligible population
- A state may not remove disabled students from their placements in response to disruptive conduct arising out of their disabilities; required that a disabled student remain in his/her placement pending completion of an IEP review proceeding
- Changed terminology from *handicapped children* to *children with disabilities*

TABLE 8.1 Selected Federal Legislation Influencing
Social Work Services in Schools: Major Principles (continued)

IDEA Amendments of 1991 (PL 102–119)

- Authorized appropriations for services to infants and toddlers with disabilities, including those living on Indian reservations
- Included training programs for parents and professionals

Improving America's Schools Act of 1993 (PL 103–382)

- Reauthorized the Elementary and Secondary Education Act
- Emphasis on high performance standards for all children, including those served under Title I
- Allowed for greater involvement by teachers and parents in decision making at the local school level

---

Goals 2000: Educate America Act 1994 (PL 103–227)

- Contained national educational goals
- Reauthorized all federal education programs
- Promoted national skills standards and certification
- Framework for education reform
- Created new initiatives, e.g., violence prevention programs, parent information and resource centers, midnight basketball

---

IDEA Amendments of 1997 (PL 105–17)

- Supported initiatives for transition services from high school to adult living
- Specified that transition planning should begin at age fourteen

---

Several studies (Allen-Meares 1977; Torres 1996) have sought to examine what social workers actually do in schools and what requisite skills and knowledge are needed for this work. Based on a national survey of social work tasks, Allen-Meares (1977) identified the following knowledge requirements of an entry-level school social work practitioner:

TABLE 8.2 National Education Goals[8]

---

1. All children in America will start school ready to learn.
2. The high school graduation rate will increase to at least 90 percent.
3. All students will leave grades 4, 8, and 12 having demonstrated competency over challenging subject matter including English, mathematics, economic, science, foreign languages, civics, and government, and in every school America will ensure that all students learn to use their minds well, so that they may be prepared for responsible citizenship, further learning, and productive employment in our nation's modern economy.
4. The nation's teaching force will have access to programs for the continued improvement of their professional skills and the opportunity to acquire the knowledge and skill needed to instruct and prepare all American students for the next century.
5. United States students will be the first in the world in mathematics and science achievement.
6. Every adult American will be literate and possess the knowledge and skills necessary to compete in a global economy and execise the rights and responsibilities of citizenship.
7. Every school in the United States will be free of drugs, violence, and unauthorized presence of firearms and alcohol and will offer a disciplined environment conducive to learning.
8. Every school will promote partnerships that will increase parental involvement and participation in promoting the social, emotional, and academic growth of children.

- knowing fundamental administrative and professional tasks (e.g., confidentiality, recording keeping),
- serving as liaison between home and school,
- helping children make best use of school, and
- facilitating and advocating family's use of community resources.

It would appear that those activities most directly linked to direct service roles with children and families continue to characterize social work services in schools. However, the push of educational reform initiatives toward local team decisionmaking may shift primary social work roles to those of mediator, facilitator, or advocate. In fact, depending upon the assessment of the child, the school, and the environment, any number of goals and targets for intervention may be appropriate, as table 8.3 illustrates.

TABLE 8.3 Examples of Goals and Targets for Social Work Services in Schools[9]

- Teach social skills or competencies to children, parents, families, or teachers (e.g., friendship skills, behavior management skills)
- Identify and develop new and innovative resources or programs within the school to meet changing needs (e.g., grandparents or kinship care support group, sober home room)
- Develop relationships between the school and community resources and services (e.g., crisis intervention team, violence prevention task force)
- Increase teaching staff knowledge and understanding about selected target groups of children (child abuse and neglect, homelessness, adoption)
- Develop school wide policies and procedures to address specific issues (truancy, student conflict, student rights and discipline).

Most social workers in schools will find that on any given day they may deal with situations at many different levels of intervention and that the ability to be flexible and shift gears quickly is essential when working in a school.

Another way to conceptualize social work intervention in schools is offered by Durlak (1995) in a discussion of school-based prevention programs. Interventions can be considered primarily person or environment focused or, more likely, a combination of the two. Likewise the target group for intervention can range from broad application (universal) to a narrower focus. Specific services or programs may be limited to selected high-risk groups (e.g., children of substance-abusing families, abused or neglected children) or to those students undergoing transitions in their home or school life (e.g., children of recently divorced parents, children entering junior high). Take as an example a group of students undergoing a transition, such as students who are new to the school, either new to the school district or transfers from another school. Person-oriented interventions might consist of orientation groups for new students or individual help with school adjustment. Environment-oriented interventions might include putting up a poster or bulletin board with pictures of new students or offering information and tips to teachers regarding typical reactions to change and subsequent behaviors of new students in the classroom.

As in all social work practice, the choice of intervention should be based on an accurate assessment of the situation or issue of concern. As suggested in chapter 5, this assessment needs to

- consider both person and environment factors,
- be gathered from a variety of sources and perspectives, and
- include strengths and coping resources as well as deficits.

Two other important characteristics for assessment are that the process itself be culturally sensitive and that it be client centered. The framework employed and the level of detail expected in a social work assessment varies depending on the setting and the job responsibilities of the social worker. In the next section we examine the types of information and the assessment methods that are particularly useful when working in a school setting. Also, appendix 5 includes a variety of electronic resources useful for such assessment.

Assessment of Children within the Context of the School

School-age children may be referred for social work services for any number of reasons. Some children are referred because of learning or behavior problems in the classroom. Others are referred because of home or family factors that are related to problems in the classroom. Still other children are considered to be at risk of developing further problems unless services are provided.

The specific approach to assessment will vary greatly depending on whether or not the social worker is housed within the school or providing services under an agency partnership with the school. However, basic information will be needed about the individual student, family, classroom, school, and community. The goal of helping the child deal with the school setting effectively must be kept in mind, as this will limit the type and extent of information to be generated.

The following summary of pertinent information is based on the framework developed by Allen-Meares, Washington, and Welsh (2000) regarding the types and sources of data useful for assessment.[1]

- *Information to be gathered about the student*: Name, age, grade, birth date, school history, medical history, developmental history, friendship and peer network, social support system, previous services provided, strengths, and resources.

  Sources of information: School records, parent and teacher interviews, behavior rating scales, observation of the child at school, interviews with child, ecomap, social network map.

• *Information to be gathered about the family*: Basic identifying information (names and birth dates of members, dates of deaths and marriages, race/ethnicity/culture, religion, and language spoken in the home), citizenship status and special issues surrounding geographic relocations, presence and role of extended family, family structure and environment, family history; family functioning in such areas as decision making, communication, and child rearing, family's previous experience with schools, strengths and coping resources.

  Sources of information: Home visits, family meetings, genogram, ecomap, culturagram (as described in chapter 5 and in appendix 1).

• *Information to be gathered about the classroom*: Demographic information about the students (number, ages, academic level, sex, race, culture, handicapping conditions), information about the teacher (age, sex, race, culture/ethnicity, teacher preparation and experience, teaching style), classroom climate (teacher-student relationships, student-student relationships, group process), relationship of classroom to rest of school (teacher-teacher relationships, teacher-principal relationships).

  Sources of information: direct observation, teacher and other support staff interviews, ecomap, and sociogram.

• *Information to be gathered about the school*: School physical plant and facilities, organizational structure, administrative style, teaching, professional support, clerical and maintenance staff, student population demographics, curriculum, extracurricular and special programs offered, policies and procedures in regard to students rights and discipline, resources and supports available to teachers, level and types of parent involvement.

  Sources of information: Participant observation, interviews with administration and staff, written information about the school, contacts with school board members and parents, focus groups, and surveys.

• *Information to be gathered about the community*: History of the local community, demographic and diversity information, assets and resources, relationship of school and community (extent to which educational goals and values are shared, perception of school in community, joint projects undertaken, communication patterns), strengths and barriers to school-community partnerships.

Sources of information: Participant observation, focus groups, surveys, interviews with key informants, data bases, community capacity or asset mapping.

Unique Features of School-Based Practice

For those agency-based social workers less familiar with practice within a school setting, we present three features of school-based practice that are important to consider.

Interdisciplinary Team Approaches in Intervention

Many school social workers will conduct assessment and intervention within the context of an interdisciplinary team (Torres 1996). Team composition and structure will vary across school districts, but it is common for teams to include school social workers, school psychologists, school guidance counselors, school nurses, principals and teachers, among others. Particular forms of teamwork, as in developing an IEP (Individualized Educational Plan) or site-based management teams, highlight the important role and participation of family members.

Intervention assistance teams offer another way to organize and structure interdisciplinary work. In this approach, used with children who may be in need of special services, the teacher is first asked to try to resolve the problem on his or her own. The next step is teacher-teacher consultation. Failing that, the concern is brought to the attention of the school's support staff. If no resolution is reached, the teacher then contacts the team representative. The teacher will be asked to

- specify the academic, behavioral, or social concerns in behaviorally specific language,
- convey general academic screening information to the team, e.g., reading, math level,
- identify what steps were taken to resolve the problem, and
- list what special services are currently provided to the child.

The team members will consider all the information provided and, together with the teacher and parent, work to understand the problem, gather baseline information, and develop needed interventions.

The above approach is an effective use of team time and expertise. It requires good communication and problem-solving skills from all participants. Like all teamwork, often the group process yields a higher quality and more valid assessment and intervention plan than would any one person working alone. Team approaches also remind us that school social work services are not offered in isolation but as an essential component of the educational process (Allen-Meares, Washington, and Welsh 2000).

Engagement Issues with Students, Families, and School Staff

One important feature of social work services in schools is that the worker provides services in a host setting. Whenever a social worker works in a host setting, it is important to establish relationships within and be knowledgeable about that setting; otherwise, he or she may be treated as the "outsider" in the system. For this reason the preparation of school social workers includes course work and field practice on the nature of the educational process and the school as a social system. Having some knowledge of how schools operate and how teachers teach makes it easier to begin work within the educational system. Also, social workers in schools quickly learn that the relationship with the principal is vital to their ability to provide services in the school. It is important for all school staff to regard the social worker as a visible, competent presence in the life of the school. The principal's endorsement and support increase the chances that the social worker will gain that level of acceptance.

In addition, social workers need to provide a great deal of information about their role and function within the school; they may otherwise find themselves assigned tasks (e.g., attendance) to which they are unable to apply their best skills and resources or, even worse, not be called upon to help at all. Information can be conveyed to parents, teachers, and other school staff through informal discussions, in-service presentations, and/or informational brochures and pamphlets designed for a specific school. The Midwest School Social Work Council as well as the School Social Work Section of the National Association of Social Workers produce brochures explaining what school social workers do and who might benefit from school social work services. (*Information on these organizations is listed in appendix 6.*)

Berrick and Duerr (1996) offer a number of practical suggestions for social workers in maintaining positive school relationships:

- fit into the existing structure,
- build rapport with the principal,
- communicate through regular meetings,
- be clear about whom you serve,
- be visible and provide prompt feedback, and
- involve the teacher in the plan.

While these suggestions may seem commonsense, they are often difficult to carry out within the context of a busy day interrupted by one crisis after another and in a setting where there may be only one social worker. Many school social workers find no set process and structure for their services within the school. Consequently, developing a plan, format, and structure for the services to be provided is essential to beginning work in the school. Generally, the overall plan for service will be developed with the principal and will be based on the needs and resources of the school.[2]

Written sets of instructions and a brief instrument or format for teacher referrals are also often helpful in organizing the work and explaining the service. The information to be contained in a referral generally includes basic identifying information about the student, the reason for referral or behavior that is causing concern in behaviorally specific terms (e.g., Sarah appears sad as evidenced by her not participating in class, crying during lunch by herself almost daily, having difficulty turning in work on time, and staring out the window during group activities), the desired outcome, student strengths and weaknesses, and relevant family or medical information. It is important that the person making the referral know how he or she will get feedback on what was done in response to the referral.

Determining Who the Client Is

A final feature of social work services in schools is not unfamiliar to social work — that of determining who the client is. Social workers in schools will be in contact with a variety of people: students, students' families, teaching staff, other school support and administrative staff, and community groups and agencies. Each of these parties may facilitate the assessment and intervention process or may be the target of assessment and intervention. In other words, the "client" could be a student, a teacher, or an entire school. Or the "client" may be all three, as in the following example:

A social worker noticed a large number of referrals of children in foster care in one elementary school. The social workers provided a variety of direct services to the children and families, particularly to help the foster child adjust to a new school, family, and community. At the same time, an in-service presentation on typical reactions and behaviors of children in foster care was offered to teaching staff. The social worker also began to develop a schoolwide plan to reach out to this group of children and foster families upon their initial entrance to school.

It is essential to be clear about who the client is and to engage with all client systems effectively. Often, the child and/or family will present as involuntary clients, having been viewed as having a problem by someone else. In these instances all of the social work skills of working with involuntary/nonvoluntary clients can be applied (Hepworth, Rooney, and Larsen 1997; Rooney 1992).

Overview of School-Based Intervention Approaches

Given the unique features of school-based practice noted above, this section explores the range and types of interventions typically carried out within school settings. This list is not exhaustive, but is offered to stimulate thinking about social work roles in schools.

Social Work with Individual Students

In general, the goal of working with individual students is to help with student learning and behavior. Typically, the social worker works closely with the teacher and family in conducting an assessment, developing targets for change, and implementing interventions. Social workers may help with behavior management, self-esteem issues, communication, and problem-solving skills, among others. Social skills or prosocial skills training is often a component of work with students, as in developing friendship, adjusting to a group setting where sharing and turn taking are a requirement, and using words (versus behavior) to communicate feelings and needs (McGinnis and Goldstein 1984).

Depending on the situation and the availability of staff, a case management component may be required in the intervention, as in referring the child and family to needed community resources, accessing other needed assessments or evaluations, and helping to coordinate the overall plan. As noted above, much of the work directed toward individual children will be provided in conjunction with other school team members. The staff resources of most school districts are such that long-term services are usually provided outside the school.

Social Work with Families

As in work with students in general, school social work services with families are directed toward helping the family to be an active participant in their child's learning and to connect with the school and with needed community resources. Oftentimes, social workers help the family understand the child's learning needs and the school system's approach to education; at the same time, they help the school understand the family's position and their view of the child.

Social workers have an especially important role in helping the school understand and respond to diverse family backgrounds and lifestyles. For example, one social worker provided a great deal of information to an interdisciplinary team working with a young child with physical disabilities from a Southeast Asian refugee family — typical foods eaten within the culture, culturally based explanations for disability and disease, and religious practices and worldviews. Without this information the team's services to the child would simply not have made sense to the family. Another social worker offered a support group to grandparents raising grandchildren; the group was well received by a number of families providing kinship care. A final example is interpreting typical classroom behaviors of homeless children living in shelters (poor attention span, avoiding peer friendships, and losing or not completing homework), as a direct consequence of a transient lifestyle, instability, overcrowding, and lack of privacy (Wall 1996).

Parent Education

One component of working with families may take the form of parent education. Parent education can offer support, information, and resources to help parents cope with stressful situation situations, participate more effectively on behalf of their child's learning, and understand child development and child-rearing techniques. Parent education programs may be offered to the entire school population (as in helping with homework at home or family math nights) or be directed to a defined target group (adoptive parents, parents of teens, parents of children with disabilities). A number of curriculum programs are available for purchase;[3] however, most parent educators find that the curriculum must be tailored to their particular group.

It is a challenge to find culturally appropriate parent training resources, especially in line with demographic changes in the population over the last decade. Parent education approaches must adapt to these changes. For example, as discussed in chapter 1, families that have recently migrated to the U.S. from developing countries have special needs and face special challenges. Traditional didactic approaches do not recognize the diversity of learning styles, the complexity of family life and the stressors that these and other families face today. Programs offering information and skills that focus on the prevention of problems and the wellness of families and that are accessible in terms of time, travel, language, and staffing have a better chance of succeeding (Kagan 1995; Griffin-Wiesner 1996). For example, a parent training program offered on an Indian reservation utilized elders as group facilitators, since they were traditionally turned to and respected for their knowledge of child rearing.

Group Approaches

Oftentimes, group approaches with children are a developmentally appropriate means to provide support, information, and skills training. Group approaches are also cost and time effective, particularly in a school setting since children are already in groups. Group approaches may be targeted to an entire classroom, as in a prevention program, or selected students may be drawn together to form a group. As is always the case, the child's parents/guardians must give permission for the child to participate. Groups offered in many elementary schools illustrate typical student concerns: "banana splits," a divorce and separation group, "lunch bunch," a social skills training group, grief and loss group, friendship skills group, peer mediation training, "extra step" group for at-risk youth, and parents and grandparents support groups. Groups also can be an effective way to reach adolescents, as the following example shows.

Sister Sister Let's Talk

Sister Sister Let's Talk is a group for young women ages fourteen to eighteen that has been organized by a school social worker in a large, public, inner-city school in Connecticut. The group was launched because of the social worker's concern about the high number of referrals she was receiving of young women at risk of dropping out of school because of low attendance, school fights, and pregnancy. At first the group was small; four students would meet in the social worker's office to discuss their concerns. Guests from community agencies would be invited to provide information and resources the students needed.

Gradually the group began to grow as the young women told their friends. And, they began to meet more often, including before school for discussion over breakfast. The activities began to broaden as well. One project, a "penny drive," was started to raise money for a program that serves babies who have HIV/AIDS. Money was also raised to help a young woman suffering from sickle-cell anemia. Sister Sister Let's Talk currently meets biweekly for one hour and consists of approximately forty members. Parents and family members are welcome to attend and support the group.

Sister Sister Let's Talk is aimed at developing well-rounded young women. Group meetings focus on discussions of family life, health concerns, relationship issues, and important choices in everyday life. Guest speakers have included representatives from special projects that emphasize school retention and youth opportunities and from recreational programs such as scouting. These guests provide positive role models as well as useful information about resources in their community. In addition to meeting at the school, the group has gone on several all-day field trips: workshops at a nearby college, out-of-state trips to a New York City museum to view a hip hop exhibit, and a trip to a college in a nearby state to attend an African American festival during Black History month. Events currently being planned include a mother/daughter tea and an end-of-the-year overnight retreat.

Sister Sister Let's Talk is an interactive opportunity for the young women to learn, grow, and become active in their planning for their own future, as well as one that provides an environment for increased self-esteem and empowerment. The young women are excited about their participation and find the group a positive place to belong.

Work with Teachers and Other School Staff

Social workers in schools typically communicate and work closely with teachers and other school staff as part of service provision to children and families. Services may also be provided to school staff in the form of in-service training and consultation. Some examples include providing training to an entire school staff about children's reactions to natural disasters (e.g., flooding, hurricanes), responding to a sudden tragedy such as a child's death due to a car accident, or consulting with a teacher on the development of a behavior management plan for a specific child.

Work with the Community and Other Social Agencies

An additional component of school social work services is mobilizing and accessing community resources on behalf of the student and family. This may include traditional resource and referral services in which the social worker connects the child or family with needed resources. Work in this area also includes community organizer and developer roles. Some examples might include participation in a community task force for violence prevention, developing relationships with mental health crisis intervention services, collaborating with a child welfare agency to provide optimal services to children in out-of-home care, and forming partnerships with other service systems, as in developing an "adoptive" relationship between an elementary school and a nursing home.

Prevention Approaches

Schools serve as natural sites for prevention programs because they provide access to large numbers of children at critical periods of development (Tracy and Rondero 1998). Of all the school-based preventive interventions, drug prevention programs are perhaps the most commonly implemented (Botvin 2000; Durlak 1995; and Sanders 2000). Federal legislation, such as the Drug Free Schools and Communities Act of 1996 and the Improving America's Schools Act of 1993, recognize the school as a logical site for educating youth about substance abuse. With many schools now developing "zero tolerance" policies for drug-related activities on school grounds, social work involvement in drug prevention will continue to be needed (Edwards et al. 1995). In fact, many school social work positions are dedicated in full or part to drug prevention programs.

These programs are designed to enhance protective factors (those associated with reduced potential for use) and to reverse or reduce risk factors (factors associated with greater potential for use). Based on the knowledge to date of risk and protective factors for drug use, the targets for intervention need to include family relationships, peer relationships, the school environment, and the community environment (Hawkins, Catalano, and Miller 1992; National Institute of Drug Abuse 1997). Prevention programs also need to target all forms of drug use, including the use of tobacco, inhalants, and alcohol (legal drugs), as the use of these substances is typically associated with later use of illegal drugs (marijuana being usually the first). Table 8.4 provides a checklist of best practice principles to be used in selecting school-based drug prevention programs.[4] (Also see appendix 10 for resources on alcohol and substance abuse.)

Selected Target Populations

In general, children who would benefit from social services in schools are those who do not learn or achieve their potential (Downs et al. 2000). The reasons for school difficulties may be due to child, family, or other

TABLE 8.4 Practice Principles for School-Based Drug Prevention Programs[10]

- Do the school-based programs reach children from kindergarten through high school? If not, do they at least reach children during the critical middle school or junior high years?
- Do the programs contain multiple years of intervention?
- Do the programs use a well-tested, standardized intervention with detailed lesson plans and student materials?
- Do the programs teach drug-resistance skills through interactive methods?
- Do the programs foster prosocial bonding to the school and community?
- Do the programs:

  teach social competence and drug resistance skills that are culturally and developmental appropriate?
  promote positive peer influence?
  promote antidrug social norms?
  include an adequate dosage (ten to fifteen sessions in a year and another ten to fifteen booster sessions)?

---

environmental factors, or more typically a combination of factors. School-related behaviors such as the following may suggest the need for a referral to school social work services:

- failure to complete school work,
- excessive shyness,
- aggressiveness or impulsivity,
- frequent physical complaints,
- poor peer relationships,
- substance abuse,
- irregular school attendance,
- persistent tardiness,
- depression,
- school age pregnancy,
- suicidal ideation/gestures, and
- need for community resources or concrete services (adapted from Midwest School Social Work Council n.d.).

Additional groups of children who may be in need of or targeted for school social work services would include children who have — or have been exposed to — HIV-AIDS, children who have experienced abuse or neglect and are in need of mandated reporting or supportive services through the school (American Humane Association n.d.; Gustavsson 1991), children from diverse family backgrounds and lifestyles (Wardle 1991), children undergoing life transitions (e.g., National Adoption Information Clearinghouse n.d.), and children with mental health, chronic health, or substance abuse problems (Freeman 1998; Schmitz and Hilton 1996). A school may also decide to target schoolwide needs, as through intervention to improve attendance or tardiness (Ford and Sutphen 1996).

Ensuring Equal Educational Opportunity: The School Social Work Role

School social workers play a vitally important role in ensuring that children and families receive all the educational services to which they are entitled and that all children are treated fairly within the school system. Several groups of children are legally recognized for focused attention by federal and state laws.

Children with Special Educational Needs

The major thrust of legislation regarding children with disabilities has been to ensure each and every child, regardless of type or extent of disabilities, access to a free appropriate public education. The social work role with children with disabilities is established in federal legislation (Individuals with Disabilities Education Act [IDEA] of 1990, PL 101–476). Social work is a related service in special education and includes

- preparing social or developmental histories on children with disabilities,
- providing group and individual counseling to children and their families,
- working with problems in children's living situations (home, school, and community) that affect their adjustment in school, and
- mobilizing school and community resources to organize students' potential to learn in their educational programs.

Social workers are typically part of the team that prepares an Individualized Educational Plan (IEP) for each child in special education. Social services may also include developing and/or consulting with teachers on behavior management plans, providing case management services, and working with parents to facilitate understanding of their child and use of school and community resources. Some students, while not eligible for special education, may by nature of other disabling conditions be covered under Section 504 of the Vocational Rehabilitation Act of 1973. These students are eligible for reasonable accommodations in order to benefit from school, and the social worker may be part of the team that prepares this plan.[5]

Discrimination Based on Language, Race, Gender

A number of studies have pointed out that not all children fare equally well in the American school system. The gap in educational achievement between high- and low-income groups, and between minority and nonminority students, is cause for concern (Chavkin 1993). Children whose primary language is other than English have not always fared well in school. Educational practices have reinforced sex role stereotypes for girls and boys and denied girls access to full educational opportunity (Allen-Meares, Washington, and Welsh 2000). While federal legislation has been enacted in the areas of language, gender, and racial discrimination, a great deal of change is required on the part of all school staff to remove racist, sexist, and other biased influences from the school, nor is there always agreement on the parts of the community as to how best to address these issues.

A number of roles are available to social workers in schools, including consciousness-raising with teachers, systematic review of the curriculum for biases/inequities, interpreting the requirements of laws and acting as advocate for children or parents, working with students who have been disadvantaged at school, and providing training to promote better relationships within the school (Allen-Meares, Washington, and Welsh 2000). These roles are consistent with the ethical responsibilities of social workers to promote effective services for vulnerable children and families, as elaborated in chapters 4 and 9.[6]

Other groups of children also require a watchful eye for equity issues in schools, such as children from a variety of religious and cultural backgrounds, gay and lesbian youths, children of immigrant and refugee families, migrant children, homeless children, children in foster family or group care, and low-income children. Social workers in schools are in a unique position to identify and address barriers to full educational opportunity as well as to help various groups of children and families to better understand and interact respectfully with one another.

As an example, gay and lesbian children and youths not only face recurring crises but are also poorly understood and inadequately served. Among the stressors they face are the following:

- developing constructive relationships with their parents, family members, and peers (Mallon 2000),
- confronting the lack of family or educational supports or, in some cases, the consequences of breakdown of the family system (Mallon 1997; Stein 1996),
- understanding their rights in regard to school, employment, and federal and state laws (Mallon 2000), and
- being at greater risk than other youths for school dropout, prostitution, depression, and suicide (Proctor and Groze 1994).

There are also challenges for the birth parents and foster parents of these youths, including understanding and coping with the young person's sexual orientation. At worst, in some situations parents may relinquish their parental roles, overtly or covertly force the young persons out of the house, and withdraw emotionally from them (Saltzburg 2001). Starting in the elementary grades, gay and lesbian youths may experience bullying and harassment in school. For example, one junior high girl told the school social worker, "No one talks to me at school — they call me a man." Schoolwide responses are called to set zero tolerance for any form of hate speech or symbols, to react promptly to emergency situations, and to respond to the victims of discrimination (Southern Poverty Law Center 1999).

Special attention is also required for children who are recent immigrants and who, therefore, need help to adjust to — and benefit from — the American educational system. Below is an example of an effective program for these children.

The New Arrival Migrant Program

This program was developed by a large, urban school system in the Northeast to serve its growing population of immigrant children, first from Caribbean countries and later from other countries such as those in eastern Europe. The program serves approximately five hundred families and their sixteen hundred children from preschool to high school age with a wide range of services. The aim is to address family and environmental issues and needs that affect children's ability to take full advantage of the educational opportunity. For example, health care services ranging from nutrition to dental care are provided. When either translation or transportation is needed to access services, these are also provided. A parent advisory council helps families to understand and become involved in meeting their children's health, social and educational needs. A preschool component offers home visits by a team of specialists to work with parents in promoting a migrant child's development.

Activities focus on cognitive skills and language, using a range of hands-on approaches. Youths in grades seven through twelve who are recent arrivals are served through a team of vocational specialists tracking their progress. There is outreach to the youths and their families to explain attendance policies and identify potential needs that may affect school attendance and learning. Youths experiencing academic problems or who appear to be at risk of dropping out of school for other reasons are referred to appropriate services. One component of the program for older children is career orientation, which includes specially planned field trips, assistance with college preparation, and linkage with other career-enhancing opportunities such as the city's Youth Commission and Peer Mediation programs.

Promoting Parent Involvement in Schools

Parent Involvement and Academic Success

Most educators today recognize the importance of family school partnerships and are working toward making schools more family friendly. Social work services in schools are often an important component of parent involvement. Research has shown that family involvement in children's education has a number of direct positive benefits on student learning (Haynes and Ben-Avie 1996; Winters 1993; Zill 1996). Family participation in school programs has been associated with improved grades and test scores, greater amounts of completed homework, and higher student attendance and graduation rates. Parent involvement in the academic life of the child is a strong predictor of student achievement across all economic groups and grade levels (Booth and Dunn 1996; Chavkin 1993; U.S. Department of Education 1994).

The home environment may account for nearly 50 percent of the variance in student achievement (Chavkin 1993). In fact, in one study of student math scores, nearly 90 percent of the variance in scores could be attributed to three factors over which parents can exercise control at home: school attendance, variety of reading materials, and amount of TV time (Barton and Coley 1992). Success in reading is heavily determined by the amount of time spent by parents in reading aloud to children at home (Anderson et al. 1985), and Epstein (1996) has shown that school efforts to involve parents in reading were associated with improved reading scores over the school year.

Parent involvement has some important benefits for parents as well. Dunlap (1996) was able to document the empowering effects on adults resulting from parent involvement in preschool education, such as use of more effective parenting techniques, increased self-sufficiency through employment or school attendance, and greater self-confidence. Winters (1993), in a study of African American mothers in urban schools, highlighted the personal growth and empowerment that typically resulted from parent involvement.

Issues in Parent Involvement

Notwithstanding what we know about the benefits of parent involvement, many schools face a number of barriers to achieving a high level of involvement. Parents of younger children tend to stay connected with the teacher and school, but participation dramatically drops off as the child grows older and enters the middle and high school environment. Practical matters of transportation, child care, work schedules, language and cultural differences all may inhibit parent involvement in schools (Booth and Dunn 1996). Some low-income and minority parents become disenfranchised from the school because of cultural or social class differences or are put off by school practices that do not encourage parent involvement (Chavkin 1993). Immigrant parents may be unfamiliar with the American educational system (Yao 1993), with potential negative consequences for their children, as seen in the following example regarding families that have immigrated to the United States from the former Soviet Union:

In the Soviet Union, schools assume considerable authority over children. Children attend school six days a week from 9 A.M. to 5 P.M. Schools also assume socialization and recreational functions. Therefore, Soviet parents consider the direction and management of a student's school problem to be primarily within the jurisdiction of the school. The greater role for parental direction and monitoring of children's education in the United States and the greater role of student autonomy confuses immigrant Soviet parents and their children. As a result, some children have become lost in the U.S. school system, resulting in truancy, continuation in school but avoidance of classes, and dropout. (Drachman 1992:72)

Few educators are trained to work with parents during their teacher preparation. Not all teachers are supportive of family involvement, and many hold a deficit view of low-income or minority families (Moles 1993). All too often, teachers contact parents only when there is a problem, which further distances the school and family; in contrast, parents are more likely to be involved when their child is doing well in school (Epstein 1996).

Those parents who as students did not like school or did not do well in school themselves may feel uncomfortable in the school setting and be unable to advocate for their child's education. Sometimes parents may not feel competent in the school environment or may lack academic or social skills needed to help out in the classroom. The following example shows how a parent may withdraw from school involvement because of a lack of skills, underscoring the importance of matching the skill level of the parent with the type of involvement expected:

When Beatrice Malcolm realized her reading skills were not sufficient for her to continue working informally with a third grade reading group, she feared telling the teacher and without notice failed to appear for a number of her scheduled group sessions. . . . After a week passed, the teacher took the initiative and suggested changing Ms. Malcolm's assignment to one that would better fit the other demands on her time. Following this, Ms. Malcom again began keeping her commitment at school but performing other tasks. Many months later, she revealed that she was taking a course in reading in the adult education program. (Winters 1993:60)

Even well-educated parents can be intimidated by the procedures and apparent expert role of the teacher in educational planning. Eccles and Harold (1996) present a model of parent involvement that shows the complexity of this process; they believe that a number of influences affect parent involvement, including parent/family characteristics, child characteristics, neighborhood characteristics, and teacher and school characteristics, beliefs, and practices. Dornbusch and Glasgow (1996) emphasize the importance of structural factors such as school organizational types, curriculum tracking, social networks, and ethnic-specific parenting practices in either strengthening or limiting family-school links. For example, they found that while Asian parents tended not to participate in "traditional" parent activities (e.g., open houses), they were very involved in reinforcing the child's learning at home. For some Hispanic and Southeast Asian immigrant families, maintaining distance from the school is actually a sign of respect; frequent contacts with the school would be viewed as a challenge to the school's authority (Moles 1993).

Lareau (1996) also found significant differences in parent-school relationships based on social class. The more parents share the same standards of school, the easier it is to negotiate the system for the benefit of their child. Lareau concluded that the meaning of school involvement differed between middle-class and working- or lower-class parents. While middle-class parents felt free, for example, to "contact the school" for any number of requests, the working and poorer parents did not presume this right and were therefore perceived by teaching staff as uninvolved in their child's education. Likewise, similar terms may hold different implications for parents. Head Start parents in one study did not understand the intent of "home visits"; this term did not represent for them a positive school-family contact but was rather viewed to be an intrusive and coercive event (Tracy and Ferguson 1993).

Yet other studies show that school practices to involve parents can overcome many of these barriers and can be more important than child and family characteristics, such as parental education, socioeconomic status, and grade level, in predicting school involvement (Dauber and Epstein 1993). Table 8.5 lists proven strategies to promote family-school partnerships.[7]

Family participation in the educational process is twice as predictive of academic learning as family socioeconomic status (Walberg 1984, cited in Chavkin 1993). Parent involvement may be an effective means to overcome the educational disadvantage experienced by children from minority and low-income backgrounds (Chavkin 1993). There is clear evidence

TABLE 8.5 Promoting Family-School Partnerships[11]

Strategies to Reduce Distrust

- Arrange contacts between teachers and parents in neutral settings
- Make sure the first contact with parents is positive (before a problem arises)
- Provide training to prepare parents to participate in parent-teacher conferences.
- Make school signs and initial contacts more welcoming (instead of the typical sign "visitors must report to the main office")
- Provide clear written guidelines for parent participation (no jargon)

Strategies to Address Barriers to Participation

- Translate written communications into parents' first languages
- Provide translators and bilingual staff for face-to-face and phone conversations
- Offer concurrent translations at parent meetings/events
- Use a variety of techniques to engage different family members (e.g., fathers, grandparents)
- Offer help with transportation and child care
- Schedule events to accommodate work schedules
- Use technology to link school and home (voice mail, electronic mail, homework hotlines, video and audio tapes)
- Provide a telephone in each classroom
- Use interactive homework assignments that involve all family members

Strategies for Staff Development

- Train teachers to work with parents
- Hire home-school coordinators
- Develop family resource centers within schools
- Offer home visits, parent workshops, and family nights
- Develop new governance systems that involve parents

from a number of studies that nearly all parents — regardless of ethnicity, race, or socioeconomic status — are concerned about their child's education, want to communicate with the teacher, and want to help in their child's learning (Chavkin and Williams 1993; Winters 1993). (*See chapter 3 for discussion of family resource centers as one strategy to involve parents in schools.*)

Assessing Parent Involvement

Social workers in school settings can contribute substantially by assessing and enhancing parental involvement. The following questions are offered as guidelines to assessing family-school connections:

- How are parents greeted when they call or visit the school?
- Does the physical environment of the school invite or discourage parent participation and presence? Is there a room set aside for parents to use?
- Does the school state explicitly that parents play a key role in the educational process?
- Is there a staff member with specific responsibility for parent involvement?
- What roles do parents have in the school?
- How does the school routinely communicate with parents?
- How is concern shown for parent's needs, e.g., childcare, transportation, language, etc.?
- What percentage of parents participates in various school events and activities?
- How representative are the parents who participate as compared with the total population of parents? What is being done to engage those parents who are underrepresented?
- To what extent and in what ways are parents involved in their child's learning at home (separate from their presence or involvement at the school)?
- How are other people and groups in the community involved in the life of the school?
- How is the school perceived in the community — as a helpful resource or as an alien presence?

- Does the school have a good or bad reputation in the community and on what basis is this formed?
- To what extent is the school environment perceived as reinforcing wider social patterns of power, oppression, and discrimination?
- What opportunities exist in the school for sharing and validating parents' culture, ethnicity, and religion? (adapted from Pryor 1996; Kemp, Whittaker, and Tracy 1997).

A clear definition and accurate assessment of parent involvement can lead to a more focused intervention plan for maximizing the role of parents in the school. A school may find that parents do attend parent-teacher conferences but lack involvement in other aspects of the school. Or a particular group of parents may be less involved than others. Data on family-school connections can be useful, then, in suggesting areas for change and in monitoring changes over time.

Emerging Issues

An emerging issue in the area of school-based intervention concerns the proper role of the school in the twenty-first century. Public schools are increasingly viewed as the central point of integration for a variety of social, health, and human services. Some see the school as the source of support not only for enrolled children and their families but for the larger neighboring community as well (Institute for Families in Society 1997). There is a variety of definitions and models, some more all-encompassing than others.

School-linked services refer to services provided through a collaboration between schools, health care providers, and social services agencies; schools are central in planning and governing the effort, and the services are located at or near the school site and coordinated by school personnel. *School-based programs* provide health, mental health, social, and/or family services through community agencies co-located in schools; this arrangement is sometimes referred to as a full-service school or one-stop shopping (Dryfoos 1994). A *family resource center* located in a school is another version of service integration within schools (Dupper and Poertner 1997; National Resource Center for Family Support Programs 1993). *Community schools,* as first described by Zigler (1989), represent an even broader service mission, that being to provide a full range of service to the entire community; community schools are typically open year round, sixteen hours a day, and include medical, dental, mental health, and other social and recreational services, such as parent education and before- and after-school care (Culler 1997; Children's Aid Society 1995).

Various approaches have been offered for linking social and educational services (Franklin and Streeter 1995; Lawson and Briar-Lawson 1997), and a number of states, notably New Jersey, Kentucky, and California, among others, have begun providing comprehensive services in school settings (National Resource Center for Family Support Programs 1993). These recent partnerships offer new roles for social workers, parents, and other teaching and support staff within schools as well as innovative ways to reach out to vulnerable youths, families, and communities. The issue of the rightful role of the school in service provision, given the primarily educational mission of the school, still gets raised (Lee 1998). What school-linked services can do, however, is involve many more people constructively in resolving the social and community-level problems facing schools (Franklin and Streeter 1998) and offer a means to integrate school and other social service system reforms (Lawson and Briar-Lawson 1997).

The school of the new century will look quite different from the school of the past century; demographic trends predict that the ethnic composition of schools will change and become increasingly more diverse and needy (Zigler 1989). At the same time, school reform movements, school-community partnerships, and increased recognition of parental involvement will impact social work services in schools. Winters and Gourdine (2000) envision expanded functions for school social work in the areas of school reform, curriculum initiatives, parent involvement, and community collaboration. School practitioners will increasingly be required to work with multiple levels of the student's environment — including change at the school, neighborhood, and community level — while being simultaneously skilled in interventions intended to serve a diverse population (Allen-Meares 1996).

It will be an exciting time for work in the schools, as social workers have the potential not only to respond to these influences but also to help shape the response in the best interests of students and their families. Moreover, social work services in schools, as elsewhere, are increasingly held to high standards of accountability in order to document their usefulness in furthering educational objectives. The next chapter therefore focuses on evaluation of practice and service delivery.

Notes

1. See appendix 1, as well as Kemp, Whittaker, and Tracy (1997), for
    further description of various assessment tools listed in this section.
2. See Allen-Meares, Washington, and Welsh (2000) for suggestions as to
    what to include in the service plan.
3. See Carpenter (1995) for an informative sourcebook on parenting and
    child care.
4. The website of the Safe and Drug Free Schools Program, www.ed.gov
    /offices/OESE/SDFS (May 1, 2001), is an excellent resource for ma-
    terials related to school safety and other prevention programs.
5. The ERIC (Educational Resources Information Clearinghouse on Dis-
    abilities and Gifted Education, http://ericec.org (May 1, 2001), provides
    links to resources for teachers and parents, including a guide to dis-
    ability rights laws and a website answering questions about federal spe-
    cial education legislation (Individuals with Disabilities Education Act):
    http://www.ideapractices.org (May 1, 2001).
6. Contact the School Social Work Association of America, http://
    www.sswaa.org (May 1, 2001), and the School Social Work Section,
    National Association of Social Workers, http://www.naswdc.org
    /sections/ssw (May 1, 2001), for current position papers on confidenti-
    ality, record keeping, and other ethical issues impacting practice.
7. The National Parent Information Network, http://npin.org (May 1,
    2001), provides access to research-based information about family in-
    volvement in education.
8. Quoted from "Goals 2000 — Educate America Act of 1994" (PL
    103–227).
9. Adapted from Allen-Meares, Washington, and Welsh (2000).
10. National Institute on Drug Abuse (1997).
11. U.S. Department of Education (1994).

Questions for Discussion

1. Interview a school-based social worker in your community. Ask about
major job responsibilities, roles, interventions used, and major challenges
experienced. Based on this interview, what are the characteristics of effective
social work services in schools?

2. Read the NASW *Standards for School Social Work* (National Association of Social Workers 1992). First developed by NASW in 1978 and revised in 1992, the standards identify minimum requirements for professional competence, professional preparation, and administrative support. How might these standards be implemented in a school in your community?

3. Select a target population (e.g., immigrant children, children of divorcing parents, or children with attention deficit disorder) and discuss the types of social work services that might be offered within a school.

4. How might teachers view the advantages and disadvantages of social work services in schools? Consider variations — if any — among elementary, middle school, and high school settings.

5. How might school administrators view social work services in schools? Consider variations — if any — among elementary, middle school, and high school settings.

6. A mother believes that her child has been unfairly disciplined in a school. What is the role of the school social worker and what steps might be appropriate for her or him to take?

Suggestions for Further Information

Allen-Meares, P., R. O.Washington, and B. L. Welsh. 2000. *Social Work Services in Schools*. 3d ed. Boston: Allyn and Bacon.

Constable, R., J. P. Flynn, and S. McDonald, eds. 1999. *School Social Work: Practice and Research Perspectives*. 4th ed. Chicago: Lyceum.

Freeman, E. M., C. G. Franklin, R. Fong, G. L. Shaffer, and E. M. Timberlake 1998. *Multisystem Skills and Interventions in School Social Work Practice*. Washington, D.C.: NASW.

House, A. E. 1999. *DSM-IV Diagnosis in the Schools*. New York: Guilford.

National Association of Social Workers. 1992. *NASW Standards for School Social Work*. Washington, D.C.: NASW.

Part 3

Looking to the Future

9 Evaluation of Practice
and Service Delivery

Social work practice and service delivery in the field of human services are constantly evolving in response to changing demands and realities. This of course is also true in the area of family and children's services, as suggested throughout this volume. As a consequence, it is incumbent upon practitioners as well as agency administrators to become involved in ongoing evaluation of practice and service delivery. Evaluation is also imperative as a result of demands by funders and others for accountability, assessment of performance, and cost effectiveness.

Building on recent evaluation studies, in this chapter we provide guidelines for evaluating family and children's services in one's agency as well as one's own practice. Formal and informal evaluation activities can be helpful "in assessing the outcome of child welfare services and stimulating the development of useful principles and guidelines" (Maluccio 1998:167). In many ways the research and evaluation process mirrors good practice principles, from gaining an understanding of the issue to gathering valid and reliable data and formulating relevant *goals* and outcome *measures*. Those closest to practice are often in the best position both to plan successful programs and help to formulate research questions and determine relevant indicators of success. Therefore, we describe ways for clients and social workers to become involved in the research endeavor as a means of refining and improving practice techniques to increase our understanding of "what helping techniques work for whom."

Evaluating an Agency's Program and Service Delivery

Assessing the effectiveness of an agency's program and service delivery is no easy task, particularly in such a complex field as family and child welfare. Yet, as emphasized by the contributors to a special issue of the journal *Child Welfare* (Curtis 1994), the field should be committed to a comprehensive research agenda that addresses the following themes:

- the field needs knowledge that is derived from rigorous research,
- the field is being challenged to use — and build on — a vast amount of data that will be gathered through greatly improved information systems and technologies,
- there is increasing emphasis on accountability and outcome evaluation in the delivery and administration of child welfare services, and
- there is a need for evaluative research that is culturally competent and that accounts for the special needs of people of color and other minorities.[1]

As emphasized by Gray and associates (1998), evaluation can be useful in promoting organizational effectiveness, empowerment, and excellence, if it is viewed and implemented as a continuous process that is integral to the organization's functioning. As these authors further indicate:

> For the ongoing health of our organizations, we need to set aside the hoop-jumping and bean-counting view of evaluation. As long as it is a single event or activity that comes at the end of the grant-funded project — and bears only on those organizations seeking such funding — then the evaluation *is* an imposition. As soon as we turn the idea around, however, and look at every aspect of the organization to determine how well we are doing overall to attain our mission while holding our vision, the imposition vanishes.
>
> (Gray and associates 1998:3)[2]

Evaluation is also critical in improving and maximizing service approaches that respond to the special needs of children of color and their families. This point is underscored by Courtney et al. (1996) in their extensive review of research on race and child welfare services. These authors found that "families and children of color experience poorer outcomes and are provided fewer services than Caucasian families and children" (125). Therefore, they concluded that there should be greater efforts in future research to acknowledge the importance of race and ethnicity in the delivery of child and family services and, in particular, to examine "the role of ethnicity in the efficacy of services" (131).

Process and Outcome Evaluation in the Human Services

Program evaluation is the use of research approaches to assess program goals, implementation, interventions, and results. It is a thoughtful and planned approach to examining both program processes and outcomes to determine whether the program's stated objectives are achieved (Turner 1993). An evaluation of a program's processes answers the questions: Is the program being implemented as planned? If not, why not? What changes need to be made or accommodated? What are the levels of resources used in a program's interventions, including activities by practitioners? (Turner 1993). Whereas the central question in process evaluation is: How well was the program carried out? In outcome evaluation the focus is: How well did the program work? Were the desired and planned results achieved? (Ginsberg 2001). Taken together, process and outcome evaluations enable the staff and evaluators to measure *effort* — the extent of resources committed to the intervention, *efficiency* — the extent to which the desired results were produced using these resources most economically, and *effectiveness* — the extent to which the desired benefits were attained.

As in other human services, an ongoing task for administrators and researchers in family and children's service settings is evaluation of service efficiency and effectiveness. Program planning and implementation can be carried out more carefully on the basis of findings from pertinent research, that is, quantitative and/or qualitative studies that examine the efficiency and effectiveness of services designed to enhance the functioning of client groups coming to the attention of the agency. Moreover, the best way to involve practitioners, and even clients, in evaluation is to do so from the start through their involvement in program planning and design, especially the specification of program objectives. Because program objectives are the cornerstone of sound program planning — they define the expected results of the program — the specification of measurable objectives when programs are being designed is a key precondition for evaluating outcomes. Well-written objectives provide clarity and coherence for program planning as well as specify what a program aims to achieve and how its success will be measured. When staff and clients work with program planners and evaluators to specify the major activities of the program in measurable terms — the process objectives (e.g., number of parent-child visits and number of hours of parent education sessions) — and also to specify the intended results in measurable terms — the outcome objectives (e.g., increased number of positive parent-child interactions) — the end result is a coherent, well-planned program with a built-in plan for evaluation.

Turner (1993:182) offers a useful framework for evaluating outcomes in human service programs focusing on "goals, inputs, operations, quantity of output, quality of output, and client and case outcomes." These components are diagrammed in figure 9.1.

Turner (1993:183–196) also delineates strategies for applying the above components to program evaluation in human service agencies, by using the following four-step process:

- planning the evaluation,
- selecting program characteristics that should be measured,
- determining the most appropriate evaluation strategies and
- reporting and using the results.

Building in part on strategies such as those delineated above, Fein and Staff (1993) describe a plan for conducting agency-based outcome evaluation that is designed to involve practitioners as well as administrators actively in the research process. The plan includes these three components:

- *research issues* — that is, the area of information gathering,
- *services provided* — that is, evaluation of effort, and
- *resulting outcomes* — that is, assessment of effectiveness.

Fein and Staff (1993) apply the above plan to evaluation of reunification services, as depicted in table 9.1. As they explain, using such a plan promotes staff involvement in the evaluation as well as eventual utilization of the findings in practice.

FIGURE 9.1 Components of Outcome Research in the Human Services

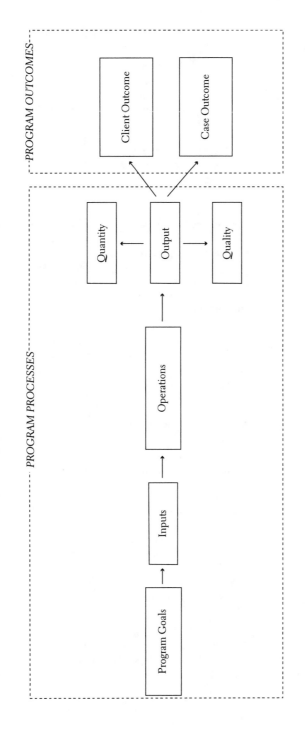

Source: J. Turner (1993), *Evaluating Family Reunification Programs*, p. 182. In B. A. Pine, R. Warsh, and A. N. Maluccio, eds., *Together Again: Family Reunification in Foster Care*, pp. 179–198. Washington, D.C.: CWLA. Reprinted with permission.

TABLE 9.1 Reunification Services: Evaluation Plan

Research Issues	Related Questions	Data Sources
Which children and families participate in reunification services?	• Can families be distinguished by their presenting diagnosis (abuse, neglect)? • What are the participants' demographic indicators (age, race, sex, etc.)?	• Case records • Family Risk Scales
What services are provided?	• What are the specifications and generalities in case plans? • What are the perceptions of each of the principals about the need for services, their adequacy, and their usefulness?	• Case records • Daily/weekly summary • Monthly goal rating • Interviews: Children, parents, and social workers
What outcomes ensue?	• What outcomes occur? • How are outcomes related to: case plans; demographics; family process (biological family), or foster family (child's success in placement)? • Reactions of the professional staff?	• Case plan • Daily/weekly summary • Monthly goal rating • Parent outcome interview • Interviews: Children, parents, and social workers
What changes take place in children and families?	• Can particular phases in reunification be defined dynamically? (Before child is returned; immediately following return; post-honeymoon) • What critical events trigger or postpone each phase? • What services or supports characterize each phase?	• Interviews: Children, parents, and social workers • Case plan • Daily/weekly summary • Monthly goal rating • Case records

Source: *The Interaction of Research and Practice in Family Reunification*, p. 203 by E. Fein and I. Staff (1993). In B. A. Pine, R. Warsh, and A. N. Maluccio (Eds.) *Together again: Family reunification in foster care.* (Pp. 199–212). Washington, D.C.: Child Welfare League of America. Reprinted by permission.

Above all, the plan exemplifies principles and strategies for conducting practice-based research. Such an orientation to evaluation "has the maximum potential for building the knowledge base in child welfare and supplying information of the greatest usefulness for developing policy and practice" (Fein and Staff 1993:24).

Guidelines and Strategies for Evaluating Family and Children's Services

In line with the above themes, evaluation of an agency's program and service delivery is best implemented if it is built into its ongoing functions as an integral component of its activities. In this way, agency staff can be fully involved in the planning and process of the evaluation and in learning from its results. Following is, first, a summary of various sets of guidelines that we have found to be useful in the field of family and children's services, as formulated by different authors. Then, we describe a range of pertinent tools for evaluation.

Greenstein (2001) focuses on helping students and practitioners to understand and use research on families. He addresses a number of essential questions:

- Why do research on families?
- What are the stages of social research?
- What are the benefits of well-conducted research?
- How is research analyzed?
- How are literature searches and reviews conducted?
- How is the Internet best used in research?

Feldman (1990) presents guidelines for delineating the target population, an early step in the process of evaluation aimed at making clear the identifiable unit to which programs are directed or carefully defining the client system. Such definition assists the evaluation in the following tasks, as described by Feldman (1990:17):

- determining whether or not the program is reaching the families to which it is addressed,
- developing a client typology — identifying the types of clients thought to be appropriate for the program,

- conducting comparisons with other client samples of the program over time,
- conducting comparisons with other programs using similar or traditional service approaches.

In his formulation of guidelines for assessing the impact of home-based services, Fraser (1990:77–101) describes a set of steps that can be helpful to administrators and others charged with carrying out the evaluation. These include

- building a conceptual framework of the various service components and skills required to achieve program outcomes,
- selecting appropriate measures to assess program outcomes, specifically measures appropriate to the program's developmental stage,
- using multiple indicators, and
- using *proximal measures* (e.g., measures of family functioning) and *distal measures* (e.g., the long-term results of intervention).

In a publication resulting from an "Outcomes and Decision-Making Project" sponsored by the Casey Family Program (American Humane Association 1998), the authors describe principles and concepts for assessing outcomes in child welfare services. Particularly noteworthy is their framework for measuring what is achieved in providing services to children and families, along with their guidelines for assisting agencies in building an outcome approach for child welfare services. The framework consists of these four major dimensions of performance measurement or core outcome indicators (American Humane Association 1998:36–38):[3]

- *Quantity of efforts*: How much was delivered by the program (e.g., number of children served)?
- *Output/effect*: How much desired change was produced (e.g., number of grade levels in which a particular child advanced in two years)?
- *Quality of effort*: How well was the service delivered (e.g., how long children waited prior to placement in a permanent family)?
- *Quality of results*: What effect or degree of change was produced for a group of families and children (e.g., number of youths who secured summer employment)?

Pecora and Maluccio (2000) apply the above guidelines in a review of studies regarding permanency planning outcomes for children and youths in foster care. On the basis of this review these authors delineate the following dimensions of program effectiveness:

- goal-oriented case planning and family involvement,
- providing youths with some voice in their care,
- focusing on independent living skills,
- facilitating child adjustment,
- agency investment in staff members who provide an array of services,
- availability of highly skilled workers,
- facilitating parent-child visitation in out-of-home placement, and
- school and community involvement as part of a system of care.

The above success factors from research on permanency planning suggest the need to select certain data on which to base plans for new interventions. In addition, Pecora et al. (1995) delineate a range of challenges and tasks in evaluation of family-based services, in such areas as evaluation designs, sampling, program efficiency, and assessment of services and their outcomes in relation to child and family functioning. Barth and Jonson-Reid (2000) consider issues and recommendations for inclusion of post–child welfare services outcome indicators, such as mortality and incarceration, in the evaluation of the performance of child welfare systems. Building on a review of recent outcome studies, Poertner, McDonald, and Murray (2000) propose definitions of outcome measures and standards for evaluating success in public child welfare. They note that "wide variations exist in both definitions and performance-standards" (808) and offer suggestions for achieving greater standardization in measurements and for using outcome data in management decision making, court monitoring, and community involvement. Pecora et al. (1996) describe specific strategies for advancing quality improvement and evaluation in child and family services.

Building on the goals of *safety*, *permanence*, and *well-being* reflected in recent federal legislation (as discussed in chapter 3), the U.S. Department of Health and Human Services (undated: 2–4 to 2–9) in its 1998 annual report of child welfare outcomes delineates the following list of desirable goals in each of the above areas for child welfare agencies throughout the country:

- reduce recurrence of child abuse and/or neglect,
- reduce the incidence of child abuse and/or neglect in foster care,
- increase permanence for children in foster care,
- reduce time in foster care prior to reunification without increasing reentry,
- reduce time in foster care prior to adoption,
- increase placement stability, and
- reduce placement of young children in group homes or institutions.

The above clearly are lofty goals toward which public and private agencies should strive. Ongoing assessment of an agency's services and their outcomes is a fundamental component of this process. Ahsan and Cramer (1998) provide a toolkit for self-assessment of family support agencies that can be adapted to various agency settings. The toolkit includes instructions for forming a community team to guide the self-assessment, along with checklists of performance indicators or measurable outcomes, in such areas as governance, outreach, casework with families and children, and monitoring and evaluation. Pecora and associates (1998) delineate a useful approach to assessing results of interventions with youths in family foster care, suggesting that agencies might want to measure the impact of their programs on young people in the following areas:

- emotional functioning,
- placement stability,
- development of cultural identity,
- use of tobacco products,
- educational competence,
- volunteer and paid employment experience, and
- illegal behaviors.

In addition to the guidelines and examples delineated above, we would highlight the following strategies for conducting agency-based evaluations of agency programs:[4]

- encouraging the participation of citizens from the agency's community in evaluation research,
- involving parents, youths, and direct service workers in identify-

ing appropriate program outcomes and setting the research agenda,

- specifying measurable process and outcome objectives during the program planning and design stages,
- focusing on important program outcomes that are directly related to agency goals, functions, and services,
- using an evaluation design appropriate to the research question and the developmental stage of the service or agency,
- including both process and outcome evaluations,
- considering treatment fidelity as an important issue — ensuring that the intervention is carried out as planned,
- using multiple methods of measurement from multiple sources,
- using culturally appropriate measures and indicators, and
- focusing on several levels of intervention: individual, family, and community.

To help achieve the goal of promoting the effectiveness of agency programs in each community, Weiss and Morrill (1998) suggest the creation of *learning organizations*. They define such an organization as one that "is able to create, acquire, and transfer knowledge as well as modify its own behavior to reflect new knowledge and insights" (2). Accordingly, they propose a model for developing a "continuous learning system" through a learning organization. The model consists of the following five steps (Weiss and Morrill 1998:3–4):

- engaging key stakeholders in strategic planning in setting activities, goals, and standards,
- learning from experience and research and incorporating lessons into the design of programs and policies,
- engaging in innovation, monitoring, and evaluation,
- learning from evaluation and comparisons with other organizations and making corrections on an ongoing basis, and
- applying lessons that are learned to program revisions and delineating knowledge gaps requiring further research and implementation.[5]

The case example provided in a later section of this chapter regarding evaluation of family certification illustrates these concepts and guidelines.

Tools for Evaluation

Various texts are available as aids in conducting evaluation of an agency's program and service delivery as well as in assessing social work practice in general (see, for example, Bloom, Fischer, and Orme 1999; Cournoyer and Klein 2000; Nugent, Sieppert, and Hudson 2001; Reamer 1998c; and Unrau, Gabor, and Grinnell 2001). In addition, we recommend for practitioners and administrators in family and child welfare agencies the tools described below. We include three national reports that agencies can use to measure trends in the communities they serve (Children's Defense Fund 2000; Federal Interagency Coordinating Council 2000; and U.S. Department of Health and Human Services, Public Health Service 2000).

Ansell-Casey Life Skills Assessment (Ansell and the Casey Family Programs 1997).

The Ansell-Casey Life Skills Assessment (ACLSA) consists of a set of tools developed following extensive testing to measure the life skill competencies of preadolescents and adolescents in foster care. The purpose is to identify areas in which these young people need help to develop or strengthen such skills in preparation for living successfully in the community upon emancipation.

The above tools consist of separate reports completed by the youths and their caregivers and cover the following domains, with different versions for different age groups:

- physical development and self-care,
- educational and vocational development,
- social development,
- community and housing issues, and
- moral development.[6]

Assessing Children's Exposure to Community Violence (Guterman and Cameron 1997)

Describes an assessment framework for examining the impact of community violence on children and youths. The framework consists of four interrelated domains:

- Identification of the young person's involvement in community violence and characterization of the nature of the involvement.
- Sequelae assessment to determine the impact of community violence on the young person.
- Lethality assessment to determine the degree to which the young person is in imminent or ongoing danger.
- Ecological assessment to best understand the presence of risks and protective factors shaping outcomes in the client's life (Guterman and Cameron 1997:500).

Behavioral and Emotional Rating Scale (BERS) (Pro-Ed 1998)[7]

This scale, which is completed by professionals involved with the child, reflects a strength-based approach to assessment. It is used to rate a child's behaviors and emotions in a positive way. Each statement (e.g., "Accepts a hug" and "Completes homework regularly") describes the child's status in the previous three months.

Caldwell HOME Inventory for Infants (Caldwell and Bradley 1984)

A widely used instrument to measure cognitive stimulation and emotional support of infants and young children. It consists of both interview and observation on six subscales:

- mother's emotional and verbal responsivity;
- use of punishment;
- physical environment;
- availability of play materials;
- quality of maternal/child interaction; and
- child's opportunities for variety.

Child and Adolescent Functional Assessment Scale (Hodges 1994)[8]

This is used to assess a youth's functional impairment in the areas of *role performance* (school/work, home, and community) and *moods/self-harm* (emotions and self-harmful behaviors).

Cultural Competence Self-Assessment Instrument (Child Welfare League of America 1993)

This is a practical and easy-to-use management tool to help agencies assess, in a structured way, their delivery of culturally competent child welfare services. This self-assessment instrument:

> provides a framework for determining whether an agency's existing policies, practices, and programs are designed to achieve and promote cultural competence in the areas of governance, program development, administration and management, and service delivery.
>
> (ix)

By using the above instrument, agencies can develop and implement a strategic plan for integrating principles of cultural competence into their services. Especially useful is a list of suggested procedures for accomplishing such tasks as the following:

- designating a coordinator and organizing an "Assessment Committee";
- compiling relevant agency documents;
- determining procedures for self-assessment;
- conducting the self-assessment; and
- analyzing, recording and reporting the findings.

Evaluating Comprehensive Community Change (Annie E. Casey Foundation 1998b)

This report of a conference on conducting evaluation of comprehensive community initiatives outlines recommendations for dealing with concerns about study design and methodology, data collection and management, and interpretation and dissemination of findings. Suggestions are also offered for improving such evaluations.

Evaluating the Quality of Kinship Foster Care: Evaluation Package (Agathen, O'Donnell, and Wells 1999)

The instruments contained in this volume measure quality of care in the kinship foster home, along with contextual factors that influence the kinship family's functioning and selected indicators of child functioning. Included are the following instruments:caseworker self-administered questionnaire, caregiver interview, case record review, and child interview. The instruments were reviewed by authorities with special knowledge in kinship care and experts in survey research. A literature review also prepared by the authors contains an extensive review of writings on issues related to quality in kinship care as well as descriptors in these three areas: selection and approval of families, evaluation of care, and outcomes of care.

Family to Family Tools for Rebuilding Foster Care. The need for self-evaluation: Using data to guide policy and practice (Annie E. Casey Foundation n.d.e)

This publication provides information on routinely collected data bases to track child and family experiences and outcomes across several types of service systems; data analysis techniques, such as longitudinal analyses; and guidelines for building self-evaluation teams to improve child welfare policy and practice.

Guidelines for Family Support Practice (Family Resource Coalition 1996)

Describes a set of principles for family support practice, as also reviewed in chapter 6. Each principle is explored in depth, with emphasis on the theory and research underlying it, and with examples of how programs realize those principles.

How Are We Doing? A Program Self-Assessment Toolkit for the Family Support Field (Ahsan and Cramer 1998)

Provides benchmarks and checklists to enable programs to assess their commitment to and ability to act upon principles of family support practice. For example, an agency or program can examine the ways in which outreach to families is provided and whether or not families are actively and properly engaged in service planning and delivery. *(See further description in appendix 1.)*

Kids Count Data Book: State Profiles of Child Well-Being (Annie E. Casey Foundation 2000, 2001)

In this annual publication, the Casey Foundation tracks the "state of children" in the United States on a state-by-state basis. The year 2000 edition

compares data for 2000 with corresponding data during the 1990s along the
following 10 indicators, each of which is used to rank states:

- percent low-birthweight babies;
- infant mortality rate (deaths per 1,000 live births);
- child death rate (deaths per 100,000 children ages 1–14);
- rate of teen deaths by accident, homicide, and suicide (deaths per
  100,000 teens ages 15–19);
- teen birth rate (births per 1,000 females ages 15–17);
- percent of teens who are high school dropouts (ages 16–19);
- percent of teens not attending school and not working (ages 16–19);
- percent of children living with parents who do not have full-time
  year-round employment;
- percent of children in poverty (data reflect poverty in the previous
  year);
- percent of families with children headed by a single parent.

Looking After Children (Jackson 1998; Parker et al. 1991; Ward 1998)

This instrument was originally developed in England and has more recently
been adapted for use in Australia, Canada, and various European countries.
It is clearly worth considering for use in family and child service agencies
in the United States, primarily as an evaluative tool that can be employed
to assess outcomes throughout the helping process as well as upon termination, in cases of "children in need," that is, those coming to the attention
of family and child welfare agencies.

The instrument, which has been extensively tested and revised, includes
a series of schedules, with versions for different age groups. The schedules
can be used by practitioners to measure developmental outcomes for children on their caseloads. Each schedule covers one of the following seven
dimensions, which are believed by the authors "to be important elements
in achieving a satisfactory outcome for children looked after by local authorities" (Parker et al. 1991:84):[9]

- health;
- education;
- emotional and behavioral development;

- family and peer relationships;
- self-care and competence;
- identity; and
- social skills.

Parenting Stress Index Short Form (Abidin 1990)

Assesses the level of stress in the parent-child dyad, through 36 statements organized in four subscales:

- parental stress
- difficult parent-child interaction;
- difficult child; and
- defensive responses (of parent).

Principles of Family Involvement (Federal Interagency Coordinating Council 2000)

The Federal Interagency Coordinating Council (FICC) has adopted (September 14, 2000) a policy statement on "Principles of Family Involvement," which reflects its emphasis on involving family members in policy and service delivery planning, development, implementation and evaluation. Through these principles, the FICC encourages agencies to review their programs by:

- assessing the degree to which your individual organization's policies and programs conform;
- building awareness among staff members and stakeholders of these concepts and their importance;
- facilitating individual and collective dialogue among staff members and stakeholders about the importance of these standards in your organization's mission;
- exploring the specific changes which these benchmarks imply within your own organization, agency, and in your individual work; and
- encouraging the dissemination of these strategies across the early childhood field. (Federal Interagency Coordinating Council 2000:1).

Quality Improvement and Evaluation in Child and Family Services:
Managing Into the Next Century (Pecora et al. 1996)

The authors offer practical tools and techniques pertaining to change strategies, outcome-oriented approaches to practice, program evaluation instruments, integrated information systems, and program planning.

Reconnecting Families: A Guide to Strengthening Family Reunification
Services (Warsh, Pine, and Maluccio 1996)

Describes in detail materials needed by public and private agencies to conduct a comprehensive self-assessment of their family reunification policies,
programs, and resources. Includes guidelines for setting up work teams of
agency staff members and community representatives, to identify system
strengths, recommend improvements, and carry out action plan for change.

The Social Work Ethics Audit: A Risk Management Tool (Reamer 2001a)

Presents step-by-step directions for implementing an "ethics audit" in an agency,
that is, to examine critically the agency's ethics-related practices, policies, and
procedures and determine appropriate action plans and strategies for correcting
any inadequacies or problems in ethical practice. The volume includes:

- a manual discussing a range of ethical issues that social workers
  should assess in their agencies;
- instructions for conducting the ethics audit;
- the audit instrument, which includes a scale for ranking ethics-
  related policies as well as guidelines for developing action plans
  to address risks and deficiencies; and
- a template on a computer disk useful for recording results and
  planning improvements.

The State of America's Children: Yearbook 2000 (Children's Defense
Fund 2000)

In this periodic publication the Children's Defense Fund tracks national
trends in the lives of children in the United States, on a national as well as
state-by-state basis; examines the problems affecting children and their families; and proposes an agenda for action. Covered are the following areas:

- family income;
- child health;
- child care;
- education;
- children and families in crisis; and
- juvenile justice and youth development.

Trends in the Well-Being of America's Children and Youth (U.S. Department of Health and Human Services, Office of the Assistant Secretary for Planning and Evaluation 2000)

This is an annual federal report on trends in the well-being of the nation's children and youths. The "report presents a broad and carefully chosen collection of national estimates of child and youth well-being" (9), based on the most recent and reliable estimates on over 80 indicators in the following areas:

- population, family, and neighborhood,
- economic security, including poverty, income, and employment,
- health conditions and health care,
- social development, behavioral health, and teen fertility, and
- education and academic achievement.

Evaluating a Family Reunification Program: Case Example

The following example illustrates some of the principles and guidelines discussed in this chapter as well as the use of a particular evaluative tool to involve staff and clients in assessing an agency's family reunification program.[10] The example provides a rationale for undertaking and then describes a comprehensive project for ascertaining the strengths and needs in twenty-five components of a service delivery system designed to reunify families whose children have been placed in foster care. The following areas are covered in the project:

- rationale,
- project implementing, and
- program benefits.

Rationale

It is widely known that child and family welfare agencies operate in an environment of the "permanent whitewater" of difficult and sometimes impossible decisions, changing community expectations, new legal mandates, and increasingly negative media coverage and public outrage when children in their care are hurt. Added to these, some agencies face challenges such as difficulty in recruiting and retaining foster parents, strained relationships with the legal system, high staff turnover, and the demands of responding to lawsuits brought by child and family advocates seeking legal redress to improve services.

Regardless of the challenges an individual agency faces, practitioners and administrators in child welfare must continuously strive to improve services so that families are preserved and children in placement have the best chance of returning home. Some administrators are responding through participatory management approaches — by increasing the role of staff and other stakeholders in solving agency problems, evaluating agency programs, and making recommendations about policy and operations (Pine, Warsh, and Maluccio 1998).

Why should child welfare administrators involve staff and others in what have typically been management's roles? The main reason is to improve services, especially in the face of the challenges delineated above. Participatory management approaches, as these are called, have the advantage of improving the quality and quantity of the information needed to solve problems, promoting consensus about the values and goals of the organization, and increasing stakeholder ownership of both problems and their solutions on the basis of systematic assessment of the agency's program and service delivery. Moreover, since most of these strategies involve the work of an interdisciplinary team or task force, the work charts the way for, and demonstrates the effectiveness of, a *partnership approach* that is the bedrock of successful child welfare practice.

Project Implementation

These participatory approaches can readily be applied to family reunification, as seen in the *Family Reunification Project*, an initiative in which agencies engage administrators, staff, foster parents, birth parents, legal staff, and other service providers to evaluate family reunification programs and charting a course for improving them on a systematic and ongoing basis (Warsh, Pine, and Maluccio 1996). The purpose of such a project is to help the agency conduct an assessment of the strengths and needs of its family reunification system and then develop a careful plan for agencywide change. It is both a top down and a bottom up approach that involves staff members at all levels of the agency in achieving systemic changes rather than simply making a few improvements in the provision of family reunification services. The project is a "top down" approach to making needed improvements because the agency's top-level administrators introduce it, provide leadership for its implementation, and ensure that the plan developed is actually implemented. It is also a "bottom up" approach because of the involvement of line staff, supervisors, foster parents, and others in a work team or task force that, through independent study and a series of group discussions, conducts the assessment and develops the recommendations for change.

The assessment incorporates twenty-five components of a family reunification system. Each of the components has been defined by a set of best practices drawn from research and expertise in family reunification services (Warsh, Pine, and Maluccio 1996). The components are organized into three main areas, as outlined below:

The Agency
- mission and principles
- financial management
- work environment
- workload
- recruitment
- cultural competence
- social work roles/responsibilities
- foster parent roles/responsibilities
- supervision
- staff development
- program monitoring/evaluation

Services
- assessment and goal planning
- preparing families for reunification
- preparing children for reunification

- visiting
- postreunification services
- funding sources

Interorganizational
Relations
- governmental bodies
- external reviewers
- cross-system collaboration
- court and legal systems
- community provider agencies
- law enforcement agencies
- school systems
- public relations and information

There are six steps to the Family Reunification Project, as follows:

- committing to the project,
- forming the work and management teams,
- launching the project,
- conducting the assessment,
- planning for change, and
- evaluating the project.

Program Benefits

The resulting benefits can be many. Undertaking a project aimed specifically at examining and evaluating family reunification services brings together the full range of players involved in family reunification to jointly consider current practices and work together to find ways of strengthening the service delivery system, in line with the "Framework of Needs and Resources for Family and Child Well-Being" delineated in chapter 1. The process of shared problem solving can result in a "we're in this together" attitude and an increased sense of individual responsibility for enhancing services.

Participants in all aspects of service delivery are reminded of how difficult it is to create and maintain a responsive child welfare system and their own part in shaping it. Moreover, there is much potential for learning and a renewed sense of optimism as participants have opportunities to reflect on their own work and that of others in contributing to the important goals of protecting children and preserving their families through systematic and dynamic evaluation that can lead to comprehensive and responsive programs. Most important, undertaking a comprehensive project such as that described here results in a blueprint for action — a clear plan for improving services and programs (Pine, Warsh, and Maluccio 1998).

Evaluating One's Own Practice

In addition to evaluation of an agency's program and service delivery in general, it is important to evaluate the process and outcome of the service in each case situation — not only to maximize the help provided to the family and children but also to learn how to enhance one's role and functioning in future cases. For these purposes we encourage social workers to examine and evaluate the service — including their own contributions — both periodically during the process of providing it and upon its conclusion.[11]

Evaluation Questions

Evaluation of one's practice in each case situation includes questions such as the following:

- What refinements are indicated in the assessments of the case?
- What are the strategies that are most effective in the intervention?
- What changes are indicated in the intervention?
- How can other agencies and/or community representatives be involved more actively and meaningfully on behalf of the family?
- What has the practitioner learned about each family's background, culture, and lifestyle that can enhance her or his ability to provide culturally sensitive and appropriate services?
- What has been learned about informal helping resources for this client (or within the community)? What changes might be suggested to involve informal helpers more effectively?
- What have the service delivery systems learned from this particular case that may be applied to other situations? What changes might be needed at the system level to support changes in practice?

Evaluation Strategies

In the efforts to address evaluative questions such as the above in the course of their practice in particular cases or upon their termination, practitioners can follow a number of guidelines for monitoring, reassessment, and outcome evaluation that have been delineated by Rothman (1994:173–190) in his examination of practice with "highly vulnerable clients." Foremost among these are the following:

- using formal or standardized instruments such as forms, rating scales, questionnaires, and checklists (such as those included in appendix 1);
- using informal techniques such as correspondence, everyday observation, scanning case records, and contacts with members of the client's support network;
- focusing on different levels, from the client to the informal network as well as the formal service system;
- using forms to aid monitoring, such as index cards to keep track of contacts with clients and their support network (as described in appendix 1);
- tracking changes in the child or family through use of management information systems;
- examining the implementation of the treatment or service plan, assessing progress toward goal attainment and specific outcomes or changes achieved, and reexamining the validity of the intervention plan; and
- reassessing the process and outcome of intervention upon termination, so as to derive implications for further service within the agency or elsewhere, as considered in chapter 6.

Gambrill (1997:475–509) also emphasizes the value of assessing outcomes as an integral component of one's practice in specific cases. Toward this end, she offers a number of guidelines regarding evaluation activities. The latter should be:

Relevant: Meaningful to clients and significant to others.
Specific: Clearly described.

Sensitive: Reflect changes that occur.

Feasible: Possible to obtain.

Unintrusive: Not interfere with service provision.

Valid: Measure what they are supposed to measure.

Reliable: Show consistency over different measurements in the absence of change.

Cost effective (Gambrill 1997:478).

We would also like to call attention to the usefulness of single-system designs in the evaluation of family and children's services (Nugent, Sieppert, and Hudson 2001). Such designs "refer to a set of empirical procedures used to observe changes in an identified target (a specified problem or objective of the client) that is measured repeatedly over time" (Bloom, Fischer, and Orme 1999:5). These designs are particularly valuable in that they can actively involve the clients in the evaluation and can be applied to any level of the client system — from an individual or family to a group or community.

Obtaining Consumer Feedback[12]

We also urge that workers obtain the views of clients regarding their helping efforts throughout the helping process, and particularly during the termination phase. Consumer feedback can accomplish various purposes. First, the systematic gathering of clients' views and impressions serves as a means of monitoring social work practice and as an essential component of program planning and evaluation. One study of client feedback, for example, generated a number of practice implications in areas such as the role of client and social worker expectations in the initial phase of the helping process, the dynamic nature of client-social worker contracting, the need for systematic collaboration between formal and informal helpers, and the significance of social networks and support systems in the client's environment (Maluccio 1990). In another study in the United Kingdom, children in placement offered many suggestions for improving services in such areas as confidentiality, case reviews, and placement recommendations (Munro 2001).

In addition, at the agency level the systematic gathering of clients' views and impressions is valuable in monitoring social work practice and in program planning and evaluation. When client feedback is communicated to workers, it is often motivating and serves as a boost to staff morale. At the same time, essential areas for staff training and development may be identified. As one example, one family preservation program posted on a bulletin board positive comments made by client families; these comments were rewarding for *all* workers to read, especially when a worker was faced with a challenging situation. Here they were reminded of how valuable their services were to families and what skills and activities families most appreciated (Kinney, Haapala, and Booth 1991).

Obtaining client perceptions can thus help to maintain accountability, identify service gaps or deficiencies, influence policy formulation and decision making, and initiate program innovations. At the case level, emphasis on client feedback can serve to engage clients even more actively in the helping process; at the same time, it can help workers to examine and revise their approach. Obtaining feedback in each situation can help ensure that the practitioner is attuned as much as possible to the client's feelings, needs, views, and qualities. Moreover, eliciting the client's views can have positive consequences for the client — by, for instance, providing her or him with opportunities for decision making, reducing the social distance between client and worker, enhancing the sense of mutuality between them, and increasing the client's sense of power and control.

Consumer feedback can be facilitated in either individual cases or for purposes of agencywide evaluation through a variety of research approaches and strategies, such as structured or unstructured questionnaires, structured or unstructured interviews, self-reports on the part of clients, surveys, client satisfaction scales, and focus groups. We recommend, in particular, the use of qualitative methodology to help capture the richness and complexity of the client's perceptions, understanding, and feelings. Specific guidelines for conducting formal or informal evaluation of services are delineated by Marshall and Rossman (1999), Padgett (1998), Sherman and Reid (1994), and Strauss and Corbin (1998).

In line with the increasing emphasis on effectiveness and accountability in the social services, client or consumer feedback can be a prominent component of program evaluation. Obtaining such feedback routinely in the course of providing social services, as well as through more formal studies, can be of benefit to us in relation to education, research, theory building, and service delivery. By regularly obtaining the views of those whom we serve, we may be able to achieve a better understanding of social work intervention — an understanding that can lead to improvement of services.

As demonstrated in the previously noted study of client perception of services in a family counseling agency (Maluccio 1990), social workers can learn from clients through a mutually rewarding process in which both they and their clients help each other to change and grow. Clients experienced satisfaction by participating in the above study. Many expressed surprise and pleasure that someone would be interested in their views. Others indicated that the research interviews helped them to review their experience with the agency and to appreciate or consolidate their gains.

More explicit emphasis on client reactions as an integral feature of practice can serve to engage the individual, family, or group even more actively in the helping process. At the same time, it can help workers to examine and revise their methods. Client feedback can thus contribute to a mutually rewarding process of interaction and growth between practitioners and their clients. By being tuned into the clients' perspectives, social workers are better able to determine which methods are effective, which approaches may need to be modified, and which assumptions about human behavior and social work practice should be questioned.

The use of client feedback ultimately can enhance social work practice and service delivery, contribute to theory building, and enrich the education of future practitioners. By evaluating their practice on an ongoing basis, social workers can also contribute to the monitoring and assessing of services provided by their agencies. Such evaluation is essential, to help workers and agencies in being responsive to the variety and variability of families and in implementing the most effective program strategies for strengthening and enhancing family life.

The following example from the field of adoption illustrates the critical role of research results, especially client feedback, in designing program interventions.

Special needs adoption is a relatively new social welfare program in which the benefit — a permanent family — is allocated to a child who needs one. Without the intervention of special needs adoption services, children deemed to have special needs because of a serious disability are likely to remain in foster care indefinitely. The emergence of expanded medical coverage, adoption subsidy payments, and postadoption support services have all been a part of these new efforts. However, because the adoptive family is essentially the benefit, adoption policy and practice must be shaped around what the families need and want in order to be successful.

Two studies of families that adopted children with developmental disabilities examined what contributed to positive outcomes, specifically the families' success and satisfaction in rearing their children and in dealing with their special needs (Lightburn and Pine 1996). The authors used qualitative and quantitative approaches to obtain this information from the families. When results of the two studies were synthesized, several factors relating to parental satisfaction with the services and supports they were provided emerged as key to positive outcomes.

First, parents wanted to be seen as partners in the helping process; they wanted professionals to listen to them and take their parental expertise seriously. Second, the parents' assessment that the financial supports in the form of medical benefits and adoption subsidies for their children were adequate was highly correlated with positive outcomes for these adoptive families. Finally, parents needed and wanted a wide range of information supports in order to meet their children's special needs. These included information about legal issues, special education, parenting, and resources for health and mental health, recreation, advocacy, and other specialized services. When needed information was provided either directly or through adoptive parent support groups organized by adoption agencies, family and parental satisfaction was higher.

The findings in the above studies as well as other investigations underscore the importance of using both qualitative and quantitative research to obtain information from families about what service interventions they find most useful.

As we have sought to convey in this chapter, evaluation is an ongoing task for social workers and administrators — as well as a vehicle for involving clients in the helping process by obtaining their feedback on a regular basis. Although we have emphasized the roles of practitioners and administrators, evaluation is most effective if it involves joint efforts by practitioners and researchers and other stakeholders in the program: "We believe that the likelihood of successful researcher-practitioner collaboration will be enhanced greatly if researchers and practitioners share their understanding of the various knowledge needs of practice" (Rosen, Proctor, and Staudt 1999:13).

In addition to helping us in improving ongoing services at the case, agency, and even policy levels, evaluation can be instrumental in stimulating and guiding new directions in service delivery — the subject of the next and final chapter.

Notes

1. See Maluccio, Ainsworth, and Thoburn (2000) for a comprehensive, comparative review of outcome research on child welfare programs in Australia, the United Kingdom, and the United States in relation to services ranging from adoption to family preservation and including traditional services as well as more recent service initiatives.
2. See Ginsberg (2001) and Gray and associates (1998) for guidelines and strategies for conducting evaluation in human service agencies and applying evaluation as a management tool. Also, the Child Welfare League of America publishes a series of Standards of Excellence in each area of practice in child welfare agencies; the standards are revised periodically on the basis of current research and knowledge and serve as valuable tools for self-assessment by agencies. See http://www.cwla .org (March 1, 2001).
3. See American Humane Association (1998) for description of the "Outcomes and Decision-Making Project" and the outcome framework and core indicators. This material is also available on the project website: http://www.caseyoutcomes.org (March 15, 2001).
4. The following are examples of agencies with which the authors have worked that regularly undertake evaluation research focused on their programs:

Casey Family Services
One Corporate Drive
Shelton, CT 06484

The Casey Family Program
1300 Dexter Avenue North
Seattle, WA 98109

The Village for Families and Children
1680 Albany Avenue
Hartford, CT 06105

5. A free quarterly newsletter, "The Evaluation Exchange: Emerging
    Strategies in Evaluating Child and Family Services" is published by

    Harvard Family Research Project
    Harvard Graduate School of Education
    38 Concord Avenue
    Cambridge, MA 02138
    www.http://gseweb.harvard.edu/hfrp (June 1, 2001)

6. Further information regarding the Ansell-Casey Life Skills Assessment
    Forms may be obtained from

    Bavendam Research Associates
    3010 77th Avenue, SE, Suite 204
    Mercer Island, WA 98040

7. The BERS rating scale may be obtained from

    PRO-ED
    8700 Shoal Creek Boulevard
    Austin, TX 78757–6897

8. The Child and Adolescent Functional Assessment Scale may be ob-
    tained from

    Kay Hodges
    2140 Old Earhart Road
    Ann Arbor, MI 48105

9. For reports of implementation of the "Looking After Children" assess-
    ment instrument in the United Kingdom and other countries, see Ward
    (1998).
10. This section has been adapted from Pine, Warsh, and Maluccio (1998);
    and Warsh, Pine, and Maluccio (1996).

11. For a comprehensive collection of tools to measure client/family functioning and attributes, see Corcoran and Fischer (2000).
12. This section draws from Maluccio (1979, 1990).

Questions for Discussion

1. Your agency's executive director has asked you for assistance in evaluating the agency's effectiveness with clients from minorities of color. How would you proceed to respond to this request?
2. Social work colleagues in your agency are eager to learn how to evaluate their effectiveness with clients and have come to you for help. How would you respond to their request?
3. Develop a tool for examining the effectiveness of your agency's practice with children or adolescents on your agency's caseloads.
4. Analyze your practice in one or more of your cases involving populations at risk and identify ways of improving your effectiveness with comparable clients.
5. Social work colleagues in your agency question or doubt the usefulness of obtaining feedback from their clients. Make a case for obtaining such feedback.
6. Review an instrument to measure client satisfaction such as that developed by Larsen et al. (1979). Adapt it for use with clients in your program or agency.

Suggestions for Further Information

Corcoran, K. and J. Fischer 2000. *Measures for Clinical Practice: A Sourcebook.* Vols. 1, 2. 3d ed. New York: Free.

Gambrill, E. 1997. *Social Work Practice: A Critical Thinker's Guide.* New York: Oxford University Press.

Gray, S. T. and associates. 1998. *Evaluation with Power: A New Approach to Organizational Effectiveness, Empowerment, and Excellence.* San Francisco: Jossey-Bass.

Harvard Family Research Project. 1998. *The Evaluation Exchange: Emerging Strategies in Evaluating Child and Family Services.* http://gseweb.harvard.edu /nhfnp/eval (March 30, 2000).

Maluccio, A. N., F. Ainsworth, and J. Thoburn. 2000. *Child Welfare Outcome Research in the United States, United Kingdom, and Australia.* Washington, D.C.: CWLA.

Rothman, J. 1994. *Practice with Highly Vulnerable Clients: Case Management and Community-Based Service.* Englewood Cliffs, N.J.: Prentice-Hall.

U.S. Department of Health and Human Services, Administration for Children and Families. 1998. *Child Welfare Outcomes 1998: Annual Report.* Washington, D.C.: USDHHS. Also available at http://www.acf.dhhs.gov/programs/cb (April 15, 2000).

Yuan, Y.-Y. and M. Rivest, eds. 1990. *Preserving Families: Evaluation Resources for Practitioners and Policymakers.* Newbury Park, Cal.: Sage.

10   Future Challenges and Opportunities

The centenary's Janus moment provides an opportunity to compare and contrast our circumstances with those of our founders, to note the benchmarks of progress and, most important, to take a candid look not only at the gaps and needs that invite rededicated action, but also at the radical changes in our world that demand major rethinking.

(Hopps 2000:3)

In this volume we are primarily concerned with the current status of social work theory on and practice with and on behalf of families and children. In addition, as Hopps (2000) indicates above in her introduction to a collection of essays reflecting on the future of the social work profession at the beginning of the new millennium, it is also timely to look toward the future.[1] As we do so, we see a number of issues in the following areas:

- policy issues and strategies for promoting child development and functioning,
- redefining child abuse and neglect and reforming child protective services,
- extending the scope of family preservation services to encompass the employment, housing, and health needs of all families,
- enhancing family foster care outcomes through increased accountability and the use of data for planning and policy formulation,
- rethinking "orphanages" as an effective option for certain children and youths,
- expanding rigorous research on child welfare issues, and
- broadening our attention to the needs of families and children in relation to violence, war, and terrorism (Maluccio and Anderson 2000b:7).

As reflected in the above list of issues, it is apparent that social work with families and children is a rapidly changing field. The events of September 11, 2001, illustrate the rapidity with which change occurs and creates new demands on social workers and other practitioners for help and support to families. Across the nation, but especially in New York City, family service agencies and social workers were mobilized to provide help to victims of terrorist attacks and their families as well as others who were directly or indirectly affected. In this final chapter we therefore review various contemporary influences, including the impact of welfare reform, managed care, growing global interdependence, and selected federal policies and programs. We then conclude by considering implications for social work education and training.

Welfare Reform

In line with social work values regarding dignity and worth of human beings and the profession's commitment to social justice, we must ensure that a continuum of services exists in each community, along with adequate funding. Two-thirds of those who receive welfare benefits are children. With the recent reforms in welfare programs, positive and negative effects on children are likely to occur in the areas of health, schooling, and emotional and social functioning.

Korr and Brieland (2000) examine current welfare reform legislation and programs from the perspective of social justice and human rights. After raising the question of whether the poor are entitled to governmental assistance or should be dependent on private charity, they observe:

> The current conservative mindset leads people to focus on welfare, whereas the most significant issue is poverty. The United States is unlikely to go back to welfare as we have known it, but we are skeptical about loss of entitlements, substitution of block grants, and extension of local control that raise social justice questions.
>
> (Korr and Brieland 2000:85)

Similarly, Pelton (1999) decries the bias against poor families evident in recent welfare legislation as well as current legislative and administrative initiatives at the federal and state levels.

These recent changes in welfare programs, called reforms by some, clearly reflect a philosophic shift away from social support and protection for needy families (Kamerman 1996). Newly designed benefit caps, time limits, eligibility restrictions, penalties for receiving assistance for some groups (chiefly new immigrants), and work requirements reflect this shift, making the terms for welfare receipt even harsher than in the past (Soss 2000; Padilla 1997). The changes are the result of long-standing debates about public responsibility for the poor, dependency, even why people are poor, and a reigniting of resentment and anger toward the poor, blaming them for their own plight, especially poor, single mothers (Halpern 1999; Kamerman 1996). As Skoepal (1997:118) noted, "A welfare program originally conceived as 'mother's pensions' lost its legitimacy in an era of racial conflict, declining wages, and widespread female entry into the wage-labor market."

As indicated in chapter 3, the Aid to Families with Dependent Children (AFDC), a federal entitlement program, was repealed in 1996 and replaced by a block grant program, Temporary Assistance to Needy Families (TANF). Architects of the new TANF program point to its two major goals — reducing illegitimacy and welfare dependence — claiming that family values and a work ethic, more than income, influence family and child well-being in the long run (Koch 2000). Yet, as indicated in chapter 2, there is ample evidence of the role poverty plays in myriad family problems. Since the 1996 passage of PRWORA, however, the reforms have been praised for their success in reducing welfare dependence (Barth and Locklin 2001). The federal cash assistance caseload has dropped by 50 percent — from 4.4 million in August 1996 to 2.2 million in June 2000 (Acs and Loprest 2001). However, the principal, as yet unanswered, question remains: How have families leaving welfare fared? Specifically, what happens in the following situations:

- to family income when benefit caps are reached?
    do wages make up for lost cash assistance?
    does the cost of going to work result in net loss of income?
    do families lose other noncash benefits too?
    if income is reduced, what are the negative effects on families?

- when parents trade cash assistance for wages?
    do mothers spend less time with their children?
    do children respect their working mothers more?
    is the quality of alternative child care equal to (or better than) the parent's?

are there effects on families that have been separated by a child's placement in foster care?

if the increasing demand for child care providers for welfare leavers threatens the "supply"of foster care providers (Courtney and Maluccio 1999)?

if the work requirements under TANF impact on the families providing kinship foster care (Barth and Locklin 2001)?

The current welfare assistance program for families and children, TANF, is clearly designed to segregate the "deserving" from the "underserving" poor — that is, those capable of working. Under TANF, almost every recipient is pushed to find employment, regardless how menial and low paying it might be. Even those who find employment may earn wages that neither lift them out of poverty nor even above the welfare eligibility limits. Working families that continue to receive welfare face a five-year lifetime limit on benefits. While there is as yet limited information on the real impact of these new restrictions, some data are beginning to emerge. For example, a recent countrywide study in a rural New York county, where jobs are scarce and public transportation even scarcer, showed that 70 percent of the families leaving welfare were well below the poverty line of $14,000, with median incomes of only $11,000 (Sengupta 2001). The negative impact is even more severe for single-mother families, which usually have excessive child care costs (Meyers et al. 2001).

Another study, a synthesis of findings from eleven studies of former welfare recipients ("welfare leavers"), focuses on economic well-being of the families (Acs and Loprest 2001). The results show that most of the families go to work on exiting welfare — three out of five at some time within the year of leaving. They typically work full time and earn between seven and eight dollars an hour: their incomes are at about the poverty line. In terms of noncash benefits, one-third receives food stamps and less than half (two families in five) have public health insurance coverage (Acs and Loprest 2001).

The issue of noncash benefits is an important one in considering family well-being. Even when welfare benefits stop, families may still be eligible for such essential supports as food stamps and medical insurance. However, many families leaving welfare may not know this. According to one study, welfare leavers stopped getting food stamps at twice the rate of other families, even though, overall, two-thirds of leavers are still eligible for them (Zeldlewski and Brauner 1999).

It is also important to consider the impact of leaving welfare on parenting effectiveness, especially for families at risk of child abuse and neglect or families already separated by a child's placement in foster care. There is considerable overlap between the population of families receiving welfare and those receiving child welfare services; as many as 45 percent of child welfare service recipients also get cash assistance (Barth and Locklin 2001). Stress has long been associated with child maltreatment. Loss of family income is likely to produce greater stress, possibly leading to increased risk of abuse or neglect. As Barth and Locklin (2001:20) indicate, "Given the established association between poverty and maltreatment, it is incumbent upon child welfare advocates and policy makers to examine the impact of welfare reform on child welfare services" (Barth and Locklin 2001:20). On the other hand, we do not know to what extent meaningful employment (if a parent is able to find it) affects positive mental health and therefore parenting capacity. However, as reported in chapter 3, a large, countywide study of welfare leavers in Ohio showed that for parents whose children were in foster care, leaving welfare for work greatly delayed the family's reunification. As many as 75 percent of the children in foster care whose mothers left welfare for work were still in care after eighteen months, as compared to only 4 percent of children whose mothers continued to receive welfare benefits. The demands of work, especially at entry-level positions with few benefits and little flexibility, may preclude a parent's meeting the demands of the child welfare system for visiting and court appearances (Barth and Locklin 2001; Wells, Guo, and Li 2000).

As Halpern (1999) has noted, the current climate surrounding poor people has worsened considerably. Welfare reform is its most visible emblem. The full impact of welfare reform on vulnerable children and families is at this point unknown, as is the impact of other policy changes. For example, there are questions as to whether current policies, such as those embedded in the Adoption and Safe Families Act of 1997 (ASFA), will be successful in early adoptive placements that last, what the impact of increased diversity in our society is likely to be on social agencies and schools, what will be the effectiveness of new social work approaches such as permanency mediation, and what the trends in managed care are likely to be and how they will impact children and families.[2]

(See appendix 8 for description of electronic resources on system reform and advocacy for children and families.)

To counteract the current climate against poor families and children, we believe that the country needs to adopt family-supportive welfare reform strategies, such as those proposed by the Family Resource Coalition of America (1998–99:8). Such strategies are embodied in the following principles proposed by the coalition regarding reform of the welfare system:

- Foster "sustainable improvements in the lives of families."
- Recognize our society's "obligation to meet the basic needs of all people."
- "The welfare system should not penalize children."
- "The welfare system should recognize that some people will need long-term support."
- There should be continued "support for families during the transition from welfare to work."
- The system should also strive to strengthen the communities in which people live.
- The system should permit informal "supportive relationships between welfare recipients and their friends, neighbors, and families."
- The system should assist people "before they become destitute and desperate."[3]

Other Federal Legislation

As we look toward the future, we anticipate a number of additional challenges in the area of federal legislation affecting families and children. Here we list some of the more prominent examples, for further consideration by administrators, practitioners, educators, and students.[4]

- Changing population groups mean increased ethnic and racial diversity, with the consequent need to increase cultural competence in agencies and staff of family and children's service agencies (cf. Pierce and Pierce 1996).
- The impact of such recent federal legislative initiatives as the following, which were considered in chapter 3 and have also been described extensively elsewhere (cf. Downs et al. 2000; Pecora et al. 2000).

Adoption and Safe Families Act of 1997: delineates policies to promote adoption and other permanent homes, while maintaining the safety of children and youths as the paramount concern guiding child welfare services.

Multiethnic Placement Act of 1997 and the Interethnic Adoption Provisions Act of 1996: forbid foster care placement decisions primarily on the basis of race, ethnicity, or culture.

Adoption and Foster Care Analysis and Reporting System (AFCARS): establishes data collection policies regarding children in out-of-home care or adoption.

- The changes in federal policies that may result from the current Republican administration and Congress in such areas as public education, health insurance, and energy conservation, and funding, for example, for faith-based services.

Managed Care

The advent of managed care has not only produced in the United States dramatic changes in the delivery of health and mental health services but also provoked a torrent of dispute in society in general and the various professions, including social work, in particular. As Schamess and Lightburn (1998a:xvi) observe:

Many contend that managed care does not serve everyone, and that it serves unevenly. It has become increasingly evident that humane care in the managed care environment is conditional, depending on diagnosis, payer categories, service unit allowances, and available networks that are well resourced.[5]

In view of the widespread adoption and impact of managed care, however, it is incumbent on social workers in family and children's settings to become knowledgeable about it and to learn how to cope with the extensive competition evident in a managed care environment. Brach and Scallet (1998) discuss managed care challenges for children and family services, indicating that "it has taken hold in the health and mental health fields, and its impact on other systems that serve children and families is growing" (p. 99). These authors underscore the following risks, among others:

- overemphasis on a medical mode of care that is inconsistent with the psycho-social-behavioral model,
- exclusion of indigenous or community-based providers with expertise in children and families, and
- loss of opportunities for consumers to participate in the design and management of services affecting them.

At the same time, Brach and Scallet (1998:99) recognize that there are potentially positive aspects in managed care:

The attraction of managed care for children and family services lies in its potential to further goals long promoted by these systems: Reducing service fragmentation, increasing access to individualized care, establishing accountability, reducing costs, and stimulating the development of more appropriate and less restrictive community services.

Various guides are available to help administrators in responding to the challenges of a managed care environment. Emenhiser, Barker, and DeWoody (1995) address practical issues and strategies that family and child welfare agencies can consider to survive and thrive in a managed care environment, in such areas as leadership, programs, and finances. They note that managed care plans offer various advantages for agencies serving special-needs populations, including "expansions in early diagnosis and treatment, increased flexibility in treatment, and new sources of funding for community-based services such as wraparound" (xiii). But, they add, "Managed care also poses risks, however, especially for children with the most intensive service needs, who require comprehensive, long-term, and often expensive treatment" (xiii).

Drissel "presents a broad overview of managed care concepts and suggests some of the myriad challenges it raises for . . . administrators and advocates" in child and family services (n.d.:2). The above authors offer guidelines to assist state and local public officials in reviewing the existing system of services for vulnerable children and families and planning for required changes. Also, Nelson (2001) considers the potential for collaboration between family-centered services and managed care. Emenhiser et al. (1998) focus on a strategic vision for creation of networks, mergers, and partnerships in child welfare settings.[6] Pecora et al. (1996) focus on coping with changing times through techniques of quality improvement and evaluation.

Global Interdependence

In addition to the impact of federal legislation and domestic events and trends, now, and increasingly in the future, social work practice is being shaped by global events. Social problems and challenges for social workers are transcending national borders. Indeed, as Healy (2001) points out, global interdependence has dramatically reshaped social work in four important ways. First, international events, or political or economic events in one country, can result in the movement of whole populations. Wars and famine provide recent examples of the relocation of refugees to countries other than their own. In addition, economic opportunities unavailable at home may cause people to leave their own country for another. Thus, social workers are called upon to understand the migration/immigration experiences of new population groups as well as key elements of their culture and ethnic heritage in order to provide effective services to these groups.

A second influence of globalization on social work is the fact that so many social problems are shared among countries. This is particularly true during periods of global economic flux; economic recessions, for example, impact multiple nations with greater negative implications for people living in the poorest countries. Many of the problems considered in previous chapters, such as homelessness, HIV-AIDS, child maltreatment, and malnutrition, are, to varying degrees, worldwide problems. As members of an international profession, social workers are involved in helping to solve them, both in their own countries and as part of the global community.

A third and related influence of global interdependence on social work and social work practice is the fact that the actions of one country affect other countries. Economic policy, trade policy, and even domestic policies in any one country have a broad impact. For example, welfare reform legislation — a domestic policy — can, as discussed earlier, affect current and future immigrants. Immigration policy most certainly affects the movement of people from one country to another. A recent trade agreement between the United States and the European Union, reported in the *New York Times* (April 14, 2001), favoring the import of bananas from certain Central American nations is likely to have a dramatic impact on the well-being of people who live in the other banana producing countries such as those in the Caribbean, particularly when the latter are single-crop countries.[7] A more dramatic example is the American response to the terrorist attacks of September 11, 2001, which prompted bombing raids on Afghanistan and resulted in millions of Afghani refugees.

Finally, advances in technology have obscured borders, making it possible to have instant communication with people around the world. Computers, faxes, and video linkages have all made the transfer of technology — information about working to solve social problems — readily available to social workers who are willing to participate in these exchanges. Healy (2001) makes a strong case for the imperative of being an *international* social worker. She points out that American social workers must, at the very least, be able to address internationally related case and community situations. They can also have an active role in the solution of global social problems, be able to understand the impact of U.S. policies on other countries and their people, and participate in the international exchange of ideas and knowledge about social issues and problems germane to our profession.[8]

The following are examples of individual case and community situations requiring social workers to understand internationally related issues and policies.

• A family that has adopted a child from another country seeks guidance on obtaining citizenship for their child, which they have heard is an onerous process. The social worker is knowledgeable about a new policy granting automatic citizenship to adopted children under age eighteen with at least one American citizen as a parent.

• An immigrant woman seeks protection from an abusive partner at a battered women's shelter even though she is afraid that by seeking help she jeopardizes her application for legal status and may even be deported, since her partner, already a legal permanent resident, has threatened to withdraw the petition he has filed for her and report her to immigration authorities. The social worker at the shelter reassures the woman that she will help her to file her own petition under special provisions of the Federal Violence Against Women Act that enable battered women to self-petition for legal status (Mathews 1999).

• A couple who are legal immigrants seeks medical care at a local hospital for their chronically ill child. The family has no medical coverage and tells the hospital social worker that they are afraid to apply for Medicaid for fear of violating the "public charge " provision of immigration policy and jeopardizing their citizenship application. The hospital social worker, knowledgeable about immigration policy, Medicaid, and the state's Children's Health Insurance Program, assures them that enrollment in these programs is exempt from this provision (Institute of Medicine 2000).

Social Work Education and Training

The trends and challenges thus far delineated in this chapter present opportunities as well as demands in respect to social work education and training for practice and administration in family and children's services. Above all, schools of social work are being challenged to prepare social workers at all levels for practice and service delivery whose defining dimensions and characteristics are unknown and/or changing, as reflected in the preceding discussion in this chapter regarding developments and uncertainties in such areas as welfare reform, managed care, and federal legislation. In addition, in line with the competence and strength orientations delineated in chapter 1, social work education and training should include attention to enhancing resiliency of clients as well as practitioners (Norman 2000). At the same time, there should be emphasis on safeguarding and promoting the well-being and welfare of children and families, as also highlighted in chapter 1.

Although the future of family and child welfare services remains uncertain, there is no question that social workers at all levels will need to be ready for autonomous practice, to one degree or another. In light of this, in their analysis of future trends and influences in child welfare education and training, Tracy and Pine (2000) propose a comprehensive set of recommendations for formal education, in-service training, and/or continuing education of professionals who are competent in the following areas:

- involving neighborhoods, and communities in the design and delivery of services;
- collaborating with courts, members of other professions and staff in courts, health and mental health agencies, education, substance abuse programs, juvenile delinquency settings, and income maintenance systems, *among others*;

- using intervention methods that "respect and strengthen family ties and reflect the role and importance of extended families, neighborhoods, and communities" (Tracy and Pine 2000:104);
- promoting multiculturalism by emphasizing knowledge about culture and ethnicity, learning to build coalitions and networks among ethnically and racially diverse groups, and using such tools as cultural genogram and the culturagram, as discussed in chapter 5;
- incorporating into the social work curriculum the philosophy and technology of "cross-organizational management," that is, emphasis on the development of partnerships, networks, and other joint ventures aimed at using resources more efficiently and effectively to meet clients' needs (Abramson and Rosenthal 1995; Weiner 1987).
- using planning and research techniques to gather information required to develop and test program innovations;
- using computers for information, planning, and teaching;
- attending to the well-being of all children in a given community and advocating for a continuum of services that help promote healthy development of families and their children; and
- incorporating into the social work curriculum content on ethical dilemmas and decision making (Reamer 2001b).

To help in accomplishing the training objectives reflected above — and in conjunction with the Council on Social Work Education's Commission on Social Work Practice, Zlotnik, Rome, and DePanfilis (1998) have compiled a compendium of exemplary child welfare syllabi in the following areas:

- baccalaureate-level courses,
- master's-level practice courses,
- master's-level policy courses, and
- special topics such as "Research in Child Welfare" and "Social Work and the Law."

The above-noted compendium includes descriptions of courses that reflect careful attention to the contemporary scene in child welfare as well as thoughtful consideration of new directions. In addition, Leung, Cheung and Stevenson (1994) offer a useful framework for ethnically sensitive practice with children and families. In their model attitudes, knowledge and skills across seven phases of work with clients (from initial contact to termination) are explored in a cross-cultural context.[9]

Reamer's (2001b) book on teaching social work ethics, the first in a series of texts on social work education published by the Council on Social Work Education, provides guidance to faculty in developing and teaching this content. Similarly, Congress (2002) includes a curriculum resource for faculty on teaching social work values and ethics. Additionally, building on his analysis of society's social and economic injustice, Gil (1998) offers a comprehensive set of strategies for preparing and supporting social workers oriented to social and economic justice in their practice.

Competency-Based Training

Preparation of social workers along the lines described in the preceding section can be promoted through emphasis on *competency-based training*, which Warsh, Maluccio, and Pine (1994:60) have defined as "designing, delivering, and evaluating training that ties worker performance to the goals of an organization and its deployment of resources." In such an approach there is emphasis on developing curriculum content and strategies that reflect the requisite knowledge, skills, and attitudes called for in a particular area of practice. As Tracy and Pine (2000:107) have noted: "Competency-based training and education can be delivered through new and old methods: through interactive distance learning, through computer-assisted training, in the classroom, and even by reestablishing field units in child welfare agencies."

Competency-based trained can be promoted through such strategies as the following:

- clearly identifying competencies in the areas of values, knowledge, and skills that the training needs to address,
- linking training to levels or standards of performance expected of agency staff,
- including exercises that allow staff to practice skills, explore values, and give feedback to one another,
- having participants complete pre- and post-training questionnaires focusing on what they know and do well and what they can do

differently, what they ought to know, what they have learned, and how they might integrate their learning into the above-noted competencies, and

- conducting follow-up evaluation of the impact of the training on worker performance and impact on the agency's services.

There are many publications useful in offering competency-based training to prepare staff in family and children's agencies for practice that responds to future challenges and opportunities. We give selected examples here.

- *Achieving Permanency for Children in Kinship Foster Care: A Training Manual* (Bonecutter and Gleeson 1997). This research-based training manual (including videotapes) consists of six learning units focusing on preparing child welfare workers to engage the child's family members in providing kinship care. Topics range from the context of practice in kinship care to supporting permanent plans for the child.
- *Building Supervisory Skills: A Curriculum to Prepare Child Welfare Supervisors* (Blome, Wright, and Raskin 1998). This also is an extensive competency-based curriculum to prepare child welfare supervisors in public and private agencies through eight days of concentrated knowledge and skill building.
- *Changing Paradigms of Child Welfare Practice: Responding to Opportunities and Challenges* (U.S. Department of Health and Human Services 1999). This is a report of a federally sponsored child welfare training symposium, covering in particular training through partnership models involving state agencies, universities, service providers, and community representatives.
- *Child Protective Services: A Training Curriculum* (Rykus, Hughes, and Garrison 1989). This is a comprehensive, competency-based core curriculum designed particularly for caseworkers in child welfare agencies.
- *Promoting Creativity Across the Life Span* (Bloom and Gulotta 2001). This volume explores what is known about creativity and how to promote it, including using creative activities to help vulnerable children and families.
- *Curriculum Competencies for Social Work Education in Family and Children's Services* (Downs et al. 2000). The authors describe a set of curriculum competencies developed by six graduate schools of social work in Michigan.

The competencies cover knowledge, self-awareness, and practice skills for child and family services. Also included is a competency list that can be used by students as a self-assessment instrument.

- *Effective Supervisory Practice: A Confidence-Building Curriculum for Supervisors and Managers* (Alwon 2000). This is a comprehensive, competency-based training program for supervisors and other middle managers in child welfare agencies, emphasizing experiential activities, lively interaction, and group discussion.

- *Family Bound* (Lewis et al. 2000). A nine session, psycho-educationally based curriculum designed to help find temporary "resource" families and prepare adolescents in out-of-home care for permanency. Includes a manual for training group leaders and guides for families and young people.

- *Family Practice: A Curriculum Plan for Social Service* (Brown and Weil 1992). The authors delineate a family-focused curriculum for child welfare services that emphasizes family practice in these agency settings: developmental and preventive services, crisis resolution services, child protective services, including out-of-home care, and permanency planning services.

- *Field Guide to Child Welfare* (Rykus and Hughes 1998): This is a comprehensive and detailed guide to child welfare practice for workers, supervisors, and trainers, covering child protective services, placement and permanence, case planning and family-centered casework, and child development and child welfare.

- *Innovations in Practice and Service Delivery Across the Life Span* (Biegel and Blum 1999). The authors describe innovations in practice and service delivery with vulnerable groups coming to the attention of social workers and others in mental health and human service agencies.

- *Learning to Be Partners: An Introductory Training Program for Family Support Staff* (Poole, Woratsched, and Williams 1997). This is a complete set of workshop materials and exercises to introduce staff to the principles and practices of family support. Separate modules focus on such topics as family support models and practice, diversity, building relationships with families, home visiting, developing family plans, building communities, teamwork, and support groups.

- *Teaching Family Reunification: A Sourcebook* (Warsh, Maluccio, and Pine 1994). This sourcebook contains curriculum modules, handouts, and selected readings on reuniting children in foster care with their families. Also provided is a set of tools for rethinking family reunification of children in out-of-home care, based on the range of competencies required for effective practice.

Perhaps the greatest challenge for those of us involved in one way or another in family and children's services is that of contributing, with conviction and vigor, to rendering society as well as environments more responsive to the needs of children and families, in line with the "Framework of Needs and Resources for Family and Child Well-Being" to which we have frequently referred throughout this text. Many can contribute to this challenge, including

> workers who will demand to have a vote in the way they work and the way the agency operates; administrators and policy makers who will facilitate decision making and case management; foster parents and child care staff who will rise to the challenge of being members of the helping team; parents and children who will feel empowered to act on their own behalf; and practitioners with diverse competencies and backgrounds who will be ready to collaborate within a multidisciplinary framework.   (Maluccio 2000:174)

In light of the historic role of social work in practice with and on behalf of families and children, we can do no less. In addition to their direct practice duties, and in line with their ethical obligations to promote social justice and social change (Gil 1998), social workers should always seek and implement opportunities to address policy issues through such means as contacting public officials, serving on task forces, pushing for legislation, and joining international organizations that advocate for human rights and social justice.

Notes

1. A volume edited by Hopps and Morris (2000) includes original essays reflecting on the future of the profession in these areas:

    -   context and evolution of social work;
    -   challenges and visions in various fields of practice, including family and children's services; and
    -   conceptual and scientific critiques.

2. For critiques of welfare reform and its impact on family and children's services, particularly child welfare, see Balgopal (2000); Fujiwara

(1998); Halpern (1999); McGowan and Walsh (2000), and Pelton (1999). In addition, see Stein (2001)—a text on social welfare policy and its making that focuses on a wide range of policies and programs and contains extensive coverage of social services, child welfare services, and education. The author pays particular attention to the role of the courts in family and children's services.

3. See the special issue of the Family Resource Coalition of America's *FRCA Report* 17 (4) (Winter 1998–99), Strengthening families in the welfare reform era.

4. See chapter 3 for more extensive discussion of federal laws and policies affecting vulnerable children and families.

5. See Schamess and Lightburn (1998b) for extensive treatment of many aspects of managed care, including policy issues, impact on human service agencies and opportunities and challenges for social work and social work education.

6. Kluger, Baker, and Garval (1998) describe the components of a strategic business plan for non-profit organizations, which they illustrate through application in one of the oldest social service, mental health, and child welfare agencies in the country. The plan can be employed to assess the impact of managed care on the agency.

7. Mishra (2000) asserts that globalization is as much a political and ideological phenomenon as it is an economic one. He, therefore, advocates a transnational approach to social policy, to ensure that social standards rise in line with economic growth.

8. For extensive discussion of cross-national perspectives on evaluation in child and family services, see Maluccio, Canali, and Vecchiato (in press) and Vecchiato, Maluccio, and Canali (in press).

9. Also see Schmitz, Stakeman, and Sisneres (2001) for guidelines on educating social workers to understand oppression and appreciate diversity in a multicultural society.

Questions for Discussion

1. How is managed care affecting clients in your agency? What recommendations would you offer to reduce its negative impact and strengthen positive outcomes for families and their children?

2. Examine your agency's services on behalf of African American, Latino, and other families of color as well as recent immigrant groups. Consider, in

particular, how well they respond to the needs and situations of these families and also offer suggestions for improving services on their behalf.

3. Consider the implications of growing global inter-dependence for your agency. What are some recent examples of internationally-related case issues that you or other staff in your agency have dealt with?

4. In this chapter we referred to the increasing need for social workers to understand that some social problems transcend national borders. What are examples of critical social problems in your community, or the population your agency serves, that are also occurring in other countries?

5. Develop a personal action plan to become more a part of the international profession of social work. What are the first steps you might take?

6. How is training/staff development organized in your agency? Is training competency-based? How are training needs assessed? Are individual learning plans developed with each staff member on a regular (at least annual) basis? Are opportunities available for staff to self-assess their skill and knowledge needs?

Suggestions for Further Information

Gil, D.G. 1998. *Confronting Injustice and Oppression: Concepts and Strategies for Social Workers*. New York: Columbia University Press.

Healy, L. M. 2001. *International Social Work: Professional Action in an Interdependent World*. New York: Oxford University Press.

Hopps, J. G. and R. Morris, eds. 2000. *Social Work at the Millennium: Critical Reflections on the Future of the Profession*. New York: Free.

Maluccio, A. N. and G. R. Anderson, eds. 2000a. Future challenges and opportunities in child welfare, special issue of *Child Welfare* 79 (1): 1–124.

Schamess, G. and A. Lightburn, eds. 1998. *Humane Managed Care?* Washington, D.C.: NASW.

Zlotnik, J. L., S. H. Rome, and D. DePanfilis, eds. 1998. *Education for Child Welfare Practice: A Compendium of Exemplary Syllabi*. Alexandria: Council on Social Work Education.

Appendix 1

Tools and Instruments to Support Practice

This appendix contains brief descriptions of selected tools and instruments to support family-centered practice that we have found useful in our teaching, consultation, and research. Key citations are provided for those wanting further information on use and procedures for administration.

Several of these tools focus exclusively on identifying child and family strengths and are useful for case planning and evaluation purposes. Depending on the service setting and administration of the tool, these instruments and procedures may be used to address

- *child developmental needs,*
- *family needs and resources, or*
- *larger societal community needs and resources.*

In the following pages we list each tool alphabetically in one or another of the above categories according to its major focus, although some may apply to more than one category. The tools vary in terms of their reliability and validity as well, and the primary references should be consulted for information on their use for decision making, practice, and research purposes.

A. Child Developmental Needs

- *Ansell-Casey Life Skills Assessment* (D. I. Ansell and the Casey Family Programs 1997): A tool for assessing a youth's life skill competencies. There are age-based versions for preadolescents and adolescents. Available online at www.caseylifeskills.org (January 8, 2000). (*See further description of this tool in chapter 9.*)
- *Child/Adolescent Measurement Systems* (Bickman and Doucette 2000): A comprehensive, integrated measurement system for young persons be-

In compiling this appendix, we have drawn upon the following sources: Kemp, Whittaker, and Tracy (1997); Day, Robison, and Sheikh (1998); and Pecora (2000).

tween the ages of six and eighteen who are served by human service agencies, focusing on assessing youth, parent, and clinician characteristics while the child is receiving services. Assessment measures cover symptom severity, functional behavior, therapeutic alliance, parent or caregiver and child relationship, and satisfaction with services, among other areas. Available at http://www.qualifacts.com/qassms (March 8, 2001) or through the authors: Anna Doucette (adoucette@aol.com) or Leonard Bickman (Bickman@att.global.net), Center for Mental Health Policy, Vanderbilt University, 1207 18th Avenue South, Nashville, TN 37212.

- *Child Behavior Checklist.* (Achenbach 1991): Standardized assessment of children's behavioral, emotional strengths and problems. There are age-based versions, plus youth, caregiver, and teacher report forms, that may be ordered online at http://www/uvm/edu/~cbcl/
- *Child's Ecomap* (Fahlberg 1991): Ecomap designed for completion by child entering placement; covers areas such as homes the child has lived in, friends, siblings, school, dreams, worries, and feelings.
- *Child Sexual Behavior Inventory* (Faller 1993): Consists of twenty items to be assessed by parents according to how frequently their child engages in specific sexual behaviors.
- *Child Well-Being Scales* (Magura and Moses 1986): Measures factors related to risk of child abuse or neglect as well as factors that reveal levels of family functioning in various domains. Forty-three scales are rated on a six-point continuum, in such areas as health, supervision of young children, and money management.
- *Placement Genogram* (Groze, Young, and Corcran-Rumppe 1991; McMillen and Groze 1994): A diagramming technique that traces the child's placement history starting from birth and records pertinent information about each placement. For instance, the date of parental rights termination, allegations of abuse, and relationships with significant caretakers might be documented on the placement genogram.
- *Recent Exposure to Violence.* (Singer et al. 1995): A questionnaire that asks children about violence they have experienced or personally witnessed over the past year. The type of violence and the settings (home, school, or neighborhood) can be determined.
- *The Child at Risk Field* (Allen 1988): Evaluates six areas of risk and safety:

  - level of maltreatment,
  - circumstances surrounding the maltreatment,

• age-appropriateness of child functioning,
• appropriateness of parent disciplinary techniques,
• appropriateness of overall parenting behavior, and
• parent's mental health.

B. Family Needs and Resources

• *Checklist of Strengths and Resources* (Washington Risk Assessment Project 1993): Presents lists of general strength factors related to the child, family, and community domain, to be assessed by workers. Examples include social supports within the family and positive relationships with adults.
• *Children of Promise: Successful Services for Children and Families at Risk* (Organization for Economic Cooperation and Development, with assistance from TV Ontario 1996). (Available from Brookes Publishers, P.O. Box 10624, Baltimore, MD 21285–0624): This sixty-minute VHS videocassette highlights six successful programs from five different countries that aim at supporting children at risk through educational, social, environmental, economic, and public health services.
• *Cultural genogram* (Hardy and Laszloffy 1995): Describes techniques for adding cultural information to a genogram, including dimensions such as intercultural marriages and groups represented in culture of origin.
• *Culturagram* (Congress 1994): An ecomaplike assessment tool designed to gauge the impact of several different aspects of culture on the family or individual, including reasons for immigration, length of time in the community, legal or undocumented status, language spoken at home and in the community, contact with cultural institutions, health beliefs, holidays and special events as well as impact of crisis events, and values about family, education, and work. In particular, the tool also enables the worker to individualize for ethnically similar clients beyond cultural generalizations.
• *Ecomap* (Hartman and Laird 1983): A widely used method to visually document and assess relationships between the family and the outside world. Clients identify people, groups, and organizations in their social networks. These are drawn on circles on the ecomap, with lines between the circles representing the quality of relationships (stressful, tenuous, or positive). The ecomap generates useful information on resources available to the client, resources available but not fully utilized, and gaps in resources.
• *Family Access to Basic Resources* (Vosler 1990): An assessment tool completed by both the worker and family to determine the extent of stress and

stress pile-up due to inadequate or unstable basic family resources. The tool includes monthly expenses, current resources, potential family resources, and stability in the following areas: wages, child support, income transfers, housing, food, clothing, personal care and recreation, health care, education, family and developmental services, and transportation.

• *Family Assessment Form* (Children's Bureau of Southern California 1996): The Family Assessment Form (FAF) helps workers to assess families at the beginning of service, develop service plans, monitor progress, and evaluate outcomes. Using a nine-point rating scale, the FAF enables workers to complete a psychosocial assessment that is recorded in a quantitative manner and allows for monitoring family progress. The FAF can also be used as a research tool.

• *Family Resource Scale* (Dunst, Trivette, and Deal 1988): A thirty-one item self-report paper-and-pencil questionnaire to measure the adequacy of different resources in households with young children; each item is rated on a five-point scale ranging from "Not at All Adequate" to "Almost Always Adequate."

• *Family Risk Scales* (Magura, Moses, and Jones 1987): Uses twenty-six rating scales to assess the full range of family risk situations, such as financial problems and social supports.

• *Family Support Scale* (Dunst, Trivette, and Deal 1988): An eighteen-item self-report paper-and-pencil measure to assess the perceived helpfulness of various sources of support to families raising young children.

• *Genogram* (Hartman and Laird 1983): A diagram constructed by worker and family members to depict family relationships extended over the last several generations. It includes such aspects as ethnic and religious backgrounds, genealogical relationships, major family events and rituals, and occupations of family members.

• *Guidelines for Family Support Practice* (Family Resource Coalition 1996). Nine principles that state how family support premises should be carried out in family support programs. Each principle is explored in depth with the theory and research underlying it, the key practices programs that should be followed to realize it, and practice examples to illustrate how it is done. A companion guide was published in 1997 as a special double issue of the *Family Resources Coalition Report*.

• *Learning to Be Partners: An Introductory Training Program for Family Support Staff* (Poole, Woratsched, and Williams 1997): This ready-to-use training program contains activities, handouts, discussion ideas, and mini-lectures to help staff begin to develop the skills and knowledge they need to act as true partners with families. The training incorporates a videotape, "Our Families, Our Future," that is also available from Family Support America.

- *Multi-Cultural Guidelines for Assessing Family Strengths and Risk Factors in Child Protective Services* (Washington Risk Assessment Project 1993): Incorporates multicultural assessment guidelines into Washington State's risk matrix, encouraging workers to consider the cultural factors that may influence their assessment of risk.
- *North Carolina Family Assessment Scale* (Reed-Ashcraft, Kirk, and Fraser 2001): An instrument designed for family assessment and outcome measurement in child welfare and family preservation services. There is strong support for the internal consistency and construct validity of this scale.
- *Preventing Bullying: A Manual for Schools and Communities* (Dwyer and Osher 2000): Describes bullying and a comprehensive action program to combat it.
- *Preventing Drug Abuse Among Children and Adolescents: A Research-Based Guide* (National Institute on Drug Abuse 1997): Presents information on risks and protective factors in drug abuse and steps communities can undertake to implement prevention programs. Includes descriptions of research-based drug abuse prevention programs.
- *Protecting Children in Substance-Abusing Families* (Kropenske and Howard 1994): Risk assessment formats for use with biological families and relative caregivers of children prenatally exposed to drugs or alcohol.
- *Routine Screening for Domestic Violence* (Ganley and Schecter 1996): Contains seven questions to be asked of each family reported for risk of child abuse or neglect, in such areas as previous threats or assaults on family members.
- *Safeguarding Our Children: An Action Guide for Implementing Early Warning, Timely Response* (U.S. Department of Education n.d.; http://www.ed.gov/(August 2, 2001): Presents research-based strategies for school safety that involve principals, teachers, counselors, parents, and students.
- *Treatment Improvement Protocol (TIP) Series*: Presents best practice guidelines, protocols and tools for the treatment of substance abuse (provided as a service of the U.S. Department of Health and Human Services, Substance Abuse and Mental Health Services Administration, Center for Substance Abuse Treatment). Available online at http://text.nlm.nih.gov (September 13, 2001) or by calling the National Clearinghouse for Alcohol

and Drug Information: 1–800–729–6682. The protocols (TIPS) include, among others:

TIPs no. 2: Pregnant, substance-using women

TIPs no. 5: Improving treatment for drug-exposed infants

TIPs no. 6: Family-centered treatment of adolescents with alcohol, drug abuse, and mental health problems

TIPs no. 35: Enhancing motivation for change in substance abuse treatment

TIPs no. 36: Substance abuse treatment for persons with child abuse and neglect issues

C. Societal and Community Needs and Resources

• *Community Interaction Checklist* (Wahler, Leske, and Rogers 1979): A self-observational listing of types of interactions occurring in the past twenty-four hours (or other) time period with members of the social network outside immediate household members; the nature and positive or negative rating of each interaction are recorded by the client.

• *Environmental Assessment Index* (Poresky 1987): A forty-four-item instrument to assess the educational/developmental quality of children's home environments via information gathered through a home interview with the caretaker and direct observation by the practitioner.

• *Essential Allies* (Jeppson and Thomas 1995): Information and tools to involve families as program advisers and consultants in meaningful ways. Includes innovative approaches for recruiting parents as well as ways to provide training to support parent involvement and address barriers to family participation in program development and implementation.

• *How Are We Doing? A Program Self-Assessment Toolkit for the Family Support Field* (Ahsan and Cramer 1998): Descriptions of specific benchmarks that family support programs can use to help them enact the principles of family support in day-to-day practice. This kit provides detailed checklists so that programs can work with a community team to assess their own performance systematically in any — or all — of ten areas: governance, outreach/engaging families, programs and activities, parent education and child development, working one-on-one with families, relationships with the community, agency environment, home visiting, staff roles and capacities, and monitoring and evaluation.

• *Inventory of Social Support* (Dunst, Trivette, and Deal 1988): A paper-and-pencil matrix of personal social network in terms both of source and type of support; respondents indicate whom they would go to or receive help from for each of twelve different types of child-rearing supports.

• *Know Your Community: A Step-by-Step Guide to Community Needs and Resources Assessment* (Samuels, Ahsan, and Garcia 1998): This complete manual guides the process of getting important community information — including hidden resources. Includes a family survey, data-collection worksheets, and progress charts.

• *Mapping Community Capacity* (McKnight and Kretzmann 1990): A format for assessing the assets and capacities existing within communities, at three levels:

> assets and capacities located inside the neighborhood and largely under neighborhood control (e.g., individual assets of residents and local resident-controlled associations and organizations),
> assets located within the community but largely controlled by outsiders (e.g., private and nonprofit organizations, physical resources, public institutions and services), and
> resources originating outside the neighborhood and controlled by outsiders (e.g., welfare expenditures, public capital improvement expenditures, and public information).

• *Saint Louis Neighborhood Network Common Assessment Tool* (Day, Robison, and Sheikh 1998): A strengths-based assessment form for use with families. It consists of four parts:

> family information,
> family assessment (strengths inventory, concerns, service needs, relationships to community, genogram),
> family plan, and
> family life book.

• *Social Network Map* (Tracy and Whittaker 1990): Gathers information about the size and composition of a client's personal social network, the types of support exchanged within that network, and the quality of network relationships (closeness, reciprocity, and criticalness). Network members are listed for each of seven domains (e.g., family, friends, neighbors). A series of questions is then asked about the nature of network relationships.

Appendix 2

National Child Welfare Resource Centers

The national child welfare resource centers listed below were established through federal legislation and funding to assist states, tribes, and public child welfare agencies in their efforts to ensure the safety, well-being, and permanent placement of children who come to the attention of the child welfare system. In collaboration with other resource centers and organizations, the national child welfare resource centers provide technical assistance, conduct needs assessment, and disseminate information on best practices aimed at promoting permanency planning for children and youths.

National Child Welfare Resource Center for Family-Centered Practice
Learning Systems Group
1150 Connecticut Avenue, NW, Suite 1100
Washington, DC 20036
(202) 638–7922
FAX: (202) 628–3812
info@cwresource.org
http://www.cwresource.org

National Child Welfare Resource Center for Organizational Improvement
Edmond S. Muskie Institute
University of Southern Maine
P.O. Box 15010
Portland, ME 04112
(207) 780–5810
FAX: (207) 780–5817
patn@usm.maine.edu
http://www.muskie.usm.maine.edu/helpkids

National Child Welfare Resource Center on Legal and Judicial Issues
ABA Center on Children and the Law
740 15th Street, NW, 9th Floor
Washington, DC 20005–1009
(202) 662–1746
FAX: (202) 662–1755
ctrchildlaw@abanet.org
http://www.abanet.org/child

National Resource Center for Foster Care and Permanency Planning
Hunter College School of Social Work
129 E. 79th Street, Room 802
New York, NY 10021
(212) 452–7053
FAX: (212) 452–7051
nrcfcpp@hunter.cuny.edu
http://guthrie.hunter.cuny.edu/socwork/nrcfcpp

National Resource Center for Information Technology in Child Welfare
Child Welfare League of America
440 First Street, NW, Third Floor
Washington, DC 20001–2085
(202) 662–4285
FAX: (202) 638–4004
nrcitcw@cwla.org
http://www.nrcitcw.org

National Resource Center for Special Needs Adoption
Spaulding for Children
16250 Northland Drive, Suite 120
Southfield, MI 48075
(248) 443–7080
FAX: (248) 443–7099
sfc@spaulding.org
http://www.spaulding.org

National Resource Center for Youth Development
University of Oklahoma
College of Continuing Education
202 W. 8th Street
Tulsa, OK 74119–1419
(918) 585–2986
FAX: (918) 592–1841
hlock@ou.edu
http://www.nrcys.ou.edu/nrcyd.htm

National Resource Center on Child Maltreatment
Child Welfare Institute
1349 W. Peachtree Street, NE, Suite 900
Atlanta, GA 30309–2956
(404) 881–0707
FAX: (404) 876–7949
nrccm@gocwi.org
http://gocwi.org/nrccm

Appendix 3

Other Resource Centers and Information Sources

In this section we include additional resource centers as well as information sources in the area of family and child welfare.

American Association of Retired Persons
Grandparents Information Center
601 E. Street, NW
Washington, DC 20049
(202) 434–2296
http://www.aarp.org/contacts/programs/gic.html

American Bar Association Center on Children and the Law
740 15th Street, NW
Washington, DC 20005
(202) 662–1740
http://www.abanet.org/child

ARCH National Resource Center for Respite and Crisis Care Services
Chapel Hill Training-Outreach Project
800 Eastowne Drive, Suite 105
Chapel Hill, NC 27514
(800) 473–1727
FAX: (919) 490–4905
ylayden@intrex.net
http://www.chtop.com

Child Care Action Campaign
330 7th Avenue
New York, NY 10001
(212) 239–0138
FAX: (212) 268–6515
http://www.childcarereaction.org

Children Awaiting Parents, Inc.
700 Exchange Street
Rochester, NY 14608
(716) 232–5110
http://www.ggw.org/cap

Children's Defense Fund
25 E Street, NW
Washington, DC 20001
(202) 628–8787
http://www.childrensdefense.org

Child Welfare League of America
440 First Street, NW, 3rd Floor
Washington, DC 20001–2085
(202) 638–2952
FAX: (202) 638–4004
http://www.cwla.org

Evan B. Donaldson Adoption Institute
130 Wall Street, 20th Floor
New York, NY 10005–3902
(202) 269–5080
http://www.adoptioninstitute.org

Faces of Adoption
http://www.adopt.org

Families International, Inc.
11700 West Lake Park Drive
Milwaukee, WI 53224–3099
(414) 359–1040
FAX: (414) 359–1074
fis@alliance1.org

Family Builders Adoption Network
3766 Fishcreek Road, no. 276
Stow, OH 44224
(330) 673–2680

Foster Family-Based Treatment Association
1415 Queen Anne Road
Teaneck, NJ 07666
(800) 414–3382
FAX: (201) 862–0331
ffta@ffta.org
http://www.ffta.org

"Friends" National Resource Center for Community-Based Family Resource and Support Programs
Chapel Hill Training-Outreach Project
800 Eastowne Drive, Suite 105
Chapel Hill, NC 27514
(800) 888–7970
FAX: (919) 968–8879
jldenniston@intrex.net

Gay, Lesbian, and Straight Education Network
121 West 27th Street
Suite 804
New York, NY 10001–6207
(212) 727–0135
http://www.glsen.org

Harvard Family Research Project
38 Concord Avenue
Cambridge, MA 02138
(617) 495–9108
hfrp_pubs@harvard.edu
http://www.gseweb.harvard.edu/~hfrp

Lambda Legal Defense and Education Fund
120 Wall Street, Suite 1500
New York, NY 10005
(212) 809–8585
http://www.lambdalegal.org

National Abandoned Infants Assistance Resource Center
Family Welfare Research Group

University of California at Berkeley
School of Social Welfare
1950 Addison Street, Suite 104
Berkeley, CA 94704–1182
(510) 643–8390
FAX: (510) 643–7019

National Adoption Center
1500 Walnut Street, Suite 701
Philadelphia, PA 19102
(877) 648–4400
http://www.adopt.org

National Adoption Information Clearinghouse
330 C Street, SW
Washington, DC 20447
(703) 352–3488 or (888) 251–0075
http://www.calib.com/naic

National Association for the Education of Young Children
1509 16th Street, NW
Washington, DC 20036
(800) 424–2460
FAX: (202) 328–1846
http://www.naeyc.org

National Association for Family-Based Services
6824 5th Street, NW
Washington, DC 20012
(202) 291–7587
FAX: (202) 291–7667

National Association for Family Child Care
P.O. Box 10373
Des Moines, IA 50306
(515) 282–8192
FAX: (515) 282–9117
http://www.nafcc.org

National Association of Child Care Resource and Referral Agencies
1319 F Street, NW, Suite 500
Washington, DC 20004
(202) 393–5501
FAX: (202) 393–1109
http://www.naccrra.org

National Black Child Development Institute
1101 15th Street, NW, Suite 900
Washington, DC 20005
(202) 833–2220
FAX: (202) 833–8222
http://www.nbcdi.org

National Center for Children in Poverty
Joseph L. Mailman School of Public Health of Columbia University
154 Haven Avenue
New York, NY 10032
(212) 304–7100
FAX: (212) 544–4200
http://cpmcnet.columbia.edu/dept/nccp/

National Center on Family Group Decision Making
American Humane Association
63 Inverness Drive East
Englewood, CO 80112
(303) 925–9421
(800) 227–4645
http://www.fgdm.org

National Clearinghouse on Child Abuse and Neglect Information
330 C Street, SW
Washington, DC 20447
1–800–394–3366
http://www.nncanch@calib.com

National Court Appointed Special Advocate Association
100 W. Harrison Street

North Tower, Suite 500
Seattle, WA 98119–4123
(206) 270–0072
http://www.nationalcasa.org

National Family Preservation Network
3971 North 1400 East
Buhl, ID 83116
(888) 498–9047
FAX: (208) 543–6080
http://www.nfpn.org

National Foster Parent Association
P.O. Box 81
Alpha, Ohio 45301–0081
(800) 557–5238
http://www.kidsource.com/nfpa/index.html

National Indian Child Welfare Association
3611 SW Hood, Suite 201
Portland, Oregon 97204
(503) 222–4044
FAX: (503) 222–4007

National Practitioners Network for Fathers and Families
1003 K Street, NW, Suite 565
Washington, DC 20001
(202) 737–6680
FAX: (202) 737–6683
http://www.npnff.org

North American Council on Adoptable Children
970 Raymond Avenue, Suite 106
St. Paul, MN 58114–1149
(651) 644–3036
http://www.nacac.org/

Parents and Friends of Lesbians and Gays, Inc.
P.O. Box 27605

Washington, DC 20038
http://www.pflag.org

Research and Training Center on Family Support and Children's Mental Health
Regional Research Institute for Human Services
Portland State University
P.O. Box 751
Portland, OR 97207–0751
(503) 725–4175
FAX: (503) 725–4180
http://www.rtc.pdx.edu

U.S. Department of Health and Human Services
Administration for Children and Families
Administration on Children, Youth and Families, Children's Bureau
330 C Street, SW
Washington, DC 20447
http://www.calib.com/cbexpress

Appendix 4

Electronic Resources on Family and Children's Services

In this appendix we briefly describe selected websites and Internet addresses of general interest in the area of family and children's services. Additional sites can be found in the listings of resource centers and information sources in previous appendixes.

• Center for Adoption Research, University of Massachusetts: http://www.umassmed.edu/service/adoption/

Provides background information on foster care and adoption research, and current related activities, as well as an adoption guidebook. There is also a link to other University of Massachusetts Public Services and to the New England Newborn Screening Program.

• Center for Multilingual, Multicultural Research: http://www.usc.edu/dept/education/CMMR/

Source for information on multilingual education and English as a second language. Includes links to African American, Asian-Pacific Island, Latino/Hispanic, and Native American resources. Site of the University of Southern California.

• Children, Youth, and Family Links: http://www.cyfc.umn.edu/cyfclinks.html

Site of the Child, Youth and Family Consortium of the University of Minnesota, with a wide range of resources for children and families available on the web. Topics include, among many others, interracial adoption, special needs adoption, divorce, attachment, attention deficit hyperactivity disorder, fatherhood, chemical dependency, and domestic violence.

• Children's Bureau, Administration for Children and Families, Department of Health and Human Services: http://www.acf.dhhs.gov/programs/cb/stats/afcars

Provides data on foster care and related services for children and youths and their families, as gathered from each state through the Adoption and Foster Care Analysis and Reporting System (AFCARS).

- Children's Bureau Express: http://www.calib.com/cb/express/
  Provides a free monthly electronic digest for professionals in the areas of child abuse and neglect, adoption, and other aspects of child welfare. It is produced and disseminated by the National Clearinghouse on Child Abuse and Neglect Information and the National Adoption Information Clearinghouse on behalf of the Children's Bureau, Administration for Children and Families, U.S. Department of Health and Human Services.

- Children's Defense Fund: http://www.childrensdefense.org/states/data.html
  Provides information on child care, the black community, publications pertaining to children's issues (especially federal legislation and advocacy), and data on population and family characteristics, economic security, and federal program participation.

- Child Trends, Inc.: http://www.childtrends.org/
  A nonprofit organization that conducts research on children, youths, and families. The site offers comprehensive data on the impact of welfare reform on children and their families.

- Child Welfare League of America: http://www.cwla.org
  The CWLA operates a site that includes sections related to recent developments in the delivery of child and family services, in addition to information on its publications on related topics as well as forthcoming conferences and training programs.

  In cooperation with state child welfare agencies and other organizations, CWLA also offers the National Data Analysis System: http://ndas.cwla.org/. This is a free online service for child welfare professionals, legislators, media, students, and others interested in statistics and other information on child abuse and neglect, including state-by-state data.

- Clearinghouse on International Developments in Child, Youth, and Family Policy: http://www.childpolicyintl.org
  Contains a database of comparative information on crossnational policies, programs, benefits, and services from the twenty-two leading industrialized

countries, covering child-related social policy issues affecting education and care, child support, parental leave, child health, and adolescent development.

• Coalition for Asian American Children and Families: http://www .cacf.org/
Advocates for social policies and programs supportive of Asian American families. Disseminates information about needs of Asian American Families.

• Families and Work Institute: http://www.familiesandwork.org
Addresses the changing nature of work and family life, focusing on research-based strategies that promote mutually supportive connections among workplaces, families, and communities.

• Family Support America: http://www.familysupportamerica.org: http:// www.familysupportamerica.org/content/home/htm
Assists states, tribal organizations and municipalities in accessing sources of information and support and developing community-based family resource programs and networks. In addition, this organization encourages family unity through online chats, useful websites, and focus on family support issues in such areas as adoption, foster care, and parenting education.

• Family Violence Prevention Fund: http://www.fvpf.org/
Information and advocacy to end domestic violence. Programs address health care, children and child welfare, immigrant women, and economic independence, among other areas.

• Father and Family Link: http://fatherfamilylink.gse.upenn.edu
This project of the National Center of Fathers and Families at the University of Pennsylvania provides current information on programs, policy, and research related to the roles of fathers in families.

• Georgia Academy for Children and Youth Professionals, Inc. and others: http://www.promisingpractices.net
This site is produced through a partnership of the Georgia Academy for Children and Youth Professionals, Inc., RAND, California Foundation Consortium, Colorado Foundation for Families and Children, and the Missouri Family Investment Trust. Its purpose is to provide information on exemplary

programs that produce positive results for children and families. Each program is described in detail.

- Hall of Multiculturalism: http://www.tenet.edu/academia/multi.html
Contains links to resources specific to African Americans, Asian Americans, Latino, Chicano, Hispanic and Mexican Americans, Native Americans, and other indigenous peoples worldwide.

- Harvard Family Research Project: http://gseweb.harvard.edu/~hfrp
Offers access to family involvement tools and resources via the FINE network (Family Involvement Network of Educators) and provides both html and pdf versions of its quarterly newsletter, the *Evaluation Exchange*. The newsletter covers promising strategies for evaluating child and family services, summaries of related publications, and description of electronic resources.

- National Alliance for Hispanic Health: http://www.hispanichealth.org /yfp.html
Information and advocacy for health insurance coverage for Hispanic youth.

- National Association for Family-Based Services: http://nafbs.org
Offers information to promote effective, culturally appropriate services to families through public policy and support for state family-based services. A complete listing of state associations can be found as well as links to other family centered publications and resources.

- National Center on Family Group Decision Making: http://www .fgdm.org
Provides information and resources for implementing and evaluating family group decision making and family empowerment models. Includes online interactive discussion groups, publications, video listings and bibliography.

- National Child Care Information Center: http://www.nccic.org
The center, a unit of the Children's Bureau Administration, U.S. Department of Health and Human Services, responds to requests for child care

information from states, territories and tribes, policymakers, parents, programs, organizations, service providers and the public.

• National Child Welfare Resource Center for Family-Centered Practice: http://www.cwresource.org
Provides numerous links to other resource centers, training for child welfare agencies, information on positive family-centered practice, and consultation. Also offers easily accessible publications relating to child welfare issues.

• National Foster Parent Association: http://www.kidsource.com/nfpa/index .html
Contains information on becoming a foster parent, explains the purpose of the National Foster Parent Association, provides membership information, and includes "Kid-Source," a site that offers information on infants, children, and adolescents in foster care.

• National Indian Child Welfare Association: http://www.nicwa.org
This organization helps tribes in the United States to deliver quality child welfare services, including information on community development and public policy.

• National Institute of Child Health and Human Development: http:// www.nichd.nih.gov/
Administers a multidisciplinary program of research, research training, and public information on the topics of prenatal development and maternal, child, and family health.

• National Parent Information Network: http://www.npin.org
This network offers resources from ERIC Clearinghouse on Elementary and Early Childhood Education and the ERIC Clearinghouse on Urban Education, in addition to a virtual library for parents and those who work with parents. A collection of full text resources for urban/minority families can also be accessed.

• National Resource Center for Health and Safety in Child Care: http:// nrc.uchsc.edu
Promotes and provides information on health and safety in out-of-home

child care settings throughout the nation, contains the licensure regulations from the fifty states and the District of Columbia, and includes directions to other child care websites and information on topics of current interest.

• North American Council on Adoptable Children: http://www.nacac.org
   Offers information about the North American Council on Adoptable Children (NACAC) and information and materials on adoption and NACAC publications.

• U.S. Bureau of the Census: Children: http://www.census.gov/populations /www/soc/demo/children.html
   This site describes and provides links to U.S. government census data and also offers recent reports on children and issues affecting children.

Appendix 5

Electronic Resources on Children's Special Needs and Exceptionalities

Here we list websites for national organizations as well as resources on special needs and exceptionalities of children.

National Information Center for Children and Youth with Disabilities
http://www.nichcy.org

Council for Exceptional Children
http://www.cec.sped.org

American Psychiatric Association
http://www.psych.org

Special education resources
http://www.hood.edu/seri/serihome.htm

Lead poisoning
http://www.nsc.org/ehc/lead

Neural Tube Defects
http://www.uhl.uiowa.edu/services.AFP.dfects.htlm

Bipolar disorder in children
http://www.bpkids.org

Spina Bifida Association of America
http://www.sbaa.org

Osteogenesis Imperfecta Foundation
http://www.osteogenesisimperfecta.org

For information on Tourette's syndrome
http://www.neuro-www2.mgh.harvard.edu/tsa/tsamain.nclk

For information on oppositional defiant disorder
http://www.odd/htm

For a guide to treating children with obsessive-compulsive disorder
http://www.psychguides.com

For a list of appropriate school-based accommodations and interventions with children who have ADHD
http://www.add.org/content/school/list.htm

For a list of myths and facts about ADHD
http://www/catalog.com/chadd/doe/doe_myth.htm

National Fragile X Foundation
http://www.fragilex.org

National Office of Birth to Three, early interventions service
http://www.birth23.org

Appendix 6

Electronic Resources on Schools and Children's Education

Following is a list of electronic resources on schools and children's education.

Council for Exceptional Children. Designed primarily for professionals in the field of special education. Committed to the advancement of education for individuals with special needs. Includes links to other websites focusing on children with exceptionalities, as well as a resource catalog and list of journals for special education teachers. Discusses upcoming training and events. http://www.ced.sped.org/

Educational Resource Information Center (ERIC). Resource for educational research and information. Provides easy access to full text resources through an extensive database. http://www.access.eric.org

Family Education Network. Designed specifically for parents, in collaboration with the National Parent-Teacher Association and the American Association of Administrators. It contains resources, an online community, and links to other sites. http://www.familyeducation.com

This site also offers access to family involvement tools and resources via the FINE network (Family Involvement Network of Educators) and offers both html and pdf versions of its quarterly newsletter, the *Evaluation Exchange.*

Harvard Family Research Project. Offers an exhaustive listing of its publications on early childhood care and education, family, school and community issues, evaluation and accountability, information and professional development, with many available for free download. http://www.gseweb.harvard.edu/~hfrp

National Center for Schools and Communities. Integrates social work and education professionals through training seminars in order to strengthen public school networks. Center website includes newsletter and online database. http://fordham.edu/gse/facil/htm

National Coalition for Parent Involvement in Education. Advocates for parent and family involvement in education. Includes information on father

involvement, family/school partnerships, and publications. http://www
.ncpie.org

National Community Education Association. Advocates for strengthening
education in communities, with emphasis on parent and community
involvement. Provides leadership to professionals in the education field and
includes lists of published articles with links to other organizations. http://
www.ncea.com/

National Parent Information Network. Provides access to educational information of particular interest to family members through its virtual library.
http://npin.org

School Social Work Section, National Association of Social Workers. Website contains information on school social work, grant funding, current topics
and links of interest to school social workers. http://www.socialworkers.org
/sections/ssw

School Social Work Association of America. Provides links to regional
school social work associations and state departments of education and publications on school social work. http://www.sswaa.org

Schools of the Twenty-first Century. Provides crucial support for families,
particularly in promoting school readiness in children. http://www.yale
.edu/21c

U.S. Department of Education. Publishes information for all those interested in education. Includes an online ordering system and access to biblio-
graphic databases. http://www.ed.gov/pubs/index.html

Appendix 7

Electronic Resources on Health of Children and Adults

Following is a list of electronic resources in the area of health for children and adults.

Agency for Health Care Policy Research
P.O. Box 8547
Silver Spring, MD 20907–8547
http://www.ahcpr.gov

American Academy of Pediatrics
141 Northwest Point Blvd., P.O. Box 927
601 13th Street, NW
Elk Grove Village, IL 60009–0927
(847) 228–5005
Suite 400 North
(800) 433–9016
Washington, DC 20005
(202) 347–8600
http://www.aap.org

American Medical Association
515 N. State Street
Chicago, IL 60610
(312) 464–5000
http://www.ama-assn.org

California Center for Health Improvement
1321 Garden Highway, Suite 210
Sacramento, CA 95833–9576
(916) 646–2149
FAX: (916) 646–2151
http://www.policymakers.org

Center for Health Policy Research
George Washington University
2021 K Street, NW, Suite 800
Washington, DC 20006
(202) 296–6922
FAX: (202) 296–0025
http://www.gwumc.edu/chpr

Center for the Advancement of Health
2000 Florida Avenue, NW, Suite 210
Washington, DC 20009–1231
(202) 387–2829
FAX: (202) 387–2857
cfah@cfah.org
http://www.cfah.org

Families USA Foundation
1334 G Street, NW, Third Floor
Washington, DC 20005–3169
(202) 628–3030
FAX: (202) 347–2417
http://www.familiesusa.org

Foundation for Accountability
520 SW Sixth Avenue, Suite 700
Portland, OR 97204
(503) 223–2228
FAX: (503) 223–4336
http://www.facct.org

Health Systems Research, Inc.
1200 18th Street, NW, Suite 700
Washington, DC 20036
(202) 828–5100
FAX: (202) 728–9469
http://www.mchneighborhood.igjp.edu/hsr

National Adolescent Health Information Center
University of California San Francisco

1388 Sutter Street, Suite 605-A
San Francisco, CA 94109
(415) 502–4856
FAX: (415) 502–4858
http://www.ucsf.edu/youth

National Association of County & City Health Officials
1100 17th Street, NW, Second Floor
Washington, DC 20036
(202) 783–5550
FAX: (202) 783–1583
http://www.naccho.org

National Committee for Quality Assurance
2000 L Street, NW, Suite 500
Washington, DC 20036
(202) 955–3500
FAX: (202) 955–3599
http://www.ncqa.org

Physicians for a National Health Program
332 S. Michigan Avenue, Suite 500
Chicago, IL 60604
(312) 554–0382
FAX: (312) 554–0383
http://www.puhp.org

Universal Health Care Action Network
2800 Euclid Avenue, Suite 520
Cleveland, OH 44115–2418
(216) 241–8422
(800) 634–4442
FAX: (216) 241–8423
http://www.uhcan.org

Washington Business Group on Health
777 North Capitol Street, NE, Suite 800
Washington, DC 20002
(202) 408–9320
http://www.wbgh.org

Appendix 8

Electronic Resources on System Reform and Advocacy for Children and Families

There is an extensive number of federal and voluntary electronic resources pertaining to reform efforts and advocacy on behalf of children and families. Following is a list of selected sites.

- Annie E. Casey Foundation: http://www.aecf.org
Informative website on critical issues affecting disadvantaged children and their families and services to strengthen practice and policy.

- FirstGov: http://firstgov.gov
First-ever government website to provide the public with one-stop access to *all* online U.S. federal government resources.

- Institute for Women Policy Research: http://www.iwpr.org
Covers welfare reform and information on domestic violence, reproduction, education, and issues that affect women in relation to welfare reform, in addition to an online forum for interested individuals to discuss welfare reform.

- National Center for Children in Poverty: http://www.cpmcnet.columbia.edu/dept/nccp/
Promotes policies and programs aimed at reducing child poverty, also providing statistics about children along with information on the impact upon them of welfare reform.

- Urban Institute: Assess the New Federalism: http://newfederalism.urban.org
In addition to information about all aspects of welfare reform, the site offers extensive research specifically related to families and children as well as a data base covering each state's welfare reform activities.

- United States Department of Health and Human Services, Administration for Families and Children: http://www.acf.dhhs.gov

Provides technical information and statistical data on welfare reform and related topics.

- Welfare Information Network: http://www.welfareinfo.org
Provides information on welfare reform, including policies on immigrants, welfare-to-work programs, domestic violence, and child welfare. The network also offers information on policy issues relating to teen parents and teen pregnancy: http://www.welfareinfo.org/teen.htm

In addition to the above, the following Internet sites provide data on child and family welfare that are useful in relation to policy and advocacy.

- Administration for Children and Families. http://www.acf.dhhs .gov/programs/acyf
- American Public Human Services Association. http://www.apwa .org
- Center for Law and Social Policy. http://www.epn.org/clasp.html
- Children's Defense Fund. http://www.childrensdefense.org/index .html
- Children, Youth, and Family Education and Research Network. http://www.cyfernet.mes.umn.edu/index.html
- Child Trends. http://www.childtrends.org
- Child Welfare League of America. http://www.cwla.org
- Families & Work Institute. http://www.familiesandworkinst.org
- Family Life Development Center. http://child.cornell.edu/fldc .home.html
- Juvenile Justice Clearinghouse. http://www.fsu.edu/-crimdo /jjclearinghouse/jjclearinghouse.html
- Kids Count. http://www.aecf.org
- National Association of Social Workers. http://www.nasw.org
- National Center for Children in Poverty. http://www.cpmcnet .columbia.edu/dept/nccp
- National Center on Child Abuse and Neglect Clearinghouse. http://www.calib.com/nccanch/
- Office of Juvenile Justice and Delinquency Prevention. http:// www.ncjrs.org/ojjhome.html
- Urban Institute. http://www.urban.org
- United States Congress. http://thomas.loc.gov
- U.S. General Accounting Office. http://www.gao.gov

Appendix 9

Electronic Resources on Mentoring and Support Groups

American Self-Help Clearinghouse Search Engine. Informative data base includes a list of national self-help support groups with contact information as well as a guide for starting groups. http://mentalhelp.net /selfhelp/

National Self-Help Clearinghouse. Provides access to self-help groups and full-text articles pertaining to support groups and research issues. http:// www.selfhelpweb/org/

One to One/The National Mentoring Partnership. Provides access to current resources and information on mentoring and upcoming training events for mentors and practitioners. http://www.mentoring.org, nmp@mentoring.org

Peer Research Laboratory. Discusses the importance of peer tutoring within the school systems and the implications for the success rate of a new tutor-centered model. http://www.selfhelp.org/peer.html

Appendix 10

Information and Training Materials on Alcohol and Substance Abuse

Here we describe a range of videotapes on informational and training materials in the area of alcohol and substance abuse, with emphasis on the impact on children and families.

Alcohol and Other Drugs: A Competency-Based Training (ACT). Thirty-six-hour two-module training curriculum accompanied by eight videos to help child welfare agencies better recognize and address AOD problems. Available: Child Welfare League of America, 440 First Street, NW, Suite 310, Washington, DC 20001–2085.

Caring for Drug-Affected Infants (running time: twenty minutes) Available: Visions Video Productions, Evanston, IL 60202 (800–323–9084). Information about the problems that drug-exposed infants experience and the techniques that can be used to care for and soothe them.

Cocaine Mothers: Beyond the Guilt (running time: twenty-five minutes) Available: Visions Video Productions, Evanston, IL 60202 (800–323–9084), $295. Discussion of addiction to cocaine and the special issues facing women who abuse cocaine. Treatment options and recovery issues discussed from a mother's point of view.

Cocaine Update (running time: thirty-three minutes) Available: FMS Productions, Santa Monica, CA. Overview of the physiological and social consequences of cocaine use and addiction. Implications for treatment.

The Door to Recovery: Community Drug Abuse Treatment (running time: twenty-five minutes; 1994).* NCADI, no. VHS24. This video tape helps answer questions about how communities can benefit from drug abuse treatment centers. Designed to inform the public about types of treatment and aftercare programs and to refute myths spread by people who oppose such centers.

Drug Abuse and the Brain (running time: twenty-six minutes;1993).* NCADI, no.VHS57 Intended primarily for drug abuse counselors, this detailed look at the biological basis of drug addiction is presented throughanimation and interviews with experts in the field. Viewers learn how the brain's reward system operates and how drug abuse can cause fundamental changes in the way the brain works.

Drug Abuse and HIV: Reaching Those at Risk (running time: seventeen minutes; 1995).* NCADI, no.VHS74, Three intervention models show how to educate out-of-treatment injection drug users about AIDS, the behaviors that transmit the disease and strategies that reduce the risk of contracting AIDS.

Drug Babies (running time: thirty-two minutes) Available: Parsons/Runyon/Arts and Entertainment, Santa Barbara, CA 93101 (800–888–7817), $295. Physical and emotional problems of children prenatally exposed to alcohol and other drugs. The problems of mothers involved with drugs, social services, foster care, and treatment are explored.

Family Power: Building Skills for Families with HIV and Drug-Affected Children. Designed for health and human service providers working with families at risk for or currently living with drug- or HIV-affected children. Available: Family Welfare Research Group, School of Social Welfare, University of California Berkeley, 1950 Addison Street, Suite 104, Berkeley, CA 94704.

Methadone: Where We Are (running time: twenty-four minutes; 1993).* NCADI, no.VHS59, Issues examined include the use and effectiveness of methadone as a treatment, the biological effects of methadone, the role of the counselor in treatment, and society attitudes and stigmas regarding methadone treatment and methadone patients.

National Training Center for Drug-Exposed and HIV-Infected Children and Their Families. For information on projects and training programs contact the above center at 1800 Columbus Avenue, Roxbury, MA 02119.

Reasonable Efforts Training (running time: eighteen minutes). A video notebook, cassette no. 3: Service Needs of Drug-Exposed Mothers and Infants. Other cassettes in this series deal with a number of child welfare issues: bonding and attachment, separation and loss, family preservation services, role of the court in dependency hearings. Available: National Council of Juvenile and Family Court Judges, P.O. Box 8970, Reno, NV 89507.

Straight from the Heart: Stories of Mothers Recovering from Addiction (running time: twenty-eight minutes), $280. Seven women in recovery talk about their addictions, their families, and their process of recovery. Available:Vida Health Communications, 6 Bigelow Street, Cambridge, MA 02139 (617–864–4334).

---

* These tapes are available from the National Clearinghouse on Alcohol and Drug Information (NCADI). To order, call NCADI at 800–729–6686.

Victims at Birth (running time: thirty-five minutes). Three-part video dealing with issues affecting pregnancy: (1) inadequate health insurance,
(2) use of alcohol and other drugs, and (3) teenage pregnancy. Each segment runs approximately twelve minutes. Available: University of California Extension Media Center (415–642–0460).

References

Abandoned Infants Assistance Resource Center. 2000. *Shared Family Care*. Berkeley: Abandoned Infants Assistance Resource Center.

Abidin, R. 1990. *Parenting Stress Index Short Form*. Charlottesville: Pediatric Psychology.

Abramovitz, M. 1986. Social policy and the female pauper: The family ethic and the U.S. welfare state. In N. Van Den Bergh and L. B. Cooper, eds., *Feminist Visions for Social Work*, pp. 211–228. Silver Spring: National Association of Social Workers.

Abramovitz, M. 1988. *Regulating the Lives of Women*. Boston: South End.

Abramovitz, M. 1993. Should all social work students be educated for social change? Yes. *Journal of Social Work Education* 29 (1): 6–11.

Abramovitz, M. 1997. Temporary assistance to needy families. In R. L. Edwards, ed., *Encyclopedia of Social Work: 1997 Supplement*, pp. 311–330. 19th ed. Washington, D.C.: NASW.

Abramson, J. S. and B. B. Rosenthal. 1995. Interdisciplinary and interorganizational collaboration. In R. E. Edwards and J. G. Hopps, eds., *Encyclopedia of Social Work* 2:1479–1489. 19th ed. Washington, D.C.: NASW.

Achenbach, T. M. 1991. *Manual for Child Behavior Checklist*. Burlington: University of Vermont, Department of Psychiatry.

Acs, G. and P. Loprest. 2001. *Initial Synthesis Report of the Findings from ASPE's "Leavers" Grants*. Washington, D.C.: Urban Institute. http://aspe.hhs.gov/hsp/leavers99/synthesis01/ (June 21, 2001).

Agathen, J. M., J. O'Donnell, and S. J. Wells. 1999. *Evaluating the Quality of Kinship Foster Care: Evaluation Package*. Urbana, Ill.: Children and Family Research Center, School of Social Work, University of Illinois at Urbana-Champaign.

Ahsan, N. and L. Cramer. 1998. *How Are We Doing? A Program Self-Assessment Toolkit for the Family Support Field*. Chicago: Family Support America.

Aldgate, J. 1980. Identification of factors influencing children's length of stay in care. In J. Triseliotis, ed., *New Developments in Foster Care and Adoption*, pp. 32–40. Boston: Routledge and Kegan Paul.

Aldgate, J. 1990. Foster children at school: Success or failure? *Adoption and Fostering* 14:38–49.

Allen, T. 1988. *Evaluation Results: South Carolina Child at Risk Field Implementation*. Denver: Action for Child Protection.

Allen, R. I. and C. G. Petr. 1998. Rethinking family-centered practice. *American Journal of Orthopsychiatry* 68:4–15.

Allen-Meares, P. 1977. Analysis of tasks in school social work. *Social Work* 22 (3): 196–201.

Allen-Meares, P. 1996. Social work services in schools: A look at yesteryear and the future. *Social Work in Education* 18 (4): 202–208.

Allen-Meares, P., R. O. Washington, and B. L. Welsh. 2000. *Social Work Services in Schools*. 3d ed. Boston: Allyn and Bacon.

Alwon, F. 2000. *Effective Supervisory Practice: A Confidence-Building Curriculum for Supervisors and Managers*. Washington, D.C.: CWLA.

American Humane Association. N.d. *Guidelines for Schools to Help Protect Abused and Neglected Children*. Englewood, Col.: AHA.

American Humane Association. 1992. *Emotional Abuse*. AHA Fact Sheet no. 3 (October. Englewood, Col.: AHA.

American Humane Association. 1993a. *America's Children: How Are They Doing?* AHA Fact Sheet no. 8 (May). Englewood, Col.: AHA.

American Humane Association. 1993b. *Child Sexual Abuse*. AHA Fact Sheet no. 4 (May). Englewood, Col.: AHA.

American Humane Association. 1994a. *Child Neglect Information Sheet*. Englewood, Col.: AHA.

American Humane Association. 1994b. *Childhood Fatalities Due to Child Abuse and Neglect, Information Sheet*. Englewood, Col.: AHA.

American Humane Association. 1998. *Assessing Outcomes in Child Welfare Services: Principles, Concepts, and a Framework of Core Indicators*. Englewood, Col.: AHA, Children's Division.

Amodeo, M. 1995. *National Association of Social Workers Curriculum Module on Alcohol and Other Drugs*. Washington, D.C.: Center for Substance Abuse Prevention, Substance Abuse and Mental Health Services Administration.

Anderson, E. 1991. Neighborhood effects on teenage pregnancy. In C. Jencks and P. E. Peterson, eds., *The Urban Underclass*. Washington, D.C.: Brookings Institution.

Anderson, G. R., A. S. Ryan, and B. R. Leashore, eds. 1997. *The Challenge of Permanency Planning in a Multicultural Society.* New York: Haworth.

Anderson, G. R., C. Ryan, S. Taylor-Brown, and M. White-Gray, eds. 1998. HIV/AIDS and children, youths, and families: Lessons learned. Special issue. *Child Welfare* 77:99–271.

Anderson, R. C., E. H. Heibert, J. A. Scott, and I. A. G. Wilkinson. 1985. *Becoming a Nation of Readers: The Report of the Commission on Reading.* Washington, D.C.: National Academy of Education.

Andrews, A.B., and Ben-Arieh, A. 1999. Measuring and monitoring children's well-being across the world. *Social Work* 44 (2): 105–115.

Annie E. Casey Foundation. N.d.a. *Family to Family Tools for Rebuilding Foster Care. Safety First: Dealing with the Daily Challenges of Child Welfare.* Part 1. Baltimore: Annie E. Casey Foundation.

Annie E. Casey Foundation. N.d.b. *Family to Family Tools for Rebuilding Foster Care. Team Decision Making: Involving the Family and Community in Child Welfare Decisions. Building Community Partnerships in Child Welfare.* Part 1. Baltimore: Annie E. Casey Foundatio.

Annie E. Casey Foundation. N.d.c. *Family to Family Tools for Rebuilding Foster Care. People Helping People: Partnerships Between Professionals and Natural Helpers. Building Community Partnerships in Child Welfare.* Part 4. Baltimore: Annie E. Casey Foundation.

Annie E. Casey Foundation. N.d.d. *Family to Family Tools for Rebuilding Foster Care. The Resiliency Workshop: A Tool to Lessen Burnout in Child Welfare. Building Support for Child Welfare's Frontline Workers.* Part 2. Baltimore: Annie E. Casey Foundation.

Annie E. Casey Foundation. N.d.e. *Family to Family Tools for Rebuilding Foster Care. The Need for Self-Evaluation: Using Data to Guide Policy and Programs.* Baltimore: Annie E. Casey Foundation.

Annie E. Casey Foundation. N.d.f. *Family to Family Tools for Rebuilding Foster Care. Back from the Brink: Women, Crack, and the Child Welfare System.* Baltimore: Annie E. Casey Foundation.

Annie E. Casey Foundation. 1998a. *Improving Economic Opportunities for Young People Served by the Foster Care System: Three Views of the Path to Independent Living — Phase 1.* Baltimore: Annie E. Casey Foundation.

Annie E. Casey Foundation. 1998b. *Evaluating Comprehensive Community Change.* Baltimore: Annie E. Casey Foundation.

Annie E. Casey Foundation. 2000. *Kids Count Data Book: States Profiles of Child Well-Being.* Baltimore: Annie E. Casey Foundation.

Annie E. Casey Foundation. 2001. *Kids Count Data Book: States Profiles of Child Well-Being.* Baltimore: Annie E. Casey Foundation.

Ansell, D. I. and the Casey Family Programs. 1997. *Ansell-Casey Life Skills Assessment: 1 Through 3*. Mercer Island, Wa.: Bavendam Research Associates.

Antonovsky, A. 1994. The sense of coherence: An historical and future perspective. In H. Z. McCubbin, E. A. Thompson, A. I. Thompson, and J. E. Fromer, eds., *Sense of Coherence and Resilience: Stress, Coping, and Health*, pp. 3–21. Madison: University of Wisconsin System.

Apfel, R. J. and B. Simon, 1996. *Minefields in Their Hearts: The Mental Health of Children in War and Communal Violence*. New Haven: Yale University Press.

Arroyo, W. and S. Eth.1996. Post-traumatic stress disorder and other stress reactions. In R. J. Apfel and B. Simon, eds., *Minefields in Their Hearts: The Mental Health of Children in War and Communal Violence*, pp. 52–74. New Haven: Yale University Press.

Avery, N. 1998. *Public Agency Adoption in New York State: Phase I Report. Foster Care Histories of Children Freed for Adoption in New York State: 1980–1993*. Ithaca: Cornell University.

Azzi-Lessing, L. and L. J. Olsen. 1996. Substance abuse–affected families in the child welfare system: New challenges, new alliances. *Social Work* 41 (1): 15–23.

Babb, L. A. 1999. *Ethics in American Adoption*. Westport, Conn.: Bergen and Harvey.

Bailey, J. 2000. Study reveals irony faced by former welfare moms. *CWRU Campus News*, October 19, pp. 1, 4.

Baladarian, N. 1994. Abuse and neglect of children with disabilities. *Arch Fact Sheet*. Chapel Hill: Arch National Resource Center for Crisis Nurseries and Respite Care Services.

Balgopal, P.R. 2000. *Social Work Practice with Immigrants and Refugees*. New York: Columbia University Press.

Bane, M. J. and D. T. Ellwood. 1994. *Welfare Realities from Rhetoric to Reform*. Cambridge: Harvard University Press.

Banks, H. 2001. Grants for inner-city asthma awarded by CDC. Washington, D.C.: CWLA. http://www.wer4kdz (February 16, 2001).

Barnett, W.S. 1995. Long-term effects of early childhood programs on cognitive and school outcomes. *Future of Children* 5 (3): 25–50.

Barrerra, M. 1986. Distinctions between social support concepts, measures, and models. *American Journal of Community Psychology* 14:413–455.

Barth, R. P. and M. Berry. 1994. Implications of research on the welfare of children under permanency planning. In R. P. Barth, J. D. Berrick, and N. Gilbert, eds., *Child Welfare Research Review* 1:323–368. New York: Columbia University Press.

Barth, R. P. and M. Jonson-Reid. 2000. Outcomes after child welfare services: Implications for the design of performance measures. *Children and Youth Services Review* 22 (9/10): 763–788.

Barth, R. P. and E. Locklin. 2001. *Administrative Data on the Well-Being of Children*

on and off Welfare. Washington, D.C.: National Academies. http://www4
.nationalacademies.org/cb (July 8, 2001).

Barton, P. E. and R. J. Coley, 1992. *America's Smallest School: The Family.* Princeton: Educational Testing Service.

Beaty, Cynthia 1997. *Parents in Prison: Children in Crisis.* Washington, D.C.: CWLA.

Beeman, S. 1997. Reconceptualizing social support and its relationship to child neglect. *Social Service Review* 71:421–440.

Belle, D. 1982. *Lives in Stress: Women and Depression.* Beverly Hills: Sage.

Belle, D. 1994. Social support issues for "latchkey" and supervised children. In F. Nestmann and K. Hurrelmann, eds., *Social Networks and Social Support in Childhood and Adolescence,* pp. 293–304. New York: Aldine de Gruyter.

Benard, B. 1994. Applications of resilience. Paper presented at a conference on the Role of Resilience in Drug Abuse, Alcohol Abuse, and Mental Illness, December 5–6. Washington, D.C. Cited in D. Saleebey 1997.

Benard, B. 1997. Fostering resiliency in children and youth: Promoting protective factors in the school. In D. Saleebey, ed., *The Strengths Perspective in Social Work,* pp. 167–182. 2d ed. New York: Longman.

Benedict, M., S. Zuravin, D. Brandtd, and H. Abbey. 1994. Types and frequency of child maltreatment by family foster care providers in an urban population. *Child Abuse and Neglect* 18:577–585.

Berg, I. 1994. *Family-Based Services: A Solution-Focused Approach.* New York: Norton.

Berrick, J. D. and M. Duerr. 1996. Maintaining positive school relationships: The role of the social worker vis-à-vis full service schools. *Social Work in Education* 18 (1): 53–58.

Berrick, J. D., B. Needell, R. P. Barth, and M. Johnson-Reid. 1998. *The Tender Years: Toward Developmentally Sensitive Child Welfare Services for Very Young Children.* New York: Oxford University Press.

Berry, M. F. 1993. *The Politics of Parenthood: Child Care, Women's Rights, and the Myth of the Good Mother.* New York: Viking Penguin.

Berry, M. 1997. *The Family at Risk: Issues and Trends in Family Preservation Services.* Columbia: University of South Carolina Press.

Berry, M., J. S. Cash, and J. P. Brook. 2000. Intensive family preservation services: An examination of critical service components. *Child and Family Social Work* 5:191–203.

Besharov, D. J. 1990. Crack children in foster care: Re-examining the balance between children's rights and parent's rights. *Children Today,* July-August, pp. 21–25.

Bickman, L. and A. Doucette. 2000. *Child/Adolescent Measurement Systems.* Nashville: Vanderbilt University.

Biegel, D.E. and A. Blum, eds. 1999. *Innovations in Practice and Service Delivery Across the Life Span.* New York: Oxford University Press.

Billingsley, A. 1968. *Black Families in White America*. Englewood Cliffs, N.J.: Prentice-Hall.

Billingsley, A. and J. Giovannoni. 1972. *Children of the Storm: Black Children and American Child Welfare*. New York: Wiley.

Blank, H. and G. Adams. 1997. *State Developments in Child Care and Early Education*. Washington, D.C.: Children's Defense Fund.

Blome, W. W. 1997. What happens to foster kids: Educational experiences of a random sample of foster care youth and a matched group of nonfoster care youth. *Child and Adolescent Social Work Journal* 14 (1): 41 – 53.

Blome, W. W., L. Wright, and M. Roskin 1998. *Building Supervisory Skills: A Curriculum to Prepare Child Welfare Supervisors*. Washington, D.C.: CWLA.

Bloom, B. 1995. Imprisoned mothers. In K. Gabel and D. Johnston, eds., *Children of Incarcerated Parents*, pp. 21–30. Boston: Lexington.

Bloom, B. and D. Steinhart. 1993. *Why Punish the Children? A Reappraisal of the Children of Incarcerated Mothers in America*. San Francisco: National Council on Crime and Delinquency.

Bloom, M., J. Fischer, and J. G. Orme. 1999. *Evaluating Practice: Guidelines for the Accountable Professional*. 3d ed. Boston: Allyn and Bacon.

Bloom, M. and T. P. Gulotta, eds. 2001. *Promoting Creativity Across the Life Span*. Washington, D.C.: CWLA.

Blythe, B. J., M. P. Salley, and S. Jayaratne. 1994. A review of intensive family preservation research. *Social Work Research* 18 (2): 213–224.

Blythe, B. J., E. M. Tracy, and A. Kotovsky 1992. Organizational supports to sustain intensive family preservation programs. *Families in Society: The Journal of Contemporary Human Services* 73:463–470.

Bok, M. and J. Morales. 1997. The impact and implications of HIV on children and adolescents: Social justice and social change. *Journal of HIV-AIDS Prevention and Education for Adolescents and Children* 1 (1): 9–34.

Bonecutter, F. J. and J. P. Gleeson. 1997. *Achieving Permanency for Cchildren in Kinship Foster Care: A Training Manual*. Chicago: University of Illinois at Chicago, Jane Adams College of Social Work.

Booth, A. and J. F. Dunn, eds. 1996. *Family-School Links: How Do They Affect Educational Outcomes?* Mahwah, N.J.: Lawrence Erlbaum.

Botvin, G. 2000. Preventing drug abuse in schools: Social and competence enhancement approaches targeting individual-level etiologic factors. *Addictive Behaviors* 25 (6): 887–897.

Brach, C. and L. C. Scallet. 1998. Managed care challenges for children and family services. In G. Schamess and A. Lightburn, eds., *Humane Managed Care?* pp. 99–108. Washington, D.C.: NASW.

Bradley, J. 1997. *Runaway Youth: Stress, Social Support, and Adjustment*. New York: Garland.

Brandwein, R.A. 1986. A feminist approach to social policy. In N. Van Den Bergh, and L. B. Cooper, eds., *Feminist Visions for Social Work*, pp. 250–261. Silver Spring: National Association of Social Workers.

Brayfield, A., S. Deich, and S. L. Hofferth. 1993. *Caring for Children in Low-Income Families*. Washington, D.C.: Urban Institute Press.

Brissett-Chapman, S. 2000. How do I consider cultural factors when assessing risk and safety? In H. Dubowitz and D. DePanfilis, eds., *Handbook for Child Protection Practice*, pp. 233–239. Thousand Oaks, Cal.: Sage.

Brissett-Chapman, S. and M. Issacs-Shockley. 1997. *Children in Social Peril: A Community Vision for Preserving Family Care of African-American Children and Youths*. Washington, D.C.: CWLA.

Bronfenbrenner, U. 1979. *The Ecology of Human Development*. Cambridge: Harvard University Press.

Bronfenbrenner, U. 1986. Ecology of the family as a context for human development: Research perspectives. *Developmental Psychology* 22 (6): 723–742.

Brown, J. H. and M. Weil, eds. 1992. *Family Practice: A Curriculum Plan for Social Service*. Washington, D.C.: CWLA

Brown, V. A. 2002. *Child Welfare: Case Studies*. Boston: Allyn and Bacon.

Burford, G. and J. Hudson. 2000. *Family Group Conferences: New Directions in Community-Centered Child and Family Practice*. New York: Aldine de Gruyter.

Burford, G., J. Pennell, and S. MacLeod. 1999. Family group decision making. In B. R. Compton and B. Galaway, *Social Work Processes*, pp. 278–283. 6th ed. Pacific Grove, Cal.: Brooks/Cole.

Burnette, D. 1997. Grandparents raising grandchildren in the inner city. *Families in Society: The Journal of Contemporary Human Services* 78 (5): 489–501.

Butler, J., N. Brigham, and S. Schultheiss. 1992. *No Place Like Home: A Study of In-Home and Relative Child Day Care*. Providence: Rosenblum.

Buzzi, M. 2000. New statistics show only small percentage of eligible families receive child care help. *ANE-Bulletin*. http://www.cwla.org/wer4kolz (December 8, 2000).

Cadoret, R. J., W. R. Yates, E. Troughton, G. Woodworth, and M. A. Stewart. 1995. Genetic-environmental interactions in the genesis of agressivity and conduct disorders. *Archives of General Psychiatry* 52:916–924.

Caldwell, B. and R. Bradley. 1984. *Home Observation for Measurement of the Environment*. Little Rock: University of Arkansas at Little Rock.

Caldwell, C. H., A. D. Greene, and A. Billingsley. 1994. Family support programs in black churches, a new look at old functions. In S. L. Kagan and B. Weissbourd, eds., *Putting Families First: America's Family Support Movement and the Challenge of Change*, pp. 137–160. San Francisco: Jossey-Bass.

Cameron. G. 2000. Parent mutual aid organizations in child welfare demonstration project: A report of outcomes. *Children and Youth Services Review* 22 (6): 421–440.

Cameron, G. and J. Vanderwoerd, 1997. *Protecting Children and Supporting Families: Promising Programs and Organizational Realities*. New York: Aldine de Gruyter.

Campbell, S. 2001. The housing disaster. *Hartford Courant*, February 24, 2001, pp. D1, D5.

Carbino, R. 1991. Advocacy for foster families in the United States facing child abuse allegations: How social agencies and foster parent organizations are responding to the problem. *Child Welfare* 70:131–149.

Carpenter, K. H. 1995. *Sourcebook on Parenting and Child Care*. Phoenix: Oryx.

Carter, B., and M. McGoldrick, eds. 1999. *The Expanded Family Life Cycle: Individual, Family, and Social Perspectives*. 3d ed. Boston: Allyn and Bacon.

Carter, L. S., L. A. Weithorn, and R. E. Behrman. 1999. Domestic violence and children: Analysis and recommendations. *Future of Children* 9 (3): 4–20.

Center for Substance Abuse Prevention. 1993. *Alcohol, Tobacco, and Other Drugs Resource Guide: Elementary Youth*. Washington, D.C.: Center for Substance Abuse Prevention.

Center for Substance Abuse Prevention. 1996. *Keeping Youth Drug-Free: A Guide for Parents, Grandparents, Elders, Mentors, and Other Caregivers*. 422–180/ 60521. Washington, D.C.: Government Printing Office.

Center for Youth Development and Policy Research. N.d. What is youth development? http://aed.org/us/cyd/whatis.html (June 9, 2001).

Chalk, R. and P. A. King, eds. 1998. *Violence in Families: Assessing Prevention and Treatment Programs*. Washington, D.C.: National Academy Press.

Chandler, S. M. 1986. The hidden feminist agenda in social development. In N. Van Den Bergh and L. B. Cooper, eds., *Feminist Visions for Social Work*, pp. 149–162. Silver Spring: National Association of Social Workers.

Chasnoff, I. J., H. Landress, and M. Barrett. 1990. The prevalence of illicit-drug or alcohol use during pregnancy and discrepancies in mandatory reporting in Pinellas County, Florida. *New England Journal of Medicine* 322:1202.

Chavkin, N. F., ed. 1993. *Families and Schools in a Pluralistic Society*. Albany: State University of New York Press.

Chavkin, N. F. and D. L. Williams Jr. 1993. Minority parents and the elementary school: Attitudes and practices. In N. F. Chavkin, ed., *Families and Schools in a Pluralistic Society*, pp. 73–83. Albany: State University of New York Press.

Cheung, K. M. 1996. Cultural adjustment and differential acculturation among Chinese new immigrant families in the United States. In S. Lau, ed., *Growing Up the Chinese Way: Chinese Child and Adolescent Development*, pp. 321–355. Hong Kong: Chinese University Press.

Children's Aid Society. 1995. *Building a Community School: A Revolutionary Design in Public Education*. New York: Children's Aid Society.

Children's Bureau of Southern California. 1996. *Family Assessment Form*. Washington, D.C.: CWLA.

Children's Defense Fund. N.d. *Fourteen Things You Should Know About the New Child Health Program*. Washington, D.C.: Children's Defense Fund.

Children's Defense Fund. 1989. Homeless families: mired in misfortune. *CDF Reports* 10 (12): 1–2, 8.

Children's Defense Fund. 1992. *The State of America's Children*. Washington, D.C.: Children's Defense Fund.

Children's Defense Fund. 1999. *Extreme Child Poverty Rises by More Than Four Hundred Thousand in One Year*. Washington, D.C.: Children's Defense Fund. http://www.childrensdefense.org/release990822/.htm (June 30, 2001).

Children's Defense Fund. 2000. *The State of America's Children: Yearbook 2000*. Washington, D.C.: Children's Defense Fund.

Children's Defense Fund. 2001. *New Data Show High Poverty Levels for Children in Every State*. Washington, D.C.: Children's Defense Fund. http://www.childrensdefense.org/release010806.htm (October 25, 2001).

Child Welfare League of America. 1989. *Standards for Services to Strengthen and Preserve Families with Children*. Washington, D.C.: CWLA.

Child Welfare League of America. 1993. *Cultural Competence Self-Assessment Instrument*. Washington, D.C.: CWLA.

Child Welfare League of America. 1994. *Kinship Care: A Natural Bridge*. Washington, D.C.: CWLA.

Child Welfare League of America 1995. *Standards of Excellence for Family Foster Care*. Washington, D.C.: CWLA.

Child Welfare League of America. 1998. *Breaking the Link Between Substance Abuse and Child Maltreatment: An Issue Forum*. Washington, D.C.: CWLA.

Child Welfare League of America. 2000a. New statistics show only small percentages of families receive child care help. *WeR4Kdz* (e-bulletin; December 8), no. 4.

Child Welfare League of America. 2000b. *CWLA Standards of Excellence for Kinship Care Services*. Washington, D.C.: CWLA.

Cicarelli, V. G. 1969. *The Impact of Head Start: An Evaluation of the Effects of Head Start on Children's Cognitive and Affective Development*. Athens: Ohio University and New York: Westinghouse Learning Corporation.

Cohen, N. A., ed. 1992. *Child Welfare: A Multicultural Focus*. Needham Heights, Mass.: Allyn and Bacon.

Cohen, S., and T. A. Wills. 1985. Stress, social support, and the buffering hypothesis. *Psychological Bulletin* 98 (2): 310–357.

Cole, E. and J. Duva. 1990. *Family Preservation: An Orientation for Administrators and Practitioners*. Washington, D.C.: Child Welfare League of America.

Collins, A. and B. Carlson. 1998. *Child Care by Kin and Kin-Supporting Family, Friends, and Neighbors Caring for Children*. New York: National Center for Children in Poverty.

Collins, J. and P. Messerschmidt. 1993. Epidemiology of alcohol-related violence. *Alcohol Health and Research World* 17 (2): 93–100.

Comer, E. W. and M. W. Fraser. 1998. Evaluation of six family-support programs: Are they effective? *Families in Society: The Journal of Contemporary Human Services* 79 (2): 134–148.

Compton, B. R. and B. Galaway. 1999. *Social Work Processes*. 6th ed. Pacific Grove, Cal.: Brooks/Cole.

Congress, E. 1994. The use of culturagrams to assess and empower culturally diverse families. *Families in Society: The Journal of Contemporary Human Services* 75: 531–540.

Congress, E. 2002a. *Teaching Social Work Values and Ethics: A Curriculum Resource*. Alexandria, Va.: Council on Social Work Education.

Congress, E. 2002b. Using the culturagram with culturally diverse families. In A. R. Roberts and G. Greene, eds., *Social Work Desk Reference*, pp. 57–61. New York: Oxford University Press.

Connolly, M. and M. McKenzie. 1999. *Effective Participatory Practice: Family Group Conferencing in Child Protection*. New York: Aldine de Gruyter.

Coohey, C. 1996. Child maltreatment: Testing the social isolation hypothesis. *Child Abuse and Neglect* 20 (3): 241–254.

Coohey, C. 1998. Home alone and other inadequately supervised children. *Child Welfare* 77:291–310.

Corcoran, K. and J. Fischer. 2000. *Measures for Clinical Practice: A Sourcebook*. Vols. 1, 2. 3d ed. New York: Free.

Corcoran, M. E. and A. Chaundry. 1997. The dynamics of childhood poverty. *Future of Children* 7 (2): 40–54.

Cormier, W. and L. Cormier, L. 1985. *Interviewing Strategies for Helpers*. 2d ed. Monterey, Cal.: Brooks/Cole.

Costin, L. B., ed. 1985. Toward a feminist approach to child welfare. Special issue. *Child Welfare* 64:195–320.

Cournoyer, D. E. and W. C. Klein. 2000. *Research Methods for Social Work*. Boston: Allyn and Bacon.

Courtney, M. E., R. P. Barth, J. D., Berrick, D. Brooks, B. Needell, and L. Park. 1996. Race and child welfare services: Past research and future directions. *Child Welfare* 75:99–137.

Courtney, M. E. and A. N. Maluccio. 1999. The rationalization of foster care in the twenty-first century. In P. A. Curtis, G. Dale Jr., and J. C. Kendall, eds., *The Foster Care Crisis: Translating Research Into Policy and Practice*, pp. 225–242. Lincoln: University of Nebraska Press.

Courtney, M. E. and B. Needell. 1997. Outcomes in kinship care: Lessons from California. In J. D. Berrick, R. D. Barth and N. Gilbert, eds., *Child Welfare Research Review* 2:130–149. New York: Columbia University Press.

Cox, K.L. 2000. Parenting the second-time around for parents in recovery: Parenting class using the twelve-step recovery model. *Sources* 10 (1): 11–14. National Abandoned Infants Assistance Resource Center.

Crittenden, P. M. 1985. Social networks, quality of child rearing and child development. *Child Development* 56:1299–1313.

Crosson-Tower, C. 2001. *Exploring Child Welfare: A Practice Perspective.* Boston: Allyn and Bacon.

Crumbley, J. and R. L. Little. 1997. *Relatives raising children: An overview of kinship care.* Washington, D.C.: CWLA.

Culler, T. 1997. Community schools: Where the children are. *Children's Voice* 7 (1): 8–9, 21.

Culross, P. L. 1999. Health care system responses to children exposed to domestic violence. *Future of Children* 9 (3): 111–121.

Curtis, P. A., ed. 1994. *A Research Agenda for Child Welfare.* Special issue. *Child Welfare* 73 (5): 355–655.

Daley, D. and T. Gorske. 2000. Improving treatment adherence for mothers with substance abuse problems. *Sources* 10 (1): 1–5. National Abandoned Infants Assistance Resource Center.

Danzy, J., and Jackson, S.M. 1997. Family preservation and support services: A missed opportunity for kinship care. *Child Welfare* 76:31–44.

Daro, D. and K. McCurdy. 1991. *Current Trends in Child Abuse Reporting and Fatalities: The Results of the 1989 Annual Fifty-State Survey.* Chicago: National Center on Child Abuse Prevention Research, National Committee for Prevention of Child Abuse.

Dauber, S. L. and J. L. Epstein, 1993. Parents' attitudes and practices of involvement in inner-city elementary and middle schools. In N. F. Chavkin, ed., *Families and Schools in a Pluralistic Society,* pp. 53–71. Albany: State University of New York Press.

Davidson, J. R. and L. Davidson. 1998. Confidentiality and managed care: Ethical and legal concerns. In G. Schamess and A. Lightburn, eds., *Humane managed care?* pp. 281–292. Washington, D.C.: NASW.

Davis, I. P., J. Landsverk, R. Newton, and W. Ganger. 1996. Parental visiting and foster care reunification. *Children and Youth Services Review* 18:363–382.

Davis, L.V. 1995. Domestic violence. In R. L. Edwards and J. G. Hopps, eds., *Encyclopedia of Social Work* 1:780–789. 19th ed. Washington, D.C.: NASW.

Day, P., S. Robison, and L. Sheikh. 1998. *Ours to Keep: A Guide to Building a Community Assessment Strategy for Child Protection.* Washington, D.C.: CWLA.

DePalma, A. 2001. Dole says trade accord on bananas favors rival. *New York Times,* April 14, 2001, p. C2.

DePanfilis, D. 1996. Social isolation of neglectful families: a review of social support assessment and intervention models. *Child Maltreatment* 1 (1): 37–52.

Department of Health, England–Department for Education and Employment, Home Office. 2000. *Framework for the Assessment of Children in Need and Their Families.* London: Stationery Office.

Devaney, B. L, M. R. Ellwood, and J. M. Love. 1997. Programs that mitigate the effects of poverty on children. *Future of Children* 7 (2): 88–112.

Developmental Disabilities Assistance and Bill of Rights Act of 2000. Public Law 106–402. 114 Stat. 1677.

Devore, W. and E. G. Schlesinger. 1996. *Ethnic-Sensitive Social Work Practice.* 4th ed. Boston: Allyn and Bacon.

Dickson, D. T. 1998. *Confidentiality and Privacy in Social Work: A Guide to the Law for Practitioners and Students.* New York: Free.

DiLeonardi, J. W. 1993. Families in poverty and chronic neglect of children. *Families in Society: The Journal of Contemporary Human Services* 74: 557–562.

DiNitto, D. M. 1995. Hunger, nutrition, and food programs. In R. Edwards and J. G. Hopps, eds., *Encyclopedia of Social Work* 1:1428–1437. 19th ed. Washington, D.C.: NASW.

DiNitto, D. M. and T. Dye. 1987. *Social Welfare Politics and Public Policy.* Englewood Cliffs, N.J.: Prentice-Hall.

Dore, M. M. 1999. Emotionally and behaviorally disturbed children in the child welfare system: Points of intervention. *Children and Youth Services Review* 66:335–348.

Dornbusch, S. M. and K. L. Glasgow. 1996. The structural context of family-school relations. In A. Booth and J. F. Dunn, eds., *Family-School Links: How Do They Affect Educational Outcomes?* pp. 35–44. Mahwah, N.J.: Lawrence Erlbaum.

Doucette-Dudman, D. and J. R. LaCure. 1996. *Raising Our Children's Children.* Minneapolis: Fairview.

Downs, S. W., E. Moore, E. J. McFadden, and L. B. Costin. 2000. *Child Welfare and Family Services: Policies and Practice.* 6th ed. Boston: Allyn and Bacon.

Drachman, D. 1992. A stage-of-migration framework for service to immigrant populations. *Social Work* 37 (1): 68–72.

Drachman, D. 1995. Immigration statuses and their influence on service provision access and use. *Social Work* 40:188–197.

Drachman, D., Y. H. Kwon-Ahn, and A. Paulino. 1996. Migration and resettlement experiences of Dominican and Korean families. *Families in Society: The Journal of Contemporary Human Services* 77:626–638.

Dreier, M. and M. Lewis. 1991. Support and psychoeducation for parents of hospitalized mentally ill children. *Health and Social Work* 16:11–18.

Drissel, A. N.d. *Managed Care and Children and Family Services: A Guide for State and Local Officials*. Baltimore: Annie E. Casey Foundation.

Dryfoos, J. G. 1994. *Full-Service Schools: A Revolution in Health and Social Services for Children, Youth, and Families*. San Francisco: Jossey-Bass.

Dubos, R. 1968. *So Human an Animal*. New York: Scribners.

Dubowitz, H. and D. DePanfilis, eds. 2000. *Handbook for Child Protection Practice*. Thousand Oaks, Cal.: Sage.

Dunlap, E. 1992. The impact of drugs on family life and kin networks in the inner-city African-American single-parent household. In A. F. Harrell and A. E. Peterson, eds., *Drugs, Crime, and Social Isolation: Barriers to Urban Opportunity*, pp. 181–207. Washington, D.C.: Urban Institute.

Dunlap, K. M. 1996. Supporting and empowering families through cooperative preschool education. *Social Work in Education* 18 (4): 211–221.

Dunst, C. J., C. M. Trivette, and A. G. Deal. 1988. *Enabling and Empowering Families: Principles and Guidelines for Practice*. Cambridge: Brookline.

Dupper, D. R. and J. Poertner 1997. Public schools and the revitalization of impoverished communities: School-linked, family resource centers. *Social Work* 42 (5): 415–422.

Durlak, J. A. 1995. *School-Based Prevention Programs for Ch ildren and Adolescents*. Thousand Oaks, Cal.: Sage.

Dwyer, K. and D. Osher. 2000. *Preventing Bullying: A Manual for Schools and Communities*. U.S. Department of Education. http://www.ed.gov/ (April 15, 2001).

Early, T. J. 2001. Measures for practice with families from a strengths perspective. *Families in Society: The Journal of Contemporary Human Services* 82:225–232.

Early, T. J. and L. F. GlenMaye. 2000. Valuing families: Social work practice with families from a strength perspective. *Social Work* 45:118–130.

Eccles, J. S. and R. D. Harold. 1996. Family involvement in children's and adolescents' schooling. In A. Booth and J. F. Dunn, eds., *Family-School Links: How Do They Affect Educational Outcomes?* pp. 3–34. Mahwah, N.J.: Lawrence Erlbaum.

Edin, K. 1995. Single mothers and child support: The possibilities and limits of child support policy. *Children and Youth Services Review* 17 (1/2): 203–230.

Edmunds, M. and M. J. Coye, eds. 1998. *America's Children: Health Insurance and Access to Care*. Washington, D.C.: National Academy Press.

Edna McConnell Clark Foundation. 1993. *Keeping Families Together: Facts on Family Preservation Services*. New York: Edna McConnell Clark Foundation.

Emenhiser, D., R. Barker, and M. DeWoody. 1995. *Managed Care: An Agency's Guide to Surviving and Thriving*. Washington, D.C.: CWLA.

Emenhiser, D. L., D. W. King, S. A. Joffe, and K. S. Penkert. 1998. *Networks,*

Mergers, and Partnerships in a Managed Care Environment. Washington, D.C.: CWLA.

Endres, J. 2000. Family development matrix outcomes model for measuring family progress. *Prevention Report* 1:3–7.

Edwards, E. D., J. R. Seaman, J. Drews, and M. E. Edwards. 1995. A community approach for Native American drug and alcohol prevention programs: A logic model framework. *Alcoholism Treatment Quarterly* 13 (2): 43–62.

Epstein, J. L. 1996. Perspectives and previews on research and policy for school, family, and community partnerships. In A. Booth and J. F. Dunn, eds., *Family-School Links: How Do They Affect Educational Outcomes?* pp. 209–246. Mahwah, N.J.: Lawrence Erlbaum.

Erikson, E. H. 1963. *Childhood and Society.* 2d ed. New York: Norton.

Everett, J. 1995. Relative foster care: An emerging trend in foster care placements policy and practice. *Smith College Studies in Social Work* 65:239–254.

Everett, J. E. 1997. Theoretical, policy, research and clinical perspectives for social work practice with African Americans. Special issue. *Smith College Studies in Social Work* 67 (3): 255–643.

Everett, J. E., S. S. Chipungu, and B. R. Leashore, eds. 1991. *Child Welfare: An Africentric Perspective.* New Brunswick, N.J.: Rutgers University Press.

Ewalt, P. L., E. M. Freeman, and A. E. Fortune, eds. 1999. *Multicultural Issues in Social Work: Practice and Research.* Washington, D.C.: NASW.

Ezell, M. 2001. *Advocacy in the Human Services.* Belmont, Cal.: Wadsworth/Thompson Learning.

Fahlberg, V. I. 1991. *A Child's Journey Through Placement.* Indianapolis: Perspectives.

Faithfull, J. 1997. HIV-positive and AIDS-infected women: Challenges and difficulties of mothering. *American Journal of Orthopsychiatry* 67 (1): 144–151.

Faller, K. 1993. *Child Sexual Abuse: Intervention and Treatment Issues.* Washington, D.C.: DHHS, Administration for Children and Families.

Family Resource Coalition of America. 1996. *Guidelines for Family Support Practice.* Chicago: Family Resource Coalition of America.

Family Resource Coalition of America. 1998–99. Strengthening families in the welfare reform era. *FRCA Report* 17 (4) (Winter): 4–46.

Family Violence Prevention Fund. 1999–2001. Children and domestic violence. http://www.fvpf.org/kids/index.htm (June 11, 2001).

Fantuzzo, J. W. and W. K. Mohr. 1999. Prevalence and effects of child exposure to domestic violence. *Future of Children* 9 (3): 21–32.

Farmer, S. and D. Galaris. 1993. Support groups for children of divorce. *American Journal of Family Therapy* 21(1): 40–50.

Federal Interagency Coordinating Council. 2000. *Principles of Family Involvement.* http://www.fed.icc.org/policy/fam_inv.htm (June 1, 2001).

Feig, L. 1990. *Drug-Exposed Infants and Children: Service Needs and Policy Questions*. Washington, D.C.: DHHS.

Fein, E. and Maluccio, A.N. 1992. Permanency planning: Another remedy in jeopardy. *Social Service Review* 66:335–348.

Fein, E., A. N. Maluccio, and M. P. Kluger. 1990. *No More Partings: An Examination of Long-Term Foster Care*. Washington, D.C.: CWLA.

Fein, E. and I. Staff. 1993. The interaction of research and practice in family reunification. In B. A. Pine, R. Warsh, and A. N. Maluccio, eds., *Together Again: Family Reunification in Foster Care*, pp. 199–212. Washington, D.C.: CWLA.

Feldman, L. 1990. Target population definition. In Y.-Y. T. Yuan and M. Rivest, eds., *Preserving Families: Evaluation Resources for Practitioners and Policymakers*, pp. 16–38. Newbury Park, Cal.: Sage.

Feldman, L. 1991. *Assessing the Effectiveness of Family Preservation Services in New Jersey Within an Ecological Context*. Trenton: New Jersey Division of Youth and Family Services, Bureau of Research, Evolution, and Quality Assurance.

Ferguson, S. A., E. M. Tracy, and D. Simonelli. 1993. *Parent Network Project Manual: Training Head Start Parent Advisors to Strengthen the Support Systems of Low-Income Parents*. Cleveland: Center for Practice Innovations, Mandel School of Applied Social Sciences, Case Western Reserve University.

Figueira-McDonough, J. 1993. Policy practice: The neglected side of social work intervention. *Social Work* 38 (2): 179–187.

Fine, P. 1995. *A developmental network approach to therapeutic foster care*. Washington, D.C.: CWLA.

Finkelhor, D. 1979. What's wrong with sex between adults and children? Ethics and the problem of sexual abuse. *American Journal of Orthopsychiatry* 47 (4): 692–698.

Fischer, C. S. 1982. *To Dwell Among Friends: Personal Networks in Town and City*. Chicago: University of Chicago Press.

Folman, R. D. 1998. "I was tooken." How children experience removal from their parents preliminary to placement into foster care. *Adoption Quarterly* 2:7–35.

Fong, R. and S. Furuto. 2001. *Culturally Competent Practice: Skills, Intervensions, and Evaluations*. Boston: Allyn and Bacon.

Fontana, V. J. 2000. Troubled children in a troubled society. *Children's Voice*, March, pp. 28–29.

Ford, J. and R. D. Sutphen. 1996. Early intervention to improve attendance in elementary school for at-risk children: A pilot program. *Social Work in Education* 18 (2): 95–102.

Ford, M. E. and J. B. Schwamm, 1992. Expanding eligibility for supplemental security income based on childhood disability: The Zebley decisions. *Child Welfare* 71:307–318.

Franklin, C. and C. L. Streeter. 1995. School reform: Linking public schools with human services. *Social Work* 40 (6): 773–782.

Franklin, C. and C. L. Streeter. 1998. School-linked services as interprofessional collaboration in student education. *Social Work* 43 (1): 67–69.

Franklin, C., J. Biever, K. Moore, D. Clemons, and M. Scanardo. 2001. The effectiveness of solution-focused therapy with children in a school setting. *Research on Social Work Practice* 11:411–434.

Franks, F. and S. A. Faux. 1990. Depression, stress, mastery, and social resources in four ethnocultural women's groups. *Research in Nursing and Health* 13 (5): 283–292.

Fraser, C. 1995. Suffering children and the Christian Science Church. *Atlantic Monthly*, April, pp. 105–120.

Fraser, M. W. 1990. Program outcome measures. In Y.-Y. T. Yuan and M. Rivest, eds., *Preserving Families: Evaluation Resources for Practitioners and Policymakers*, pp. 77–101. Newbury Park, Cal.: Sage.

Fraser, M. W., ed. 1997a. *Risk and Resilience in Childhood: An Ecological Perspective*. Washington, D.C.: NASW.

Fraser, M. W. 1997b. The ecology of childhood: A multi-systems perspective. In M. W. Fraser, ed., *Risk and Resilience in Childhood: An Ecological Perspective*, pp. 1–9. Washington, D.C.: NASW.

Fraser, M. W., P. J. Pecora, and D. A. Haapala. 1991. *Families in Crisis: The Impact of Intensive Family Preservation Services*. New York: Aldine de Gruyter.

Freed, A. O. 1985. Linking developmental, family, and life cycle theories. *Smith College Studies in Social Work* 65:169–182.

Freedberg, S. 1989. Self determination: Historical perspectives and effects on current practice. *Social Work* 34 (1): 33–38.

Freeman, E. M. 1998. Many ways of knowing: The implications for practice with youths related to substance abuse issues. *Social Work in Education* 20 (1): 3–9.

Freeman, E. M., C. G. Franklin, R. Fong, G. L. Schaffer, and E. M. Timberlake. 1998. *Multisystem Skills and Interventions in School Social Work Practice*. Washington, D.C.: NASW.

Freeman, E. M., S. L. Logan, and E. A. Gowdy. 1992. Empowering single mothers. *Affilia: Journal of Women and Social Work* 7:123–141.

Freud, S. 1988. Cybernetic epistemology. In R. A. Dorfman, ed., *Paradigms of Clinical Social Work*, pp. 356–387. New York: Brunner/Mazel.

Fried, S. E. 2000. Bullying: Children abusing children. *Children's Voice*, March, pp. 24–27.

Frisino, J. M. and D. Pollack. 1997. HIV testing of adolescents in foster care. *Journal of HIV/AIDS Prevention and Education for Adolescents and Children* 1 (1): 53–70.

Fuchs, D. 2000. Social network theory, research, and practice: Implications for family group conferencing. In G. Burford and J. Hudson, eds., *Family Group Conferencing: New Directions in Community-Centered Child and Family Practice*, pp. 131–139. New York: Aldine de Gruyter.

Fujiwara, L. H. 1998. The impact of welfare reform on Asian immigrant communities. *Social Justice* 25 (1): 82–104.

Fuligni, A. J. 1998. The adjustment of children from immigrant families. *Current Directions in Psychological Science* 7 (4): 99–103.

Gabel, K. and D. Johnston, eds. 1995. *Children of Incarcerated Parents*. Boston: Lexington.

Gaffney, S. and S. Dubey. 1997. Time series analysis of the implementation of child support enforcement policies in federal region V states. *Journal of Sociology and Social Welfare* 24 (4): 57–94.

Galanter, M. and H. D. Kleber. 1999. *Textbook of substance abuse treatment*. 2d ed. Washington, D.C.: American Psychiatric.

Gambrill, E. 1997. *Social Work Practice: A Critical Thinker's Guide*. New York: Oxford University Press.

Ganley, A. and S. Schecter.1996. *Domestic Violence: A National Curriculum for Child Protective Services*. San Francisco: Family Violence Prevention Fund.

Garbarino, J. 1992. *Children and Families in the Social Environment*. 2d ed. New York: Aldine de Gruyter.

Garbarino, J., N. Dubrow, K. Kostelny, and C. Pardo. 1992. *Children in Danger: Coping with the Consequences of Community Violence*. San Francisco: Jossey-Bass.

Garbarino, J. and K. Kostelny. 1994. Neighborhood-based programs. In G. B. Melton and F. D. Barry, eds., *Protecting Children from Abuse and Neglect: Foundations for a New National Strategy*, pp. 131–181. New York: Guilford.

Garbarino, J. and K. Kostelny. 1996. What do we need to know to understand children in war and community violence? In R. J. Apfel and B. Simon, eds., *Minefields in Their Hearts: The Mental Health of Children in War and Communal Violence*, pp. 33–51. New Haven: Yale University Press.

Garfinkel, I., M. S. Melli, and J. G. Robertson. 1994. Child support orders: A perspective on reform. *Future of Children* 4 (1): 84–100.

Garmezy, N. 1994. Reflections and commentary on risk, resilience, and development. In R. J. Haggerty, L. R. Sherrod, N. Garmezy, and M. Rutter. *Stress, Risk, and Resilience in Children: Processes, Mechanisms, and Interventions*, pp. 1–18. Cambridge: Cambridge University Press.

Gates, B. 1980. Assessing barriers to utilization: The problem of access. In B. Gates, *The Implementation of Social Policy*, pp. 141–172. Englewood Cliffs, N.J.: Prentice-Hall.

Gaudin, J. M. 1993. *Child Neglect: A Guide for Intervention*. Washington, D.C.: DHHS, National Center on Child Abuse and Neglect.

Gaudin, J. M. and H. Dubowitz. 1997. Family functioning in neglectful families. In R. Barth and N. Gilbert, eds., *Child Welfare Research Review* 2:28–62. New York: Columbia University Press.

Gaudin, J. M., N. A. Polansky, and A. C. Kilpatrick. 1996. Family functioning in neglectful families. *Child Abuse and Neglect* 20:363–377.

Gaudin, J. M., J. S. Wodarski, M. K. Arkinson, and L. S. Avery. 1990/1991. Remedying child neglect: Effectiveness of social network interventions. *Journal of Applied Social Sciences* 15:97–123.

Geismar, L. L. 1980. *Family and Community Functioning*. 2d ed. Metuchen, N.J.: Scarecrow.

Gelles, R. 1996. *The Book of David: How Preserving Families Can Cost Children's Lives*. New York: Basic.

Generations United.1998. *Grandparents and Other Relatives Raising Children: An Intergenerational Action Agenda*. Washington, D.C.: Generations United.

Gephart, M. A. 1997. Neighborhoods and communities as contexts for development. In J. Brooks-Gunn, G. J. Duncan, and J. L. Aver, eds., *Neighborhood Poverty: Contexts and Consequences for Children*. Vol. 1. New York: Russell Sage Foundation.

Germain, C. B. and M. Bloom. 1999. *Human Behavior in the Social Environment: An Ecological View*. 2d ed. New York: Columbia University Press.

Germain, C. B. and A. Gitterman. 1996. *The Life Model of Social Work Practice: Advances in Theory and Practice*. 2d ed. New York: Columbia University Press.

Giele, J. Z. 1979. Social policy and the family. *Annual Review of Sociology* 5:275–302.

Gil, D. G. 1998. *Confronting Injustice and Oppression: Concepts and Strategies for Social Workers*. New York: Columbia University Press.

Gilgun, J. F. 1999. An ecosystemic aproach to assessment. In B. R. Compton and B. Galaway, eds., *Social Work Processes*, pp. 66–82. 6th ed. Pacific Grove, Cal.: Brooks/Cole.

Gilligan, R. 1998. The importance of schools and teachers in child welfare. *Child and Family Social Work* 3(1): 13–25.

Gilligan, R. 2001. *Promoting Resilience: A Resource Guide on Working with Children in the Care System*. London: British Agencies for Adoption and Fostering.

Ginsberg, L. H. 2001. *Social Work Evaluation: Principles and Methods*. Boston: Allyn and Bacon.

Gitterman, A., ed. 2001. *Handbook of Social Work Practice with Vulnerable and Resilient Populations*. 2d ed. New York: Columbia University Press.

Gitterman, A. and L. Shulman, eds. 1994. *Mutual Aid Groups, Vulnerable Populations, and the Life Cycle*. 2d ed. New York: Columbia University Press.

Gleeson, J. P. and C. F. Hairston, eds. 1999. *Kinship Care: Improving Practice Through Research*. Washington, D.C.: CWLA.

Goals 2000 Educate America Act. 1994. PL 103–227, 108 Stat. 125.

Goldstein, J., A. J. Solnit, S. Goldstein, and A. Freud 1996. *The Best Interests of the Child: The Least Detrimental Alternative.* New York: Free.

Gomby, D. S., P. L. Culross, and R. E. Behrman. 1999. Home visiting: Recent program evaluations, analysis and recommendations. *Future of Children* 9 (1): 4–26.

Gould, K. H. 1985. A minority-feminist perspective on child welfare issues. *Child Welfare* 64:291–305.

Government Accounting Office. 2000. *Oral Health: Dental Disease Is a Chronic Problem Among Low Income Populations.* HEHS-00–72, April 12. Washington, D.C.: GAO.

Grant, R. and L. Maggio. 1997. The impact of medicaid managed care on school-based clinics. *Research in the Sociology of Health Care* 14:289–303.

Gray, S. T. and associates. 1998. *Evaluation with Power: A New Approach to Organizational Effectiveness, Empowerment, and Excellence.* San Francisco: Jossey-Bass.

Graybeal, G. 2001. Strengths-based social work assessment: Transforming the dominant paradigm. *Families in Society: The Journal of Contemporary Human Services* 82:233–242.

Green, J. W. and J. W. Leigh. 1989. Teaching ethnographic methods to social service workers. *Practicing Anthropology* 11:8–10.

Greenspan, S. I. with B. L. Benderly. 1997. *The Growth of the Mind and the Endangered Origins of Intelligence.* Reading, Mass.: Addison-Wesley.

Greenstein, T. N. 2001. *Methods of Family Research.* Thousand Oaks, Cal.: Sage.

Gresenz, C. R., K. Watkins, and D. Podus 1998. Supplemental Security Income (SSI), Disability Insurance (DI) and substance abusers. *Community Mental Health Journal* 34 (4): 337–350.

Griffin-Wiesner, J. 1996. What makes parent education programs work? *Youth Update* 1 (Summer): 5–6.

Groze, V. 1996. *Successful Adoptive Families: A Longitudinal Study of Special Needs Adoption.* Westport, Conn.: Praeger.

Groze, V., J. Young, and K. Corcran-Rumppe. 1991. *Post adoption resources for training, networking and evaluation services (PARTNERS): Working with special needs adoptive families in stress.* Washington, D.C.: DHHS, Adoption Opportunities, prepared with Four Oaks, Inc., Cedar Rapids, Iowa.

Gruszniski, R. J., J. C. Brink, and J. L. Edleson. 1988. Support and education groups for children of battered women. *Child Welfare* 67 (5): 431–444.

Guarnaccia, P. J. and S. Lopez. 1998. The mental health and adjustment of immigrant and refugee children. *Child and Adolescent Psychiatric Clinics of North America* 7 (3): 537–553.

Gustavsson, N. S. 1991. The school and the maltreated child in foster care: A role for the school social worker. *Social Work in Education* 13 (4): 224–235.

Gustavsson, N. S. and E. A. Segal 1994. *Critical issues in child welfare.* Thousand Oaks, Cal.: Sage.

Guterman, N. B. and M. Cameron, 1997. Assessing the impact of community violence on children and youths. *Social Work* 42 (5): 495–505.

Gutheil, I. A. and E. Congress. 2000. Resiliency in older people: A paradigm for practice. In E. Norman, ed., *Resiliency Enhancement: Putting the Strengths Perspective Into Social Work Practice*, pp. 40–52. New York: Columbia University Press.

Gutiérrez, L. M. and E. A. Lewis. 1999. *Empowering Women of Color.* New York: Columbia University Press.

Haas, L. J. 1991. Hide-and-seek or show-and-tell? Emerging issues of informed consent. *Ethics and Behavior* 1 (3): 175–189.

Haas, L. J. and J. L. Malouf. 1995. *Keeping Up the Good Work: A Practitioner's Guide to Mental Health Ethics.* Sarasota, Fla.: Professional Resource Exchange.

Hackl, K., A. Somlai, J. Kelly, and S. Kalichman. 1997. Women living with HIV/ AIDS: The dual challenge of being a patient and a caregiver. *Health and Social Work* 22 (1): 53–62.

Haggerty, R. J., L. R. Sherrod, N. Garmezy, and M. Rutter. 1994. *Stress, Risk, and Resilience in Children and Adolescents: Processes, Mechanisms, and Intervention.* Cambridge: Cambridge University Press.

Halpern, R. 1999. *Fragile Families, Fragile Solutions: A History of Supportive Services for Families in Poverty.* New York: Columbia University Press.

Handler, J. F. 1995. *The Poverty of Welfare Reform.* New Haven: Yale University Press.

Hanmer, J. and D. Statham. 1989. *Women and Social Work: Towards a Woman-Centered Practice.* Chicago: Lyceum.

Hardin, M. with E. Cole, J. Mickens, and R. Lancour. 1996. *Family Group Conferences in Child Abuse and Neglect Cases: Learning from the Experience of New Zealand.* Washington, D.C.: ABA Center on Children and the Law.

Hardy, K. V. and T. A. Laszloffy. 1995. The cultural genogram: Key to training culturally competent family therapists. *Journal of Marital and Family Therapy* 21:227–237.

Harms, T., A. R. Ray, and P. Rolandelli. 1998. *Preserving Childhood for Children in Shelters.* Washington, D.C.: CWLA.

Harris, I. B. 1996. *Children in Jeopardy.* New Haven: Yale Child Study Center.

Hartford Courant. 2000. More children should be insured. *Hartford Courant,* August 28, p. A8.

Harting, J. M. and J. R. Henig, 1997. Housing vouchers and certificates as a vehicle for deconcentrating the poor: Evidence from the Washington, D.C. metropolitan area. *Urban Affairs Review* 32 (3): 403–419.

Hartman, A. 1979. The extended family as a resource for change: Ecological approach to family-centered practice. In C. B. Germain, ed., *Social Work Practice: People and Environments*, pp. 239–266. New York: Columbia University Press.

Hartman, A. 1994. Diagrammatic assessment of family relationships. In B. R. Compton and B. Galaway, eds., *Social Work Processes*, pp. 154–165. Pacific Grove, Cal.: Brooks/Cole.

Hartman, A. and J. Laird. 1983. *Family-Centered Social Work Practice*. New York: Free.

Hartmann, H. 1958. *Ego Psychology and the Problem of Adaptation*. New York: International Universities Press.

Hassall, I. 1996. Origin and development of family group conferences. In J. Hudson, A. Morris, G. Maxwell, and B. Galaway, eds., *Family Group Conferences: Perspectives on Policy and Practice*, pp. 17–36. Monsey, N.Y.: Willow Tree.

Hawkins, J. D., R. F. Catalano, and J. Y. Miller. 1992. Risk and protective factors for alcohol and other drug problems in adloescence and early adulthood: Implications for substance abuse prevention. *Psychological Bulletin* 112 (1): 64–105.

Haynes, N. M. and M. Ben-Avie. 1996. Parents as full partners in education. In A. Booth and J. F. Dunn, eds., *Family-School Links: How Do They Affect Educational Outcomes?* pp. 45–56. Mahwah, N.J.: Lawrence Erlbaum.

Healy, L. M. 2001. *International Social Work: Professional Action in an Interdependent World*. New York: Oxford University Press.

Hegar, R. L. and M. Scannapieco, eds. 1999. *Kinship Foster Care: Policy, Practice, and Research*. New York: Oxford University Press.

Henggeler, S. W., S. K. Schoenwald, C. M. Borduin, M. D. Rowland, and P. B. Cunningham, 1998. *Multisystemic Treatment of Antisocial Behavior in Children and Adolescents*. New York: Guilford.

Henkin, N. and E. Kingson, eds. 1998–1999. Keeping the promise: Intergenerational strategies for strengthening the social compact. Special issue. *Generations* 22 (9): 1–110.

Hepworth, D. H., R. Rooney, and J. A. Larsen. 1997. *Direct Social Work Practice: Theory and Skills*. 5th ed. Belmont, Cal.: Brooks/Cole.

Hess, P. M. and K. O. Proch. 1988. *Family Visiting in Out-of-Home Care: A Guide to Practice*. Washington, D.C.: CWLA.

Hess, P. M. and K. O. Proch. 1993. Visiting: The heart of family reunification. In B. A. Pine, R. Warsh, and A. N. Maluccio, eds., *Together Again: Family Reunification in Foster Care*, pp. 119–139. Washington, D.C.: CWLA.

Hill, I. A. 1992. The role of Medicaid and other government programs in providing medical care for children and pregnant women. *Future of Children* 2 (2): 134–153.

Hill, M. and J. Aldgate, eds. 1996. *Child Welfare Services: Developments in Law, Policy, Practice, and Research*. London: Kingley.

Hill, R. B. 1972. *The Strengths of Black Families*. New York: Emerson Hall.

Hill, R. B. 1997. *The Strengths of African American Families: Twenty-five Years Later.* Washington, D.C.: R and B.

Hirsch, B. J., R. Boerger, A. E. Levy, and M. Mickus. 1994. The social networks of adolescents and their mothers: Influence on Blacks and Whites in single- and two-parent families. In F. Nestmann and K. Hurrelmann, eds., *Social Networks and Social Support in Childhood and Adolescence,* pp. 305–322. New York: Aldine de Gruyter.

Hodges, K. 1994. *Child and Adolescent Functional Assessment Scale.* Ann Arbor: Hodges.

Hodges, V.G. 1991. Providing culturally sensitive intensive family preservation services to ethnic minority families. In E. M. Tracy, D. A. Haapala, J. Kinney, and P. J. Pecora, eds., *Intensive Family Preservation Services: An Instructional Sourcebook,* pp. 95–116. Cleveland: Mandel School of Applied Social Sciences, Case Western Reserve University.

Hodges, V. G. and P.J. Pecora 2000. What is strengths-based service planning? In H. Dubowitz and D. DePanfilis, eds., *The Handbook for Child Protection Practice,* pp. 379–383. Newbury Park, Cal.: Sage.

Hofferth, S. L. A. Brayfield, S. Deich, and P. Holcomb. 1991. *National Child Care Survey: 1990.* Washington, D.C.: Urban Institute Press.

Hohman, M. M. 1998. Motivational interviewing: An intervention tool for child welfare case workers working with substance-abusing parents. *Child Welfare* 77:275–289.

Hohman, M. M. and R. L. Butt. 2001. How soon is too soon? Addiction recovery and family reunification. *Child Welfare* 80 (1): 53–67.

Holder, W. 2000a. How do I assess risk and safety? In H. Dubowitz and D. DePanfilis, eds., *Handbook for Child Protection Practice,* pp. 227–232. Thousand Oaks, Cal.: Sage.

Holder, W. 2000b. How do I assess the risk of maltreatment in foster care and kinship care? In H. Dubowitz and D. DePanfilis, eds., *Handbook for Child Protection Practice,* pp. 267–270. Thousand Oaks, Cal.: Sage.

Holder, W. and M. Corey. 1987. *Child Protective Services and Risk Management: A Decision-Making Handbook.* Charlotte, NC: Action for Child Protection.

Hopps, J. G. 2000. Social work: A contextual profession. In J. G. Hopps and R. Morris, eds., *Social Work at the Millennium: Critical Reflections on the Future of the Profession,* pp. 3–17. New York: Free.

Hopps, J. G. and R. Morris, eds. 2000. *Social Work at the Millennium: Critical Reflections on the Future of the Profession.* New York: Free.

Hudson, J. and B. Galaway, eds. 1995. *Child Welfare in Canada: Research and Policy Implications.* Toronto: Thompson Educational.

Iglehart, A. P. and R. M. Becerra. 1995. *Social Services and the Ethnic Community.* Boston: Allyn and Bacon.

Ingoldsby, B. B. and S. Smith, eds. 1995. *Families in Multicultural Perspective.* New York: Guilford.

Institute for Families in Society. 1997. Linking schools and family support services. *Family Futures* 1 (1).

Institute for Urban and Minority Education. 1999. *Choices Briefs*, no. 4. New York: Teacher's College, Columbia University.

Institute of Medicine 2000. *America's Health Care Safety Net: Intact But Endangered.* Washington, D.C.: National Academy Press.

Jacobson, D. E. 1986. Types and timing of social support. *Journal of Health and Social Behavior* 27:250–264.

Jackson, S. 1998. Looking after children: A new approach or just an exercise in formfilling? A response to Knight and Caveney. *British Journal of Social Work* 28:45–56.

Jackson, S., and S. Brissett-Chapman, eds. 1997. Perspectives on serving African American children, youths, and families. Special issue. *Child Welfare* 76 (1): 3–278.

Jackson, S., J. Matthews, and R. Zuskin. 1998. *Supporting the Kinship Triad: A Training Curriculum.* Washington, D.C.: CWLA.

Jencks, C. 1991. Is the underclass growing? In C. Jencks and P. E. Peterson, eds., *The Urban Underclass.* Washington, D.C.: Brookings Institution.

Jeppson, E. S. and J. Thomas. 1995. *Essential Allies: Families As Advisors.* Bethesda: Institute for Family-Centered Care.

Johnson-Powell, G. and J. Yamamoto, eds. 1997. *Transcultural Child Development: Psychological Assessment and Treatment.* New York: Wiley.

Johnston, D. 1992. *Children of Offenders.* Pasadena, Cal.: Pacific Oakes Center for Children of Incarcerated Parents.

Johnston, D. 1995. Effects of parental incarceration. In K. Gabel and D. Johnston, eds., *Children of Incarcerated Parents*, pp. 59–88. Boston: Lexington.

Johnston, D. and Gabel, K. 1995. Incarcerated parents. In K. Gabel and D. Johnston, *Children of Incarcerated Parents*, pp. 3–20. Boston: Lexington.

Johnston, L. D., P. M. O'Malley, and J. G. Bachman. 2000. *The Monitoring the Future: National Results on Adolescent Drug Use.* Bethesda: National Institute on Drug Abuse,

Jordan, C. and C. Franklin. 1995. *Clinical Assessment for Social Workers: Quantitative and Qualitative Methods.* Chicago: Lyceum.

Kagan, S. L. 1995. The changing face of parenting education. ERIC Digest (EDO-PS-95-7). Urbana: University of Illinois, Clearinghouse on Elementary and Early Childhood Education.

Kagan, S. L. and B. Weissbourd, eds. 1994. *Putting Families First: America's Family*

Support Movement and the Challenge of Change. San Francisco, Cal.: Jossey-Bass.

Kamerman, S. B. 1985. Child care services: An issue for gender equity and women's solidarity. *Child Welfare* 64:259–272.

Kamerman, S. B. 1996. The new politics of child and family policies. *Social Work* 41 (5): 453–465.

Karger, H. J. and D. Stoesz. 1990. *American Social Welfare Policy: A Structural Approach*. New York: Longman.

Karger, H. J. and D. Stoesz. 2002. *Social Welfare Policy: A Pluralistic Approach*. 4th ed. Boston: Allyn and Bacon.

Katz, L. 1999. Concurrent planning: Benefits and pitfalls. *Child Welfare* 78:71–87.

Keigher, S. M. 1997. America's most cruel xenophobia. *Health and Social Work* 22 (3): 232–237.

Kelleher, K., M. Chaffin, J. Hollenberg, and E. Fischer. 1994. Alcohol and drug disorders among physically abusive and neglectful parents in a community-based sample. *American Journal of Public Health* 84:1586–1591.

Kemp, S. P., J. K. Whittaker, and E. M. Tracy. 1997. *Person-Environment Practice: The Social Ecology of Interpersonal Helping*. New York: Aldine de Gruyter.

Kettner, P. M, R. M. Moroney, and L. L. Martin. 1999. *Designing and Managing Programs: An Effectiveness-Based Approach*. Thousand Oaks, Cal.: Sage.

Kinney, J., D. Haapala, and C. Booth 1991. *Keeping Families Together: The Homebuilders Model*. New York: Aldine de Gruyter.

Kirby, L. D. and M. W. Fraser. 1997. Risk and resilience in childhood. In M. W. Fraser, ed., *Risk and Resilience in Childhood: An Ecological Perspective*, pp. 10–33. Washington, D.C.: NASW.

Kisker, E. and C. Ross. 1997. Arranging child care. *Future of Children* 7 (1): 99–109.

Klerman, L. 1992. Nonfinancial barriers to the receipt of medical care. *Future of Children* 2 (2): 171–185.

Kluger, M. P., W. A. Baker, and H. S. Garval, 1998. *Strategic Business Planning: Securing a Future for the Non-Profit Organization*. Washington, D.C.: CWLA.

Koch, K. 2000. Welfare reform and child poverty. *Issues in Social Policy: Selections from the CQ Researcher*, pp. 97–115. Washington, D.C.: Congressional Quarterly.

Koocher, G. P. and P. C. Keith-Spiegel. 1990. *Children, Ethics and the Law: Professional Issues and Cases*. Lincoln: University of Nebraska Press.

Korr, W. S. and D. Brieland. 2000. Social justice, human rights, and welfare reform. In J. G. Hopps and R. Morris, eds., *Social Work at the Millennium: Critical Reflections on the Future of the Profession*, pp. 73–85. New York: Free.

Koyanagi, C. 1994. Is there a national policy for children and youth with serious emotional disturbance? *Policy Studies Journal* 22 (4): 669–680.

Kretzmann, J. P. and J. L. McKnight. 1993. *Building Communities from the Inside*

Out: A Path Toward Finding and Mobilizing a Community's Assets. Evanston: Northwestern University, Center for Urban Affairs and Policy Research.

Kropenske, V. and J. Howard. 1994. *Protecting Children in Substance-Abusing Families*. Washington, D.C.: DHHS, Administration for Children and Families, National Center on Child Abuse and Neglect. Available from the Clearinghouse on Child Abuse and Neglect Information, P.O. Box 1182, Washington, D.C. 20013.

Kryder-Coe, J. H., L. M. Salamon, and J. M. Molnar. 1991. *Homeless Children and Youth: A New American Dilemma*. New Brunswick, N.J.: Transaction.

Kuo, W. H. and Y. M. Tsai, 1986. Social networking, hardiness, and immigrant's mental health. *Journal of Health and Social Behavior* 27:133–149.

Kupsin, M. M. and D. D. Dubsky. 1999. Behaviorally impaired children in out-of-home care. *Child Welfare* 78:297–310.

Laird, J. 1995. Family-centered practice: Feminist, constructivist, and cultural perspectives. In N. Van Den Bergh, ed., *Feminist Practice in the Twenty-first Century*, pp. 20–40. Washington, D.C.: NASW.

Lambert, Craig. 1999. The women of cell block B: Chains of violence. *Harvard Magazine*, September/October, pp. 19–20.

Land, H. 1995. Feminist clinical social work in the twenty-first century. In N. Van DenBergh, ed., *Feminist Practice in the Twenty-first Century*, pp. 3–10. Washington, D.C.: NASW.

Lang, M. H. 1989. *Homelessness Amid Affluence: Structure and Paradox in the American Political Economy*. New York: Praeger.

Lareau, A. 1996. Assessing parent involvement in schooling: A critical analysis. In A. Booth and J. F. Dunn, eds., *Family-School Links: How Do They Affect Educational Outcomes?* pp. 57–66. Mahwah, N.J.: Lawrence Erlbaum.

Larkin, E. 1999. The intergenerational response in child care and after-school care. *Generations* 22:33–36.

Larner, M. 1995. Linking family support and early childhood programs: Issues, experiences, opportunities. *Commissioned Paper 1: Best Practices Project*. Chicago: Family Resource Coalition.

Larsen, D. L., C. C. Atkinson, W. A. Hargreaves, and T. D. Ngveyn, 1979. Assessment of client patient satisfaction: Development of a general scale. *Evaluation and Program Planning* 2:197–207.

Lashley, M. 2000. The unrecognized social stressors of migration and reunification in Caribbean families. *Transcultural Psychiatry* 37 (2): 201–215.

Lawson, H. and K. Briar-Lawson. 1997. *Connecting the Dots: Progess Toward the Integration of School Reform, School-Linked Services, Parent Involvement, and Community Schools*. Oxford, Ohio: Danforth Foundation and the Institute for Educational Renewal at Miami University.

Lee, J. A. B. 2000. *The Empowerment Approach to Social Work Practice*. 2d ed. New York: Columbia University Press.

Lee, W. C. 1998. Balancing the educational needs of students with school-based or school linked services. *Social Work* 43 (1): 65–66.

Lehman, J. and S. Danziger. 1997. Ending welfare, leaving the poor to face new risk. *Forum for Applied Research and Public Policy* 12 (4): 6–17.

LeProhn, N., K. Wetherbee, E. Lamont, T. Achenbach, and P. J. Pecora, eds. 2001. *Assessing Youth Behaviors Using the Child Behavior Checklist in Family and Children's Services*. Seattle: Casey Family Programs.

Leung, P., K. F. Cheung, and K. M. Stevenson. 1994. A strengths approach to ethnically sensitive practice for child protective service workers. *Child Welfare* 73:707–721.

Levenson, D. 1998. Immigration statutes: Law, ethics collide. *NASW News* 43 (7): 3.

LeVine, E. S. and A. L. Sallee. 1999. *Child Welfare: Clinical Theory and Practice*. Dubuque: Eddie Bowers.

Levy, E. F. 1995. Violence against women. In N. Van Den Bergh, ed., *Feminist Practice in the Twenty-first Century*, pp. 312–329. Washington, D.C.: NASW.

Lewis, R. G., T. Stovell, S. Landers, and R. Warsh. 2000. *Family Bound Curriculum*. Southfield, Mich.: National Resource Center for Special Needs Adoption, Spaulding for Children.

Lewit, E., C. S. Larson, D. S. Gomby, P. H. Shiono, and R. E. Behrman. 1992. Recommendations. *Future of Children* 2 (2): 6–24.

Lightburn, A. In press. Family service centers: Lessons from national and local evaluations. In A. N. Maluccio, Cinzia Canali, and T. Vecchiato, eds, *Assessing Outcomes in Child and Family Services: Comparative Design and Policy Issues*. New York: Aldine de Gruyter.

Lightburn, A. and S. Kemp. 1994. Family support: Opportunities for community-based practice. *Families in Society: The Journal of Contemporary Human Services* 75 (1): 16–26.

Lightburn, A. and B. A. Pine. 1996. Supporting and enhancing the adoption of children with developmental disabilities. *Children and Youth Services Review* 18:139–162.

Lindblad-Goldberg, M., M. M. Dore, and L. Stern. 1998. *Creating Competence Out of Chaos*. New York: Norton.

Link, R. 1999. Infusing global perspectives into social work values and ethics. In C. S. Ramanathan and R. J. Link, *All Our Futures: Principles and Resources for Social Work Practice in a Global Era*. Belmont, Cal.: Brooks/Cole.

Linzer, N. 1999. *Resolving Ethical Dilemmas in Social Work Practice*. Boston: Allyn and Bacon.

Littell, J. H., L. B. Alexander, and W. K. Reynolds. 2001. Client participation: Central and under-investigated elements of intervention. *Social Service Review* 75:1–28.

Littell, J. and J. Schuerman. 1995. *A Synthesis of Research on Family Preservation and Family Reunification.* http://hhs.gov/hsp/cyp/fplitrev.htm (April 1, 1999).

Littell, J. H., J. R. Schuerman, and A. Chak. 1994. *What Works Best for Whom in Family Preservation? Relationship Between Service Characteristics and Outcomes for Selected Subgroups of Families.* Discussion paper no. 054. Chicago: Chapin Hall Center for Children.

Litzelfelner, P. 2000. The effectiveness of CASAs in achieving positive outcomes for children. *Child Welfare* 79:179–193.

Locke, E. A. and S. M. Taylor. 1991. Stress, coping, and the meaning of work. In A. Monat and R.S. Lazarus, eds., *Stress and Coping: An Anthology,* pp. 140–157. 3d ed. New York: Columbia University Press.

Loewenberg, F. M., R. Dolgoff, and D. Harrington. 2000. *Ethical Decisions for Social Work Practice.* 6th ed. Itasca, Ill.: Peacock.

Lorion, R. P., A. E. Brodsky, and M. Cooley-Quille. 1999. Exposure to urban violence: A framework for conceptualizing risky settings. In D. E. Biegel and A. Blum, eds., *Innovations in Practice and Service Delivery Across the Life Span,* pp. 124–143. New York: Oxford University Press.

Lynm, J. M. 1985. Support networks developed by immigrant women. *Social Science Medicine* 21 (3): 327–333.

McCardy, L. W. and M. Hofford, eds. 1998. *Family Violence: Emerging Programs for Battered Mothers and Their Children.* Reno: National Council of Juvenile and Family Court Judges.

McCroskey, J. and W. Meezan. 1997. *Family Preservation and Family Functioning.* Washington, D.C.: CWLA.

McCubbin, H. I. and M. A. McCubbin. 1988. Typologies of resilient families: Emerging roles of social class and ethnicity. *Family Relations* 37:247–254.

McCubbin, H. I., E. A. Thompson, A. I. Thompson, and J. Fromer, eds. 1998. *Stress, Coping, and Health in Families: Sense of Coherence and Resiliency.* Thousand Oaks, Cal.: Sage.

McDonald, T. P., R. I. Allen, A. Westerfelt, and I. Piliavin. 1996. *Assessing the Long-Term Effects of Foster Care: A Research Synthesis.* Washington, D.C.: CWLA.

MacFarlane, K., J. Waterman, S. Conerly, L. Damon, M. Durfee, and S. Long. 1986. *Sexual Abuse of Young Children.* New York: Guilford.

McGinnis, E. and A. P. Goldstein. 1984. *Skillstreaming the Elementary School Child: A Guide for Teaching Prosocial Skills.* Champaign, Ill.: Research.

McGowan, B. G. and E. M. Walsh. 2000. Policy challenges for child welfare in the new century. *Child Welfare* 79 (1): 11–27.

Mackey, R. A., B. A. O'Brien, and E. Mackey. 1997. *Gay and Lesbian Couples: Voices from Lasting Relationships.* Westport, Conn.: Praeger.

McKenzie, B., ed. 1994. *Current Perspectives on Foster Family Care for Children and Youth*. Toronto: Wall and Emerson.

McKenzie, R. B., ed. 1998. *Rethinking Orphanages for the Twenty-first Century*. Thousand Oaks, Cal.: Sage.

McKnight, J. L. and J. P. Kretzmann. 1990. *Mapping Community Capacity*. Evanston, Ill.: Northwestern University, Center for Urban Affairs and Policy Research.

McMillen, J. C. and V. Groze. 1994. Using placement genograms in child welfare practice. *Child Welfare* 72:307–318.

McRoy, R. G., Z. Oglesby, and H. Grape. 1997. Achieving same-race adoptive placements for African-American children: Culturally sensitive practice approaches. *Child Welfare* 76:85–104.

Magura, S., and B. Moses. 1986. *Outcome Measures for Child Welfare Services: Theory and Applications*. Washington, D.C.: CWLA.

Magura, S., B. Moses, and M. Jones. 1987. *Assessing Risk and Measuring Change in Families: The Family Risk Scales*. Washington, D.C.: CWLA.

Mallon, G. P. 1997. Toward a competent child welfare service delivery system for gay and lesbian adolescents and their families. In G. A. Anderson, A. S. Ryan, and B. R. Leashore, eds., 1997. *The Challenge of Permanency Planning in a Multicultural Society*, pp. 177–197. New York: Haworth.

Mallon, G. P. 2000. *Let's Get Straight: A Gay- and Lesbian-Affirming Approach to Child Welfare*. New York: Columbia University Press.

Maluccio, A. N. 1979. *Learning from Clients: Interpersonal Helping as Viewed by Clients and Social Workers*. New York: Free Press.

Maluccio, A. N., ed. 1981. *Promoting Competence in Clients: A New/Old Approach to Social Work Practice*. New York: Free Press.

Maluccio, A. N. 1990. Client feedback and creativity in social work. In H. H. Weissman, ed., *Serious Play: Creativity and Innovation in Social Work*, pp. 223–230. Washington, D.C.: NASW.

Maluccio, A. N. 1998. Assessing child welfare outcomes: The American perspective. *Children and Society* 12 (3): 161–168.

Maluccio, A. N. 1999. Action as a vehicle for promoting competence. In B. R. Compton and B. Galaway, *Social Work Processes*, pp. 354–365. 6th ed. Pacific Grove, Cal.: Brooks/Cole.

Maluccio, A. N. 2000. A competence-centered perspective on child and family welfare. In J. G. Hopps and R. Morris, eds., *Social Work at the Millennium: Critical Reflections on the Future of the Profession*, pp. 160–174. New York: Free Press.

Maluccio, A. N., F. Ainsworth, and J. Thoburn. 2000. *Child Welfare Outcome Research in the United States, United Kingdom, and Australia*. Washington, D.C.: CWLA.

Maluccio, A. N. and G. R. Anderson. 2000. Future challenges and opportunities in child welfare. *Child Welfare* 79:3–9.

Maluccio, A. N., C. Canali, and T. Vecchiato, eds. In press. *Assessing Outcomes in Child and Family Services: Comparative Design and Policy Issues*. New York: Aldine de Gruyter.

Maluccio, A. N., R. Krieger, and B. A. Pine. 1990. *Preparing Adolescents for Life After Foster Care: The Central Role of Foster Parents*. Washington, D.C.: CWLA.

Maluccio, A. N., B. A. Pine, and R. Warsh, 1994. Protecting children by preserving their families. *Children and Youth Services Review* 16 (5/6): 295–307.

Maluccio, A. N., R. Warsh, and B. A. Pine. 1998. Teaching family preservation. *Journal of Teaching in Social Work* 16:3–17.

Manning, S. S. 1997. The social worker as moral citizen: Ethics in action. *Social Work* 42 (3): 223–230.

Marans, S., M. Berkman, and D. Cohen. 1996. Child development and adaptation to catastrophic circumstances. In R. J. Apfel and B. Simon, eds., *Minefields in Their Hearts: The Mental Health of Children in War and Communal Violence*, pp. 104–127. New Haven: Yale University Press.

Marsh, P. and G. Crow. 1997. *Family Group Conferences in Child Welfare*. Oxford: Blackwell.

Marshall, C. and G. B. Rossman, 1999. *Designing Qualitative Research*. Thousand Oaks, Cal.: Sage.

Martin, F. E. and T. Palmer. 1997. Transitions to adulthood: A child welfare youth perspective. *Community Alternatives: International Journal of Community Care* 9:29–60.

Mason, S. 1998. Custody planning with HIV-Affected families: Considerations for child welfare workers. *Child Welfare* 77:161–179.

Masten, A. S., K. M. Best, and N. Garmezy. 1991. Resilience and development: Contributions from the study of children who overcame adversity. *Development and Psychopathology* 2:425–444.

Mather, J. H. and P. B. Lager, 2000. *Child Welfare: A Unifying Model*. Belmont, Cal.: Brooks/Cole.

Mathews, M. A. 1999. The impact of federal and state laws on children exposed to domestic violence. *Future of Children* 9 (3): 50–66.

Mattaini, M. A. 1999. *Clinical Intervention with Families*. Washington, D.C.: NASW.

Maza, P. L. and J. A. Hall. 1998. *Homeless Children and Their Families: A Preliminary Study*. Washington, D.C.: CWLA.

Mayers, A. and L. Spiegel. 1992. A parental support group in a pediatric AIDS clinic: Its usefulness and limitations. *Health and Social Work* 17:183–191.

Mech, E. V. and J. R. Rycraft, eds. 1995. *Preparing Foster Youths for Adult Living: Proceedings of an Invitational Research Conference*. Washington, D.C.: CWLA.

Merkel-Holguin, L. 1996a. Putting families back into the child protection partnership: Family group decision making. *Protecting Children* 12 (3): 4–7.

Merkel-Holguin, L. 1996b. *Children Who Lose Their Parents to HIV-AIDS: Agency Guidelines for Adoptive and Kinship Placement*. Washington, D.C.: CWLA.

Meyer, C. H. 1985. A feminist perspective on foster family care: A redefinition of the categories. *Child Welfare* 64:249–258.

Meyer, D. R. 1995. Supplemental security income. In R. L. Edwards and J. G. Hopps, eds., *Encyclopedia of Social Work* 2:2379–2385. 19th ed. Washington, D.C.: NASW

Meyers, M. K., W. J. Han, J. Waldfogel, and I. Garfinkel. 2001. Child care in the wake of welfare reform: The impact of government subsidies on the economic well-being of single-mother families. *Social Service Review* 75:1–28.

Midwest School Social Work Council. N.d. *School Social Work Services: Linking School, Home and Community*. Available from Midwest School Social Work Council, 759 Fifth Avenue, Lake Odessa, MI 48849.

Mika, K. L. 1996. *Program Outcome Evaluation: A Step-by-Step Handbook*. Milwaukee: Families International.

Miller, J. C. 1991. Child welfare and the role of women: A feminist perspective. *American Journal of Orthopsychiatry* 61:592–598.

Milner, J. S. 1994. Is poverty a key contributor to child maltreatment? No. In E. Gambrill and T. J. Stein, eds., *Controversial Issues in Child Welfare*, pp. 23–26. Boston: Allyn and Bacon.

Mishra, R. 2000. *Globalization and the Welfare State*. Williston, Vt.: Elgar.

Mitchell, A., E. Cooperstein, and M. Larner. 1992. *Child Care Choices, Consumer Education, and Low-Income Families*. New York: National Center for Children in Poverty.

Moles. O. C. 1993. Collaboration between schools and disadvantaged parents: Obstacles and openings. In N. F. Chavkin, ed. *Families and Schools in a Pluralistic Society*, pp. 21–49. Albany: State University of New York Press.

Monat, A. and R. S. Lazarus, eds. 1991. *Stress and Coping: An Anthology*. 3d ed. New York: Columbia University Press.

Moore-Kirkland, J. 1981. Mobilizing motivation: From theories to practice. In A. N. Maluccio, ed., *Promoting Competence in Clients: A New/Old Approach to Social Work Practice*, pp. 27–54. New York: Free.

Morgan, G. 1983. Child day care policy in chaos. In E. F. Zigler; S. L. Kagan, and E. Klugman, eds., *Children, Families, and Government-Perspectives on American Social Policy*, pp. 249–265. New York: Cambridge University Press.

Morin, R. C. and E. Seidman. 1986. A social network approach and the revolving door patient. *Schizophrenia Bulletin* 12:262–273.

Morris, M. and J. B. Williamson. 1986. *Poverty and Public Policy*. New York: Greenwood.

Mulroy, E. A. 1995a. Housing. In R. Edwards and J. G. Hopps, eds., *Encyclopedia of Social Work* 2:1377–1384. 19th ed. Washington, D.C.: NASW.

Mulroy, E. A. 1995b. *The New Uprooted: Single Mothers in Urban Life*. Westport, Conn.: Greenwood.

Munro, E. 2001. Empowering looked-after children. *Child and Family Social Work* 6:129–137.

Murphy, J. M., M. Jellinek, D. Quinn, G. Smith, F. G. Poitrast, and M. Goshko. 1991. Substance abuse and serious child maltreatment: Prevalence, risk, and outcome in a court sample. *Child Abuse and Neglect* 15:7–211.

Nash, K. A. 1999. *Cultural Competence: A Guide for Human Service Agencies*. Washington, D.C.: CWLA.

National Adoption Information Clearinghouse. N.d. *Adoption and School Issues*. Washington, D.C.: National Adoption Information Clearinghouse.

National Association of Social Workers. 1992. *NASW Standards for School Social Work*. Washington, DC: NASW.

National Association of Social Workers. 1996a. Supreme court to hear privilege case. *NASW News* 41 (1) 2–3.

National Association of Social Workers.1996b. Supreme court upholds social work privilege. *NASW News* 41 (8): 1, 10.

National Association of Social Workers. 1999. *Code of Ethics of the National Association of Social Workers*. Washington, D.C.: NASW. http://www.naswdc.org /Code/ethics.htm (January 15, 2000).

National Black Child Development Institute. 1989. *Who Will Care When Parents Can't: A Study of Black Children in Foster Care*. Washington, D.C.: National Black Child Development Institute.

National Center for Children in Poverty. 1996. *One Child in Four: America's Youngest Poor*. New York: National Center for Children in Poverty.

National Center for Children in Poverty. 1998. *Early Childhood Poverty: Research Brief*. New York: National Center for Children in Poverty.

National Center for Education Statistics. 1995. *Dropout Rates in the United States, 1995*. http://nces.ed.gov/pubs98/dropout/index.html (June 10, 1998).

National Center for Education Statistics. 1996. *Dropout Rates in the United States, 1996*. http://nces.ed.gov/pubs/dp95/97473-f.html (June 10, 1998).

National Child Welfare Resource Center for Family-Centered Practice. 2000. *Best Practice/Next Practice* 1 (1): 7–11.

National Commission on Excellence in Education. 1983. *A Nation at Risk — the Imperative Educational Reform: A Report to the Nation and the Secretary of Education*. Washington, D.C.: U.S. Department of Education, National Commission on Excellence in Education.

National Commission on Family Foster Care. 1991. *A Blueprint for Fostering Infants, Children, and Youths in the 1990s*. Washington, D.C.: CWLA with the National Foster Parents Association.

National Committee for Prevention of Child Abuse. 1989. *Fact Sheet: Substance*

Abuse and Child Abuse. Chicago: National Committee for Prevention of Child Abuse.

National Institute on Drug Abuse. 1997. *Preventing Drug Use Among Children and Adolescents: A Research-Based Guide.* Washington, D.C.: DHHS.

National Resource Center for Family Support Programs. 1993. *Family Support Programs and School-Linked Services.* Chicago: Family Resource Coalition.

National Resource Center on Child Abuse and Neglect. 1997. *Worker Safety for Human Service Organizations. A Children's Division Issue Brief.* Englewood, Col.: American Humane Association.

Needell, B. and R. P. Barth 1998. Infants entering foster care compared to other infants using birth status indicators. *Child Abuse and Neglect* 22:1179–1187.

Nelson, B. J. 1984. *Making an Issue of Child Abuse.* Chicago: University of Chicago Press.

Nelson, K. E. 2001. Shaping the future of family-centered services: Competition or collaboration? In E. Walton, P. Sandau-Beckler, and M. Mannes, eds., *Balancing Family-Centered Services and Child Well-Being: Exploring Issues in Policy, Practice, and Research,* pp. 359–376. New York: Columbia University Press.

Nelson, K. E. and M. J. Landsman. 1992. *Alternative Models of Family-Based Services in Context.* Springfield, Ill.: Charles C. Thomas.

Nestman, F. and K. Hurrelmann, eds. 1994. *Social Networks and Social Support in Childhood and Early Adolescence.* Berlin: Aldine de Gruyter.

New Haven Public Schools. 1992. *Social Development Project Evaluation, 1991–1992: Final Report.* New Haven: New Haven Public Schools.

Newman, B. M. and P. R. Newman. 1995. *Development Through Life: A Psychosocial Approach.* 6th ed. Pacific Grove, Cal.: Brooks/Cole.

Nichols-Casebolt, A. and I. Garfinkel. 1991. Trends in paternity adjudicating and child support awards. *Social Science Quarterly* 72 (1): 83–97.

Nisivoccia, D. 1996. Working with kinship foster families: Principles for practice. *Community Alternatives: International Journal of Family Care* 8 (1): 1–21.

Nollan, K. A., M. Wolf, D. Ansell, J. Burns, L. Barr, W. Copeland, and G. Paddock. 2000. Ready or not: Assessing youth's preparedness for independent living. *Child Welfare* 79:159–176.

Norman, E., ed. 2000. *Resiliency Enhancement: Putting the Strengths Perspective Into Social Work Practice.* New York: Columbia University Press.

Nugent, W. R., J. D. Sieppert, and W. W. Hudson. 2001. *Practice Evaluation for the Twenty-first Century.* Florence, Ky.: Brooks/Cole-Thomson Learning.

Nunnally, E. W., C. S. Chilman, and F. M. Cox. 1988. Introduction to the series. In E. W. Nunnally, C. S. Chilman, and F. M. Fox, eds., *Troubled Relationships* 3:7–14. Newbury Park, Cal.: Sage.

Office of the Child Advocate. 1998a. *State of Connecticut Child Fatality Review*

Panel Report on the Death of Andrew M. Hartford: Office of the Child Advocate.

Office of the Child Advocate. 1998b. *State of Connecticut Child Fatality Review Panel Report on the Death of Shanice M.* Hartford: Office of the Child Advocate.

Okun, B. F. 1996. *Understanding Diverse Families: What Practitioners Need to Know.* New York: Guilford.

O'Looney, J. 1996. *Redesigning the Work of Human Services.* Westport, Conn.: Quorum.

O'Neill, J. V. 2001. Report says youth aren't receiving adequate care. *NASW News,* March 12, 2001.

Organization for Economic Cooperation and Development. 1996. *Children of Promise: Successful Services for Children and Families at Risk.* Baltimore: Brookes.

Osofsky, J. D. 1995. The effects of exposure to violence on young children. *American Psychologist* 50:782–788.

Osofsky, J. D. 1999. The impact of violence on children. *Future of Children* 9 (3): 33–49.

Ozawa, M. N. and B. E. Hong. 1999. SSI for children with mental disorders: Backgrounds and a study of participation. *Children and Youth Services Review* 21 (6): 437–462.

Ozawa, N. 1995. Income security overview. In R. Edwards and J. G. Hopps,, eds., *Encyclopedia of Social Work* 2:1447–1464. 19th ed. Washington, D.C.: NASW.

Padgett, D. K. 1998. *Qualitative Methods in Social Work Research.* Thousand Oaks, Cal.: Sage.

Padilla, Y. C. 1997. Immigrant policy: Issues for social work practice. *Social Work* 42 (6): 595–606.

Palmer, S. E. 1995. *Maintaining Family Ties: Inclusive Practice in Foster Care.* Washington, D.C.: CWLA.

Pancoast, D. L., P. Parker, and C. Froland. 1983. *Rediscovering Self-Help: Its Role in Social Care.* Beverly Hills: Sage.

Parker, R., H. Ward, S. Jackson, J. Aldgate, and P. Wedge, eds. 1991. *Looking After Children: Assessing Outcomes in Child Care.* London: HMSO.

Parks, C. A. 1998. Lesbian parenthood: A review of the literature. *American Journal of Orthopsychiatry* 68 (3): 376–389.

Parsons, R. D. 2001. *The Ethics of Professional Practice.* Boston: Allyn and Bacon.

Parsons, R. J. and E. O. Cox. 1994. *Empowerment-Oriented Social Work Practice with the Elderly.* Pacific Grove, Cal.: Brooks/Cole.

Patten, P. 2000. How parents and peers influence children's school success. *Parent News,* vol. 5, no. 5. http://npin.org/pnews/2000/ pnew900/int900e.html (October 2, 2000).

Pecora, P. J. 1991. Investigating allegations of child maltreatment: The strengths and limitations of current risk assessment systems. *Child and Youth Services* 15 (2): 73–92.

Pecora, P. J. 2000. Promising assessment measures in child and family services: A selective review. Paper presented at the Seventh Annual California's Focus: Family Strengths Family-Centered Services Conference. Sacramento, California, August 28.

Pecora, P. J. and associates. 1998. *How Are the Children Doing? Assessing Youth Outcomes in Family Foster Care.* Seattle: Casey Family Programs.

Pecora, P. J. and A. N. Maluccio. 2000. What works in family foster care. In M. Kluger, G. Alexander, and P. Curtis, eds., *What Works in Child Welfare*, pp. 139–155. Washington, D.C.: CWLA.

Pecora, P. J., M. W. Fraser, K. E. Nelson, J. McCroskey, and W. Meezan. 1995. *Evaluating Family-Based Services.* New York: Aldine de Gruyter.

Pecora, P. J., W. R. Seelig, F. A. Zirps, and S. M. Davis, eds. 1996. *Quality Improvement and Evaluation in Child and Family Services: Managing Into the Next Century.* Washington, D.C.: CWLA.

Pecora, P. J., J. K. Whittaker, A. N. Maluccio, and R. P. Barth, 2000. *The Child Welfare Challenge: Policy, Practice, and Research.* 2d ed. New York: Aldine de Gruyter.

Pelton, L. H. 1994. Is poverty a key contributor to child maltreatment? Yes. In E. Gambrill and T. J. Stein, eds., *Controversial Issues in Child Welfare*, pp. 16–22. Boston: Allyn and Bacon.

Pelton, L. H. 1999. Welfare discrimination and child welfare. *Ohio State Law Journal* 60 (4): 1479–1492.

Pennell, J. and G. Burford. 1995. Family group decision making project: Implementation Report. Research/Evaluation Instruments. Vol. 2. St. John's, Newfoundland: Memorial University of Newfoundland, School of Social Work.

Pennell, J. and Burford, G. 2000. Family group decision making: Protecting women and children. *Child Welfare* 79:131–158.

Perez-Koenig, R. 2000. The Unitas extended family circle: Developing resiliency in Hispanic Youngsters. In E. Norman, ed., *Resiliency Enhancement: Putting the Strengths Perspective Into Social Work Practice*, pp. 143–153. New York: Columbia University Press.

Perloff, J. D. 1992. Health care resources for children and pregnant women. *Future of Children* 2 (2): 78–94.

Perrin, J., B. Guyer, and J. M. Lawrence. 1992. Health care services for children and adolescents. *Future of Children* 2 (2): 58–77.

Petr, C. G. 1998. *Social Work with Children and Their Families: Pragmatic Foundations.* New York: Oxford University Press.

Pierce, R. L. and L. H. Pierce. 1996. Moving toward cultural competence in the child welfare system. *Children and Youth Services Review* 18 (3): 713–731.

Piliavin, I., B. R. E. Wright, R. D. Mare, and A. H. Westerfelt. 1996. Exit from and return to homelessness. *Social Service Review* 70:33–57.

Pinderhughes, E. 1997. Developing diversity competence in child welfare and permanency planning. In G. R. Anderson, A. S. Ryan, and B. R. Leashore, eds., *The Challenge of Permanency Planning in a Multicultural Society*, pp. 19–38. New York: Haworth.

Pine, B. A. 1986. Child welfare reform and the political process. *Social Service Review* 60 (3): 339–359.

Pine, B. A. 1987. Strategies for more ethical decision making in child welfare practice. *Child Welfare* 66:315–326.

Pine, B. A. 1999. *Caring for Connecticut's Children: Perspectives on Informal, Subsidized Child Care*. Farmington, Conn.: Child Health and Development Institute of Connecticut.

Pine, B. A., R. Warsh, and A. N. Maluccio, 1998. Participatory management in a public child welfare agency: A key to effective change. *Administration in Social Work* 22 (1): 19–32.

Plotnick, R. D. 1997. Child poverty can be reduced. *Future of Children* 7 (2): 72–87.

Poe, L. M. 1992. *Black Grandparents As Parents*. Berkeley: Poe. Available from L. M. Poe, 2034 Blake St., Berkeley, Cal. 94704.

Poertner, J., T. P. McDonald, and C. Murray. 2000. Child welfare outcome revisited. *Children and Youth Services Review* 22 (9/10): 789–810.

Polansky, N. A., J. M. Gaudin, and P. W. Ammons. 1985. Loneliness and isolation in child neglect. *Social Casework* 66: 38–47.

Poole, L. E., F. Woratsched, and J. Williams, eds. 1997. *Leaning to Be Partners: An Introductory Training Program for Family Support Staff*. Pittsburgh: Family Support America with Center for Assessment and Policy Development and University of Pittsburgh, Office of Child Development.

Popkin, S. J., J. E. Rosenbaum, and P.M. Meaden, 1993. Labor market experiences of low income black women in middle-class suburbs: Evidence from a survey of Gautreaux program participants. *Journal of Policy Analysis and Management* 12 (3): 556–573.

Poresky, R. H. 1987. Environmental Assessment Index: Reliability, stability, and validity of the long and short forms. *Educational and Psychological Measurements* 47:969–975.

Powell, D. R. 1979. Family-environment relations and early childrearing: The role of social networks and neighborhoods. *Journal of Research and Development in Education* 13(1): 1–11.

Powell, T. J. 1995. Self-help groups. In R. L. Edwards and J. G. Hopps, eds., *Encyclopedia of Social Work* 3:2116–2123. 19th ed. Washington, D.C.: NASW.

Power, A. and A. N. Maluccio. 1999. Intergenerational approaches to helping families at risk. *Generations* 22:37–42.

Proctor, C. D. and V. Groze, 1994. Risk factors for suicide among gay, lesbian, and bisexual youths. *Social Work* 39 (5): 504–512.

Pro-Ed. 1998. *Behavioral and Emotional Rating Scale*. Austin: Pro-Ed.

Pryor, C. B. 1996. Techniques for assessing family-school connections. *Social Work in Education* 18 (2): 85–93.

Putnam, F. W., M. B. Liss, and J. Landsverk. 1996. Ethical issues in maltreatment research with children and adolescents. In K. Hoagwood, P. S. Jensen, and C. B. Fisher, eds., *Ethical Issues in Mental Health Research with Children and Adolescents*, pp. 113–132. Mahwah, N.J.: Lawrence Erlbaum.

Pynoos, R. S. and S. Eth. 1986. Witness to violence. *Journal of American Child Psychiatry* 25:306–319.

Quinn, J. 1999. Where need meets opportunity: Youth development: Programs for early teens. *Future of Children* 9 (2): 96–116.

Raphael, J. and R. M. Tolman. 1998–99. Domestic violence keeps women on welfare: New research you need to support families. *FRCA Report* 17 (4): 20–22.

Rapp, C. A. 1998. *The Strengths Model: Case Management with People Suffering from Severe and Persistent Mental Illness*. New York: Oxford University Press.

Reamer, F. G. 1983a. The concept of paternalism in social work. *Social Service Review* 57 (2): 254–271.

Reamer, F. G. 1983b. Ethical dilemmas in social work practice. *Social Work* 28 (1): 31–35.

Reamer, F. G. 1987. Informed consent in social work. *Social Work* 32 (5): 425–429.

Reamer, F. G. 1990. *Ethical Dilemmas in Social Service: A Guide for Social Workers*. 2d ed. New York: Columbia University Press.

Reamer, F. G. 1995. *Social Work Values and Ethics*. New York: Columbia University Press.

Reamer, F. G. 1998a. *Ethical Standards in Social Work: A Critical Review of the NASW Code of Ethics*. Washington, D.C.: NASW.

Reamer, F. G. 1998b. The evolution of social work ethics. *Social Work* 43 (6): 488–500.

Reamer, F. G. 1998c. *Social Work Research and Evaluation Skills: A Case-Based, User-Friendly Approach*. New York: Columbia University Press.

Reamer, F. G. 2001a. *The Social Work Ethics Audit: A Risk Management Tool*. Washington, D.C.: CWLA.

Reamer, F. 2001b. *Ethics Education in Social Work*. Washington, D.C.: Council on Social Work Education.

Reed-Ashcraft, K., R. S. Kirk, and M. W. Fraser. 2001. Reliability and validity of the North Carolina Family Assessment Scale. *Research on Social Work Practice* 11:503–520.

Regehr, C. and B. Antle. 1997. Coercive influences: Informed consent in court. Mandated social work practice. *Social Work* 42 (3): 300–306.

Reynolds, A. J., H. J. Walberg, and R. P. Weissberg, eds. 1999. *Promoting Positive Outcomes : Issues in Children's and Families' Lives*. Washington, D.C.: CWLA.

Rhodes, M. 1986. *Ethical Dilemmas in Social Work Practice*. Boston: Routledge and Kegan Paul.

Rhodes, R. 2000. What causes brutality? The people nurturing it. *Children's Voice*, March, pp. 10–11.

Rhodes, W. A., and W. K. Brown. 1991. *Why Some Children Succeed Despite the Odds*. New York: Praeger.

Richman, J. M. and G. L. Bowen. 1997. School failure: An ecological-interactional-developmental perspective. In M. W. Fraser, ed., *Risk and Resilience in Childhood: An Ecological Perspective*, pp. 95–116. Washington, D.C.: NASW.

Ricketts, E. R. and I. V. Sawhill. 1988. Defining and measuring the underclass. *Journal of Policy Analysis and Management* 7 (2): 316–325.

Rindfleisch, N., G. Bean, and R. Denby. 1998. Why foster parents continue and cease to foster. *Journal of Sociology and Social Welfare* 25:5–24.

Rion, M. 1989. *The Responsible Manager: Practical Strategies for Ethical Decision Making*. New York: Harper and Row.

Ripple, L., E. Alexander, and B. Polemis. 1964. *Motivation, Capacity, and Opportunity*. Chicago: University of Chicago, School of Social Service Administration.

Roberts, P. G. 1994. Child support orders: Problems with enforcement. *Future of Children* 4 (1): 101–120.

Roe, K. M. and M. Minkler. 1998–1999. Grandparents raising grandchildren: Challenges and responses. *Generations* 22 (4): 37–42.

Roman, N. P. and P. B. Wolfe. 1997. The relationship between foster care and homelessness. *Public Welfare* 55:4–9.

Rooney, R. 1992. *Strategies for Work with Involuntary Clients*. New York: Columbia University Press.

Rosen, A., E. K. Proctor, and M. M. Staudt. 1999. Social work research and the quest for knowledge. *Social Work* 23 (1): 4–14.

Rosenfeld, L. B., J. M. Richman, and G. L. Bowen. 2000. Social support networks and school outcomes: The centrality of the teacher. *Child and Adolescent Social Work Journal* 17 (3): 205–226.

Roskies, E. 1991. Stress management: A new approach to treatment. In A. Monat and R. S. Lazarus, eds., *Stress and Coping: An Anthology*, pp. 411–431. 3d ed. New York: Columbia University Press.

Rossi, P.H. 1990. The old homeless and the new homeless in historical perspective. *American Psychologist* 45:954–959.

Roth, J., L. F. Murry, J. Brooks-Gunn, and W. H. Foster. 1999. The potential of youth development programs. In D. J. Besharov, ed., *America's Disconnected Youth: Toward a Preventive Strategy.* Washington, D.C.: CWLA.

Rothman, J. 1994. *Practice with Highly Vulnerable Clients: Case Management and Community-Based Service.* Englewood Cliffs, N.J.: Prentice-Hall.

Rothman, J. C. 1998. *From the Front Lines: Student Cases in Social Work Ethics.* Boston: Allyn and Bacon.

Rutter, M. 1985. Resilience in the face of adversity: Protective factors and resistance to psychiatric disorders. *British Journal of Psychiatry* 147:598–611.

Rycus, J. S. and R. C. Hughes. 1998. *Field Guide to Child Welfare: Child Development and Child Welfare.* Vol. 3. Washington, D.C.: CWLA.

Rycus, J. S., R. C. Hughes, and J. K. Garrison, 1989. *Child Protective Services: A Training Curriculum.* Columbus, Ohio: Institute for Human Services.

Saleebey, D., ed. 1997a. *The Strengths Perspective in Social Work Practice.* 2d ed. New York: Longman.

Saleebey, D. 1997b. Introduction: Power in the people. In D. Saleebey, ed., *The Strengths Perspective in Social Work Practice,* pp. 3–19. 2d ed. New York: Longman.

Saleebey, D., ed. 2002. *The Strengths Perspective in Social Work Practice.* 3d ed. Boston: Allyn and Bacon.

Saltzburg, S. 2001. Learning that an adolescent child is gay or lesbian: The parent experience. Ph.D. diss., Boston College, Graduate School of Social Work.

Samuels, B., N. Ahsan, and J. Garcia. 1998. *Know Your Community: A Step-by-Step Guide to Community Needs and Resources.* Chicago: Family Support America.

Sanders, M. 2000. Community-based parenting and family support interventions and the prevention of drug abuse. *Addictive Behaviors* 25 (6): 929–942.

Sarri, R. C. 1985. Federal policy changes and the feminization of poverty. *Child Welfare* 64:235–248.

Schamess, G. and A. Lightburn. 1998a. Preface. In G. Schamess and A. Lightburn, eds., *Humane Managed Care?* pp. xv–xxi. Washington, D.C.: NASW.

Schamess, G. and A. Lightburn, eds. 1998b. *Humane Managed Care?* Washington, D.C.: NASW.

Schein, V. E. 1995. *Working from the Margins: Voices of Mothers in Poverty.* Ithaca: Cornell University Press.

Schneider, R. L. and F. E. Netting. 1999. Influencing social policy in a time of devolution: Upholding social work's great tradition. *Social Work* 44 (4): 349–357.

Schorr, L. B. 1997. *Common Purpose: Strengthening Families and Neighborhoods to Rebuild America.* New York: Anchor.

Schriver, J. M. 1995. *Human Behavior and the Social Environment: Shifting Paradigms in Essential Knowledge for Social Work Practice.* Boston: Allyn and Bacon.

Schuerman, J. R., T. L. Rzepnicki, and J. Littell. 1994. *Putting Families First: An Experiment in Family Preservation*. New York: Aldine de Gruyter.

Schwamm, J. B. 1996. Childhood disability determination for supplemental security income: Implementing the Zebley decision. *Children and Youth Services Review* 18 (7): 621–635.

Schmitz, C. L. and A. Hilton. 1996. Combining mental health treatment with education for preschool children with severe emotional and behavioral problems. *Social Work in Education* 18 (4): 237–249.

Schmitz, C. L., C. Stakeman, and J. Sisneres. 2001. A multicultural society: Understanding oppression and valuing diversity. *Families in Society: The Journal of Contemporary Human Services* 82 (6): 612–622.

School Social Work Association of America. 2001. *Position Statement on "School Social Workers and Confidentiality."* Chicago: School Social Work Association of America.

Seader, M. B. 1994. Should adoption records be opened? No. In E. Gambrill and T. J. Stein, eds., *Controversial Issues in Child Welfare*, pp. 232–237. Boston: Allyn and Bacon.

Search Institute.1996. *Developmental Assets*. Minneapolis: Search Institute.

See, L. A., ed. 1998. *Human Behavior in the Social Environment from an African American Perspective*. Binghamton, N.Y.: Haworth.

Seidel, J. F. 1991. The development of a comprehensive pediatric HIV developmental service program. *Technical report on developmental disabilities and HIV infection*, no. 7 (December). Silver Spring, Md.: American Association of University Affiliated Programs.

Selye, H. 1956. *The Stress of Life*. New York: McGraw-Hill.

Sengupta, S. 2001. Living on welfare: A clock is ticking. *New York Times*, April 29, 2001, pp. A-1, 44.

Sewell-Coker, B., J. Hamilton-Collins, and E. Fein. 1985. Social work practice with West Indian Immigrants. *Social Casework* 66 (9): 563–568.

Seymour, C. 1998. Children with parents in prison: Child welfare policy, program, and practice issues. *Child Welfare* 77:469–493.

Seymour, C. B. and C. F. Hairston, eds. 1998. Children with parents in prison. Special issue. *Child Welfare* 77:467–493.

Shartrand, A. 1996. *Supporting Latino Families: Lessons from Exemplary Programs*. Vol. 1. Cambridge: Harvard Family Research Project.

Shemmings, D. 2000. Professionals' attitudes to children's participation in decision making: Dichotomous accounts and doctrinal contests. *Child and Family Social Work* 5 (3): 235–243.

Sherman, E. and W. J. Reid, 1994. *Qualitative Research in Social Work*. New York: Columbia University Press.

Shlonsky, A. R. and J. D. Berrick. 2001. Assessing and promoting quality in kin and nonkin foster care. *Social Service Review* 75:60–83.

Skoepal, T. 1997. The next liberalism. Review of R. M. Blank's *It Takes a Nation: A New Approach Agenda for Fighting Poverty. Atlantic Monthly*, April, pp. 118–120.

Silver, J. A., B. J. Amster, and T. A. Haecker. 1999. *Young Children and Foster Care: A Guide for Professionals.* Baltimore: Paul Brookes.

Simms, M. D. and N. Halfon. 1994. The health care needs of children in foster care: A research agenda. *Child Welfare* 73:505–524.

Simms, M. D., M. Freundlich, E. S. Battistelli, and N. D. Kaufman. 1999. Delivering health care and mental health care services to children in family foster care after welfare and health care reform. *Child Welfare* 78:166–183.

Singer, M. I., T. M. Anglin, L. Y. Song, and L. Lunghafer. 1995. Adolescents' exposure to violence and associated symptoms of psychological trauma. *Journal of the American Medical Association* 273 (6): 477–482.

Smith, C. and B. E. Carlson. 1997. Stress, coping and resilience in children and youth. *Social Service Review* 71 (2): 231–256.

Smith, S. 1995. Family theory and multicultural family studies. In B. B. Ingoldsby and S. Smith, eds., *Families in Multicultural Perspective*, pp. 5–35. New York: Guilford.

Smokowski, P. R. 1998. Prevention and intervention strategies for promoting resilience in disadvantaged children. *Social Service Review* 72:337–364.

Social Legislation Information Service. 1997. *Washington Social Legislation Bulletin* 35 (23) (December 8). Washington, D.C.: Social Legislation Information Service.

Soss, J. 2000. *Unwanted Claims: The Politics of Participation in the U.S. Welfare System.* Ann Arbor: University of Michigan Press.

Southern Poverty Law Center. 1999. *Responding to Hate at School: A Guide for Teachers, Counselors, and Administrators.* Montgomery: Author. Southern Poverty Law Center.

Stack, C. B. 1974. *All Our Kin: Strategies for Survival in a Black Community.* New York: Harper and Row.

Starfield, B. 1992. Child and adolescent health status measures. *Future of Children* 2 (2): 25–39.

Starr, R. H., D. J. MacLean, and D. P. Keating. 1991. Life-span developmental outcomes of child maltreatment. In R. H. Starr and D. A. Wolfe, eds., *The Effects of Child Abuse and Neglect: Issues and Research.* New York: Guilford.

Stein, T. J. 1996. Child custody and visitation: The rights of lesbian and gay parents. *Social Service Review* 70 (3): 435–450.

Stein, T. J. 1997. *The Social Welfare of Women and Children with HIV and AIDS: Legal Protections, Policy, and Programs.* New York: Oxford University Press.

Stein, T. J. 1998. *Child Welfare and the Law*. Rev. ed. Washington, D.C.: CWLA.

Stein, T. J. 2001. *Social Policy and Policymaking by the Branches of Government and the Public-at-Large*. New York: Columbia University Press.

Stoesz, D. 2000. *A Poverty of Imagination: Bootstrap Capitalism, Sequel to Welfare Reform*. Madison: University of Wisconsin Press.

Stoney, L. and M. Greenberg. 1996. The financing of child care: Current and emerging trends. *Future of Children* 6 (2): 83–102.

Strauss, A. and J. Corbin. 1998. *Basics of Qualitative Research: Techniques and Procedures for Developing Grounded Theory*. Thousand Oaks, Cal.: Sage.

Straussner, S. L. A. 1993. Assessment and treatment of clients with alcohol and other drug abuse problems: An overview. In S. L. A. Strussner, ed., *Clinical Work with Substance-Abusing Clients*, pp. 3–30. New York: Guilford.

Streeter, C. I. and C. Franklin. 1992. Defining and measuring social support: Guidelines for social work practitioners. *Research in Social Work Practice* 2:81–98.

Studt, E. 1968. Social work theory and implications for the practice methods. *Social Work Education Reporter* 16 (2): 22–24, 42–46.

Substance Abuse and Mental Health Services Administration. 1997. *Substance Use Among Women in the United States*. Office of Applied Studies of the Department of Health and Human Services. Rockville, Md.: Substance Abuse and Mental Health Services Administration.

Summers, A. B. 1989. The meaning of informed consent in social work. Special issue. *Social Thought* 15 (3/4): 128–140.

Swenson, C. R. 1998. Clinical social work's contribution to a social justice perspective. *Social Work* 43 (6): 527–537.

Swift, K. J. 1995. *Manufacturing "Bad Mothers": A Critical Perspective on Child Neglect*. Toronto: University of Toronto Press.

Taylor, R. J., L. M. Chatters, and V. M. Mays. 1988. Parents, children, siblings, in-laws, and non-kin as sources of emergency assistance to Black Americans. *Family Relations* 37:298–304.

Taylor-Brown, S. and A. Garcia. 1995. Social workers and HIV-affected families: Is the profession prepared? *Social Work* 40 (1): 14–15.

Taylor-Brown, S., J. Teeter, E. Blackburn, L. Oinen, and L. Wedderburn. 1998. Parental loss due to HIV: Caring for children as a community issue — the Rochester, New York experience. *Child Welfare* 77:137–160.

Terr, L. C. 1991. Childhood traumas: An outline and overview. *American Journal of Psychiatry* 148 (1): 10–20.

Thompson, M. S. and W. Peebles-Wilkins. 1992. The impact of formal, informal, and societal support networks on the psychological well-being of black adolescent mothers. *Social Work* 37 (4): 322–328.

Thompson, R. A. 1995. *Preventing Child Maltreatment Through Social Support*. Thousand Oaks, Cal.: Sage.

Thompson, R. A., D. J. Laible, and J. K. Robbennolt, 1997. Child care and preventing child maltreatment. *Advances in Early Education and Day Care* 9: 173–202.

Torres, S. 1996. The status of school social workers in America. *Social Work in Education* 18 (1): 8–18.

Tower, K. D. 1994. Consumer-centered social work practice: Restoring client self determination. *Social Work* 39 (2): 191–196.

Tracy, E. M. 1994. Maternal substance abuse: Protecting the child, preserving the family. *Social Work* 39 (5): 534–540.

Tracy, E. M. 2000. What works in family support services. In M. Kluger, G. Alexander, and P. A. Curtis, eds., *What Works in Child Welfare*, pp. 3–9. Washington, D.C.: CWLA.

Tracy, E. M. 2001. Interventions: Hard and soft services. In E. Walton, P. Sandau-Beckler, and M. Mannes, eds., *Balancing Family-Centered Services and Child Well-Being: Exploring Issues in Policy, Practice, Theory, and Research*, pp. 155–178. New York: Columbia University Press.

Tracy, E. M., D. Biegel, J. Johnsen, and A. Rebeck. 1999. *Final Report: Family Stability Incentive Fund Evaluation Study*. Cleveland: Cuyahoga County Mental Health Research Institute, Mandel School of Applied Social Sciences.

Tracy, E. M. and K. J. Farkas. 1994. Preparing practitioners for child welfare practice with substance-abusing families. *Child Welfare* 73:57–68.

Tracy, E. M. and S. A. Ferguson. 1993. *Parent Network Project Final Report*. Cleveland: Mandel School of Applied Social Sciences, Case Western Reserve University.

Tracy, E. M., R. K. Green, and M. D. Bremseth. 1993. Meeting the environmental needs of abused and neglected children: Implications from a statewide survey of supportive services. *Social Work Research and Abstracts* 29 (2): 21–26.

Tracy, E. M. and B. A. Pine. 2000. Child welfare education and training: Future trends and influences. *Child Welfare* 79:93–113.

Tracy, E. M. and V. Rondero. 1998. School-based substance abuse intervention. *Issues of Substance* 3 (3): 8–9. Washington, D.C.: NASW.

Tracy, E. M. and J. K. Whittaker. 1990. The Social Network Map: Assessing social support in clinical social work practice. *Families in Society: The Journal of Contemporary Human Services* 71:461–470.

Tracy, E. M., J. K. Whittaker, F. Boylan, P. Neitman, and E. Overstreet. 1995. Network interventions with high-risk youth and families throughout the continuum of care. In I. M. Schwartz and P. AuClaire, eds., *Home-Based Services for Troubled Youth*, pp. 55–72. Lincoln: University of Nebraska Press.

Turnell, A. and S. Edwards. 1999. *Signs of Safety: A Solution and Safety-Oriented Approach to Child Protection*. New York: Norton.

Turner, J. 1993. Evaluating family reunification programs. In B. A. Pine, R. Warsh and A. N. Maluccio, eds., *Together Again: Family Reunification in Foster Care*, pp. 179–198. Washington, D.C.: CWLA.

Tyack, D. 1992. Health and social services in public schools: Historical perspectives. *Future of Children* 2 (1): 19–31.

Unrau, Y. A., P. A. Gabor, and R. M. Grinnell Jr. 2001. *Evaluation in the Human Services*. Itasca, Ill.: Peacock.

Usher, C. L., K. A. Randolph, and H. C. Gogan. 1999. Placement patterns in foster care. *Social Service Review* 78:22–36.

U.S. Bureau of the Census. 1995. *Statistical Abstracts of the United States*. Washington, D.C.: Government Printing Office.

U.S. Department of Education. 1994. *Strong Families, Strong Schools: Building Community Partnerships for Learning*. Washington, D.C.: U.S. Department of Education.

U.S. Department of Education. 2000. *Safeguarding Our Children: An Action Guide for Implementing Early Warning, Timely Response*. Washington, D.C.: U.S. Department of Education. http://www.ed.gov/ (August 2, 2001).

U.S. Department of Health and Human Services, Administration for Children and Families. N.d. *Child Welfare Outcomes 1998: Annual Report*. Washington, D.C.: DHHS.

U.S. Department of Health and Human Services, Administration for Children and Families. 1998. *Child Welfare Outcomes 1998: Annual Report*. Washington, D.C.: DHHS. http://www.acf.dhhs.gov/programs/cb (June 1, 2000).

U.S. Department of Health and Human Services, Administration for Children and Families. 1999a. *Changing Paradigms of Child Welfare Practice: Responding to Opportunities and Challenges*. Washington, D.C.: DHHS.

U.S. Department of Health and Human Services, Administration for Children and Families. 1999b. *The AFCARS Report: Current Estimates As of January 1999*. www.acf.dhhs.gov/programs/chdata (January 5, 2000).

U.S. Department of Health and Human Services, Office of the Assistant Secretary for Planning and Evaluation. 2000. *Trends in the Well-Being of America's Children and Youth*. Washington, D.C.: DHHS.

U.S. Department of Health and Human Services, Office of the Assistant Secretary for Planning and Evaluation. 2001. *Evaluation of Family Preservation and Reunification Programs (Interim Report)*. Washington, D.C.: DHHS.

U.S. Department of Health and Human Services, Substance Abuse and Mental Health Services Administration. 2000. *1999 National Household Survey on Drug Abuse*. Washington, D.C.: DHHS.

U.S. Department of Health and Human Services, Public Health Service. 2000. *Healthy People 2000: National Health Promotion and Disease Prevention Objectives*. Washington, D.C.: DHHS.

U.S. General Accounting Office. 1995. *Supplemental Security Income: Recent Growth in the Roles Raises Fundamental Program Concerns.* Testimony of Jane L. Ross before the Subcommittee on Human Resources Committee on Ways and Means, House of Representatives, January 27. GAO/T-HEHS–95–67. Washington, D.C.: GAO.

U.S. General Accounting Office. 1997. *Poverty Measurement: Issues in Revising and Updating the Official Definition.* GAO/HEHS–97–39. Washington, D.C.: GAO.

U.S. General Accounting Office. 1998. *Welfare Reform: Child Support an Uncertain Income Supplement for Families Leaving Welfare.* GAO/HEHS–98–168. Washington, D.C.: GAO.

U.S. General Accounting Office. 1999a. *Report to Congressional Committees: Children's Health Insurance Program — State Implementation Approaches Are Evolving.* GAO/HEHS–99–65. Washington, D.C.: GAO.

U.S. General Accounting Office. 1999b. *Women in Prison: Issues and Challenges Confronting U.S. Correctional Systems.* GAO/GGD–00–22. Washington, D.C.: GAO.

U.S. General Accounting Office. 2000. *Homelessness: Barriers to Using Mainstream Programs.* GAO/RCED–00–184. Washington, D.C.: GAO.

Vachon, J. M. 1985. Food stamps go electronic: Food stamps no longer are made of paper in Reading, Pennsylvania. *Public Welfare* 43 (3): 36–42.

Valentine, J. and E. F. Zigler. 1985. Headstart: A case study in the development of social policy for children and families. In E. F. Zigler, S. L. Kagan, and E. Klugman, eds., *Children, Families, and Government: Perspectives on American Social Policy*, pp. 266–280. New York: Cambridge University Press.

Van Den Bergh, N. 1995a. Feminist social work practice: Where have we been . . . Where are we going? In N. Van Den Bergh, ed., *Feminist Practice in the Twenty-first Century*, pp. xi–xxxix. Washington, D.C.: NASW.

Van Den Bergh, N., ed. 1995b. *Feminist Practice in the Twenty-first Century.* Washington, D.C.: NASW.

Van Den Bergh, N. and L. B. Cooper. 1986. Introduction. In N. Van Den Bergh and L. B. Cooper, eds., *Feminist Visions for Social Work*, pp. 1–28. Silver Spring: National Association of Social Workers.

Vaux, A., P. Burda, and D. Stewart, 1986. Orientation toward utilization of support resources. *Journal of Community Psychology* 11:159–170.

Vecchiato, T., A. N. Maluccio, and C. Canali, eds. In press. *Evaluation in Child and Family Services: Comparative Client and Program Perspectives.* New York: Aldine de Gruyter.

Voluntary Cooperative Information Systems. 1997. *Child Substitute Care: Flow Data for FY 96.* Washington, D.C.: American Public Welfare Association.

Vosler, N. R. 1990. Assessing family access to basic resources: An essential component of social work practice. *Social Work* 35 (5): 434–441.

Wahler, R. G., G. Leske, and E. S. Rogers. 1979. The insular family: A deviance support system for oppositional children. In L. A. Hamerlynch, ed., *Behavioral Systems for the Developmentally Disabled: School and Family Environments* 1:102–127. New York: Bruner/Mazel.

Wakefield, J. C. 1988. Psychotherapy, distributive justice, and social work: Distributive justice as a conceptual framework for social work. Part 1. *Social Service Review* 62 (2): 187–210.

Walker, C., P. Zangrillo, and J. Smith. 1991. *Parental Drug Abuse and African American Children in Foster Care: Issues and Study Findings.* Washington, D.C.: National Black Child Development Institute.

Walker, M. E., S. Wasserman, and B. Wellman. 1993. Statistical models for social support networks. *Sociological Methods and Research* 22 (1): 71–98.

Wall, J. C. 1996. Homeless children and their families: Delivery of educational and social services through school systems. *Social Work in Education* 18 (3): 135–144.

Wallace, H. 1996. *Family Violence: Legal, Medical, and Social Perspectives.* Boston: Allyn and Bacon.

Walsh, E. M. 1994. Should adoption records be opened? No. In E. Gambrill and T. J. Stein, eds., *Controversial Issues in Child Welfare,* pp. 239–243. Boston: Allyn and Bacon.

Walsh, F. 1998. *Strengthening Family Resilience.* New York: Guilford.

Walton, E., P. Sandau-Beckler, and M. Mannes, eds. 2001. *Balancing Family-Centered Services and Child Well-Being: Exploring Issues in Policy, Practice, and Research.* New York: Columbia University Press.

Ward, H., ed. 1998. Assessing outcomes in child care: An international perspective. Special issue. *Children and Society* 12:151–248.

Wardle, F. 1991. Interracial Children and Their Families: How School Social Workers Should Respond. *Social Work in Education* 13 (4): 215–223.

Warsh, R., A. N. Maluccio, and B. A. Pine. 1994. *Teaching Family Reunification: A Sourcebook.* Washington, D.C.: CWLA.

Warsh, R., B. A. Pine, and A. N. Maluccio. 1996. *Reconnecting Families: A Guide to Strengthening Family Reunification Services.* Washington, D.C.: CWLA.

Washington Risk Assessment Project. 1993. *Multi-cultural Guidelines for Assessing Family Strengths and Risk Factors in Child Protective Services.* Olympia: Washington Risk Assessment Project.

Watson, K. W. 1994. Should adoption records be opened? Yes. In E. Gambrill and T. J. Stein, eds., *Controversial Issues in Child Welfare,* pp. 223–230. Boston: Allyn and Bacon.

Webb, N. B. 1996. *Social Work Practice with Children.* New York: Guilford.

Webb, N. B., ed. 2001. *Culturally Diverse Parent-Child and Family Relationships: A*

Guide for Social Workers and Other Practitioners. New York: Columbia University Press.

Weil, M. and E. Sanchez. 1983. The impact of the Tarasoff decision on clinical social work practice. *Social Service Review* 57:112–124.

Weiner, M. E. 1987. Values and skills of cross-organizational management for the 1990s. In L. M. Healy, B. A. Pine, and M. E. Weiner, eds., *Social Work Leadership for Human Service Management in the 1990s: The Challenge of the New Demographic Reality,* p. 76. West Hartford: University of Connecticut, School of Social Work.

Weinreb, M. L. 1997. Be a resiliency mentor: you may be a lifesaver for a high-risk child. *Young Children,* January, pp. 14–20.

Weisman, M. 1994. When parents are not in the best interests of the child. *Atlantic Monthly* 275 (5): 43–63.

Weiss, H. B. and W. A. Morrill. 1998. Useful learning for publication. *Evaluation Exchange* 4 (3/4): 2–4, 14.

Weissbourd, B. 1994. The evolution of the family resource movement. In S. L. Kagan and B. Weissbourd, eds., *Putting Families First: America's Family Support Movement and the Challenge of Change,* pp. 28–47. San Francisco: Jossey-Bass.

Weissbourd, R. 1996. *The Vulnerable Child.* Reading, Mass.: Addison-Wesley.

Wells, K., S. Guo, and F. Li. 2000. *Impact of Welfare Reform on Foster Care and Child Welfare in Cuyahoga County, Ohio: Interim Report.* Cleveland: Mandel School of Applied Social Sciences, Case Western Reserve University.

Wells, K. and E. M. Tracy. 1996. Reorienting family preservation services to public child welfare practice. *Child Welfare* 75:667–692.

Werner, E. E. 1989. High-risk children in young adulthood: A longitudinal study from birth to thirty-two years. *American Journal of Orthopsychiatry* 59:72–81.

Werner, E. E. 1994. Overcoming the odds. *Journal of Developmental and Behavioral Pediatrics* 15:131–136.

Werner, E. E. 1995. Resilience in development. *American Psychological Society* 4:81–85.

Westat, Inc., Chapin Hall Center for Children, and James Bell Associates. 2001. *Evaluation of Family Preservation and Reunification Programs.* Washington, D.C.: DHHS, Assistant Secretary for Planning and Evaluation and the Administration for Children and Families.

Westpheling, G. 1998. AIDS, the single mother, and planning for the future. Ph.D. diss., Rutgers, State University of New Jersey.

Wetherington, C. L., V. L. Smeriglio, and L. P. Finnegan. 1996. Behavioral studies of drug-exposed offspring: Methodological issues in human and animal research. NIDA Research Monograph no. 164. Washington, D.C.: DHHS.

Whitbeck, L. B. and D. R. Hoyt. 1999. *Nowhere to Grow: Homeless and Runaway Adolescents and Their Families.* New York: Aldine de Gruyter.

White, R. W. 1963. *Ego and Reality in Psychoanalytic Theory*. New York: International University Press.

Whittaker, J. K. and J. Garbarino. 1983. *Social Support Networks: Informal Helping in the Human Services*. New York: Aldine de Gruyter.

Whittaker, J. K. and E. Tracy. 1989. *Social Treatment: An Introduction to Interpersonal Helping in Social Work Practice*. 2d ed. New York: Aldine de Gruyter.

Whittaker, J. K. and E. M. Tracy. 1990. Social Network Intervention in Intensive Family-Based Preventive Services. *Prevention in the Human Services* 9 (1): 175–192.

Wiehe, V. R. 1992. *Working with Child Abuse and Neglect*. Itasca, Ill.: Peacock.

Wilson, D. B. and S. S. Chipungu. 1996. Introduction. Special issue. *Child Welfare* 75:397.

Wilson, W. J. 1996. Work. *New York Times Magazine*, August 18, 1996, pp. 26–54.

Wilson, W. J. 1987. *The Truly Disadvantaged: The Inner City, the Underclass, and Public Policy*. Chicago: University of Chicago Press.

Winters, W.G. 1993. *African American Mothers and Urban Schools: The Power of Participation*. New York: Lexington.

Winters, W. G. and R. M. Gourdine. 2000. Social reform: A viable domain for school social work practice. In J. G. Hopps and R. Morris, eds., *Social Work at the Millennium: Critical Reflections on the Future of the Profession*, pp. 138–159. New York: Free.

W. K. Kellogg Foundation. N.d. *Families for Kids of Color: A Special Report of Challenges and Opportunities*. Battle Creek: W. K. Kellogg Foundation.

Wolin, S. J. and S. Wolin, 1994. *The Resilient Self: How Survivors of Troubled Families Rise Above Adversity*. New York: Villard.

Wright, J. D. 1991. Poverty, homelessness, health, nutrition, and children. In J. H. Kryder-Coe, L. M. Salamon, and J. M. Molnar, eds., *Homeless Children and Youth: A New American Dilemma*, pp. 71–103. New Brunswick, N.J.: Transaction.

Wright, L. 2001. *Toolbox No. 1: Using Visitation to Support Permanency*. Washington, D.C.: CWLA.

Wronka, J. 1995. Human rights. In R. L. Edwards and J. G. Hopps, eds., *Encyclopedia of Social Work* 2:1405–1418. 19th ed. Washington, D.C.: NASW.

Yao, E. L. 1993. Strategies for working effectively with Asian immigrant parents. In N. F. Chavkin, ed., *Families and Schools in a Pluralistic Society*, pp. 149–156. Albany: State University of New York Press.

Young, N. K., S. L. Gardner, and K. Dennis. 1998. *Responding to Alcohol and Other Dug Abuse Problems in Child Welfare: Weaving Together Practice and Policy*. Washington, D.C.: CWLA.

Young, N. K., K. Wingfield, and T. Klempner, eds. 2001. Serving children, youth, and families with alcohol and other drug-related problems in child welfare. Special issue. *Child Welfare* 80:103–107.

Yuan, Y.-Y. and M. Rivest, eds. 1990. *Preserving Families: Evaluation Resources for Practitioners and Policymakers.* Newbury Park, Cal.: Sage.

Zambelli, G. C. and A. P. DeRosa. 1992. Bereavement support groups for school-age children: Theory, intervention, and case example. *American Journal of Orthopsychiatry* 62 (4): 484–493.

Zastrow, C. and K. Kirst-Ashman. 1997. *Understanding Human Behavior and the Social Environment.* Chicago: Nelson-Hall.

Zeldlewski, S. R. and S. Brauner. 1999. *Are Steep Declines in Food Stamp Participation Linked to Falling Welfare Caseloads?* Washington, D.C.: Urban Institute.

Zigler, E. 1989. Addressing the nation's child care crisis: The school of the twenty-first century. *American Journal of Orthopsychiatry* 59:484–491.

Zigler, E., S. L. Kagan, and E. Klugman, eds. 1985. *Children, Families, and Government: Perspectives on American Social Policy.* New York: Cambridge University Press.

Zigler, E. and S. Muenchow. 1992. Heard Start: The inside study of America's most successful educational experiment. New York: Basic.

Zill, N. 1996. Family change and student achievement: What we have learned, what it means for schools. In A. Booth and J. F. Dunn, eds., *Family-School Links: How Do They Affect Educational Outcomes?* pp. 139–174. Mahwah, N.J.: Lawrence Erlbaum.

Zlotnik, J. L., S. H. Rome, and D. DePanfilis, eds. 1998. *Educating for Practice: A Compendium of Exemplary Syllabi.* Alexandria, Va.: Council on Social Work Education.

Zuskin, R. 2000. How do I protect children when there is a history of domestic violence in the family? In H. Dubowitz and D. DePanfilis, eds., *Handbook for Child Protection Practice,* pp. 246–249. Thousand Oaks, Cal.: Sage.

Index